AL EWING ★ SIMON SPURRIER ★ ROB WILLIAMS
Writers

SIMON COLEBY ★ HENRY FLINT
D'ISRAELI ★ CARL CRITCHLOW
Artists

HENRY FLINT
Cover Artist

Creative Director and CEO: Jason Kingsley
Chief Technical Officer: Chris Kingsley
2000 AD Editor in Chief: Matt Smith
Graphic Novels Editor: Keith Richardson
Graphic Design: Simon Parr & Sam Gretton
Reprographics: Kathryn Symes
PR: Michael Molcher
Original Commisioning Editor: Matt Smith

Published by Rebellion, Riverside House,
Osney Mead, Oxford, OX2 0ES, UK.
www.rebellion.co.uk

ISBN: 978-1-78108-145-7
Printed in Malta by Gutenberg Press
Manufactured in the EU by LPPS Ltd., Wellingborough, NN8 3PJ, UK.
1st printing: August 2013
10 9 8 7 6 5 4 3 2 1

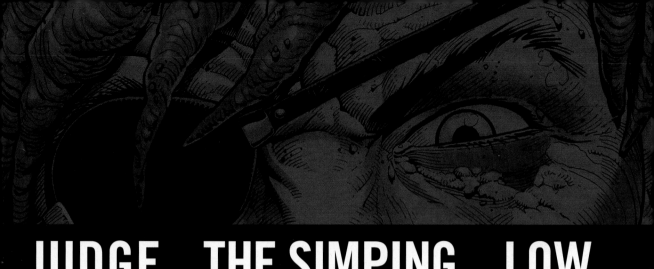

JUDGE DREDD

CREATED BY
JOHN WAGNER & CARLOS EZQUERRA

THE SIMPING DETECTIVE

CREATED BY
SIMON SPURRIER & FRAZER IRVING

LOW LIFE

CREATED BY
ROB WILLIAMS & HENRY FLINT

TRIFECTA

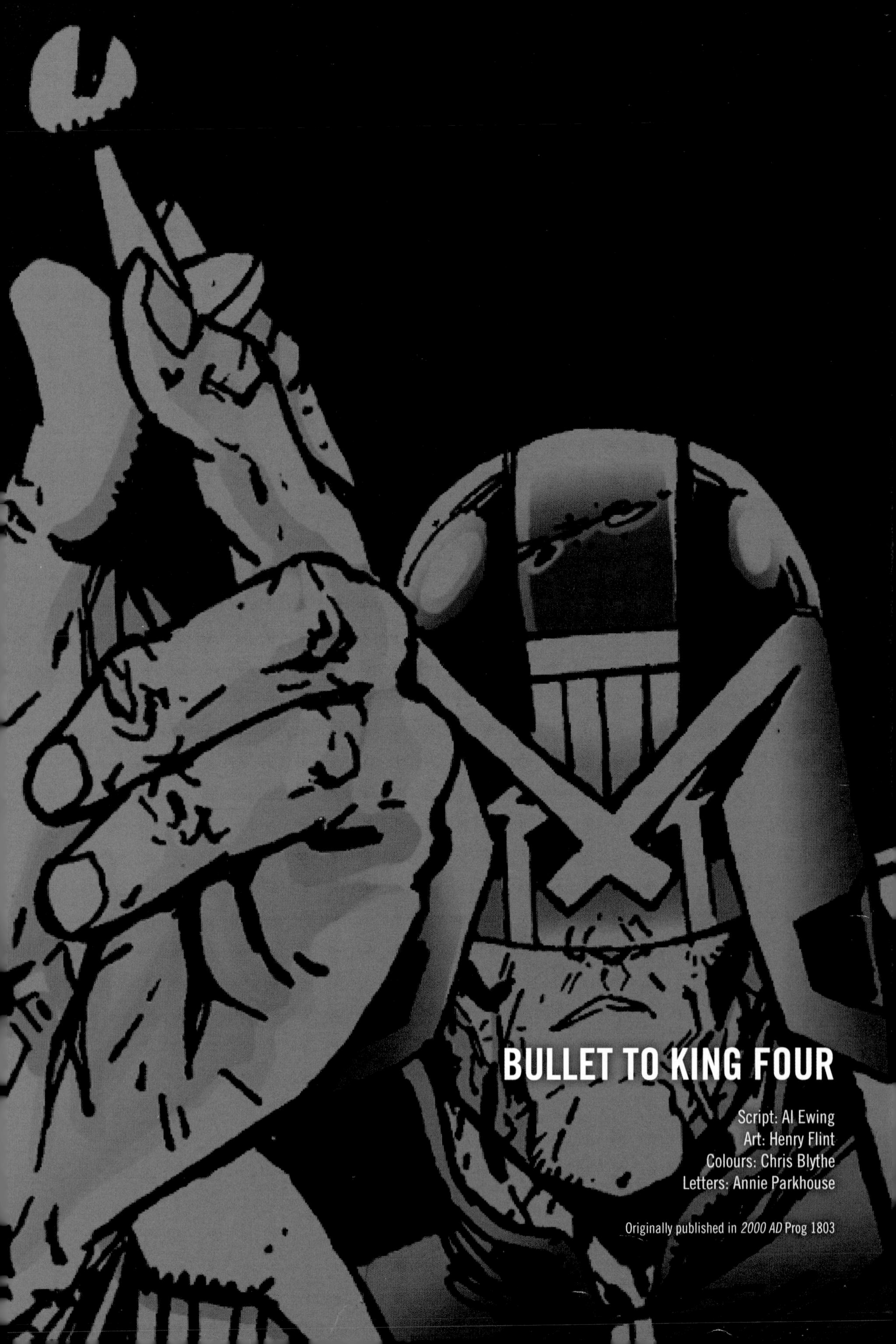

BULLET TO KING FOUR

Script: Al Ewing
Art: Henry Flint
Colours: Chris Blythe
Letters: Annie Parkhouse

Originally published in *2000 AD* Prog 1803

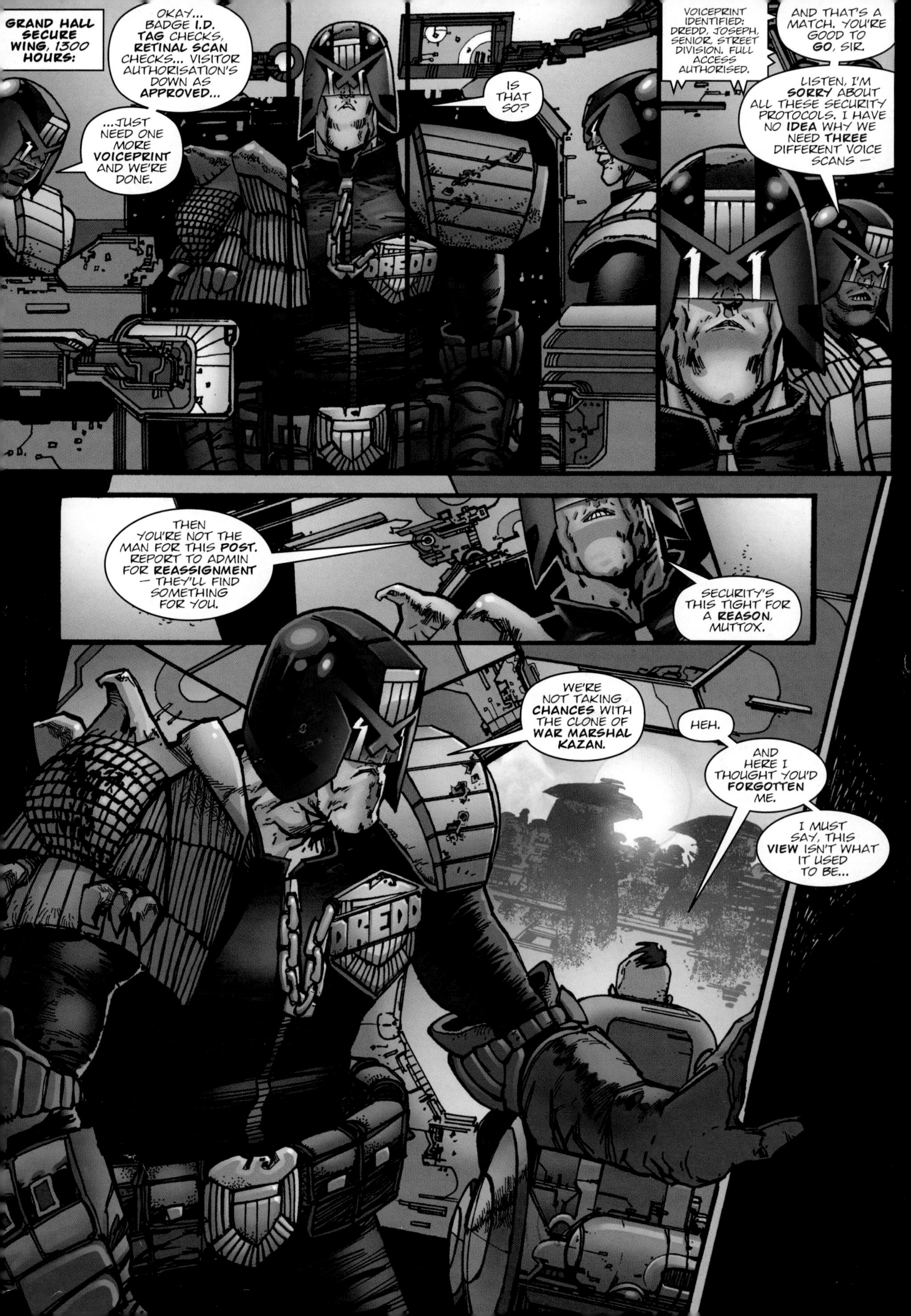

GRAND HALL SECURE WING, 1300 HOURS:
OKAY... BADGE I.D. TAG CHECKS, RETINAL SCAN CHECKS... VISITOR AUTHORISATION'S DOWN AS APPROVED...
...JUST NEED ONE MORE VOICEPRINT AND WE'RE DONE.
IS THAT SO?
VOICEPRINT IDENTIFIED: DREDD, JOSEPH, SENIOR, STREET DIVISION. FULL ACCESS AUTHORISED.
AND THAT'S A MATCH. YOU'RE GOOD TO GO, SIR.
LISTEN, I'M SORRY ABOUT ALL THESE SECURITY PROTOCOLS. I HAVE NO IDEA WHY WE NEED THREE DIFFERENT VOICE SCANS —
THEN YOU'RE NOT THE MAN FOR THIS POST. REPORT TO ADMIN FOR REASSIGNMENT — THEY'LL FIND SOMETHING FOR YOU.
SECURITY'S THIS TIGHT FOR A REASON, MUTTOX.
WE'RE NOT TAKING CHANCES WITH THE CLONE OF WAR MARSHAL KAZAN.
HEH.
AND HERE I THOUGHT YOU'D FORGOTTEN ME.
I MUST SAY, THIS VIEW ISN'T WHAT IT USED TO BE...

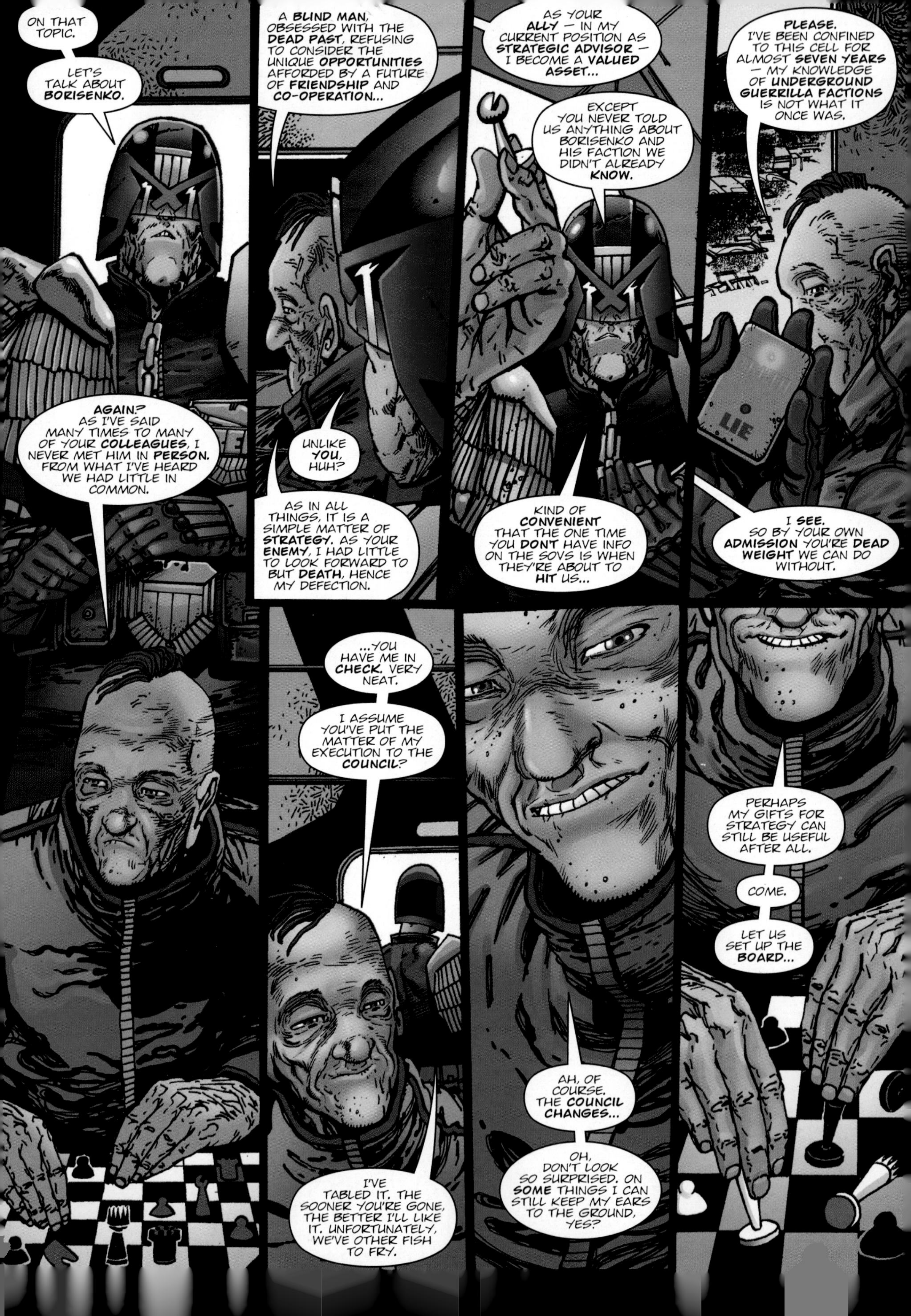
ON THAT TOPIC.
LET'S TALK ABOUT BORISENKO.
AGAIN? AS I'VE SAID MANY TIMES TO MANY OF YOUR COLLEAGUES, I NEVER MET HIM IN PERSON. FROM WHAT I'VE HEARD WE HAD LITTLE IN COMMON.
A BLIND MAN, OBSESSED WITH THE DEAD PAST, REFUSING TO CONSIDER THE UNIQUE OPPORTUNITIES AFFORDED BY A FUTURE OF FRIENDSHIP AND CO-OPERATION...
UNLIKE YOU, HUH?
AS IN ALL THINGS, IT IS A SIMPLE MATTER OF STRATEGY. AS YOUR ENEMY, I HAD LITTLE TO LOOK FORWARD TO BUT DEATH, HENCE MY DEFECTION.
AS YOUR ALLY — IN MY CURRENT POSITION AS STRATEGIC ADVISOR — I BECOME A VALUED ASSET...
EXCEPT YOU NEVER TOLD US ANYTHING ABOUT BORISENKO AND HIS FACTION WE DIDN'T ALREADY KNOW.
KIND OF CONVENIENT THAT THE ONE TIME YOU DON'T HAVE INFO ON THE SOVS IS WHEN THEY'RE ABOUT TO HIT US...
PLEASE. I'VE BEEN CONFINED TO THIS CELL FOR ALMOST SEVEN YEARS — MY KNOWLEDGE OF UNDERGROUND GUERRILLA FACTIONS IS NOT WHAT IT ONCE WAS.
LIE
I SEE. SO BY YOUR OWN ADMISSION YOU'RE DEAD WEIGHT WE CAN DO WITHOUT.
...YOU HAVE ME IN CHECK. VERY NEAT.
I ASSUME YOU'VE PUT THE MATTER OF MY EXECUTION TO THE COUNCIL?
I'VE TABLED IT. THE SOONER YOU'RE GONE, THE BETTER I'LL LIKE IT. UNFORTUNATELY, WE'VE OTHER FISH TO FRY.
AH, OF COURSE. THE COUNCIL CHANGES...
OH, DON'T LOOK SO SURPRISED. ON SOME THINGS I CAN STILL KEEP MY EARS TO THE GROUND, YES?
PERHAPS MY GIFTS FOR STRATEGY CAN STILL BE USEFUL AFTER ALL.
COME.
LET US SET UP THE BOARD...

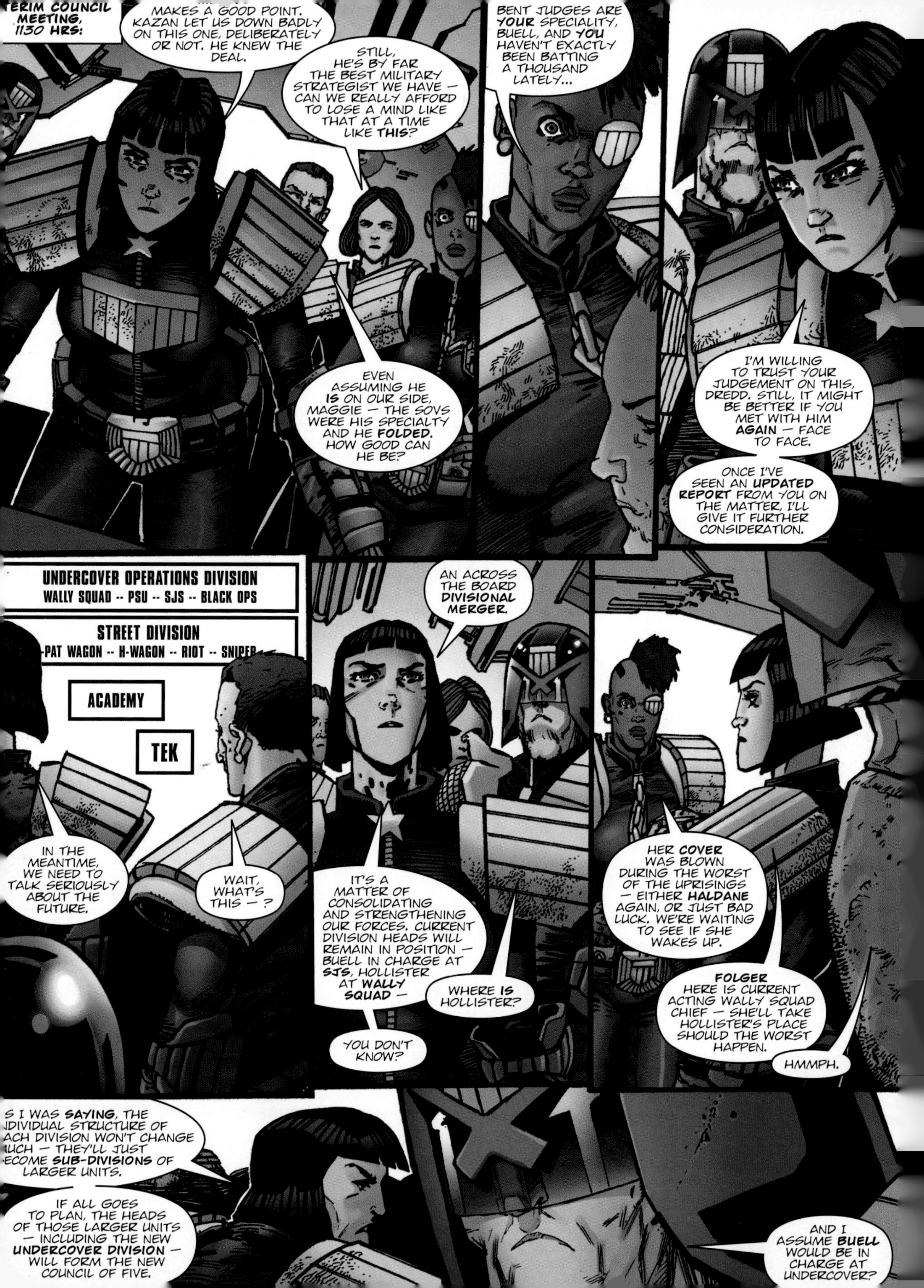

TERIM COUNCIL MEETING, 1130 HRS:
MAKES A GOOD POINT. KAZAN LET US DOWN BADLY ON THIS ONE, DELIBERATELY OR NOT. HE KNEW THE DEAL.
STILL, HE'S BY FAR THE BEST MILITARY STRATEGIST WE HAVE — CAN WE REALLY AFFORD TO LOSE A MIND LIKE THAT AT A TIME LIKE THIS?
EVEN ASSUMING HE IS ON OUR SIDE, MAGGIE — THE SOVS WERE HIS SPECIALTY AND HE FOLDED. HOW GOOD CAN HE BE?
BENT JUDGES ARE YOUR SPECIALITY, BUELL, AND YOU HAVEN'T EXACTLY BEEN BATTING A THOUSAND LATELY...
I'M WILLING TO TRUST YOUR JUDGEMENT ON THIS, DREDD. STILL, IT MIGHT BE BETTER IF YOU MET WITH HIM AGAIN — FACE TO FACE.
ONCE I'VE SEEN AN UPDATED REPORT FROM YOU ON THE MATTER, I'LL GIVE IT FURTHER CONSIDERATION.
UNDERCOVER OPERATIONS DIVISION
WALLY SQUAD -- PSU -- SJS -- BLACK OPS
STREET DIVISION
-PAT WAGON -- H-WAGON -- RIOT -- SNIPER
ACADEMY
TEK
IN THE MEANTIME, WE NEED TO TALK SERIOUSLY ABOUT THE FUTURE.
WAIT, WHAT'S THIS — ?
AN ACROSS THE BOARD DIVISIONAL MERGER.
IT'S A MATTER OF CONSOLIDATING AND STRENGTHENING OUR FORCES. CURRENT DIVISION HEADS WILL REMAIN IN POSITION — BUELL IN CHARGE AT SJS, HOLLISTER AT WALLY SQUAD —
WHERE IS HOLLISTER?
YOU DON'T KNOW?
HER COVER WAS BLOWN DURING THE WORST OF THE UPRISINGS — EITHER HALDANE AGAIN, OR JUST BAD LUCK. WE'RE WAITING TO SEE IF SHE WAKES UP.
FOLGER HERE IS CURRENT ACTING WALLY SQUAD CHIEF — SHE'LL TAKE HOLLISTER'S PLACE SHOULD THE WORST HAPPEN.
HMMPH.
S I WAS SAYING, THE NDIVIDUAL STRUCTURE OF ACH DIVISION WON'T CHANGE UCH — THEY'LL JUST ECOME SUB-DIVISIONS OF LARGER UNITS.
IF ALL GOES TO PLAN, THE HEADS OF THOSE LARGER UNITS — INCLUDING THE NEW UNDERCOVER DIVISION — WILL FORM THE NEW COUNCIL OF FIVE.
AND I ASSUME BUELL WOULD BE IN CHARGE AT UNDERCOVER?

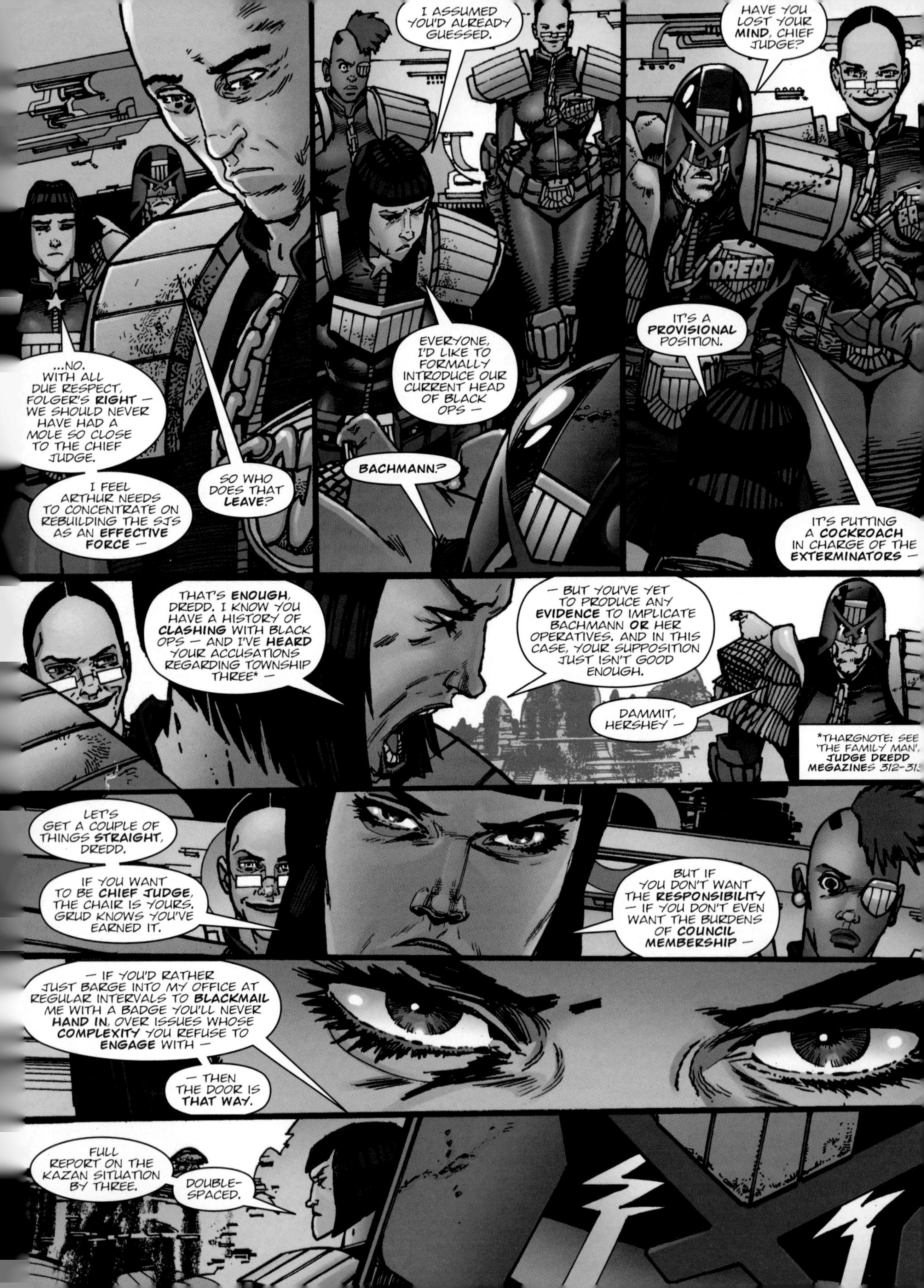
...NO. WITH ALL DUE RESPECT, FOLGER'S RIGHT — WE SHOULD NEVER HAVE HAD A MOLE SO CLOSE TO THE CHIEF JUDGE.
I FEEL ARTHUR NEEDS TO CONCENTRATE ON REBUILDING THE SJS AS AN EFFECTIVE FORCE —
SO WHO DOES THAT LEAVE?
I ASSUMED YOU'D ALREADY GUESSED.
EVERYONE, I'D LIKE TO FORMALLY INTRODUCE OUR CURRENT HEAD OF BLACK OPS —
BACHMANN?
HAVE YOU LOST YOUR MIND, CHIEF JUDGE?
IT'S A PROVISIONAL POSITION.
IT'S PUTTING A COCKROACH IN CHARGE OF THE EXTERMINATORS —
THAT'S ENOUGH, DREDD. I KNOW YOU HAVE A HISTORY OF CLASHING WITH BLACK OPS — AND I'VE HEARD YOUR ACCUSATIONS REGARDING TOWNSHIP THREE* —
— BUT YOU'VE YET TO PRODUCE ANY EVIDENCE TO IMPLICATE BACHMANN OR HER OPERATIVES. AND IN THIS CASE, YOUR SUPPOSITION JUST ISN'T GOOD ENOUGH.
DAMMIT, HERSHEY —
*THARGNOTE: SEE 'THE FAMILY MAN', JUDGE DREDD MEGAZINES 312-313
LET'S GET A COUPLE OF THINGS STRAIGHT, DREDD.
IF YOU WANT TO BE CHIEF JUDGE, THE CHAIR IS YOURS. GRUD KNOWS YOU'VE EARNED IT.
BUT IF YOU DON'T WANT THE RESPONSIBILITY — IF YOU DON'T EVEN WANT THE BURDENS OF COUNCIL MEMBERSHIP —
— IF YOU'D RATHER JUST BARGE INTO MY OFFICE AT REGULAR INTERVALS TO BLACKMAIL ME WITH A BADGE YOU'LL NEVER HAND IN, OVER ISSUES WHOSE COMPLEXITY YOU REFUSE TO ENGAGE WITH —
— THEN THE DOOR IS THAT WAY.
FULL REPORT ON THE KAZAN SITUATION BY THREE.
DOUBLE-SPACED.

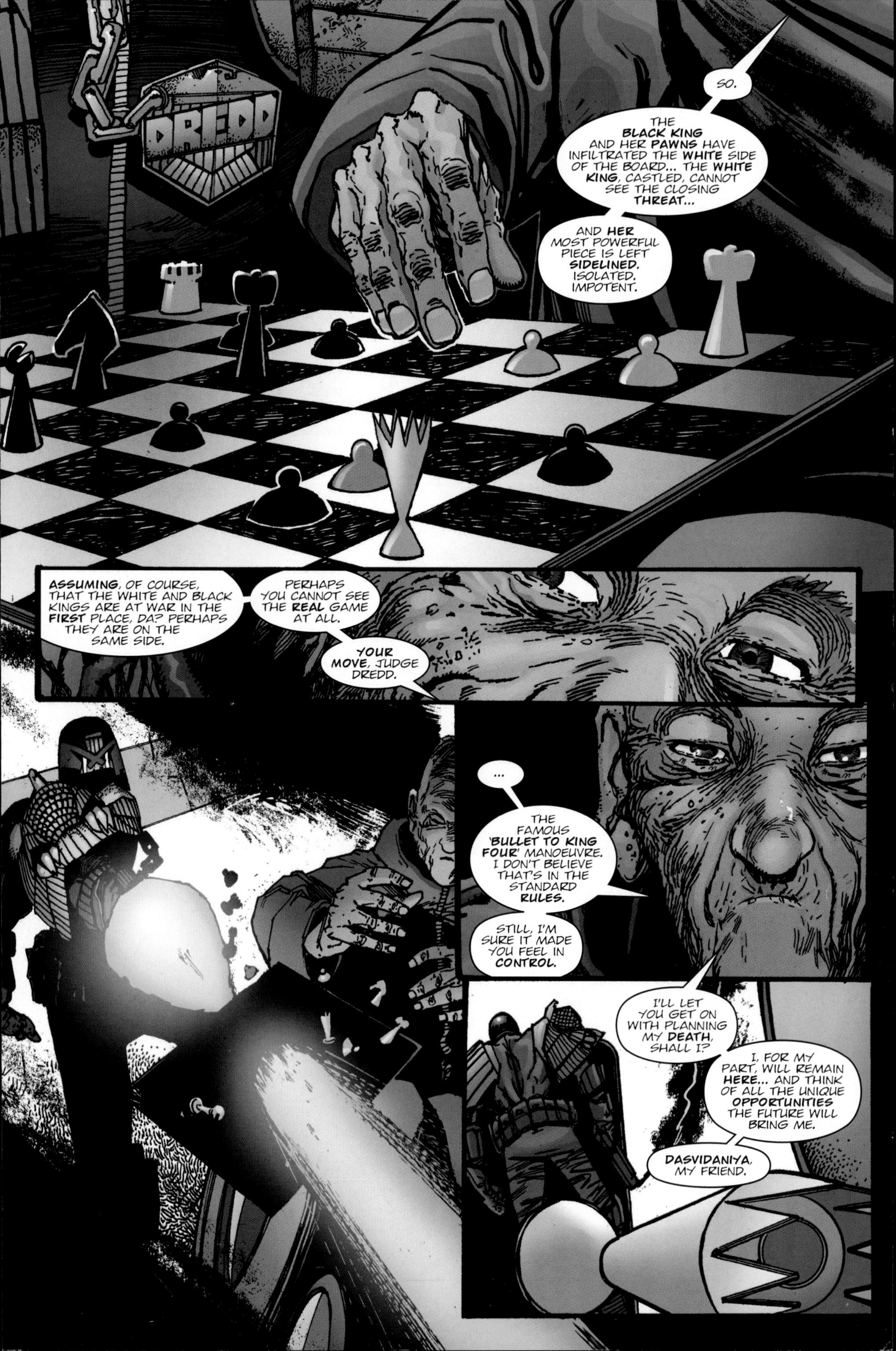
DREDD
SO.
THE BLACK KING AND HER PAWNS HAVE INFILTRATED THE WHITE SIDE OF THE BOARD... THE WHITE KING, CASTLED, CANNOT SEE THE CLOSING THREAT...
AND HER MOST POWERFUL PIECE IS LEFT SIDELINED. ISOLATED. IMPOTENT.
ASSUMING, OF COURSE, THAT THE WHITE AND BLACK KINGS ARE AT WAR IN THE FIRST PLACE, DA? PERHAPS THEY ARE ON THE SAME SIDE.
PERHAPS YOU CANNOT SEE THE REAL GAME AT ALL.
YOUR MOVE, JUDGE DREDD.
...
THE FAMOUS 'BULLET TO KING FOUR' MANOEUVRE. I DON'T BELIEVE THAT'S IN THE STANDARD RULES.
STILL, I'M SURE IT MADE YOU FEEL IN CONTROL.
I'LL LET YOU GET ON WITH PLANNING MY DEATH, SHALL I?
I, FOR MY PART, WILL REMAIN HERE... AND THINK OF ALL THE UNIQUE OPPORTUNITIES THE FUTURE WILL BRING ME.
DASVIDANIYA, MY FRIEND.

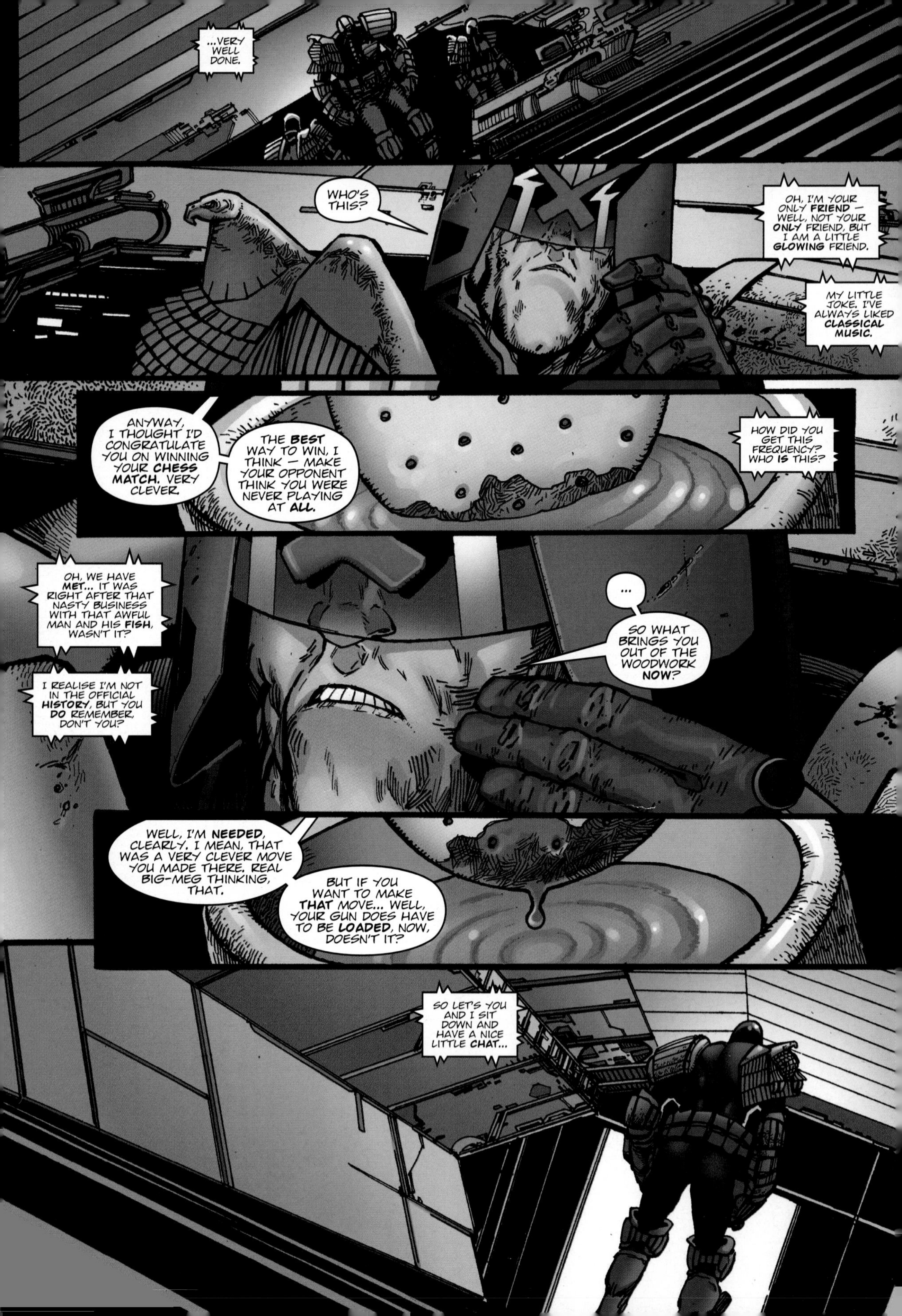

...VERY WELL DONE.
WHO'S THIS?
OH, I'M YOUR ONLY FRIEND — WELL, NOT YOUR ONLY FRIEND, BUT I AM A LITTLE GLOWING FRIEND.
MY LITTLE JOKE. I'VE ALWAYS LIKED CLASSICAL MUSIC.
ANYWAY, I THOUGHT I'D CONGRATULATE YOU ON WINNING YOUR CHESS MATCH. VERY CLEVER.
THE BEST WAY TO WIN, I THINK — MAKE YOUR OPPONENT THINK YOU WERE NEVER PLAYING AT ALL.
HOW DID YOU GET THIS FREQUENCY? WHO IS THIS?
OH, WE HAVE MET... IT WAS RIGHT AFTER THAT NASTY BUSINESS WITH THAT AWFUL MAN AND HIS FISH, WASN'T IT?
I REALISE I'M NOT IN THE OFFICIAL HISTORY, BUT YOU DO REMEMBER, DON'T YOU?
...
SO WHAT BRINGS YOU OUT OF THE WOODWORK NOW?
WELL, I'M NEEDED, CLEARLY. I MEAN, THAT WAS A VERY CLEVER MOVE YOU MADE THERE. REAL BIG-MEG THINKING, THAT.
BUT IF YOU WANT TO MAKE THAT MOVE... WELL, YOUR GUN DOES HAVE TO BE LOADED, NOW, DOESN'T IT?
SO LET'S YOU AND I SIT DOWN AND HAVE A NICE LITTLE CHAT...

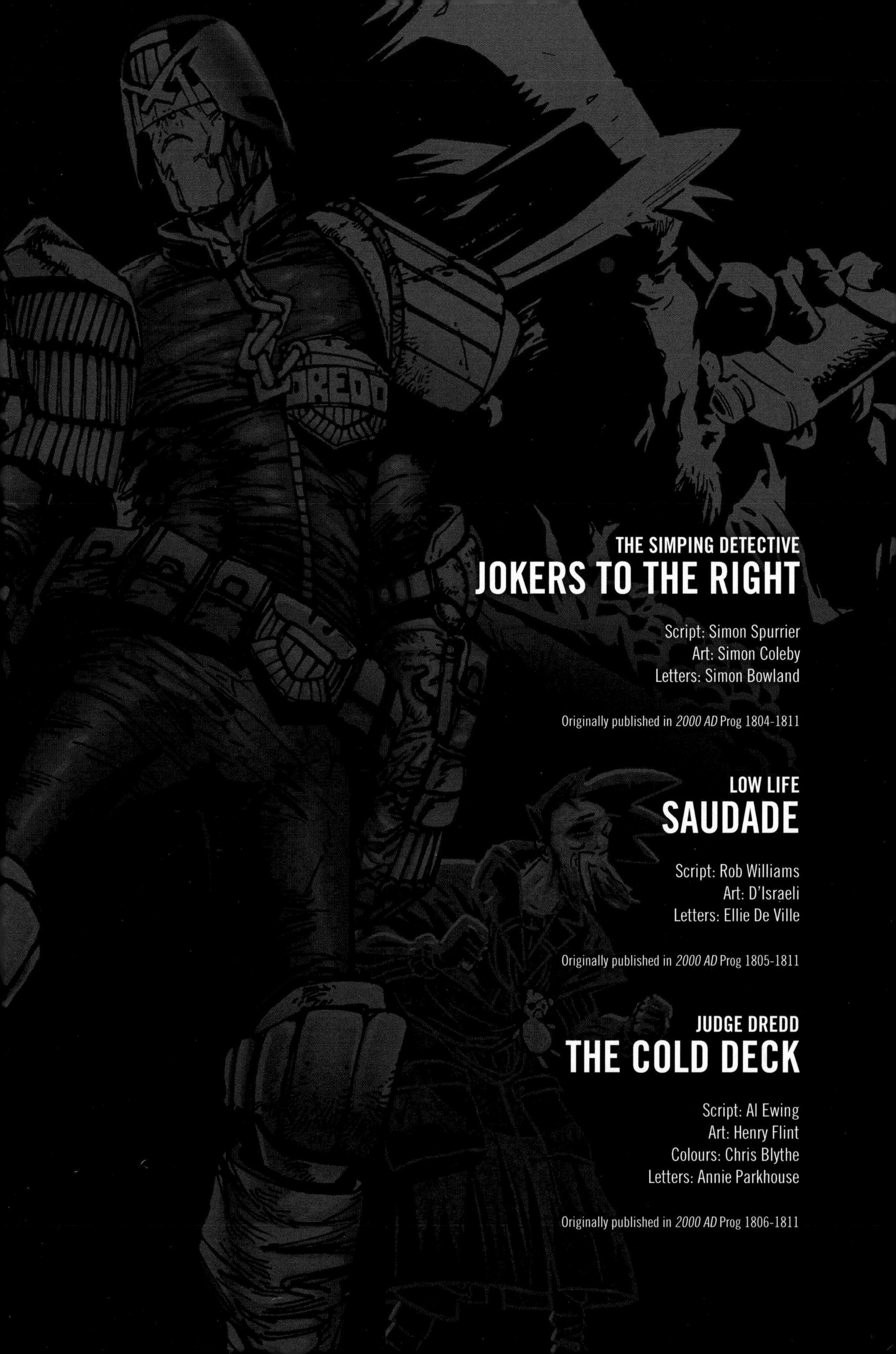

THE SIMPING DETECTIVE
JOKERS TO THE RIGHT

Script: Simon Spurrier
Art: Simon Coleby
Letters: Simon Bowland

Originally published in *2000 AD* Prog 1804-1811

LOW LIFE
SAUDADE

Script: Rob Williams
Art: D'Israeli
Letters: Ellie De Ville

Originally published in *2000 AD* Prog 1805-1811

JUDGE DREDD
THE COLD DECK

Script: Al Ewing
Art: Henry Flint
Colours: Chris Blythe
Letters: Annie Parkhouse

Originally published in *2000 AD* Prog 1806-1811

Mornin'. Step into my office.

Jack Point
Private Eye

Stommhole sector like *Angeltown*--the kinda place where the *Chaos Bug* was a drokkin' *improvement*--it's important you got a *sanctuary*. Like your own *Vatican-Virgin™* *VagiVault*, ya know?

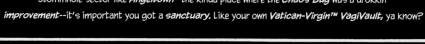

Nothin' gets in.

KL-DONK

WHATTHE*DROKK*--

Uuuuh...

Last night...last night was a *good one*, judgin' from the memories I *ain't got.*

Overhung like a cliff-climber's *anxiety dream.* Toothache like there's a *mole* in my *molar.*

It's *Monday.* It *must* be.

Name's *Jack Point.* Yeah, *Point:* as in "well-argued", "case in" and "frequently held at gun". I make *jokes.*

I'm all about the funny.

~BLEEURGH~

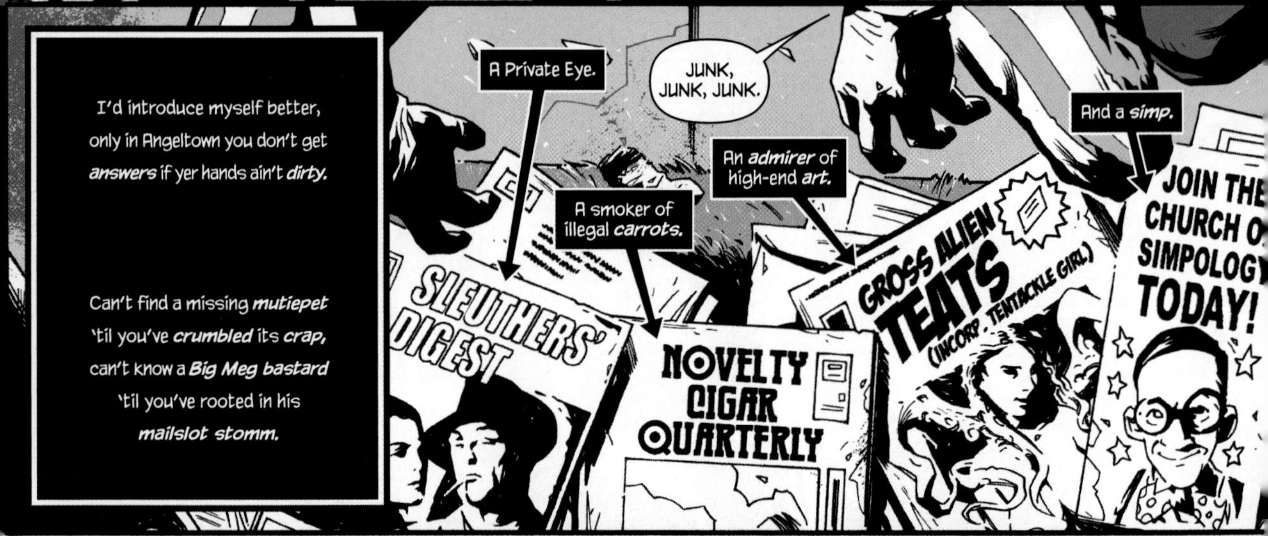
I'd introduce myself better, only in Angeltown you don't get answers if yer hands ain't dirty.
Can't find a missing mutiepet 'til you've crumbled its crap, can't know a Big Meg bastard 'til you've rooted in his mailslot stomm.
A Private Eye.
JUNK, JUNK, JUNK.
A smoker of illegal carrots.
An admirer of high-end art.
And a simp.
SLEUTHERS' DIGEST
NOVELTY CIGAR QUARTERLY
GROSS ALIEN TEATS
(INCORP. TENTACKLE GIRL)
JOIN THE CHURCH O SIMPOLOGY TODAY!

People ask why I gotta dress like a *kook.* Whole buncha answers to that, but the shortest one's ***this:***

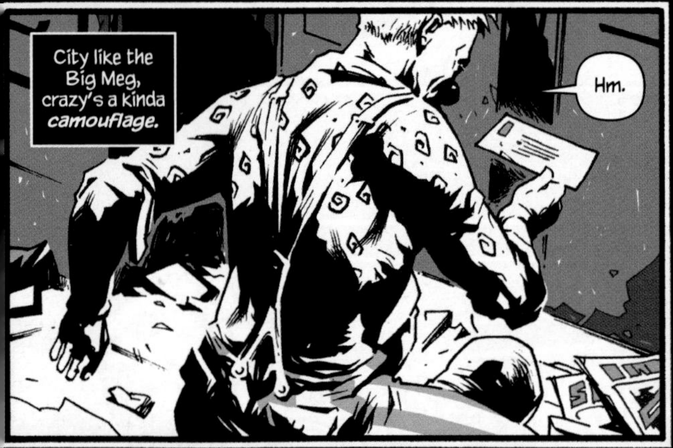
City like the Big Meg, crazy's a kinda camouflage.
Hm.

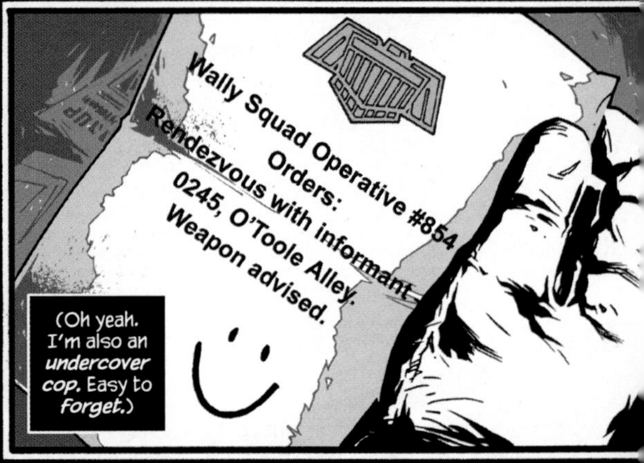
Wally Squad Operative #854
Orders:
Rendezvous with informant
0245, O'Toole Alley.
Weapon advised.
(Oh yeah. I'm also an undercover cop. Easy to forget.)

Yeah, I got more layers than a ***dyslexic dragon.*** In Angeltown that ain't unusual. You wind up in ***Sector 13,*** there's a good chance you got...***well...***

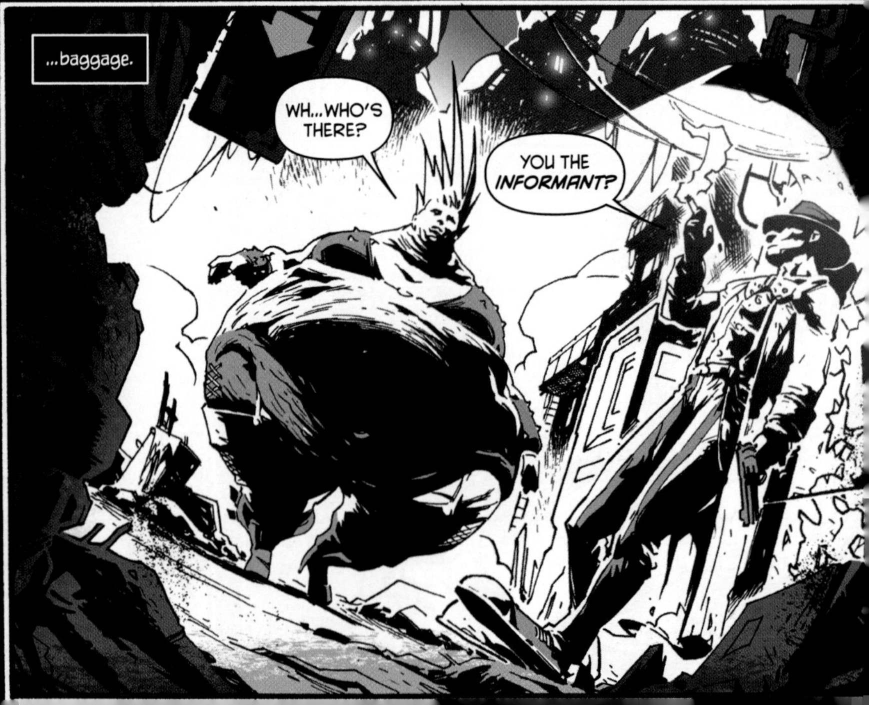
...baggage.
WH...WHO'S THERE?
YOU THE INFORMANT?

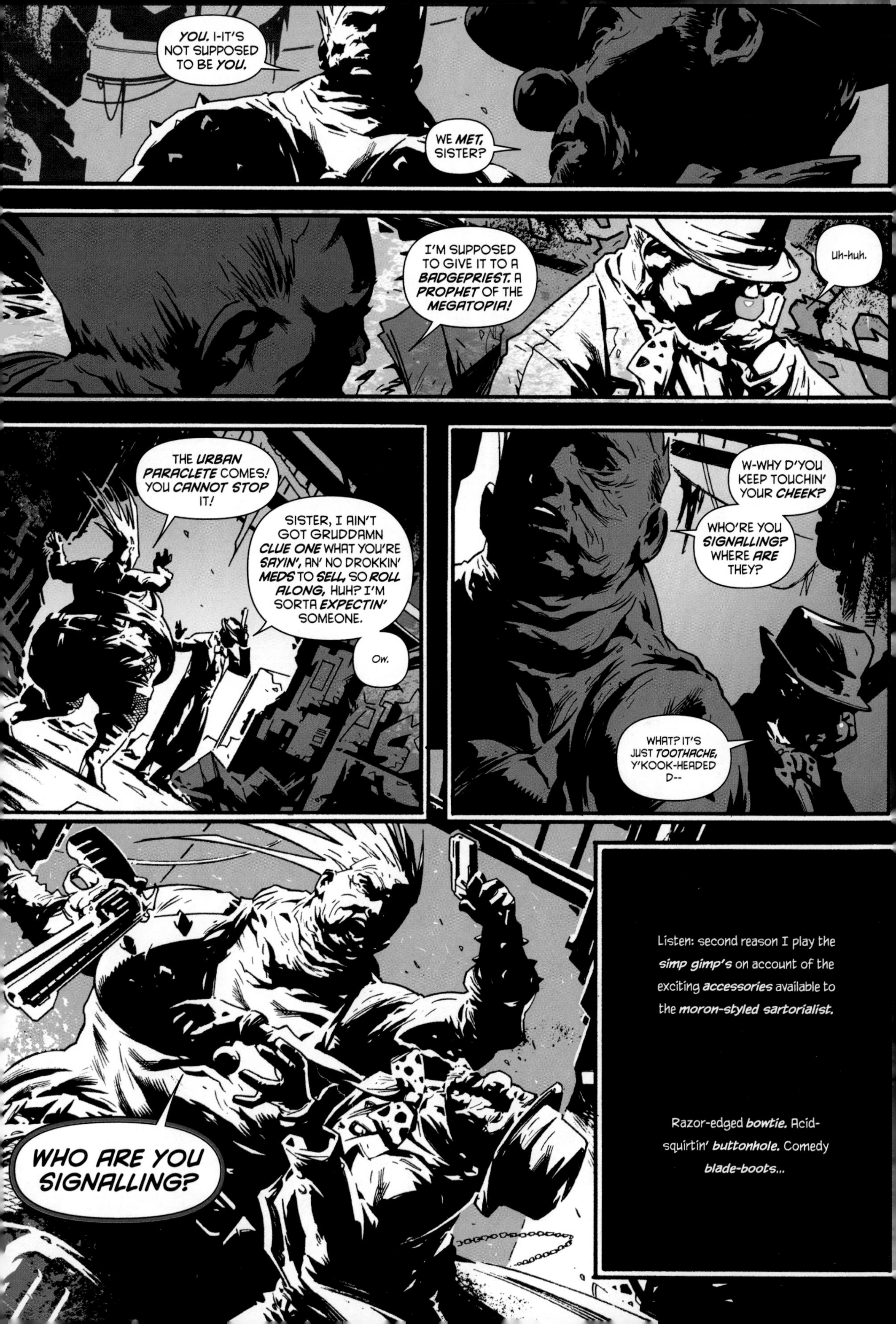
YOU. I-IT'S NOT SUPPOSED TO BE YOU.
WE MET, SISTER?
I'M SUPPOSED TO GIVE IT TO A BADGEPRIEST. A PROPHET OF THE MEGATOPIA!
Uh-huh.
THE URBAN PARACLETE COMES! YOU CANNOT STOP IT!
SISTER, I AIN'T GOT GRUDDAMN CLUE ONE WHAT YOU'RE SAYIN', AN' NO DROKKIN' MEDS TO SELL, SO ROLL ALONG, HUH? I'M SORTA EXPECTIN' SOMEONE.
Ow.
W-WHY D'YOU KEEP TOUCHIN' YOUR CHEEK?
WHO'RE YOU SIGNALLING? WHERE ARE THEY?
WHAT? IT'S JUST TOOTHACHE, Y'KOOK-HEADED D--
WHO ARE YOU SIGNALLING?
Listen: second reason I play the simp gimp's on account of the exciting accessories available to the moron-styled sartorialist.
Razor-edged bowtie. Acid-squirtin' buttonhole. Comedy blade-boots...

Mostly, in this town, that's *enough*.

WAIT, WAIT--

Mostly.

This broad's a *Boing®packed* bowling ball at the *gravplex*. She's a Black Atlantic *hyperwhale* on *Flabbon™*.

It ain't right somethin' so *big* can move quicker'n I do.

Blame it the *carro*

→*koff koff*← L-LADY, I DON'T KNOW YOU FROM *SPUG*, BUT...

...BUT IT TAKES A BIGGER SIMP'N *ME* HIT AN *ANGELTOW ALLEYDATE* WITHO *BACK-UP.*

...

WHAT'S YOUR *POINT?*

YAAAHH!

COME RIGH AFTER *JAC*

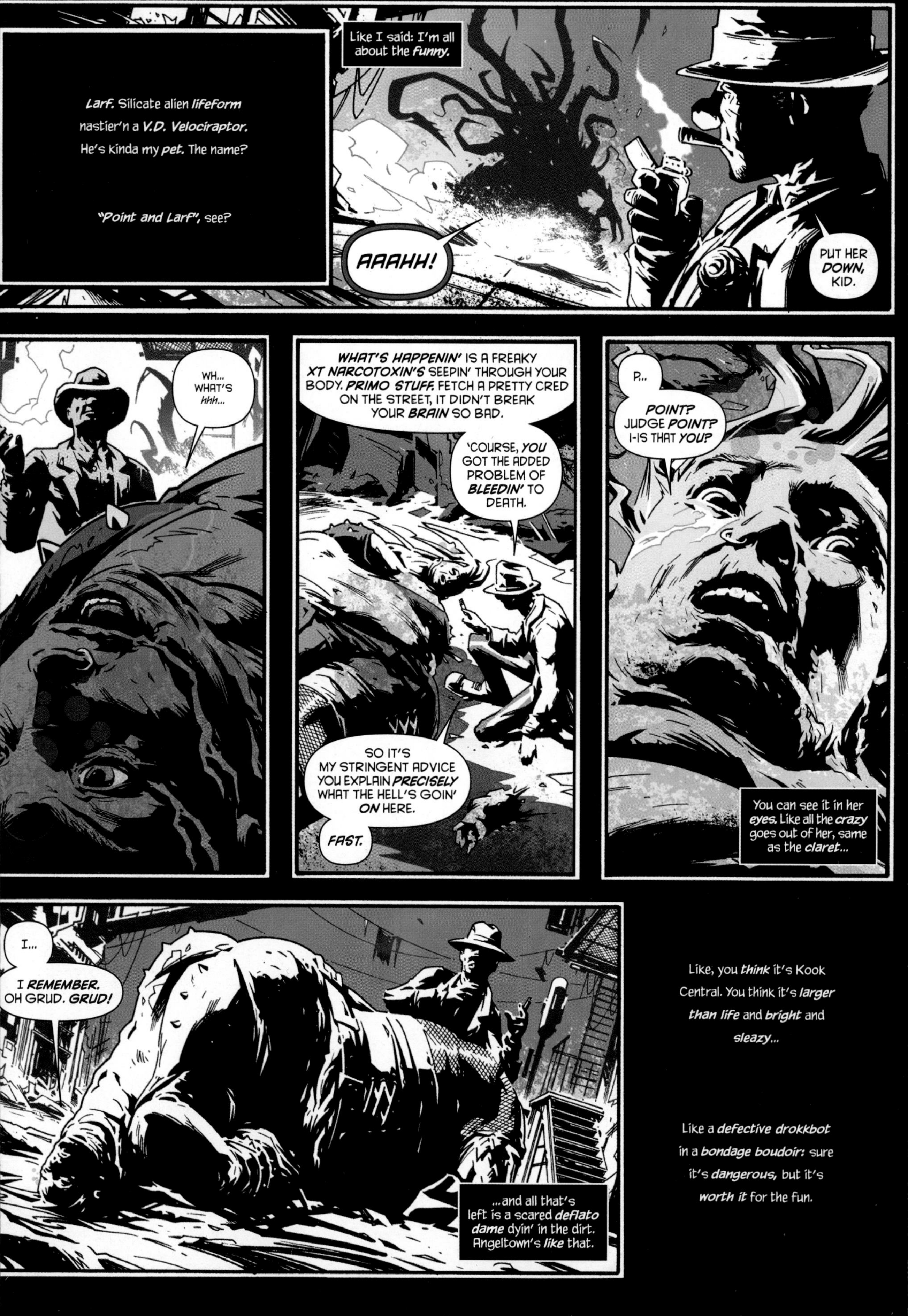

Larf. Silicate alien lifeform nastier'n a V.D. Velociraptor. He's kinda my pet. The name?
"Point and Larf", see?
Like I said: I'm all about the funny.
AAAHH!
PUT HER DOWN, KID.
WH... WHAT'S hhh...
WHAT'S HAPPENIN' IS A FREAKY XT NARCOTOXIN'S SEEPIN' THROUGH YOUR BODY. PRIMO STUFF. FETCH A PRETTY CRED ON THE STREET, IT DIDN'T BREAK YOUR BRAIN SO BAD.
'COURSE, YOU GOT THE ADDED PROBLEM OF BLEEDIN' TO DEATH.
SO IT'S MY STRINGENT ADVICE YOU EXPLAIN PRECISELY WHAT THE HELL'S GOIN' ON HERE.
FAST.
P...
POINT? JUDGE POINT? I-IS THAT YOU?
You can see it in her eyes. Like all the crazy goes out of her, same as the claret...
I...
I REMEMBER. OH GRUD. GRUD!
...and all that's left is a scared deflato dame dyin' in the dirt. Angeltown's like that.
Like, you think it's Kook Central. You think it's larger than life and bright and sleazy...
Like a defective drokkbot in a bondage boudoir: sure it's dangerous, but it's worth it for the fun.

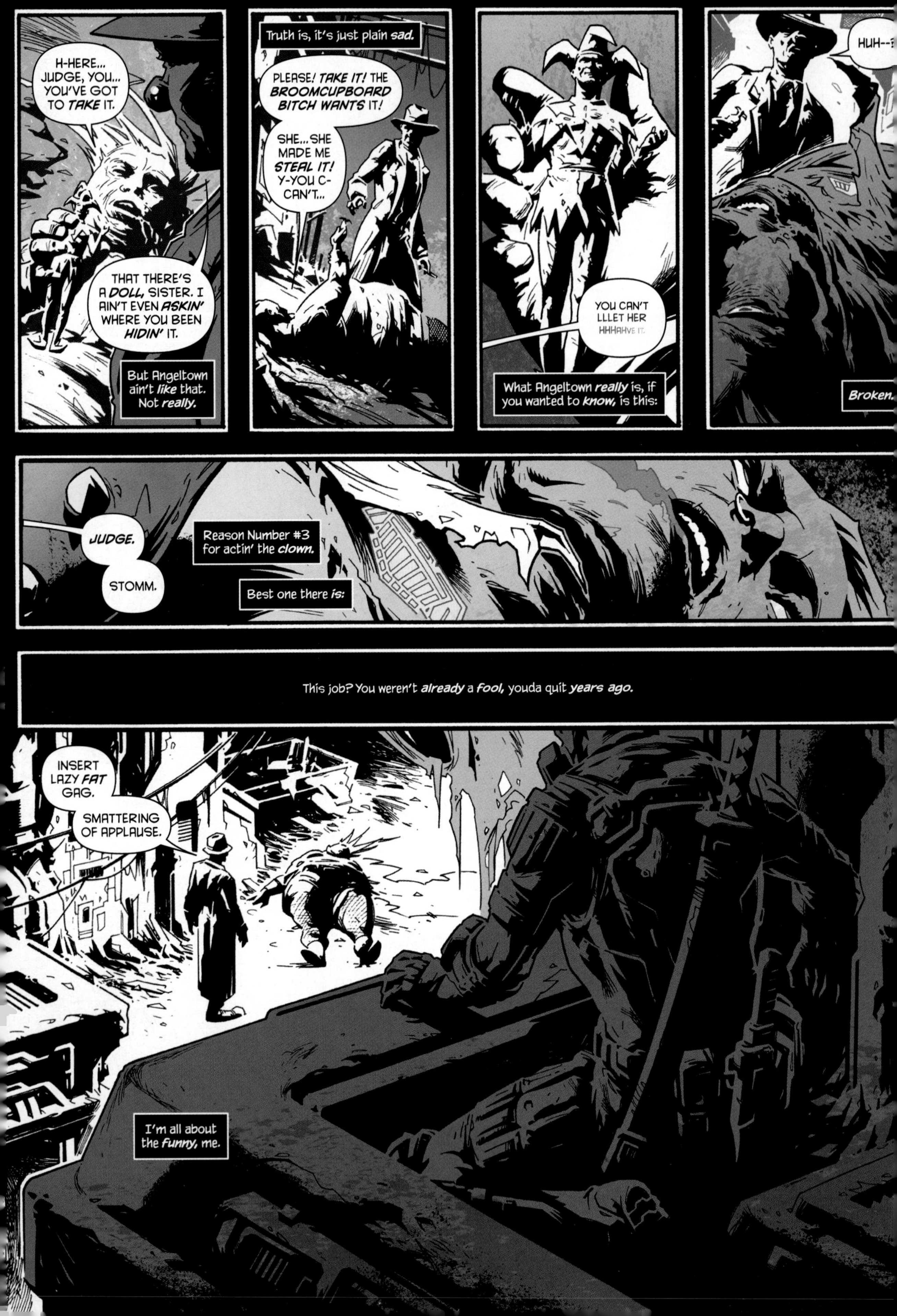
H-HERE... JUDGE, YOU... YOU'VE GOT TO TAKE IT.
THAT THERE'S A DOLL, SISTER. I AIN'T EVEN ASKIN' WHERE YOU BEEN HIDIN' IT.
But Angeltown ain't like that. Not really.
Truth is, it's just plain sad.
PLEASE! TAKE IT! THE BROOMCUPBOARD BITCH WANTS IT!
SHE... SHE MADE ME STEAL IT! Y-YOU C-CAN'T...
YOU CAN'T LLLET HER HHHAHVE IT.
What Angeltown really is, if you wanted to know, is this:
HUH--?
Broken.
JUDGE.
STOMM.
Reason Number #3 for actin' the clown.
Best one there is:
This job? You weren't already a fool, youda quit years ago.
INSERT LAZY FAT GAG.
SMATTERING OF APPLAUSE.
I'm all about the funny, me.

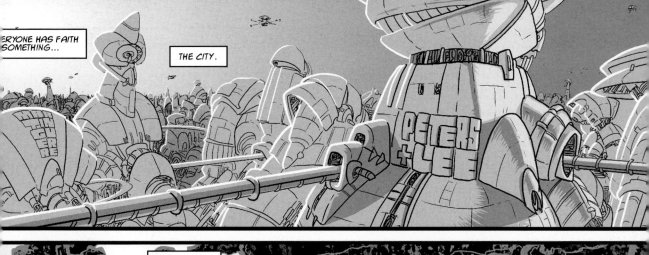

EVERYONE HAS FAITH [IN] SOMETHING...

THE CITY.

THE LOW LIFE.

SWOON!

DIRTY...

DIRTY FRANK AFFIRMED AND REDEEMED.

YAY!

DIRTY FRANK BACK ON THE MEAN STREETS OF HIS BELOVED...

HANG ON...

WHO'S **THIS** BLOKE, THEN? AND WHY HAS HE GOT IN THE WAY OF DIRTY FRANK'S EUPHORIC CELEBRATORY SEQUENCE?

JUDGE FRANK...

... YOU'RE DROOLING.

WUH!

URRR...

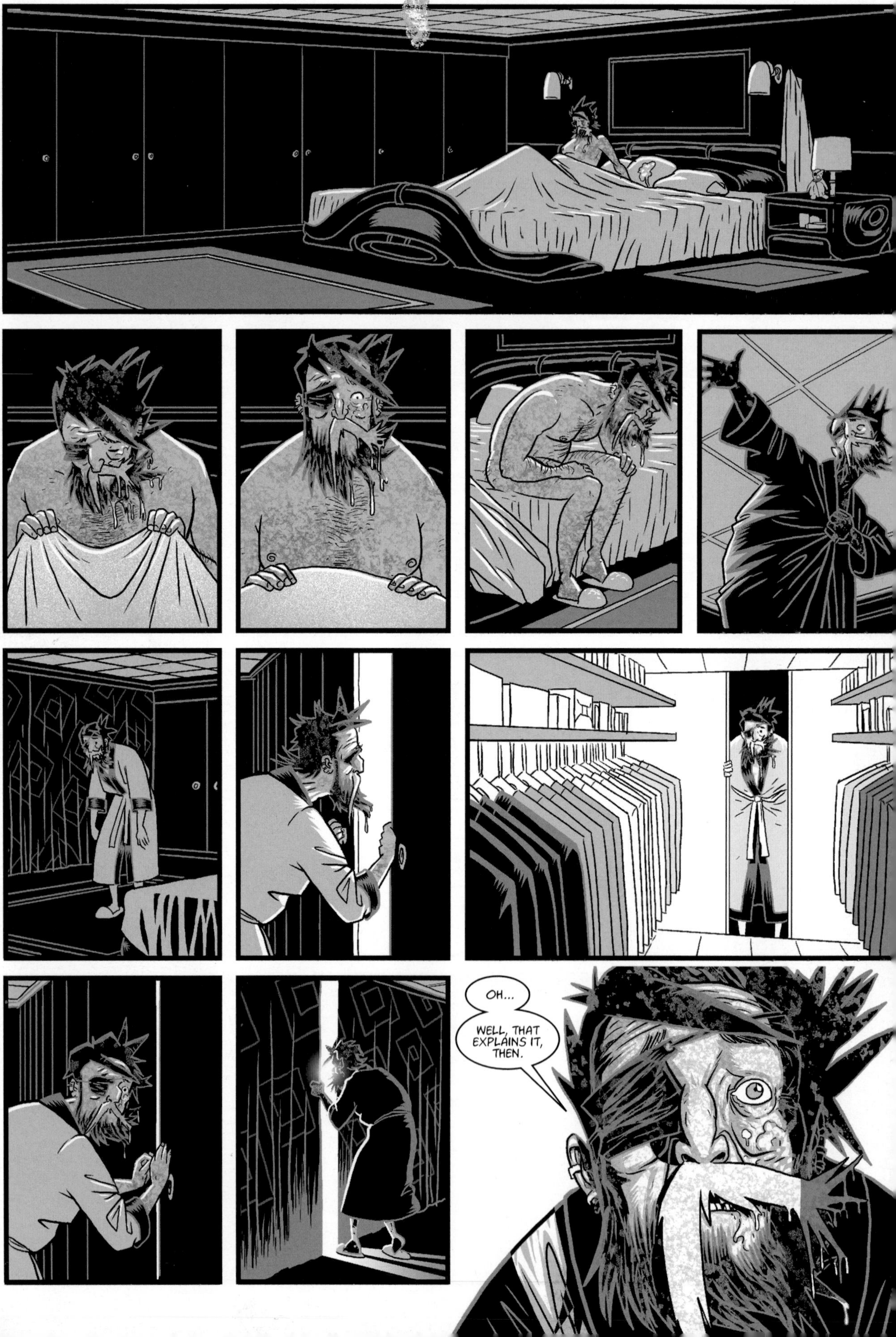
OH...
WELL, THAT EXPLAINS IT, THEN.

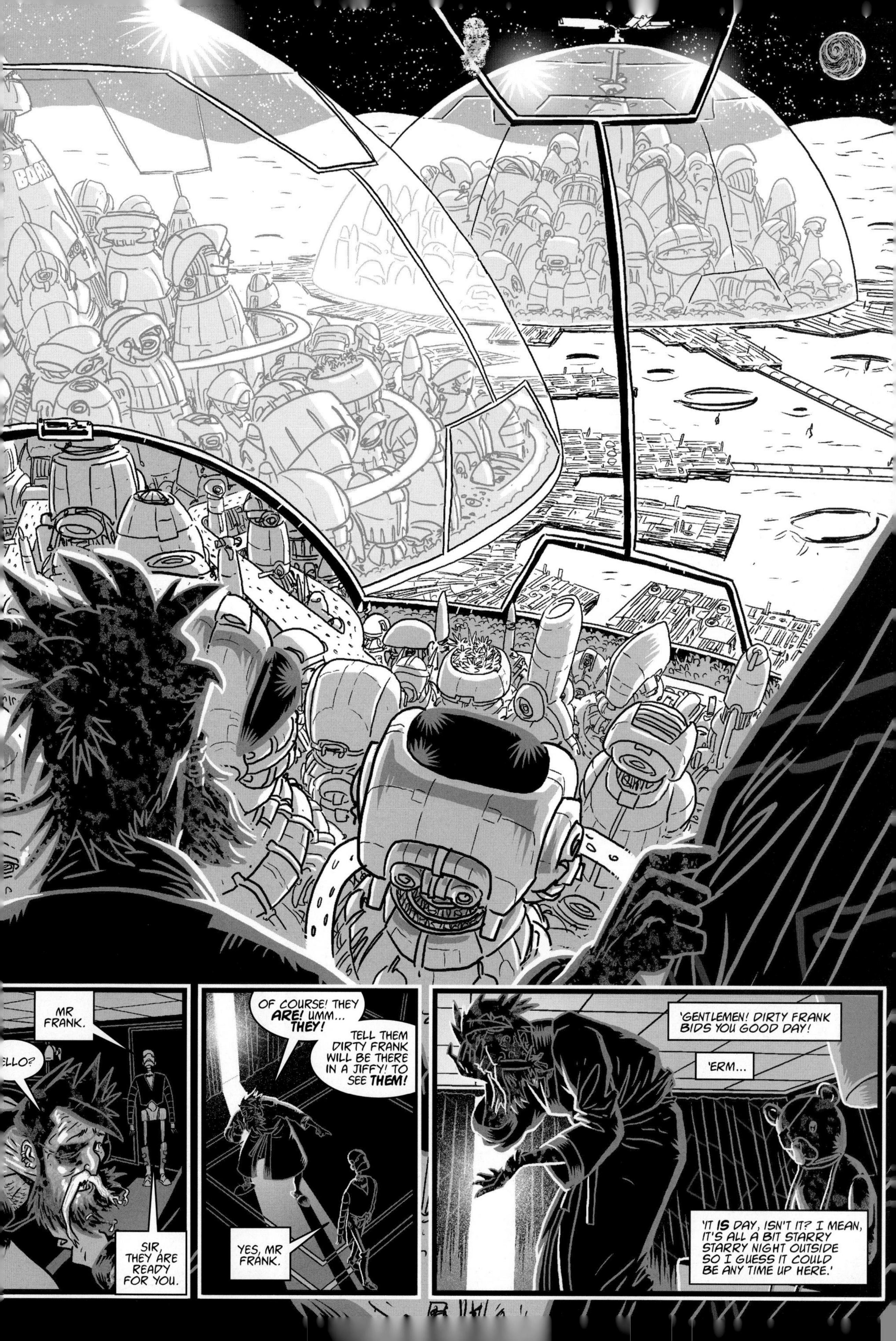
MR FRANK.
ELLO?
SIR, THEY ARE READY FOR YOU.
OF COURSE! THEY **ARE**! UMM... **THEY**!
TELL THEM DIRTY FRANK WILL BE THERE IN A JIFFY! TO SEE **THEM**!
YES, MR FRANK.
'GENTLEMEN! DIRTY FRANK BIDS YOU GOOD DAY!
'ERM...
'IT **IS** DAY, ISN'T IT? I MEAN, IT'S ALL A BIT STARRY STARRY NIGHT OUTSIDE SO I GUESS IT COULD BE ANY TIME UP HERE.'

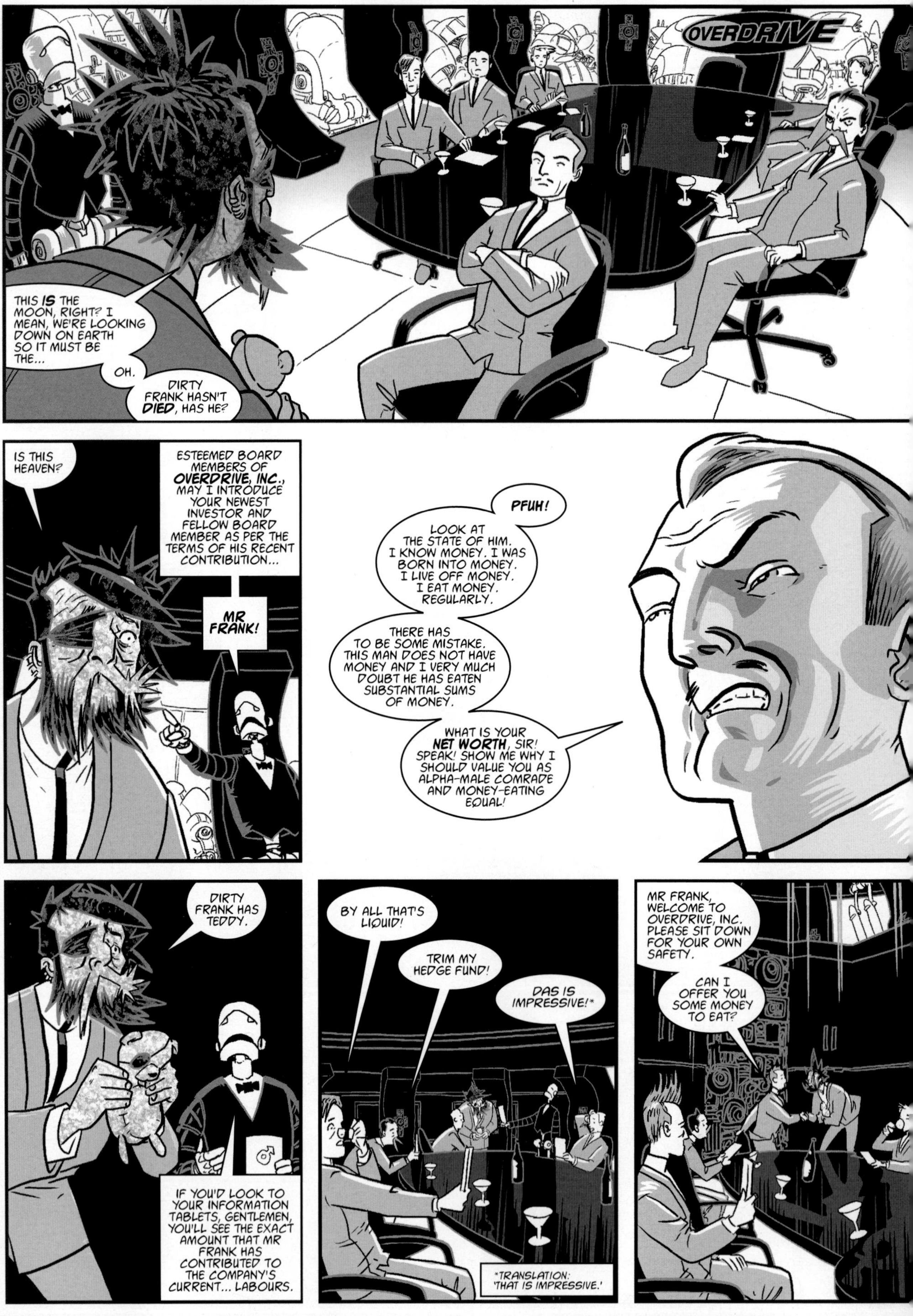

OVERDRIVE
THIS IS THE MOON, RIGHT? I MEAN, WE'RE LOOKING DOWN ON EARTH SO IT MUST BE THE...
OH.
DIRTY FRANK HASN'T DIED, HAS HE?
IS THIS HEAVEN?
ESTEEMED BOARD MEMBERS OF OVERDRIVE, INC., MAY I INTRODUCE YOUR NEWEST INVESTOR AND FELLOW BOARD MEMBER AS PER THE TERMS OF HIS RECENT CONTRIBUTION...
MR FRANK!
PFUH!
LOOK AT THE STATE OF HIM. I KNOW MONEY. I WAS BORN INTO MONEY. I LIVE OFF MONEY. I EAT MONEY. REGULARLY.
THERE HAS TO BE SOME MISTAKE. THIS MAN DOES NOT HAVE MONEY AND I VERY MUCH DOUBT HE HAS EATEN SUBSTANTIAL SUMS OF MONEY.
WHAT IS YOUR NET WORTH, SIR! SPEAK! SHOW ME WHY I SHOULD VALUE YOU AS ALPHA-MALE COMRADE AND MONEY-EATING EQUAL!
DIRTY FRANK HAS TEDDY.
IF YOU'D LOOK TO YOUR INFORMATION TABLETS, GENTLEMEN, YOU'LL SEE THE EXACT AMOUNT THAT MR FRANK HAS CONTRIBUTED TO THE COMPANY'S CURRENT... LABOURS.
BY ALL THAT'S LIQUID!
TRIM MY HEDGE FUND!
DAS IS IMPRESSIVE!*
*TRANSLATION: 'THAT IS IMPRESSIVE.'
MR FRANK, WELCOME TO OVERDRIVE, INC. PLEASE SIT DOWN FOR YOUR OWN SAFETY.
CAN I OFFER YOU SOME MONEY TO EAT?

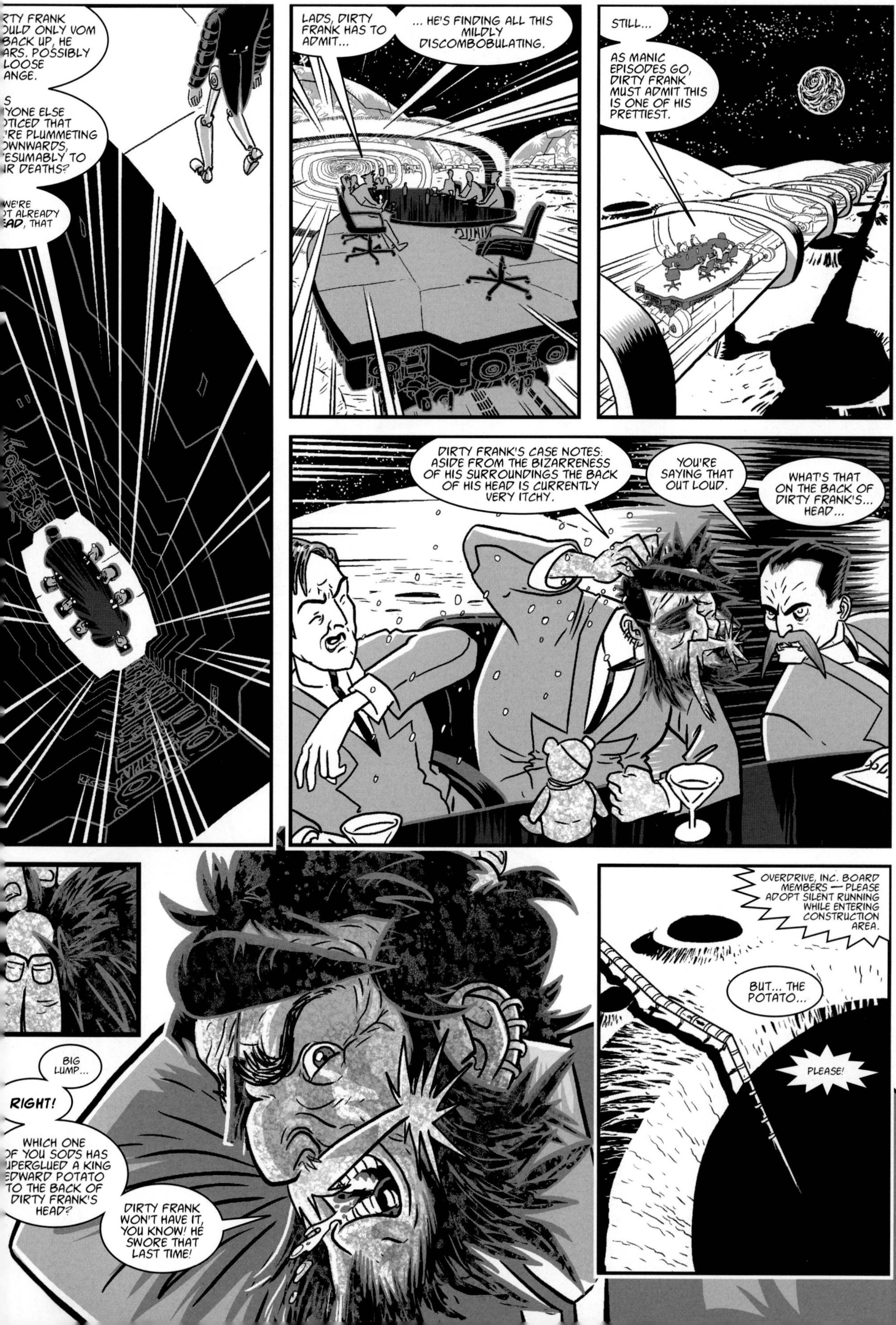

RTY FRANK
OULD ONLY VOM
BACK UP, HE
ARS. POSSIBLY
LOOSE
ANGE.
S
YONE ELSE
OTICED THAT
'RE PLUMMETING
OWNWARDS,
ESUMABLY TO
R DEATHS?
WE'RE
OT ALREADY
EAD, THAT
LADS, DIRTY FRANK HAS TO ADMIT...
... HE'S FINDING ALL THIS MILDLY DISCOMBOBULATING.
STILL...
AS MANIC EPISODES GO, DIRTY FRANK MUST ADMIT THIS IS ONE OF HIS PRETTIEST.
DIRTY FRANK'S CASE NOTES: ASIDE FROM THE BIZARRENESS OF HIS SURROUNDINGS THE BACK OF HIS HEAD IS CURRENTLY VERY ITCHY.
YOU'RE SAYING THAT OUT LOUD.
WHAT'S THAT ON THE BACK OF DIRTY FRANK'S... HEAD...
BIG LUMP...
RIGHT!
WHICH ONE
OF YOU SODS HAS
UPERGLUED A KING
EDWARD POTATO
TO THE BACK OF
DIRTY FRANK'S
HEAD?
DIRTY FRANK WON'T HAVE IT, YOU KNOW! HE SWORE THAT LAST TIME!
OVERDRIVE, INC. BOARD MEMBERS — PLEASE ADOPT SILENT RUNNING WHILE ENTERING CONSTRUCTION AREA.
BUT... THE POTATO...
PLEASE!

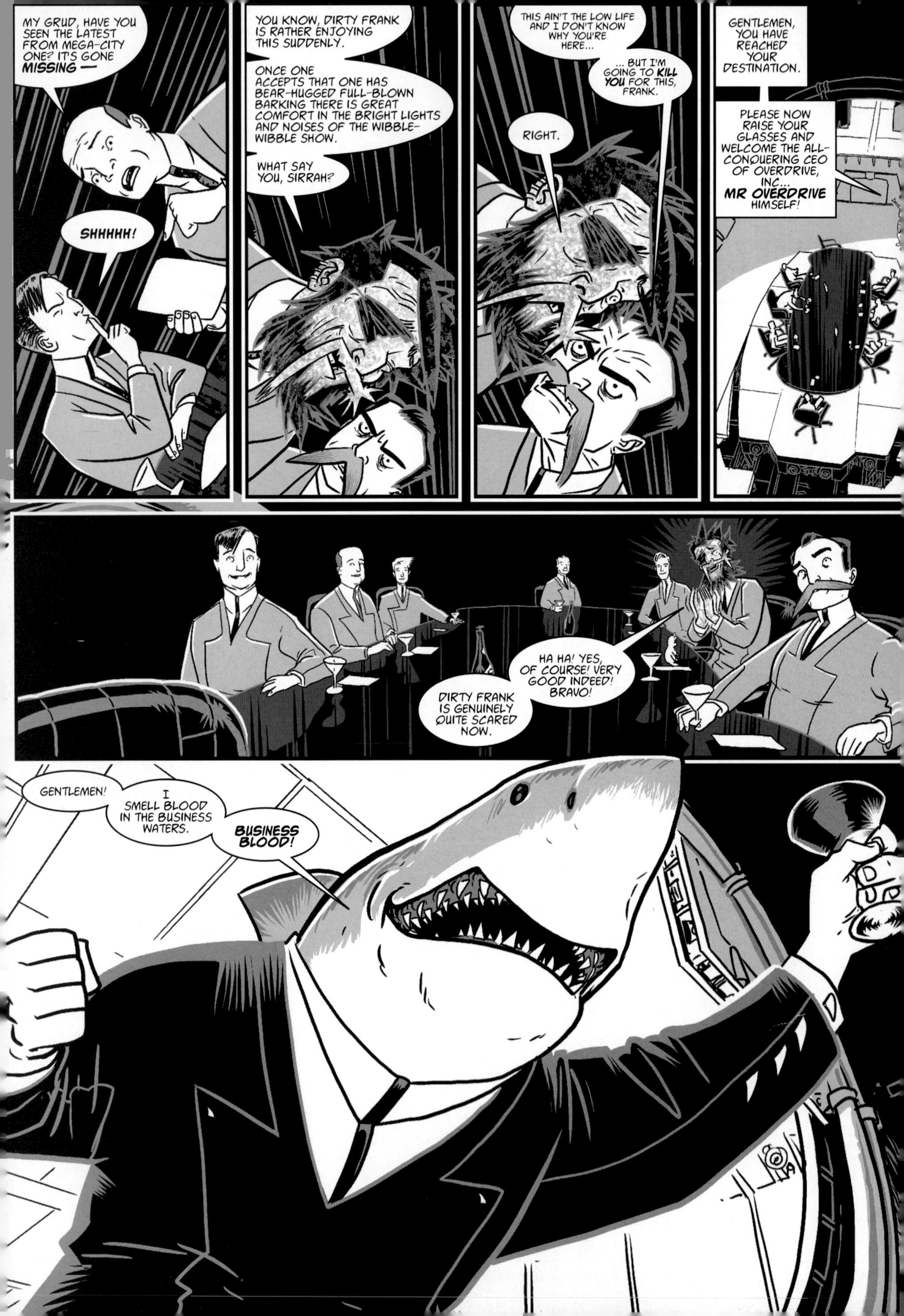

MY GRUD, HAVE YOU SEEN THE LATEST FROM MEGA-CITY ONE? IT'S GONE **MISSING** —
SHHHHH!
YOU KNOW, DIRTY FRANK IS RATHER ENJOYING THIS SUDDENLY.
ONCE ONE ACCEPTS THAT ONE HAS BEAR-HUGGED FULL-BLOWN BARKING THERE IS GREAT COMFORT IN THE BRIGHT LIGHTS AND NOISES OF THE WIBBLE-WIBBLE SHOW.
WHAT SAY YOU, SIRRAH?
THIS AIN'T THE LOW LIFE AND I DON'T KNOW WHY YOU'RE HERE...
... BUT I'M GOING TO **KILL YOU** FOR THIS, FRANK.
RIGHT.
GENTLEMEN, YOU HAVE REACHED YOUR DESTINATION.
PLEASE NOW RAISE YOUR GLASSES AND WELCOME THE ALL-CONQUERING CEO OF OVERDRIVE, INC... **MR OVERDRIVE** HIMSELF!
HA HA! YES, OF COURSE! VERY GOOD INDEED! BRAVO!
DIRTY FRANK IS GENUINELY QUITE SCARED NOW.
GENTLEMEN!
I SMELL BLOOD IN THE BUSINESS WATERS.
BUSINESS BLOOD!

ow, *corpse disposal* ain't a *keg* of
ckles at the besta times, but try doin'
with a *half-ton honey*, a *toothrot-
ggered brainstrain*, and a direct ticket
to *Titan* if you get caught.

Sure, I have my
ways. Still: been a
long drokkin' night.

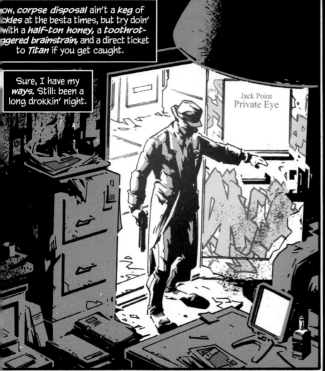

Jack Point
Private Eye

I killed a *Judge*.

Just another *stomm-stain* on the C.V.
Another reason to *throttle* the *bottle*.

HELL'RE *YOU*
LOOKIN' AT, YOU
CREEPY LITTLE
BASTARD?

THIS AIN'T
NO TIME TO
BE *SM*...

smiling

your
smiley

smile

...SAME AS I
KE MY *LINGERIE*,
R. BLACKER'N
ATAN'S *WINGS*
D PACKED WITH
SUGAR.

ANY, uh...
ANY CHANCE OF
IRISHIN' THAT
UP?

WZZZT...?

Dental displeasure. Exhaustion. Hangover like
a *cranial cremation*. And now I'm *hallucinatin'*
brainfart-bullstomm without a *hippydose high*.

Only thing could make today *worse* is--

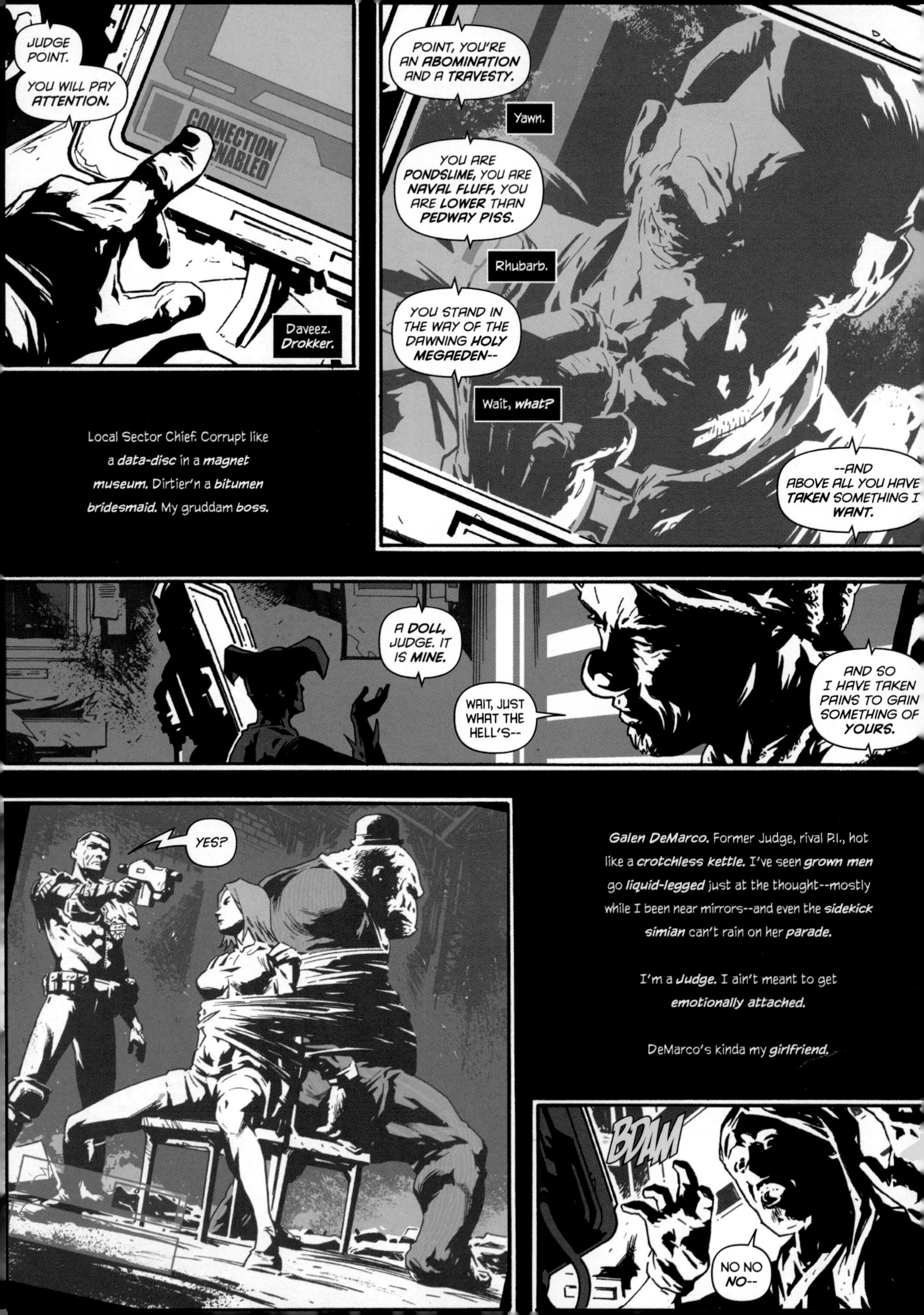
JUDGE POINT.
YOU WILL PAY ATTENTION.
CONNECTION
Daveez. Drokker.
Local Sector Chief. Corrupt like a data-disc in a magnet museum. Dirtier'n a bitumen bridesmaid. My gruddam boss.
POINT, YOU'RE AN ABOMINATION AND A TRAVESTY.
Yawn.
YOU ARE PONDSLIME, YOU ARE NAVAL FLUFF, YOU ARE LOWER THAN PEDWAY PISS.
Rhubarb.
YOU STAND IN THE WAY OF THE DAWNING HOLY MEGAEDEN--
Wait, what?
--AND ABOVE ALL YOU HAVE TAKEN SOMETHING I WANT.
A DOLL, JUDGE. IT IS MINE.
WAIT, JUST WHAT THE HELL'S--
AND SO I HAVE TAKEN PAINS TO GAIN SOMETHING OF YOURS.
YES?
Galen DeMarco. Former Judge, rival P.I., hot like a crotchless kettle. I've seen grown men go liquid-legged just at the thought--mostly while I been near mirrors--and even the sidekick simian can't rain on her parade.
I'm a Judge. I ain't meant to get emotionally attached.
DeMarco's kinda my girlfriend.
BDAM
NO NO NO--

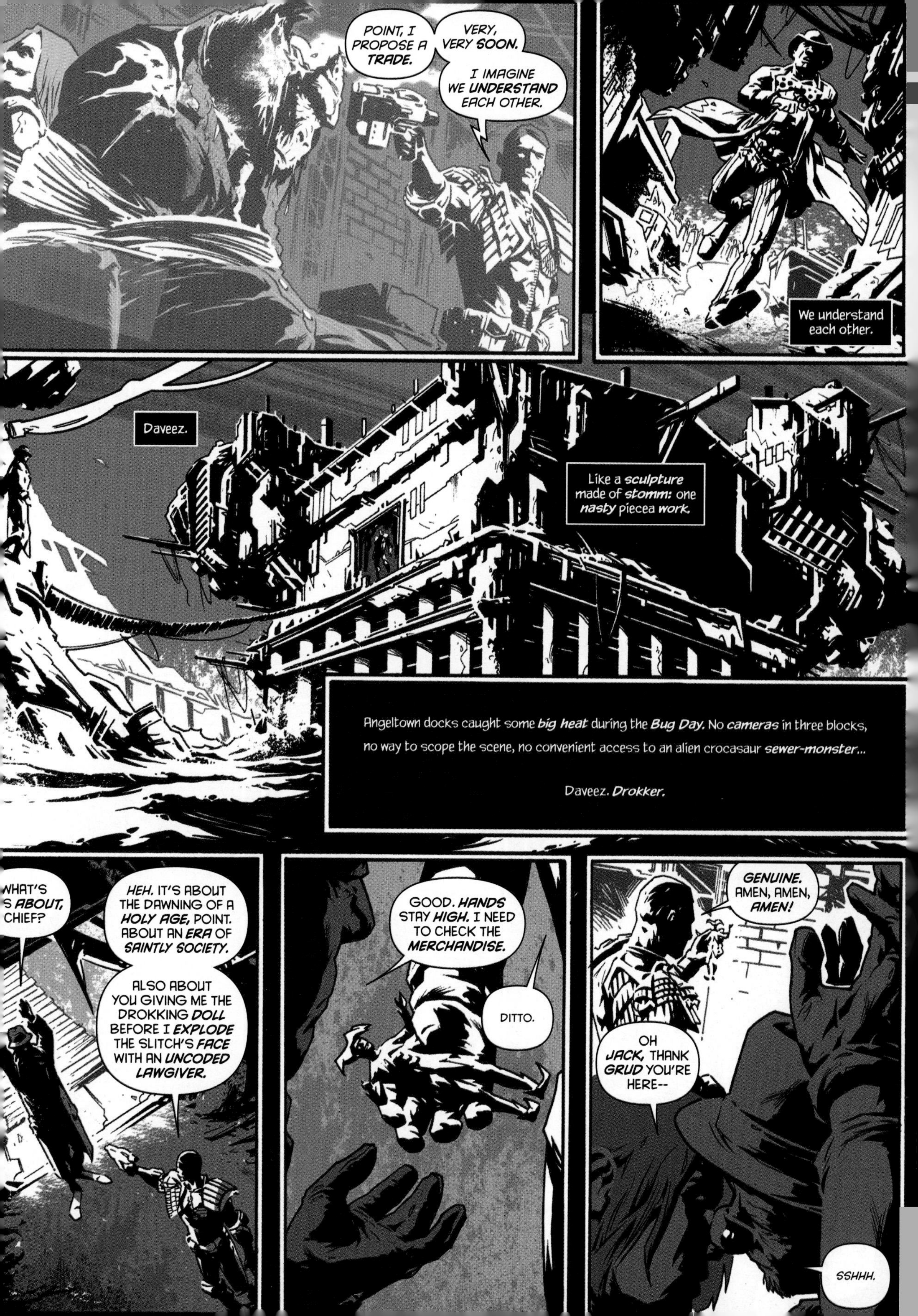
POINT, I PROPOSE A TRADE.
VERY, VERY SOON.
I IMAGINE WE UNDERSTAND EACH OTHER.
We understand each other.
Daveez.
Like a sculpture made of stomm: one nasty piecea work.
Angeltown docks caught some big heat during the Bug Day. No cameras in three blocks, no way to scope the scene, no convenient access to an alien crocasaur sewer-monster...
Daveez. Drokker.
WHAT'S
S ABOUT, CHIEF?
HEH. IT'S ABOUT THE DAWNING OF A HOLY AGE, POINT. ABOUT AN ERA OF SAINTLY SOCIETY.
ALSO ABOUT YOU GIVING ME THE DROKKING DOLL BEFORE I EXPLODE THE SLITCH'S FACE WITH AN UNCODED LAWGIVER.
GOOD. HANDS STAY HIGH. I NEED TO CHECK THE MERCHANDISE.
DITTO.
GENUINE. AMEN, AMEN, AMEN!
OH JACK, THANK GRUD YOU'RE HERE--
SSHHH.

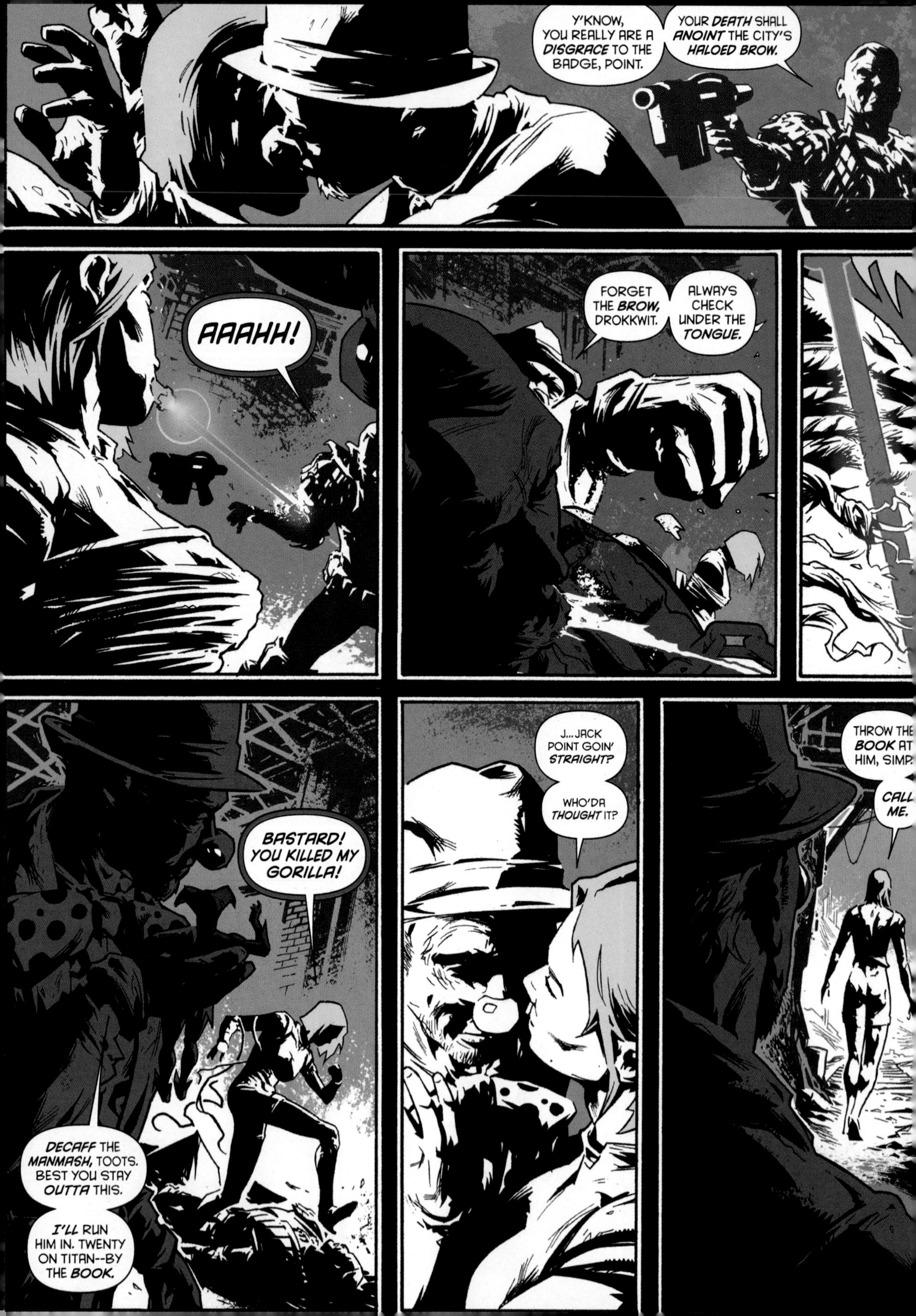
Y'KNOW, YOU REALLY ARE A DISGRACE TO THE BADGE, POINT.
YOUR DEATH SHALL ANOINT THE CITY'S HALOED BROW.
AAAHH!
FORGET THE BROW, DROKKWIT.
ALWAYS CHECK UNDER THE TONGUE.
BASTARD! YOU KILLED MY GORILLA!
DECAFF THE MANMASH, TOOTS. BEST YOU STAY OUTTA THIS.
I'LL RUN HIM IN. TWENTY ON TITAN--BY THE BOOK.
J... JACK POINT GOIN' STRAIGHT?
WHO'DA THOUGHT IT?
THROW THE BOOK AT HIM, SIMP.
CALL ME.

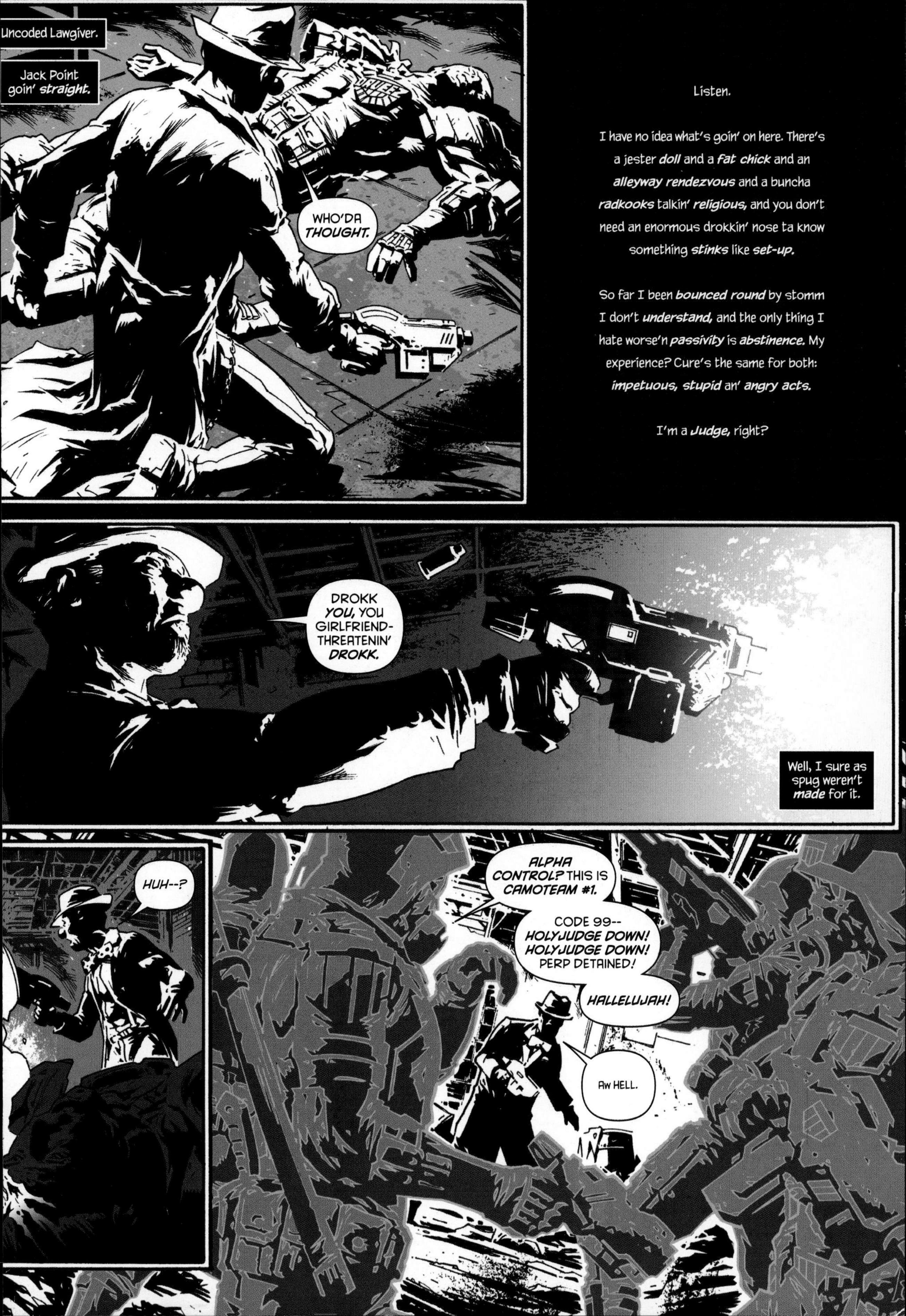

Uncoded Lawgiver.
Jack Point goin' *straight.*
WHO'DA *THOUGHT.*
Listen.
I have no idea what's goin' on here. There's a jester *doll* and a *fat chick* and an *alleyway rendezvous* and a buncha *radkooks* talkin' *religious,* and you don't need an enormous drokkin' nose ta know something *stinks* like *set-up.*
So far I been *bounced round* by stomm I don't *understand,* and the only thing I hate worse'n *passivity* is *abstinence.* My experience? Cure's the same for both: *impetuous, stupid* an' *angry acts.*
I'm a *Judge,* right?
DROKK *YOU,* YOU GIRLFRIEND-THREATENIN' *DROKK.*
Well, I sure as spug weren't *made* for it.
HUH--?
ALPHA CONTROL? THIS IS *CAMOTEAM #1.*
CODE 99-- *HOLYJUDGE DOWN! HOLYJUDGE DOWN!* PERP DETAINED!
HALLELUJAH!
AW HELL.

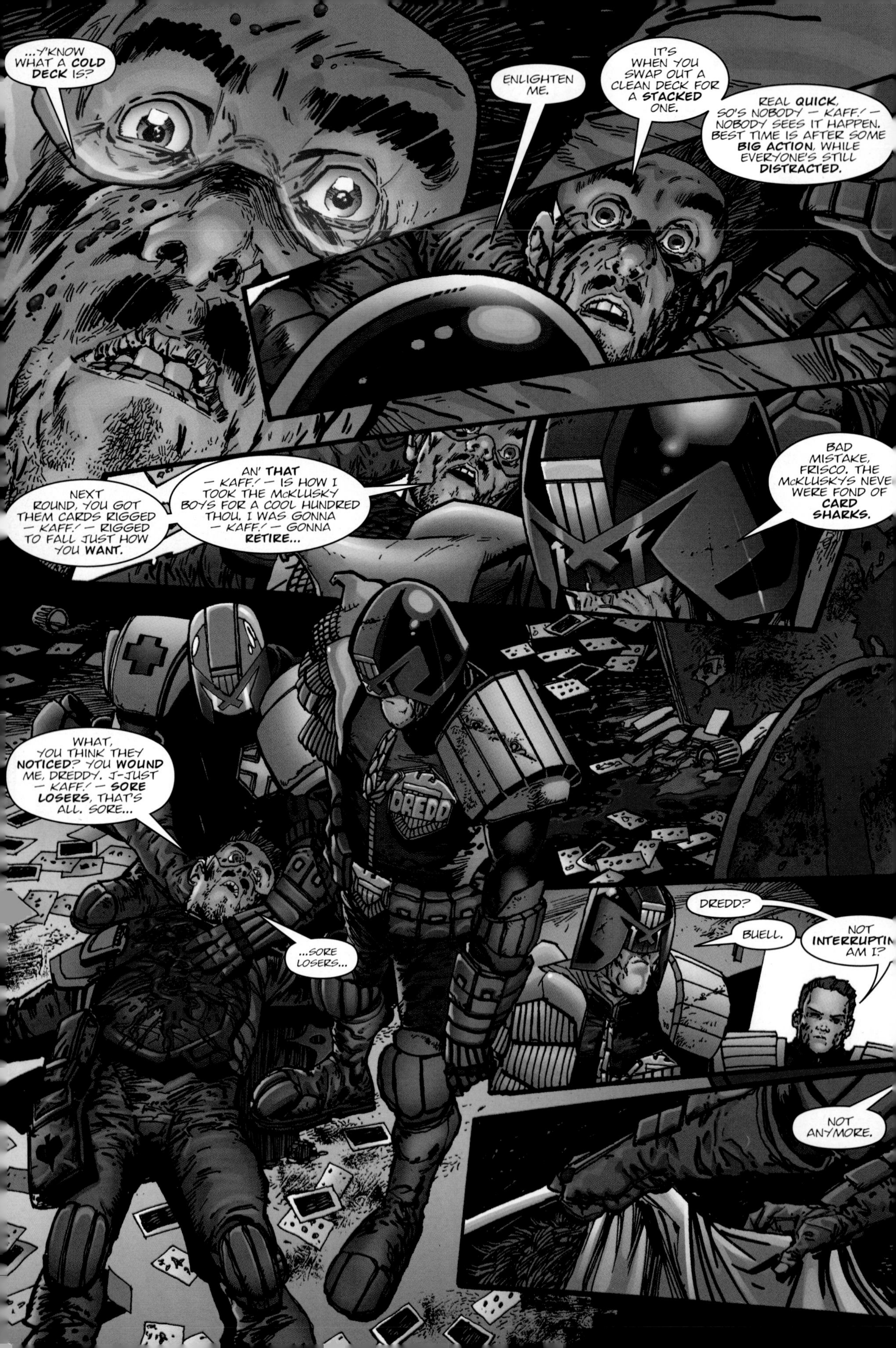
...Y'KNOW WHAT A COLD DECK IS?
ENLIGHTEN ME.
IT'S WHEN YOU SWAP OUT A CLEAN DECK FOR A STACKED ONE.
REAL QUICK, SO'S NOBODY — KAFF! — NOBODY SEES IT HAPPEN. BEST TIME IS AFTER SOME BIG ACTION, WHILE EVERYONE'S STILL DISTRACTED.
NEXT ROUND, YOU GOT THEM CARDS RIGGED — KAFF! — RIGGED TO FALL JUST HOW YOU WANT.
AN' THAT — KAFF! — IS HOW I TOOK THE McKLUSKY BOYS FOR A COOL HUNDRED THOU. I WAS GONNA — KAFF! — GONNA RETIRE...
BAD MISTAKE, FRISCO. THE McKLUSKYS NEVE WERE FOND OF CARD SHARKS.
WHAT, YOU THINK THEY NOTICED? YOU WOUND ME, DREDDY. J-JUST — KAFF! — SORE LOSERS, THAT'S ALL. SORE...
...SORE LOSERS...
DREDD?
BUELL.
NOT INTERRUPTIN AM I?
NOT ANYMORE.

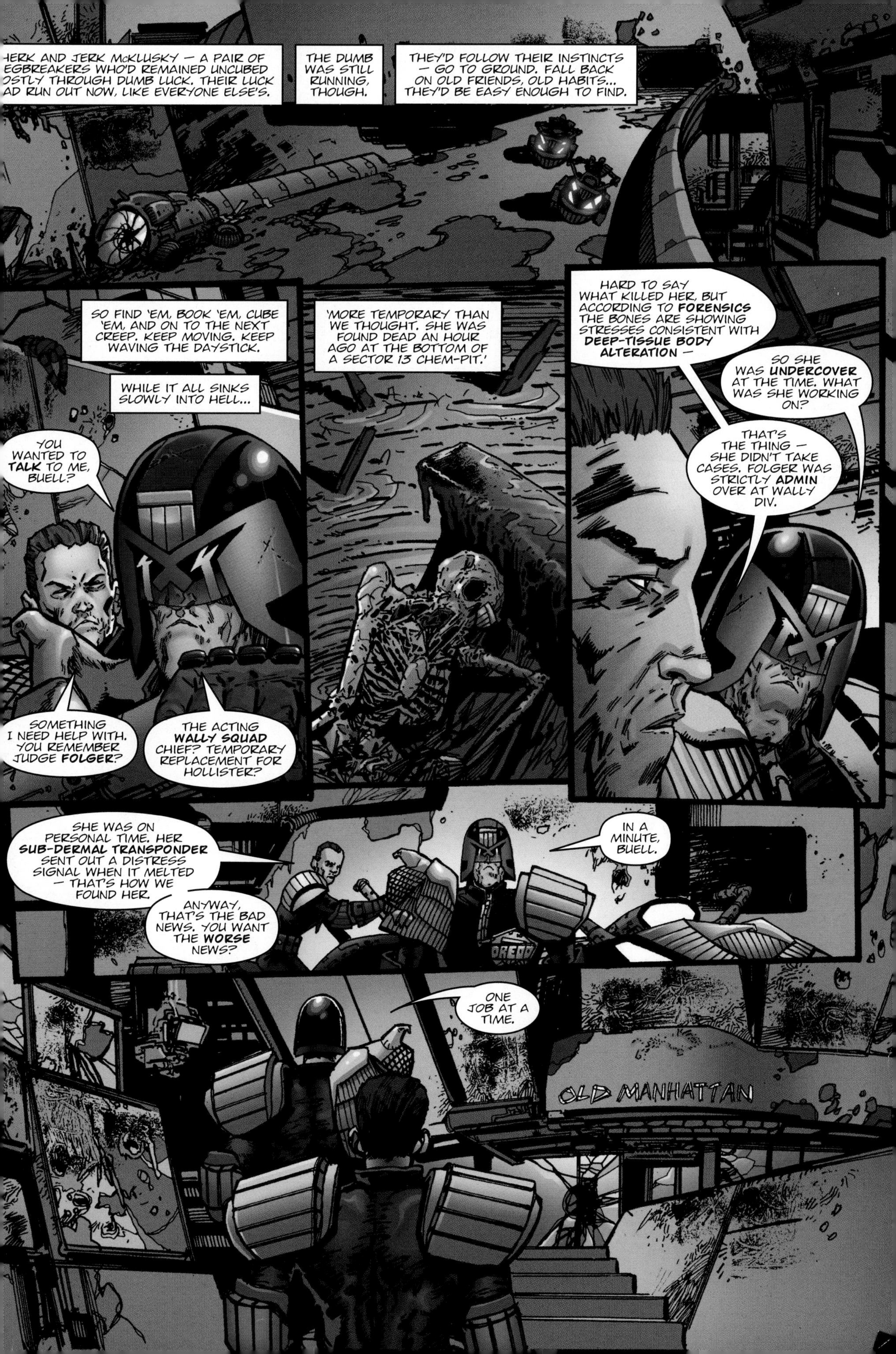

HERK AND JERK McKLUSKY — A PAIR OF EGBREAKERS WHO'D REMAINED UNCUBED OSTLY THROUGH DUMB LUCK. THEIR LUCK AD RUN OUT NOW, LIKE EVERYONE ELSE'S.
THE DUMB WAS STILL RUNNING, THOUGH.
THEY'D FOLLOW THEIR INSTINCTS — GO TO GROUND. FALL BACK ON OLD FRIENDS, OLD HABITS... THEY'D BE EASY ENOUGH TO FIND.
SO FIND 'EM, BOOK 'EM, CUBE 'EM, AND ON TO THE NEXT CREEP. KEEP MOVING. KEEP WAVING THE DAYSTICK.
WHILE IT ALL SINKS SLOWLY INTO HELL...
YOU WANTED TO TALK TO ME, BUELL?
SOMETHING I NEED HELP WITH. YOU REMEMBER JUDGE FOLGER?
THE ACTING WALLY SQUAD CHIEF? TEMPORARY REPLACEMENT FOR HOLLISTER?
'MORE TEMPORARY THAN WE THOUGHT. SHE WAS FOUND DEAD AN HOUR AGO AT THE BOTTOM OF A SECTOR 13 CHEM-PIT.'
HARD TO SAY WHAT KILLED HER, BUT ACCORDING TO FORENSICS THE BONES ARE SHOWING STRESSES CONSISTENT WITH DEEP-TISSUE BODY ALTERATION —
SO SHE WAS UNDERCOVER AT THE TIME. WHAT WAS SHE WORKING ON?
THAT'S THE THING — SHE DIDN'T TAKE CASES. FOLGER WAS STRICTLY ADMIN OVER AT WALLY DIV.
SHE WAS ON PERSONAL TIME. HER SUB-DERMAL TRANSPONDER SENT OUT A DISTRESS SIGNAL WHEN IT MELTED — THAT'S HOW WE FOUND HER.
IN A MINUTE, BUELL.
ANYWAY, THAT'S THE BAD NEWS. YOU WANT THE WORSE NEWS?
DREDD
ONE JOB AT A TIME.
OLD MANHATTAN

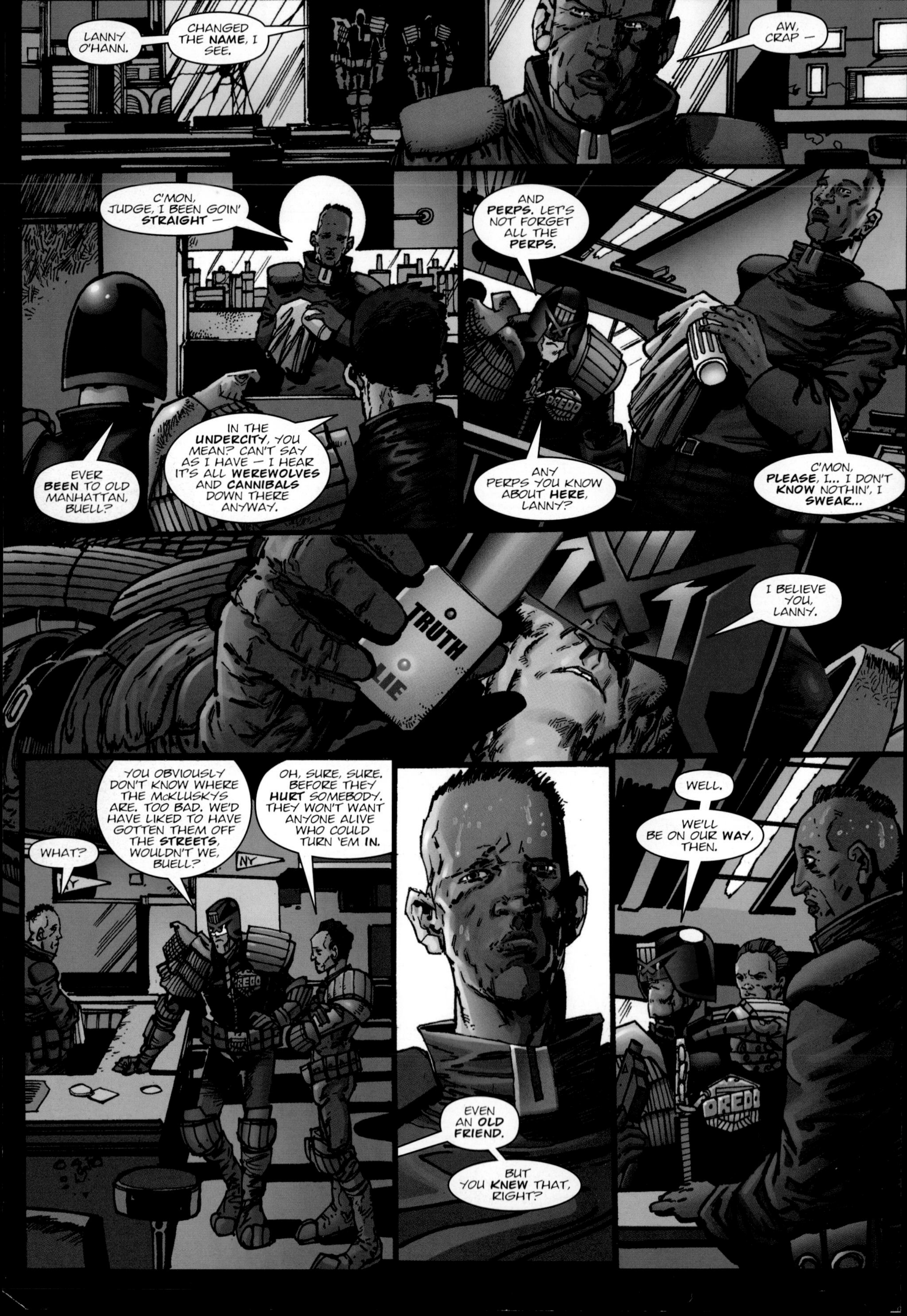
LANNY O'HANN.
CHANGED THE NAME, I SEE.
AW, CRAP —
C'MON, JUDGE, I BEEN GOIN' STRAIGHT —
EVER BEEN TO OLD MANHATTAN, BUELL?
IN THE UNDERCITY, YOU MEAN? CAN'T SAY AS I HAVE — I HEAR IT'S ALL WEREWOLVES AND CANNIBALS DOWN THERE ANYWAY.
AND PERPS. LET'S NOT FORGET ALL THE PERPS.
ANY PERPS YOU KNOW ABOUT HERE, LANNY?
C'MON, PLEASE, I... I DON'T KNOW NOTHIN', I SWEAR...
TRUTH
LIE
I BELIEVE YOU, LANNY.
YOU OBVIOUSLY DON'T KNOW WHERE THE McKLUSKYS ARE. TOO BAD. WE'D HAVE LIKED TO HAVE GOTTEN THEM OFF THE STREETS, WOULDN'T WE, BUELL?
WHAT?
OH, SURE, SURE. BEFORE THEY HURT SOMEBODY. THEY WON'T WANT ANYONE ALIVE WHO COULD TURN 'EM IN.
EVEN AN OLD FRIEND.
BUT YOU KNEW THAT, RIGHT?
WELL.
WE'LL BE ON OUR WAY, THEN.

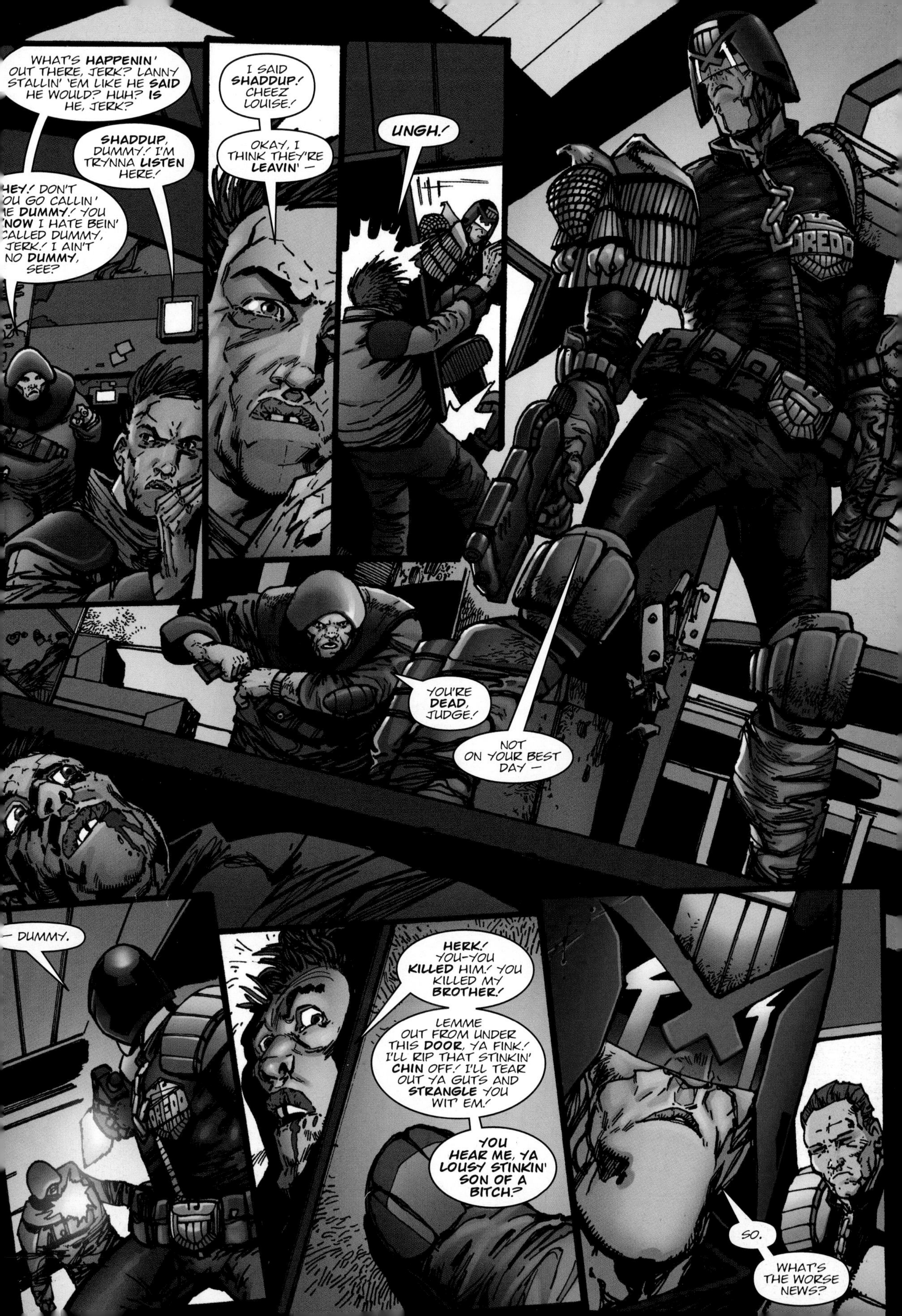

WHAT'S **HAPPENIN'** OUT THERE, JERK? LANNY STALLIN' 'EM LIKE HE **SAID** HE WOULD? HUH? **IS** HE, JERK?
SHADDUP, DUMMY! I'M TRYNNA **LISTEN** HERE!
HEY! DON'T YOU GO CALLIN' ME **DUMMY**! YOU KNOW I HATE BEIN' CALLED DUMMY, JERK! I AIN'T NO **DUMMY**, SEE?
I SAID **SHADDUP**! CHEEZ LOUISE!
OKAY, I THINK THEY'RE **LEAVIN'** —
UNGH!
YOU'RE **DEAD**, JUDGE!
NOT ON YOUR BEST DAY —
— DUMMY.
HERK! YOU-YOU **KILLED** HIM! YOU KILLED MY **BROTHER!**
LEMME OUT FROM UNDER THIS **DOOR**, YA FINK! I'LL RIP THAT STINKIN' **CHIN** OFF! I'LL TEAR OUT YA GUTS AND **STRANGLE** YOU WIT' EM!
YOU HEAR ME, YA LOUSY STINKIN' SON OF A BITCH?
SO.
WHAT'S THE WORSE NEWS?

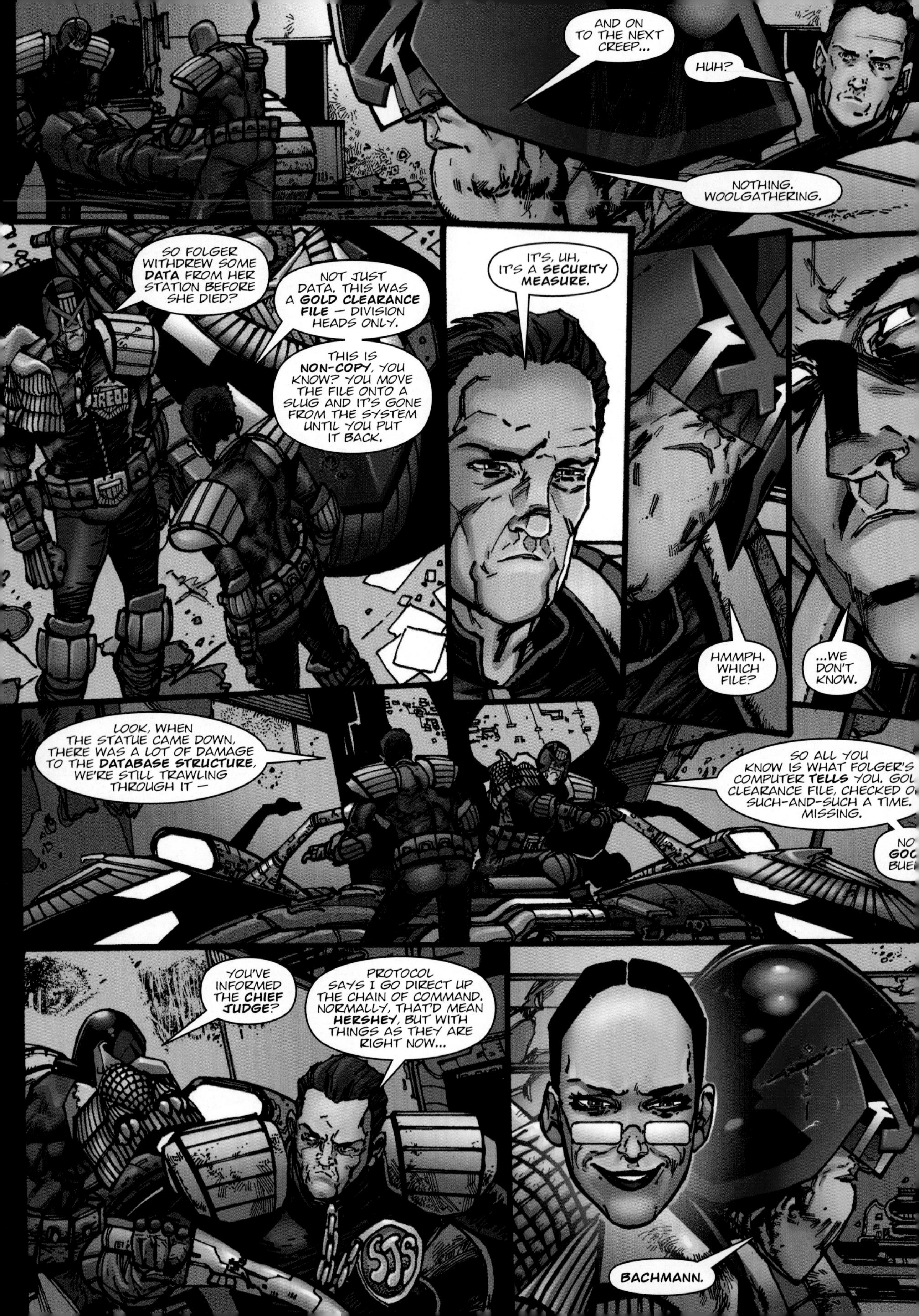

AND ON TO THE NEXT CREEP...
HUH?
NOTHING. WOOLGATHERING.
SO FOLGER WITHDREW SOME DATA FROM HER STATION BEFORE SHE DIED?
NOT JUST DATA. THIS WAS A GOLD CLEARANCE FILE — DIVISION HEADS ONLY.
THIS IS NON-COPY, YOU KNOW? YOU MOVE THE FILE ONTO A SLUG AND IT'S GONE FROM THE SYSTEM UNTIL YOU PUT IT BACK.
IT'S, UH, IT'S A SECURITY MEASURE.
HMMPH. WHICH FILE?
...WE DON'T KNOW.
LOOK, WHEN THE STATUE CAME DOWN, THERE WAS A LOT OF DAMAGE TO THE DATABASE STRUCTURE, WE'RE STILL TRAWLING THROUGH IT —
YOU'VE INFORMED THE CHIEF JUDGE?
PROTOCOL SAYS I GO DIRECT UP THE CHAIN OF COMMAND. NORMALLY, THAT'D MEAN HERSHEY, BUT WITH THINGS AS THEY ARE RIGHT NOW...
BACHMANN.

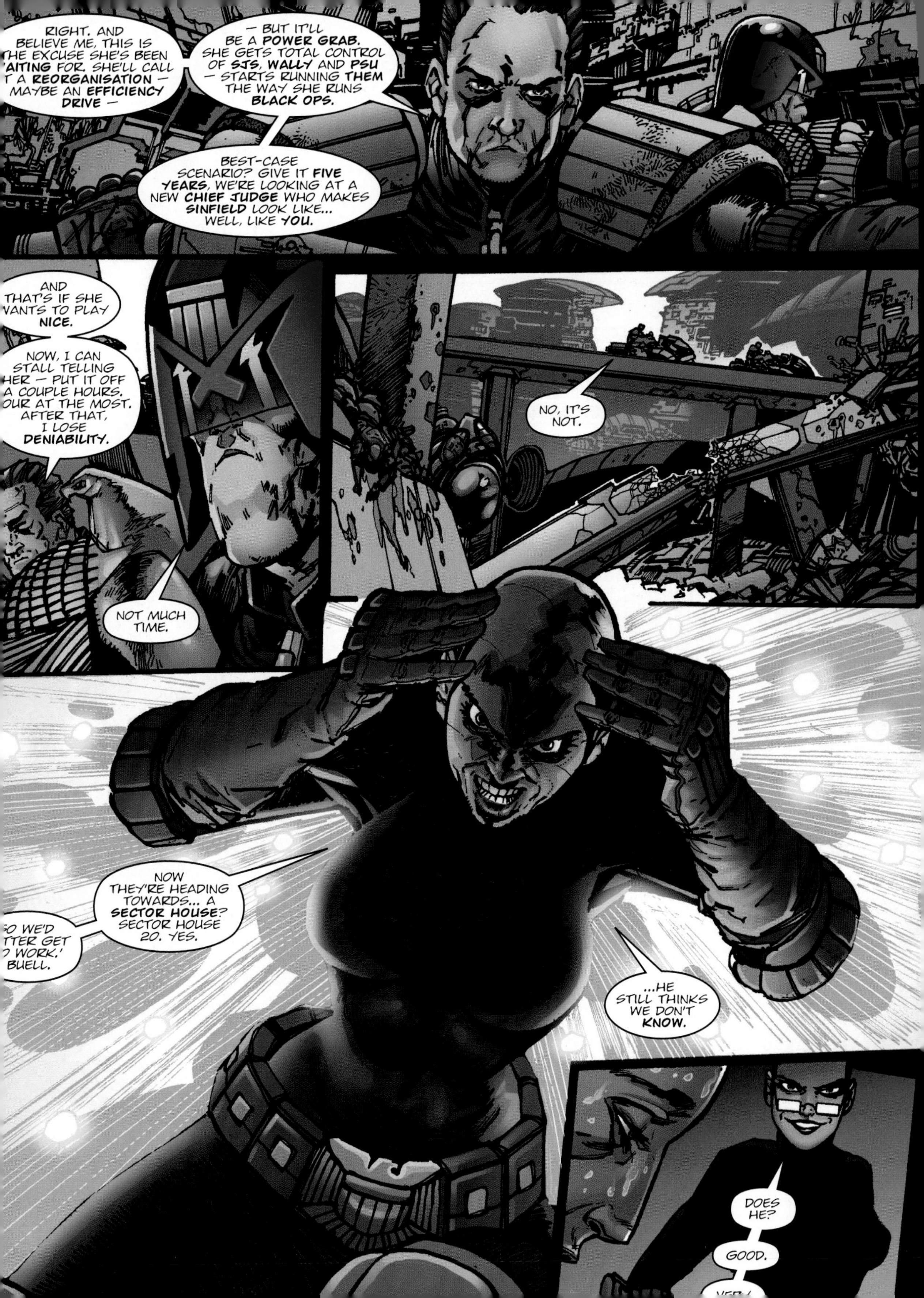
RIGHT. AND BELIEVE ME, THIS IS THE EXCUSE SHE'S BEEN AITING FOR. SHE'LL CALL T A REORGANISATION — MAYBE AN EFFICIENCY DRIVE —
— BUT IT'LL BE A POWER GRAB. SHE GETS TOTAL CONTROL OF SJS, WALLY AND PSU — STARTS RUNNING THEM THE WAY SHE RUNS BLACK OPS.
BEST-CASE SCENARIO? GIVE IT FIVE YEARS, WE'RE LOOKING AT A NEW CHIEF JUDGE WHO MAKES SINFIELD LOOK LIKE... WELL, LIKE YOU.
AND THAT'S IF SHE VANTS TO PLAY NICE.
NOW, I CAN STALL TELLING HER — PUT IT OFF A COUPLE HOURS. OUR AT THE MOST. AFTER THAT, I LOSE DENIABILITY.
NOT MUCH TIME.
NO, IT'S NOT.
NOW THEY'RE HEADING TOWARDS... A SECTOR HOUSE? SECTOR HOUSE 20. YES.
O WE'D TTER GET WORK.' BUELL.
...HE STILL THINKS WE DON'T KNOW.
DOES HE?
GOOD.

Look, survivin' *Angeltown's* a lot like playin' the *muncedog-dunk* with a Fine Freaky *Fem.* You ain't got the right *technique,* there's a *sticky end* scheduled *early.*

So count yourself lucky you got a *pro-bono pro* right here to extend the *metaphor* all to hell. Pay drokkin' *attention:*

CRIMES AGAINST *GOD!* RIGHTEOUS *EXECUTION!*

WAIT WAIT WAIT--

Tip #1: The enemy is *time.* Take a *lot* of i

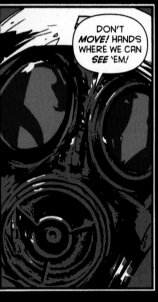

DON'T *MOVE!* HANDS WHERE WE CAN *SEE* 'EM!

DON'T MOVE! DON'T *MOVE!*

JUST... TAKIN' OFF...THE *NOSE*...SO YOU'LL *KNOW*...WHO I *AM*...

SEE? I'M A *GOOD GUY.*

Tip #2: Your *anatomy* is *apparatus.* Don't matter how *small* the relevant *parts*--

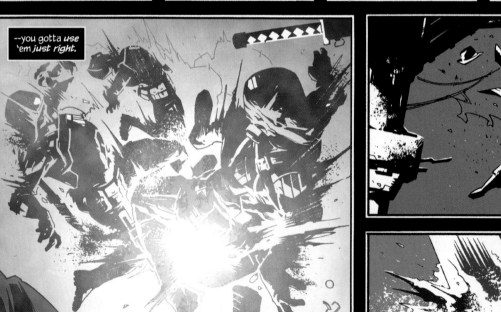

--you gotta *use* 'em *just right.*

AHHHh

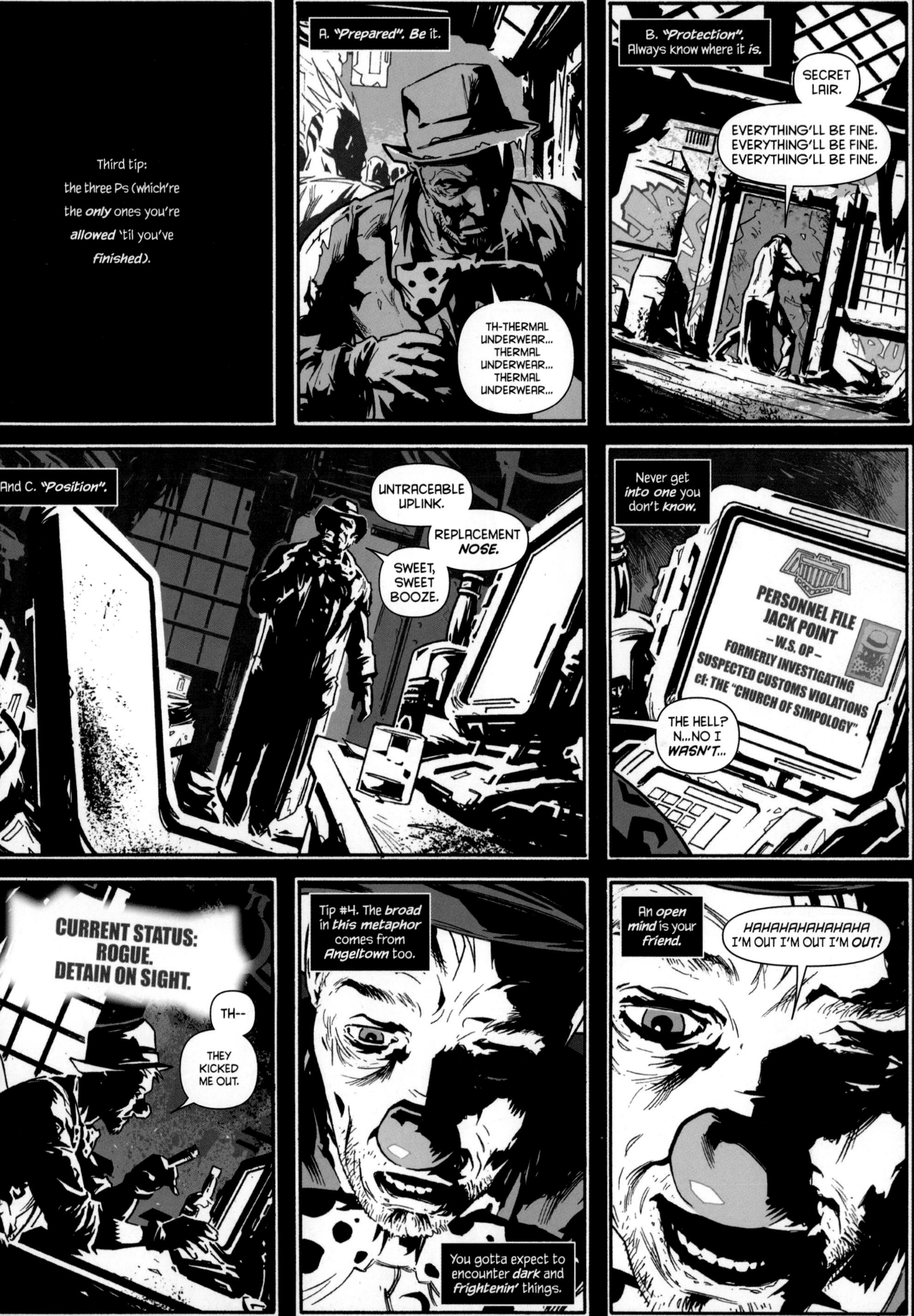

Third tip: the three Ps (which're the *only* ones you're *allowed* 'til you've *finished*).
A. *"Prepared"*. *Be* it.
TH-THERMAL UNDERWEAR... THERMAL UNDERWEAR... THERMAL UNDERWEAR...
B. *"Protection"*. Always know where it *is*.
SECRET LAIR.
EVERYTHING'LL BE FINE. EVERYTHING'LL BE FINE. EVERYTHING'LL BE FINE.
And C. *"Position"*.
UNTRACEABLE UPLINK.
REPLACEMENT *NOSE.*
SWEET, SWEET BOOZE.
Never get *into one* you don't *know*.
PERSONNEL FILE
JACK POINT
– W.S. OP –
FORMERLY INVESTIGATING
SUSPECTED CUSTOMS VIOLATIONS
cf: THE "CHURCH OF SIMPOLOGY".
THE HELL? N...NO I *WASN'T...*
CURRENT STATUS: ROGUE. DETAIN ON SIGHT.
TH--
THEY KICKED ME OUT.
Tip #4. The *broad* in *this metaphor* comes from *Angeltown* too.
You gotta expect to encounter *dark* and *frightenin'* things.
An *open mind* is your *friend*.
HAHAHAHAHAHAHAHA I'M OUT I'M OUT I'M *OUT!*

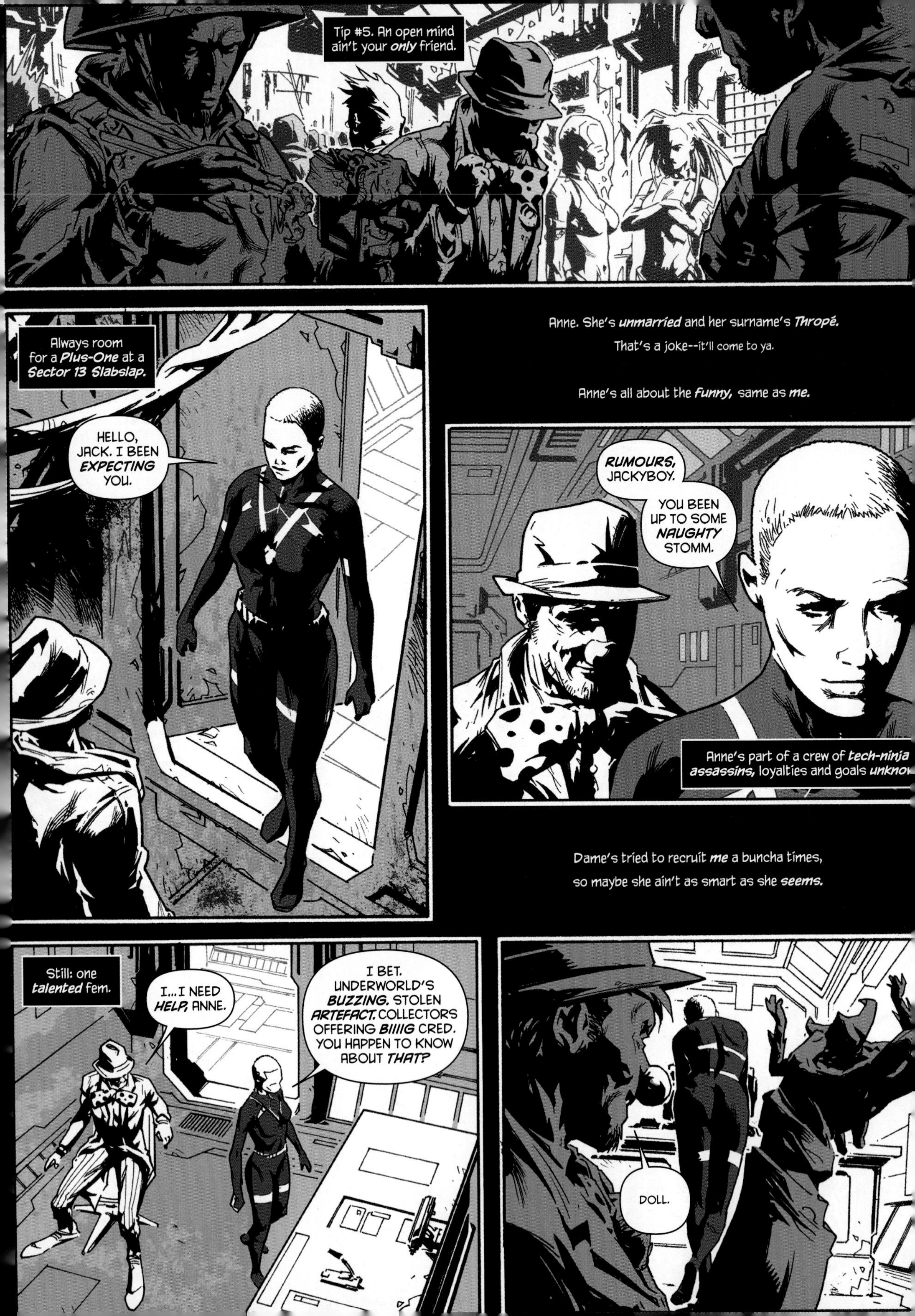

Tip #5. An open mind ain't your *only* friend.
Always room for a *Plus-One* at a *Sector 13 Slabslap.*
HELLO, JACK. I BEEN *EXPECTING* YOU.
Anne. She's *unmarried* and her surname's *Thropé.*
That's a joke--it'll come to ya.
Anne's all about the *funny,* same as *me.*
RUMOURS, JACKYBOY.
YOU BEEN UP TO SOME *NAUGHTY* STOMM.
Anne's part of a crew of *tech-ninja assassins,* loyalties and goals *unkno*
Dame's tried to recruit *me* a buncha times,
so maybe she ain't as smart as she *seems.*
Still: one *talented* fem.
I...I NEED *HELP,* ANNE.
I BET. UNDERWORLD'S *BUZZING.* STOLEN *ARTEFACT.* COLLECTORS OFFERING *BIIIIG* CRED. YOU HAPPEN TO KNOW ABOUT *THAT?*
DOLL.

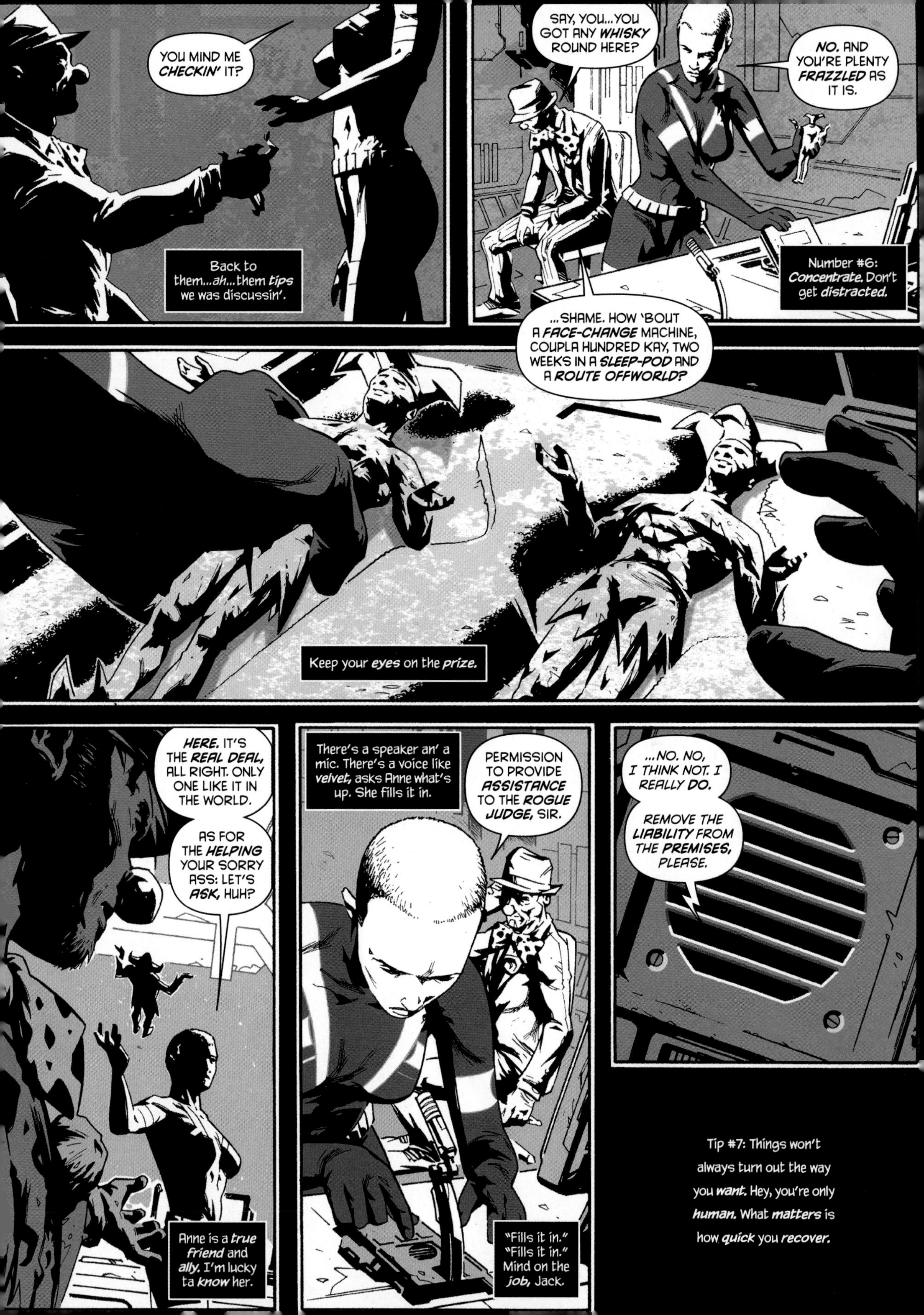
YOU MIND ME CHECKIN' IT?
Back to them...ah...them tips we was discussin'.
SAY, YOU...YOU GOT ANY WHISKY ROUND HERE?
NO. AND YOU'RE PLENTY FRAZZLED AS IT IS.
Number #6: Concentrate. Don't get distracted.
...SHAME. HOW 'BOUT A FACE-CHANGE MACHINE, COUPLA HUNDRED KAY, TWO WEEKS IN A SLEEP-POD AND A ROUTE OFFWORLD?
Keep your eyes on the prize.
HERE. IT'S THE REAL DEAL, ALL RIGHT. ONLY ONE LIKE IT IN THE WORLD.
AS FOR THE HELPING YOUR SORRY ASS: LET'S ASK, HUH?
Anne is a true friend and ally. I'm lucky ta know her.
There's a speaker an' a mic. There's a voice like velvet, asks Anne what's up. She fills it in.
PERMISSION TO PROVIDE ASSISTANCE TO THE ROGUE JUDGE, SIR.
"Fills it in." "Fills it in." Mind on the job, Jack.
...NO. NO, I THINK NOT. I REALLY DO.
REMOVE THE LIABILITY FROM THE PREMISES, PLEASE.
Tip #7: Things won't always turn out the way you want. Hey, you're only human. What matters is how quick you recover.

NOW LISTEN *HERE,* YOU DR--

JACK. *OUT.*

Y...Y'KNOW... I SWEAR I *RECOGNISED* THAT VOICE...

YOU DIDN'T.

SHAKE.

W...WHICH PART?

IDIOT.

And folks, here comes the *most important* tip of all.

#8: You wanna *survive* Angeltown--same as dancin' the *sideways-skidaddle* with its *schwingingest she-cit--*

--you're gonna need *money.*

Uh.

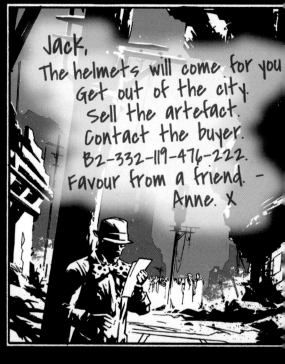

Jack,
The helmets will come for you. Get out of the city. Sell the artefact. Contact the buyer. B2-332-119-476-222. Favour from a friend. - Anne. X

Tip #9. Smoke if you *got* 'em.

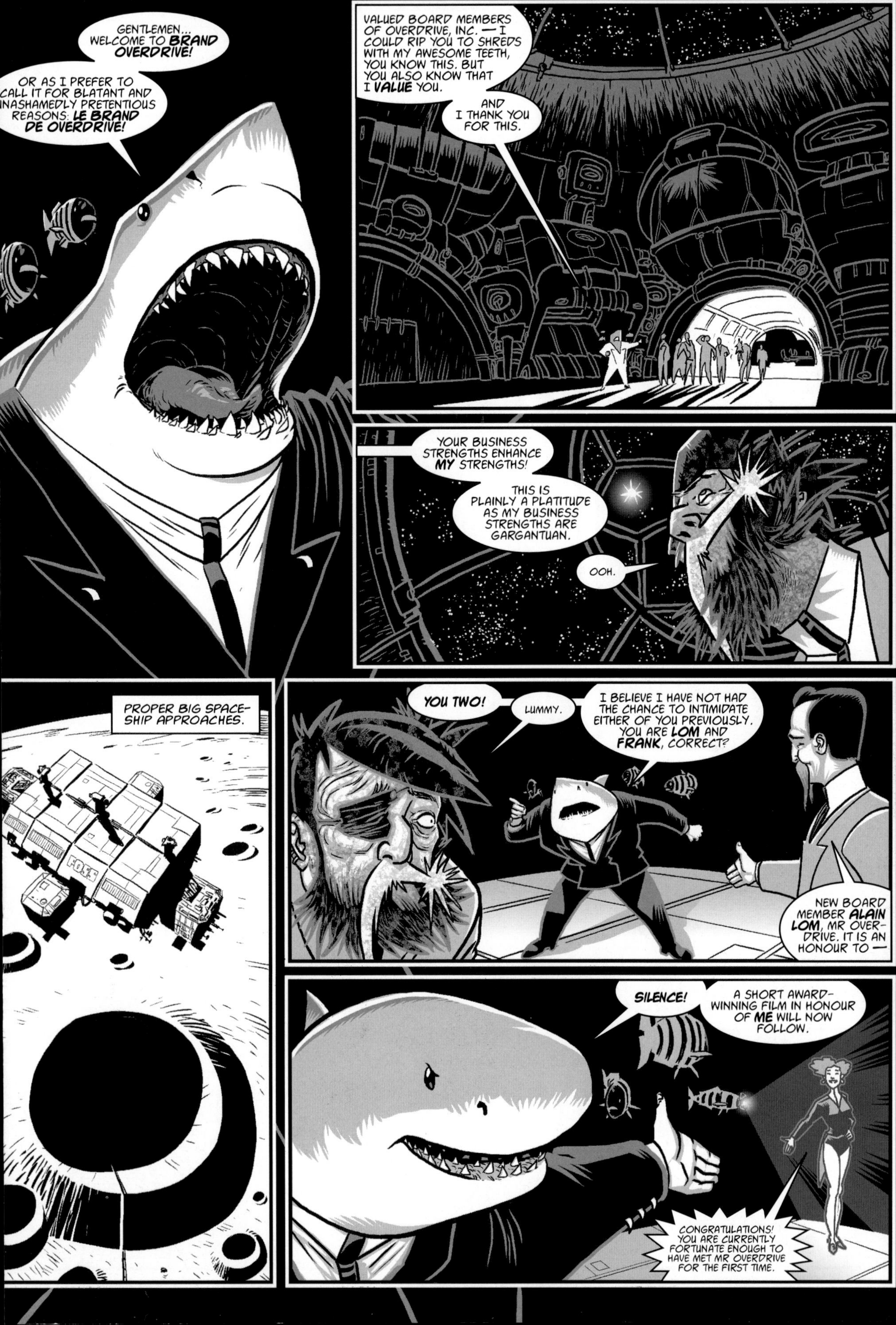
GENTLEMEN... WELCOME TO BRAND OVERDRIVE!
OR AS I PREFER TO CALL IT FOR BLATANT AND UNASHAMEDLY PRETENTIOUS REASONS: LE BRAND DE OVERDRIVE!
VALUED BOARD MEMBERS OF OVERDRIVE, INC. — I COULD RIP YOU TO SHREDS WITH MY AWESOME TEETH, YOU KNOW THIS. BUT YOU ALSO KNOW THAT I VALUE YOU.
AND I THANK YOU FOR THIS.
YOUR BUSINESS STRENGTHS ENHANCE MY STRENGTHS!
THIS IS PLAINLY A PLATITUDE AS MY BUSINESS STRENGTHS ARE GARGANTUAN.
OOH.
PROPER BIG SPACE-SHIP APPROACHES.
YOU TWO!
LUMMY.
I BELIEVE I HAVE NOT HAD THE CHANCE TO INTIMIDATE EITHER OF YOU PREVIOUSLY. YOU ARE LOM AND FRANK, CORRECT?
NEW BOARD MEMBER ALAIN LOM, MR OVER-DRIVE. IT IS AN HONOUR TO —
SILENCE!
A SHORT AWARD-WINNING FILM IN HONOUR OF ME WILL NOW FOLLOW.
CONGRATULATIONS! YOU ARE CURRENTLY FORTUNATE ENOUGH TO HAVE MET MR OVERDRIVE FOR THE FIRST TIME.

ENORMO OVERDRIVE, BORN **BARRY PENGE** — NAME CHANGED BY DEED POLL — BEGAN LIFE AS AN AMBITIOUS AND BRILLIANT MEGA-CITY ONE BUSINESSMAN.

BUT HIS PARTICULAR BRILLIANCE MARKED HIM OUT FOR BRILLIANCE.

MR OVERDRIVE MADE HIS FIRST MILLION BY PATENTING HIS INSPIRATIONAL BUSINESS MANTRA: 'DON'T BE A SHARK, BE A GREAT WHITE SHARK.'

SOON EVERYONE IN BUSINESS WAS SAYING IT.

MR OVERDRIVE THEN MADE HIS FIRST BILLION BY UPDATING THE MANTRA TO: 'DON'T BE A GREAT WHITE SHARK, BE A **GREAT** GREAT WHITE SHARK.'

A COMPETITOR ATTEMPTED TO CONTINUE THIS PATTERN BY PATENTING 'BE A GREAT, GREAT, GREAT WHITE SHARK.' BUT THIS WAS DERIDED AS BEING 'STUPID'.

MR OVERDRIVE, IN A FURTHER SHOW OF BRANDING GENIUS, THEN PAID A WORLD-RECORD SUM TO HAVE HIS **DNA** BONDED WITH THAT OF A REAL GREAT WHITE SHARK.

THIS W DEFINITELY N 'STUPID' AN WAS, IN FAC 'GREA

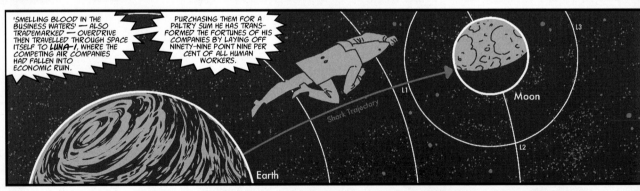

'SMELLING BLOOD IN THE BUSINESS WATERS' — ALSO TRADEMARKED — OVERDRIVE THEN TRAVELLED THROUGH SPACE ITSELF TO **LUNA-1**, WHERE THE COMPETING AIR COMPANIES HAD FALLEN INTO ECONOMIC RUIN.

PURCHASING THEM FOR A PALTRY SUM HE HAS TRANS-FORMED THE FORTUNES OF HIS COMPANIES BY LAYING OFF NINETY-NINE POINT NINE PER CENT OF ALL HUMAN WORKERS.

L3

L1

Moon

Shark Trajectory

L2

Earth

BRAVO!

WELL DOWNSIZED, SIR!

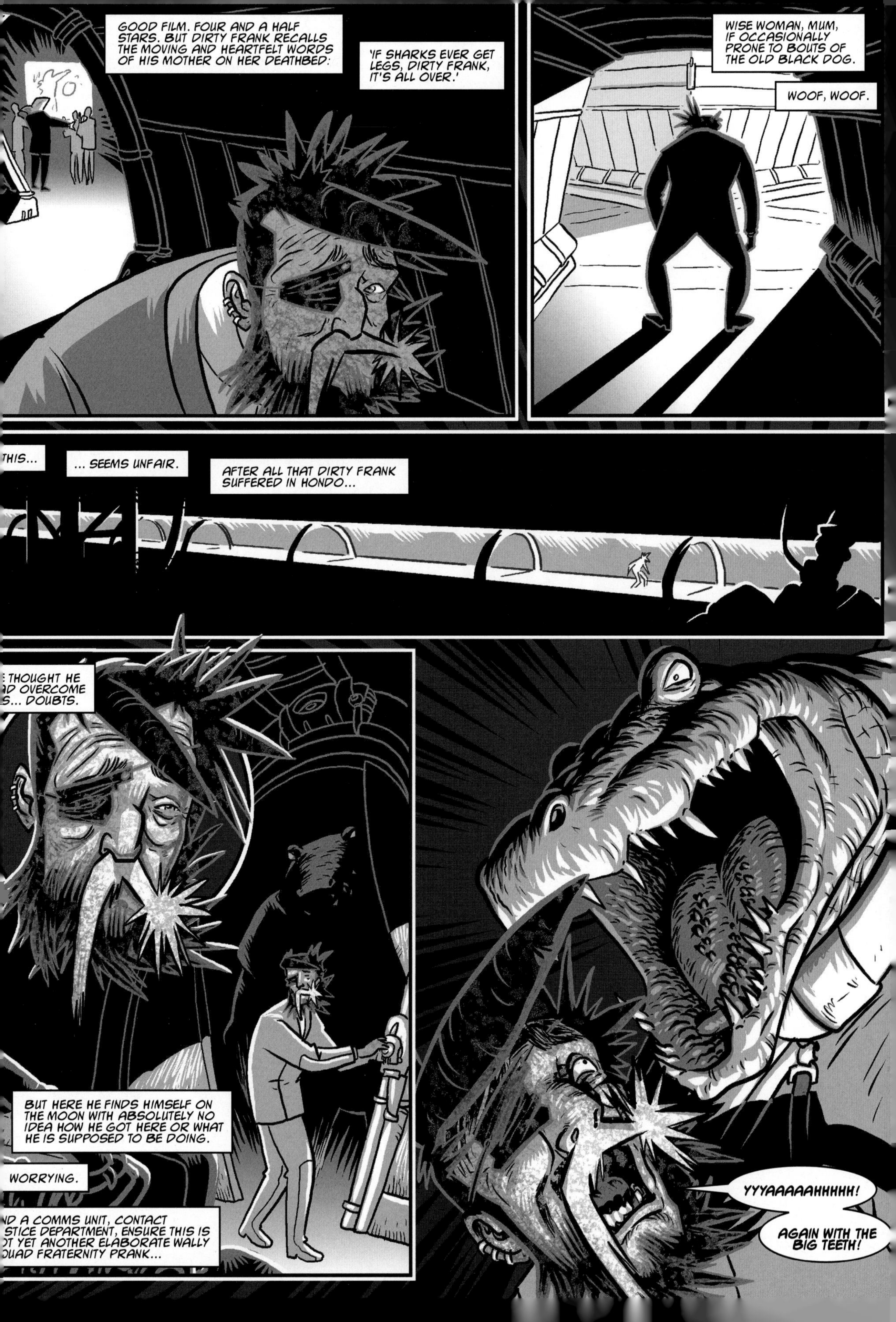
GOOD FILM. FOUR AND A HALF STARS. BUT DIRTY FRANK RECALLS THE MOVING AND HEARTFELT WORDS OF HIS MOTHER ON HER DEATHBED:
'IF SHARKS EVER GET LEGS, DIRTY FRANK, IT'S ALL OVER.'
WISE WOMAN, MUM, IF OCCASIONALLY PRONE TO BOUTS OF THE OLD BLACK DOG.
WOOF, WOOF.
THIS...
... SEEMS UNFAIR.
AFTER ALL THAT DIRTY FRANK SUFFERED IN HONDO...
THOUGHT HE AD OVERCOME S... DOUBTS.
BUT HERE HE FINDS HIMSELF ON THE MOON WITH ABSOLUTELY NO IDEA HOW HE GOT HERE OR WHAT HE IS SUPPOSED TO BE DOING.
WORRYING.
ND A COMMS UNIT, CONTACT STICE DEPARTMENT, ENSURE THIS IS OT YET ANOTHER ELABORATE WALLY QUAD FRATERNITY PRANK...
YYYAAAAAHHHHH!
AGAIN WITH THE BIG TEETH!

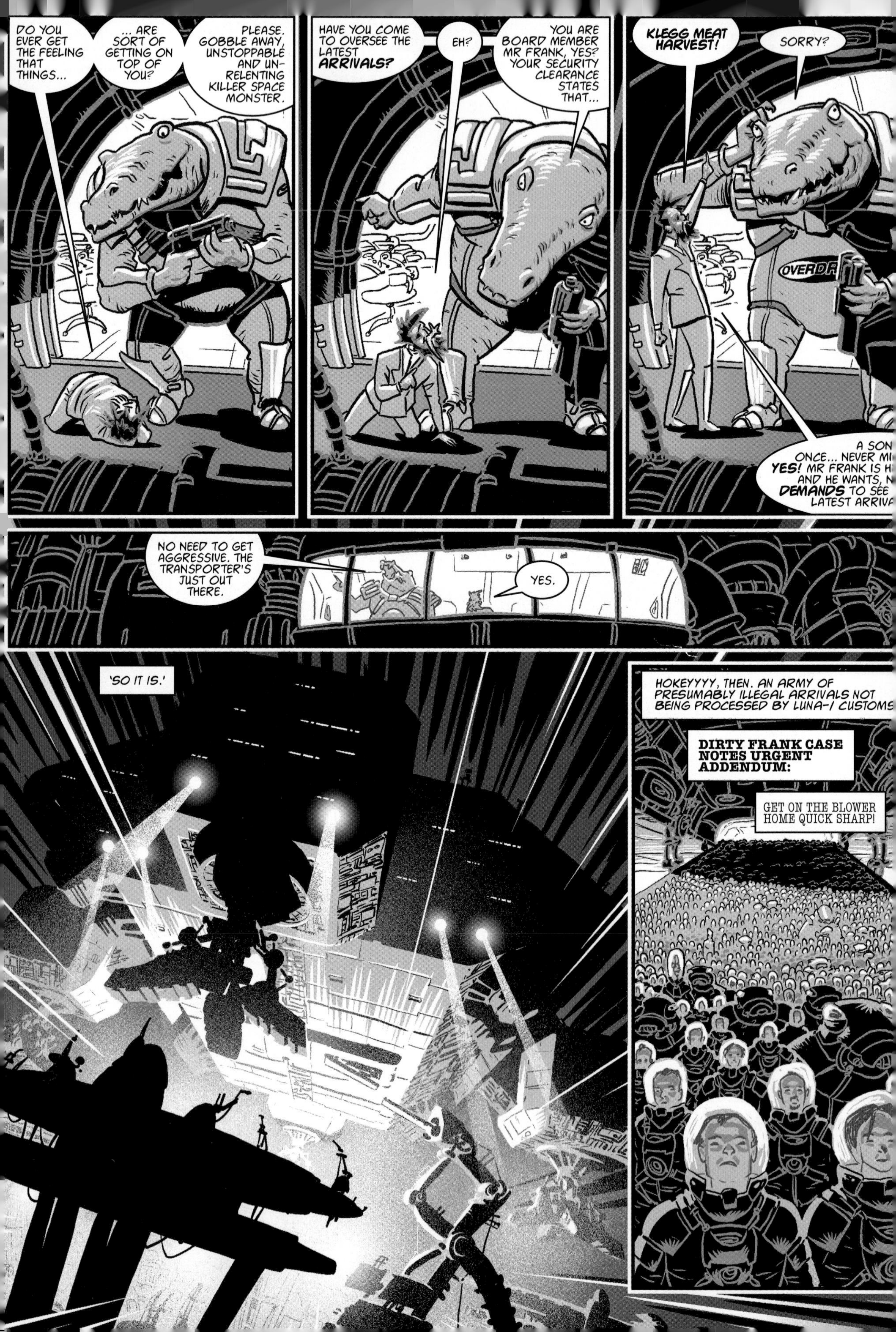

DO YOU EVER GET THE FEELING THAT THINGS...
... ARE SORT OF GETTING ON TOP OF YOU?
PLEASE. GOBBLE AWAY, UNSTOPPABLE AND UN-RELENTING KILLER SPACE MONSTER.
HAVE YOU COME TO OVERSEE THE LATEST **ARRIVALS?**
EH?
YOU ARE BOARD MEMBER MR FRANK, YES? YOUR SECURITY CLEARANCE STATES THAT...
KLEGG MEAT HARVEST!
SORRY?
OVERDR
A SON
ONCE... NEVER MI
YES! MR FRANK IS H
AND HE WANTS, N
DEMANDS TO SEE
LATEST ARRIVA
NO NEED TO GET AGGRESSIVE. THE TRANSPORTER'S JUST OUT THERE.
YES.
'SO IT IS.'
HOKEYYYY, THEN. AN ARMY OF PRESUMABLY ILLEGAL ARRIVALS NOT BEING PROCESSED BY LUNA-1 CUSTOMS
DIRTY FRANK CASE NOTES URGENT ADDENDUM:
GET ON THE BLOWER HOME QUICK SHARP!

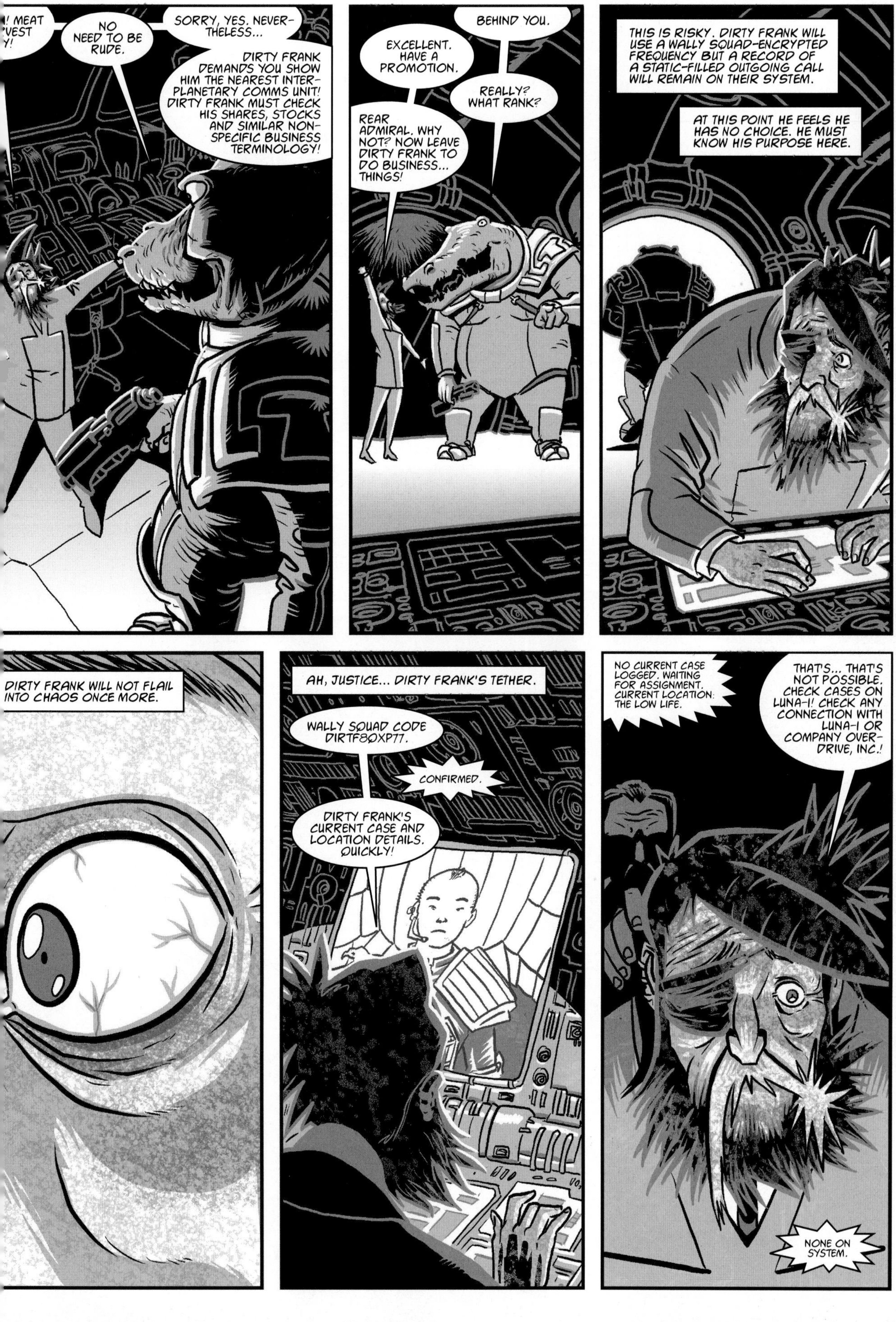
NO NEED TO BE RUDE.
SORRY, YES. NEVERTHELESS...
DIRTY FRANK DEMANDS YOU SHOW HIM THE NEAREST INTERPLANETARY COMMS UNIT! DIRTY FRANK MUST CHECK HIS SHARES, STOCKS AND SIMILAR NON-SPECIFIC BUSINESS TERMINOLOGY!
BEHIND YOU.
EXCELLENT. HAVE A PROMOTION.
REALLY? WHAT RANK?
REAR ADMIRAL. WHY NOT? NOW LEAVE DIRTY FRANK TO DO BUSINESS... THINGS!
THIS IS RISKY. DIRTY FRANK WILL USE A WALLY SQUAD-ENCRYPTED FREQUENCY BUT A RECORD OF A STATIC-FILLED OUTGOING CALL WILL REMAIN ON THEIR SYSTEM.
AT THIS POINT HE FEELS HE HAS NO CHOICE. HE MUST KNOW HIS PURPOSE HERE.
DIRTY FRANK WILL NOT FLAIL INTO CHAOS ONCE MORE.
AH, JUSTICE... DIRTY FRANK'S TETHER.
WALLY SQUAD CODE DIRTF8ØXP77.
CONFIRMED.
DIRTY FRANK'S CURRENT CASE AND LOCATION DETAILS. QUICKLY!
NO CURRENT CASE LOGGED. WAITING FOR ASSIGNMENT. CURRENT LOCATION: THE LOW LIFE.
THAT'S... THAT'S NOT POSSIBLE. CHECK CASES ON LUNA-1! CHECK ANY CONNECTION WITH LUNA-1 OR COMPANY OVER-DRIVE, INC.!
NONE ON SYSTEM.

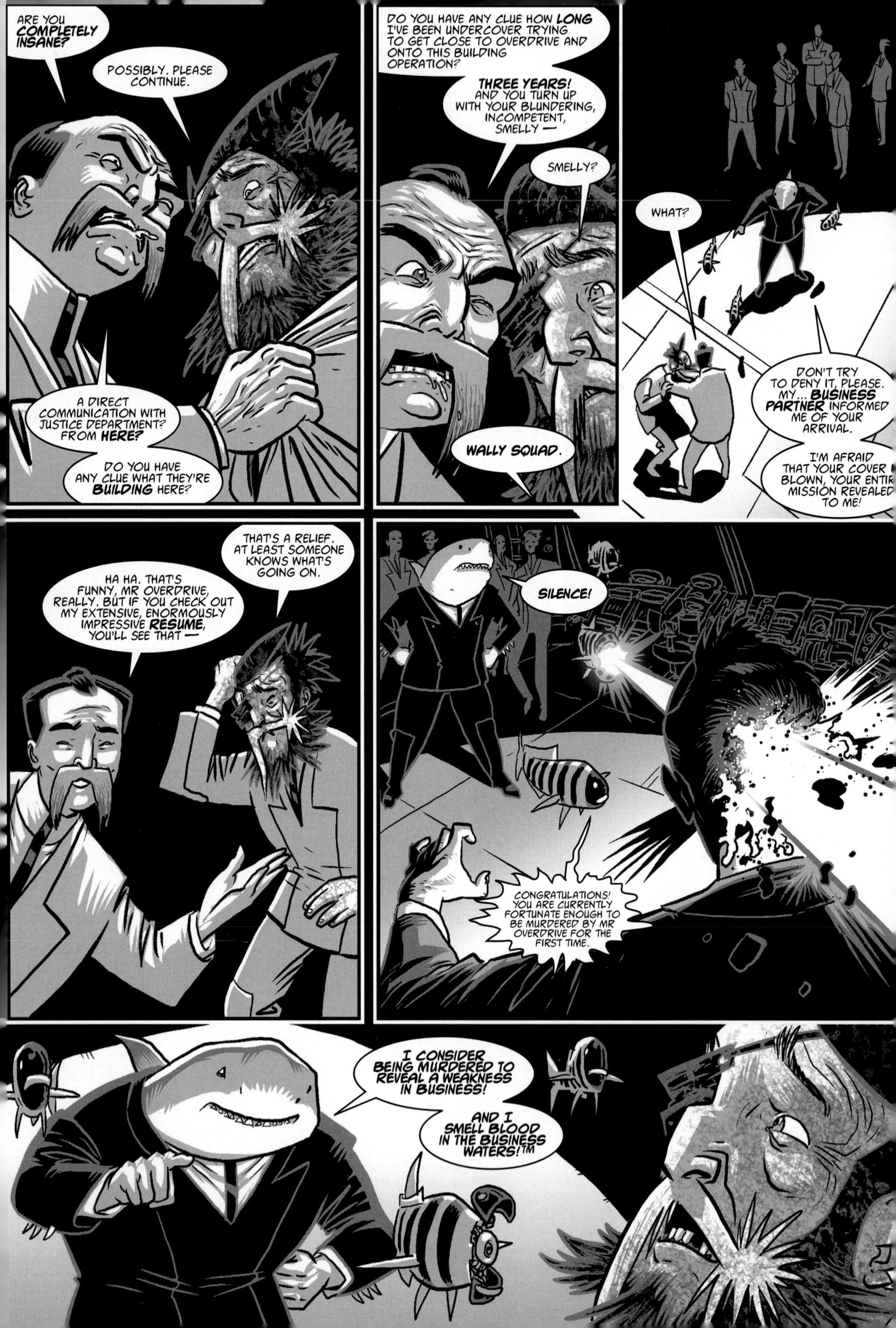
ARE YOU COMPLETELY INSANE?
POSSIBLY. PLEASE CONTINUE.
A DIRECT COMMUNICATION WITH JUSTICE DEPARTMENT? FROM HERE?
DO YOU HAVE ANY CLUE WHAT THEY'RE BUILDING HERE?
DO YOU HAVE ANY CLUE HOW LONG I'VE BEEN UNDERCOVER TRYING TO GET CLOSE TO OVERDRIVE AND ONTO THIS BUILDING OPERATION?
THREE YEARS! AND YOU TURN UP WITH YOUR BLUNDERING, INCOMPETENT, SMELLY —
SMELLY?
WALLY SQUAD.
WHAT?
DON'T TRY TO DENY IT, PLEASE. MY... BUSINESS PARTNER INFORMED ME OF YOUR ARRIVAL.
I'M AFRAID THAT YOUR COVER BLOWN, YOUR ENTIR MISSION REVEALED TO ME!
HA HA. THAT'S FUNNY, MR OVERDRIVE, REALLY. BUT IF YOU CHECK OUT MY EXTENSIVE, ENORMOUSLY IMPRESSIVE RESUME, YOU'LL SEE THAT —
THAT'S A RELIEF. AT LEAST SOMEONE KNOWS WHAT'S GOING ON.
SILENCE!
CONGRATULATIONS! YOU ARE CURRENTLY FORTUNATE ENOUGH TO BE MURDERED BY MR OVERDRIVE FOR THE FIRST TIME.
I CONSIDER BEING MURDERED TO REVEAL A WEAKNESS IN BUSINESS!
AND I SMELL BLOOD IN THE BUSINESS WATERS!™

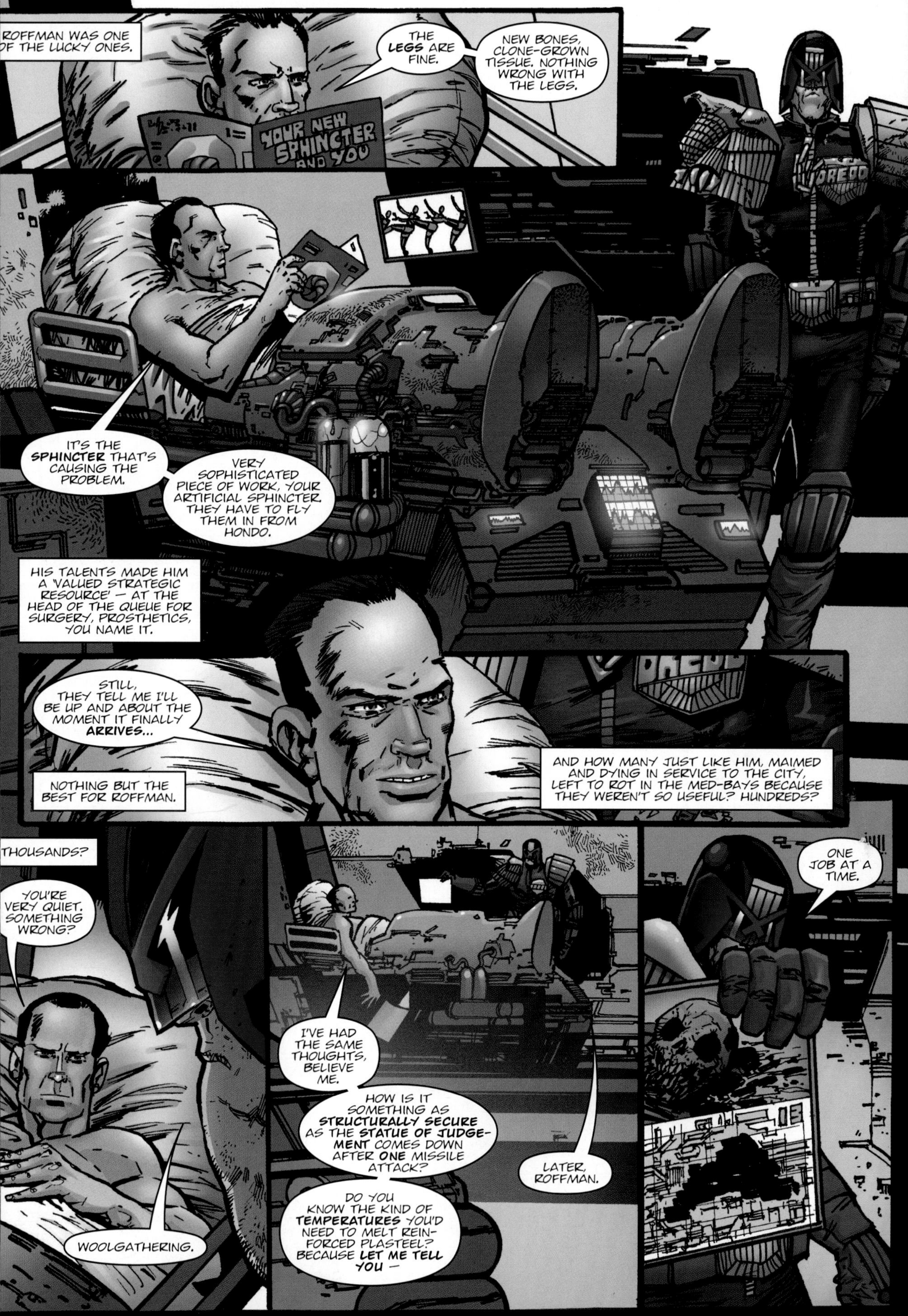
ROFFMAN WAS ONE OF THE LUCKY ONES.
YOUR NEW SPHINCTER AND YOU
THE LEGS ARE FINE.
NEW BONES, CLONE-GROWN TISSUE. NOTHING WRONG WITH THE LEGS.
IT'S THE SPHINCTER THAT'S CAUSING THE PROBLEM.
VERY SOPHISTICATED PIECE OF WORK, YOUR ARTIFICIAL SPHINCTER. THEY HAVE TO FLY THEM IN FROM HONDO.
HIS TALENTS MADE HIM A 'VALUED STRATEGIC RESOURCE' — AT THE HEAD OF THE QUEUE FOR SURGERY, PROSTHETICS, YOU NAME IT.
STILL, THEY TELL ME I'LL BE UP AND ABOUT THE MOMENT IT FINALLY ARRIVES...
NOTHING BUT THE BEST FOR ROFFMAN.
AND HOW MANY JUST LIKE HIM, MAIMED AND DYING IN SERVICE TO THE CITY, LEFT TO ROT IN THE MED-BAYS BECAUSE THEY WEREN'T SO USEFUL? HUNDREDS?
THOUSANDS?
YOU'RE VERY QUIET. SOMETHING WRONG?
WOOLGATHERING.
I'VE HAD THE SAME THOUGHTS, BELIEVE ME.
HOW IS IT SOMETHING AS STRUCTURALLY SECURE AS THE STATUE OF JUDGEMENT COMES DOWN AFTER ONE MISSILE ATTACK?
DO YOU KNOW THE KIND OF TEMPERATURES YOU'D NEED TO MELT REINFORCED PLASTEEL? BECAUSE LET ME TELL YOU —
LATER, ROFFMAN.
ONE JOB AT A TIME.

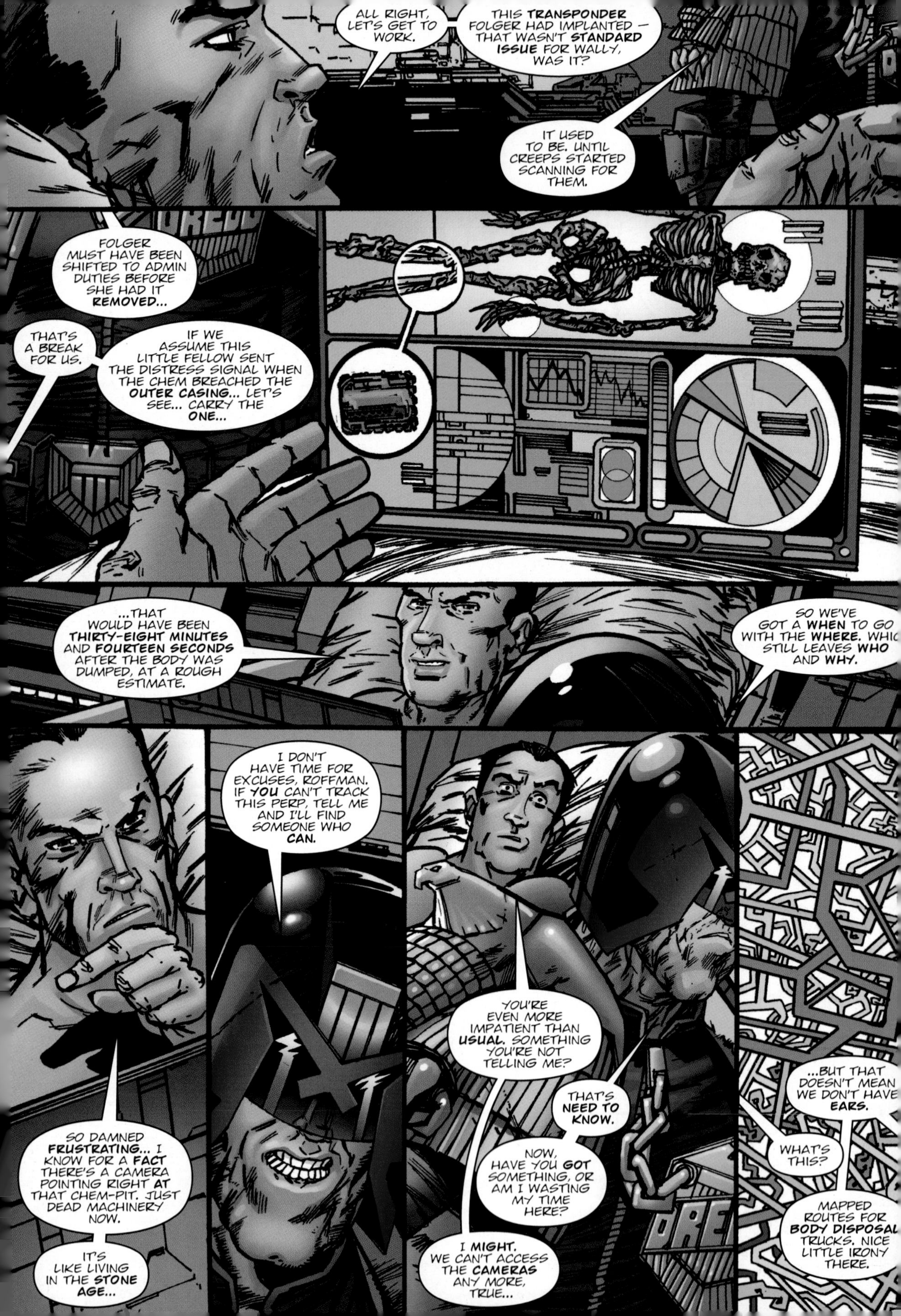
ALL RIGHT, LET'S GET TO WORK.
THIS TRANSPONDER FOLGER HAD IMPLANTED — THAT WASN'T STANDARD ISSUE FOR WALLY, WAS IT?
IT USED TO BE. UNTIL CREEPS STARTED SCANNING FOR THEM.
FOLGER MUST HAVE BEEN SHIFTED TO ADMIN DUTIES BEFORE SHE HAD IT REMOVED...
THAT'S A BREAK FOR US.
IF WE ASSUME THIS LITTLE FELLOW SENT THE DISTRESS SIGNAL WHEN THE CHEM BREACHED THE OUTER CASING... LET'S SEE... CARRY THE ONE...
...THAT WOULD HAVE BEEN THIRTY-EIGHT MINUTES AND FOURTEEN SECONDS AFTER THE BODY WAS DUMPED, AT A ROUGH ESTIMATE.
SO WE'VE GOT A WHEN TO GO WITH THE WHERE. WHIC STILL LEAVES WHO AND WHY.
SO DAMNED FRUSTRATING... I KNOW FOR A FACT THERE'S A CAMERA POINTING RIGHT AT THAT CHEM-PIT. JUST DEAD MACHINERY NOW.
IT'S LIKE LIVING IN THE STONE AGE...
I DON'T HAVE TIME FOR EXCUSES, ROFFMAN. IF YOU CAN'T TRACK THIS PERP, TELL ME AND I'LL FIND SOMEONE WHO CAN.
YOU'RE EVEN MORE IMPATIENT THAN USUAL. SOMETHING YOU'RE NOT TELLING ME?
THAT'S NEED TO KNOW.
NOW, HAVE YOU GOT SOMETHING, OR AM I WASTING MY TIME HERE?
I MIGHT. WE CAN'T ACCESS THE CAMERAS ANY MORE, TRUE...
...BUT THAT DOESN'T MEAN WE DON'T HAVE EARS.
WHAT'S THIS?
MAPPED ROUTES FOR BODY DISPOSAL TRUCKS. NICE LITTLE IRONY THERE.

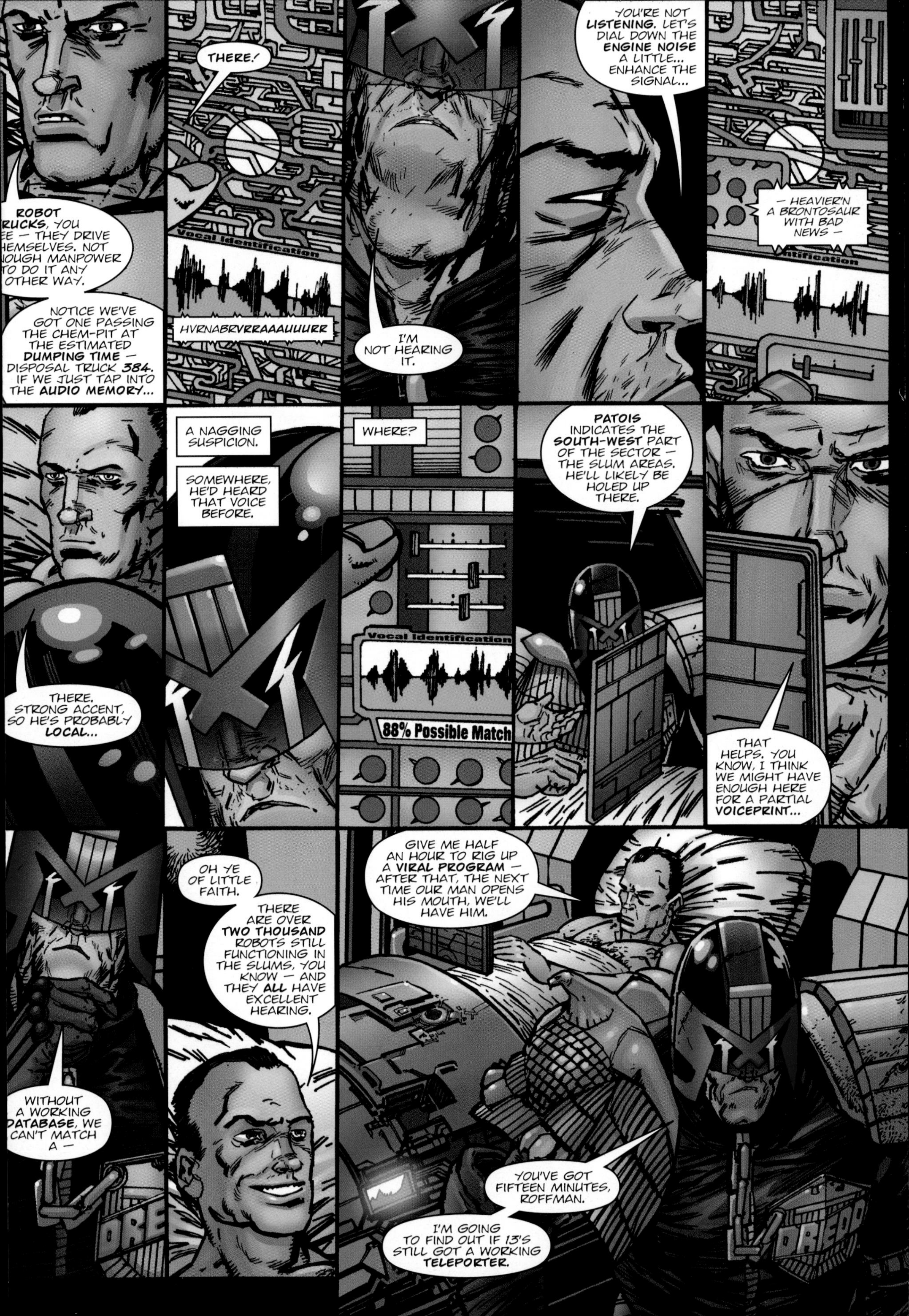
ROBOT TRUCKS, YOU SEE — THEY DRIVE THEMSELVES. NOT ENOUGH MANPOWER TO DO IT ANY OTHER WAY.
NOTICE WE'VE GOT ONE PASSING THE CHEM-PIT AT THE ESTIMATED DUMPING TIME — DISPOSAL TRUCK 384. IF WE JUST TAP INTO THE AUDIO MEMORY...
THERE!
Vocal Identification
HVRNABRVRRAAAUUURR
I'M NOT HEARING IT.
YOU'RE NOT LISTENING. LET'S DIAL DOWN THE ENGINE NOISE A LITTLE... ENHANCE THE SIGNAL...
— HEAVIER'N A BRONTOSAUR WITH BAD NEWS —
THERE. STRONG ACCENT, SO HE'S PROBABLY LOCAL...
A NAGGING SUSPICION.
SOMEWHERE, HE'D HEARD THAT VOICE BEFORE.
WHERE?
Vocal Identification
88% Possible Match
PATOIS INDICATES THE SOUTH-WEST PART OF THE SECTOR — THE SLUM AREAS. HE'LL LIKELY BE HOLED UP THERE.
THAT HELPS. YOU KNOW, I THINK WE MIGHT HAVE ENOUGH HERE FOR A PARTIAL VOICEPRINT...
WITHOUT A WORKING DATABASE, WE CAN'T MATCH A —
OH YE OF LITTLE FAITH.
THERE ARE OVER TWO THOUSAND ROBOTS STILL FUNCTIONING IN THE SLUMS, YOU KNOW — AND THEY ALL HAVE EXCELLENT HEARING.
GIVE ME HALF AN HOUR TO RIG UP A VIRAL PROGRAM — AFTER THAT, THE NEXT TIME OUR MAN OPENS HIS MOUTH, WE'LL HAVE HIM.
YOU'VE GOT FIFTEEN MINUTES, ROFFMAN.
I'M GOING TO FIND OUT IF 13'S STILL GOT A WORKING TELEPORTER.

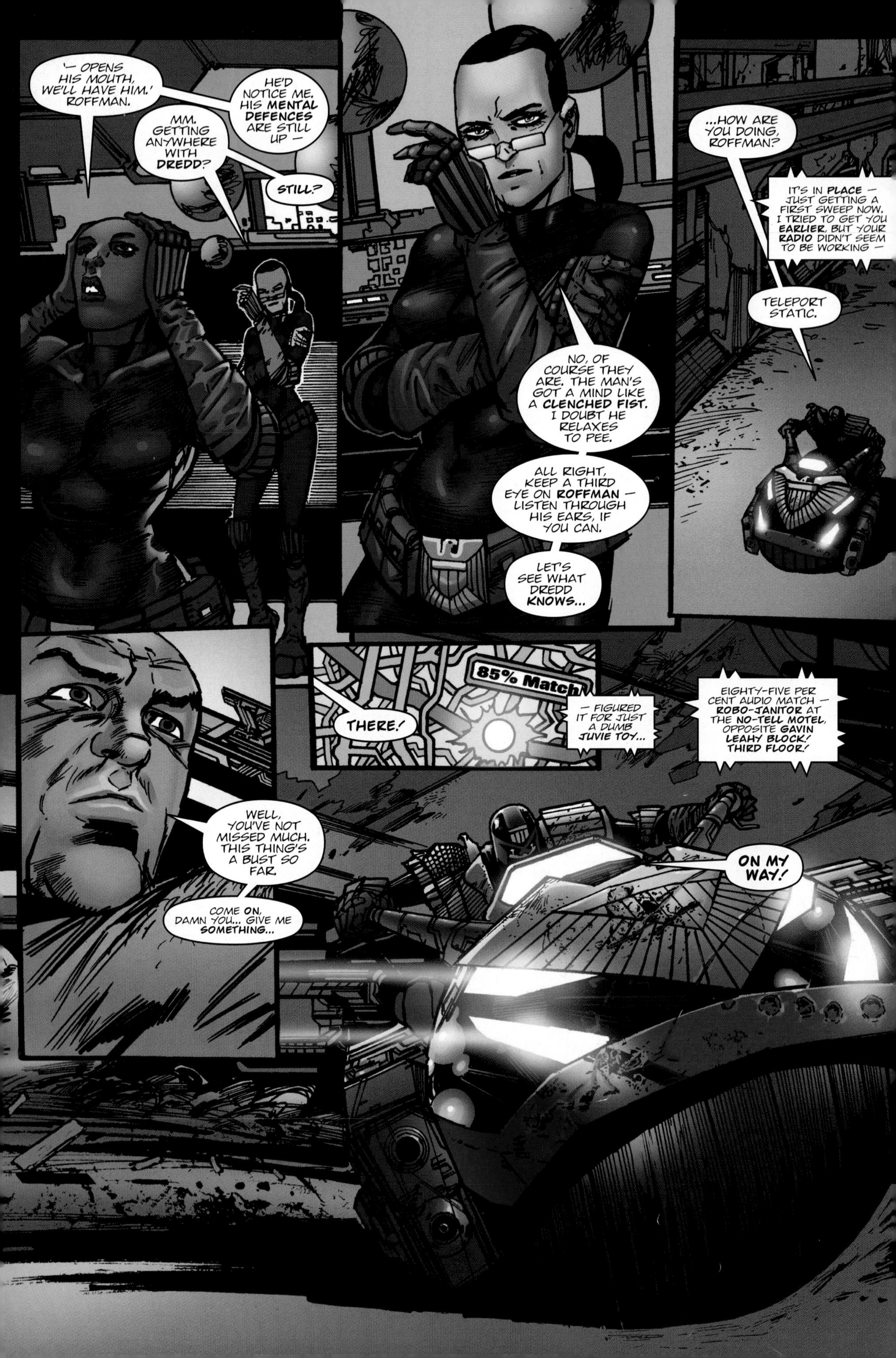
'— OPENS HIS MOUTH, WE'LL HAVE HIM.' ROFFMAN.
HE'D NOTICE ME. HIS MENTAL DEFENCES ARE STILL UP —
MM. GETTING ANYWHERE WITH DREDD?
STILL?
NO, OF COURSE THEY ARE. THE MAN'S GOT A MIND LIKE A CLENCHED FIST. I DOUBT HE RELAXES TO PEE.
ALL RIGHT, KEEP A THIRD EYE ON ROFFMAN — LISTEN THROUGH HIS EARS, IF YOU CAN.
LET'S SEE WHAT DREDD KNOWS...
...HOW ARE YOU DOING, ROFFMAN?
IT'S IN PLACE — JUST GETTING A FIRST SWEEP NOW. I TRIED TO GET YOU EARLIER, BUT YOUR RADIO DIDN'T SEEM TO BE WORKING —
TELEPORT STATIC.
WELL, YOU'VE NOT MISSED MUCH. THIS THING'S A BUST SO FAR.
COME ON, DAMN YOU... GIVE ME SOMETHING...
85% Match
THERE!
— FIGURED IT FOR JUST A DUMB JUVIE TOY...
EIGHTY-FIVE PER CENT AUDIO MATCH — ROBO-JANITOR AT THE NO-TELL MOTEL, OPPOSITE GAVIN LEAHY BLOCK! THIRD FLOOR!
ON MY WAY!

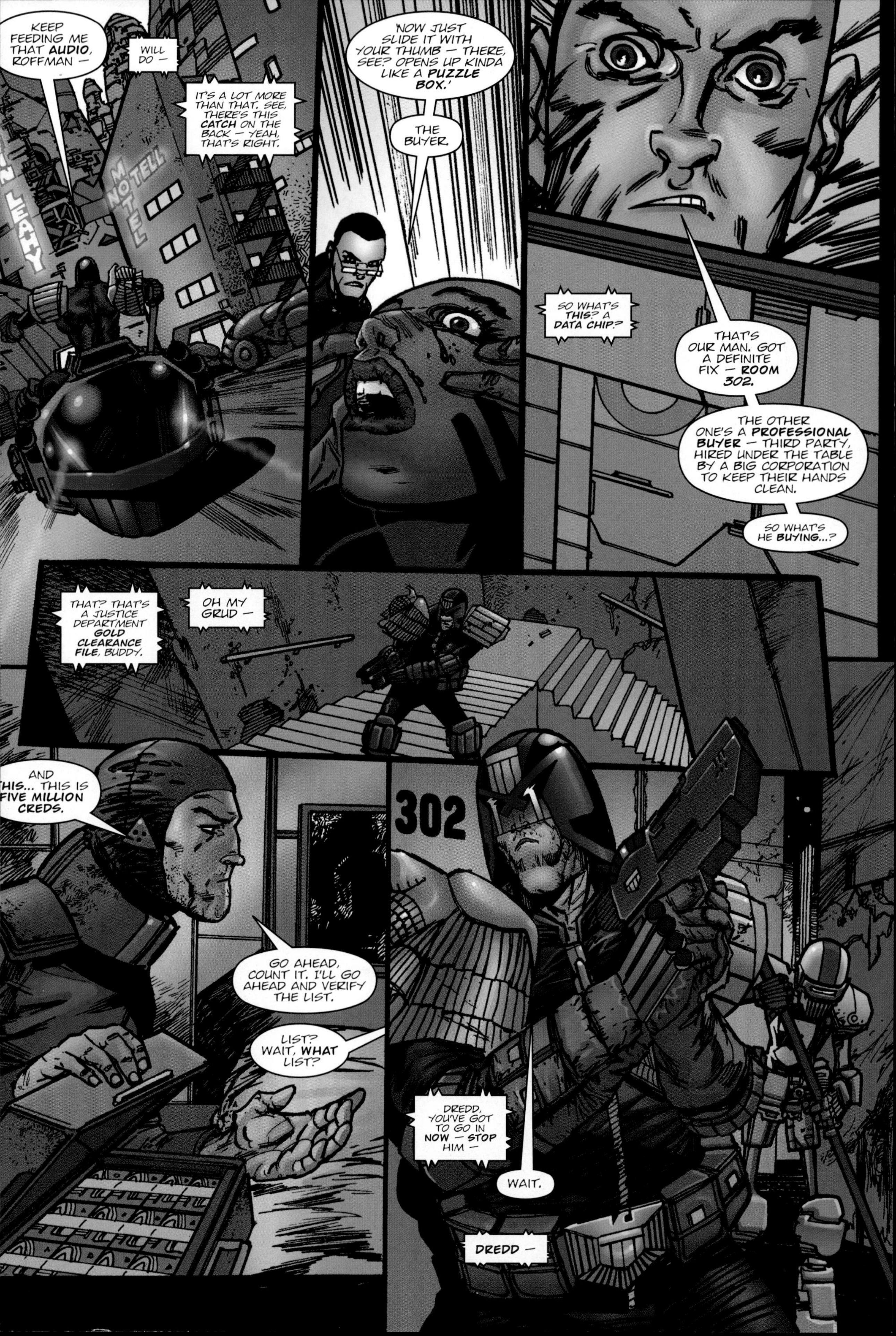

KEEP FEEDING ME THAT AUDIO, ROFFMAN —
WILL DO —
IT'S A LOT MORE THAN THAT. SEE, THERE'S THIS CATCH ON THE BACK — YEAH, THAT'S RIGHT.
'NOW JUST SLIDE IT WITH YOUR THUMB — THERE, SEE? OPENS UP KINDA LIKE A PUZZLE BOX.'
THE BUYER.
SO WHAT'S THIS? A DATA CHIP?
THAT'S OUR MAN. GOT A DEFINITE FIX — ROOM 302.
THE OTHER ONE'S A PROFESSIONAL BUYER — THIRD PARTY, HIRED UNDER THE TABLE BY A BIG CORPORATION TO KEEP THEIR HANDS CLEAN.
SO WHAT'S HE BUYING...?
THAT? THAT'S A JUSTICE DEPARTMENT GOLD CLEARANCE FILE, BUDDY.
OH MY GRUD —
AND THIS... THIS IS FIVE MILLION CREDS.
302
GO AHEAD, COUNT IT. I'LL GO AHEAD AND VERIFY THE LIST.
LIST? WAIT, WHAT LIST?
DREDD, YOU'VE GOT TO GO IN NOW — STOP HIM —
WAIT.
DREDD —

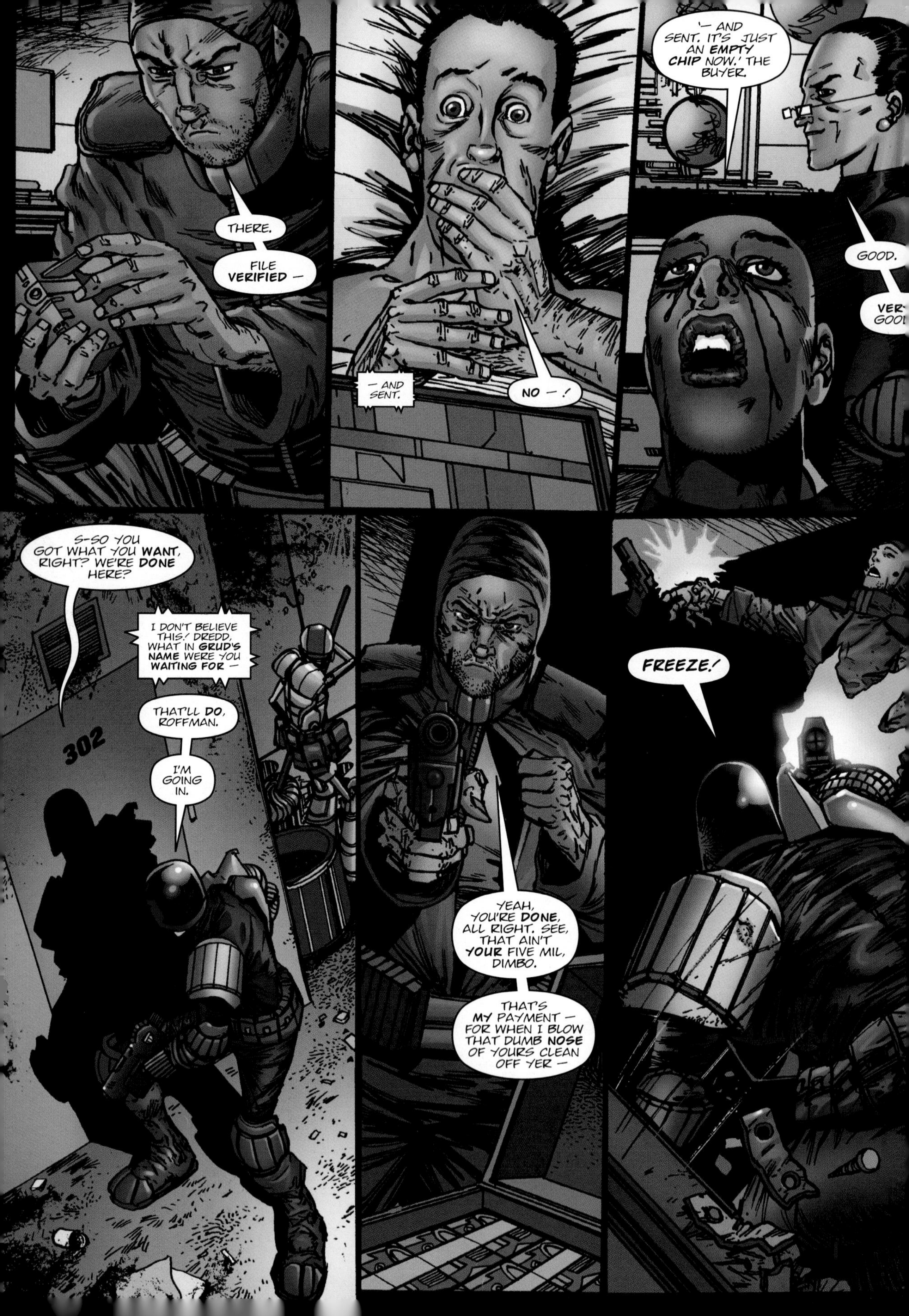
THERE.
FILE VERIFIED —
— AND SENT.
NO — !
'— AND SENT. IT'S JUST AN EMPTY CHIP NOW.' THE BUYER.
GOOD.
S-SO YOU GOT WHAT YOU WANT, RIGHT? WE'RE DONE HERE?
I DON'T BELIEVE THIS! DREDD, WHAT IN GRUD'S NAME WERE YOU WAITING FOR —
THAT'LL DO, ROFFMAN.
I'M GOING IN.
302
YEAH, YOU'RE DONE, ALL RIGHT. SEE, THAT AIN'T YOUR FIVE MIL, DIMBO.
THAT'S MY PAYMENT — FOR WHEN I BLOW THAT DUMB NOSE OF YOURS CLEAN OFF YER —
FREEZE!

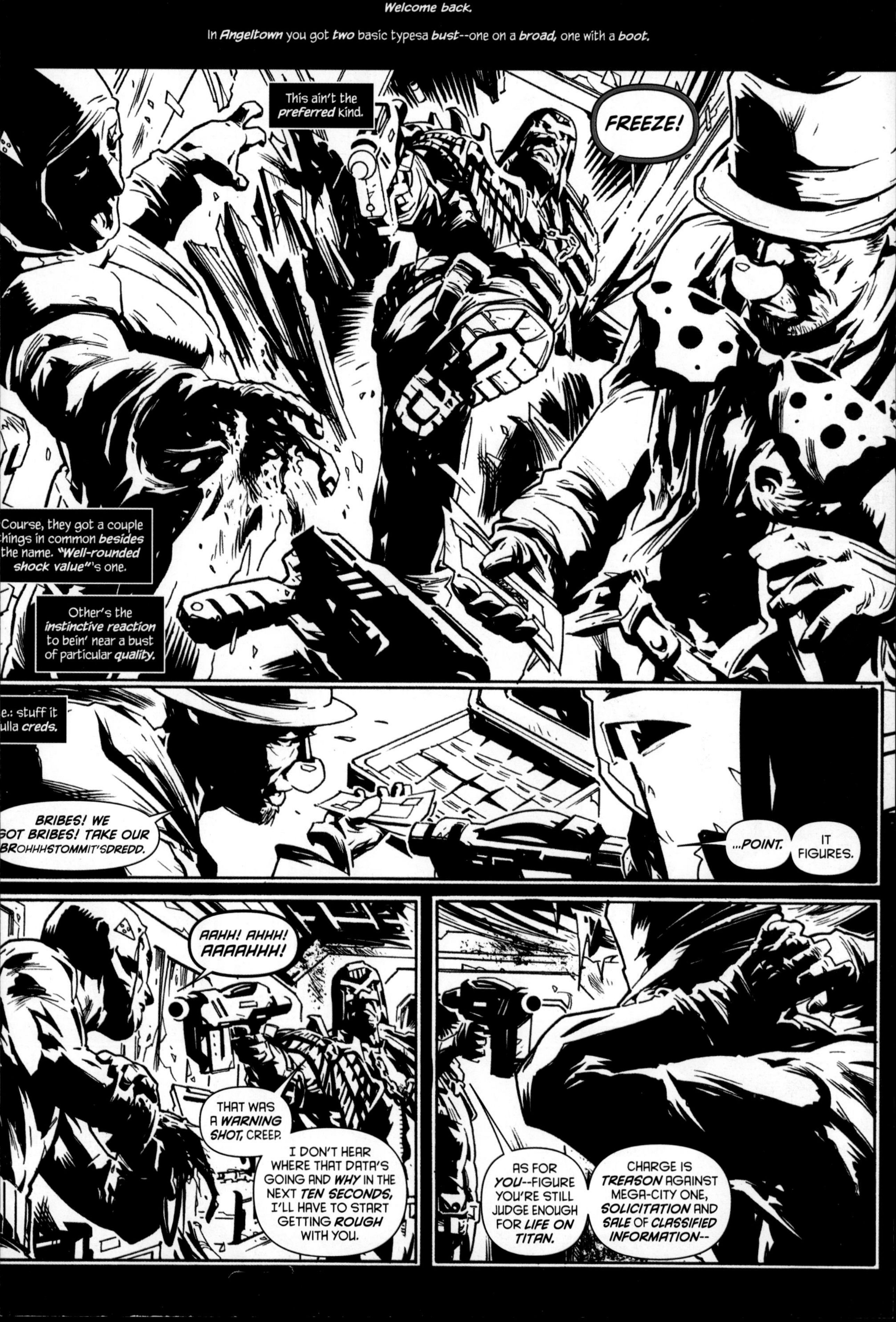
Welcome back.
In Angeltown you got two basic typesa bust--one on a broad, one with a boot.
This ain't the preferred kind.
FREEZE!
Course, they got a couple things in common besides the name. "Well-rounded shock value"'s one.
Other's the instinctive reaction to bein' near a bust of particular quality.
e.: stuff it ulla creds.
BRIBES! WE GOT BRIBES! TAKE OUR BROHHHSTOMMIT'SDREDD.
...POINT.
IT FIGURES.
AAHH! AHHH! AAAAHHH!
THAT WAS A WARNING SHOT, CREEP.
I DON'T HEAR WHERE THAT DATA'S GOING AND WHY IN THE NEXT TEN SECONDS, I'LL HAVE TO START GETTING ROUGH WITH YOU.
AS FOR YOU--FIGURE YOU'RE STILL JUDGE ENOUGH FOR LIFE ON TITAN.
CHARGE IS TREASON AGAINST MEGA-CITY ONE, SOLICITATION AND SALE OF CLASSIFIED INFORMATION--

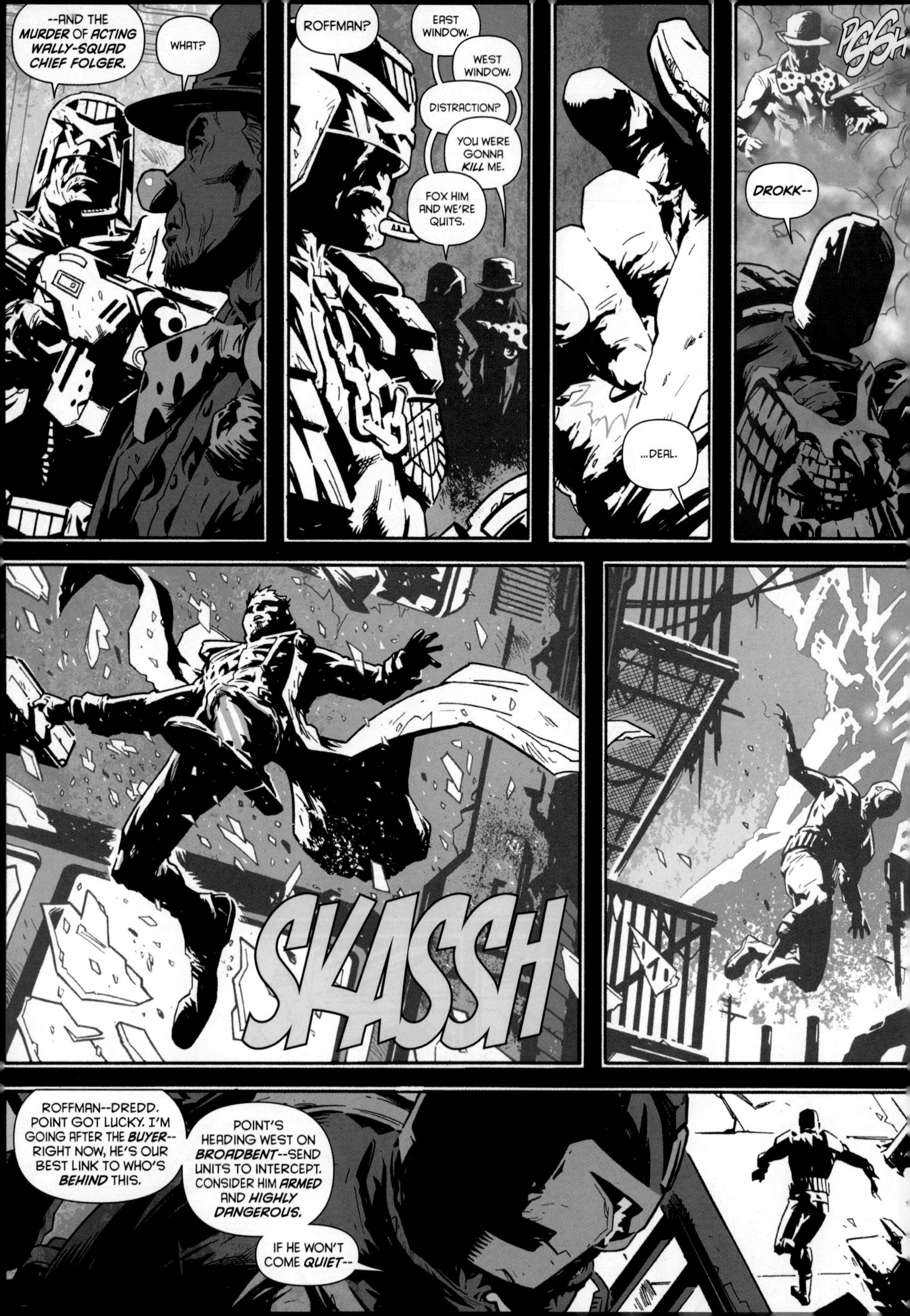
--AND THE MURDER OF ACTING WALLY-SQUAD CHIEF FOLGER.
WHAT?
ROFFMAN?
EAST WINDOW.
WEST WINDOW.
DISTRACTION?
YOU WERE GONNA KILL ME.
FOX HIM AND WE'RE QUITS.
...DEAL.
PSSH
DROKK--
SKASSH
ROFFMAN--DREDD. POINT GOT LUCKY. I'M GOING AFTER THE BUYER--RIGHT NOW, HE'S OUR BEST LINK TO WHO'S BEHIND THIS.
POINT'S HEADING WEST ON BROADBENT--SEND UNITS TO INTERCEPT. CONSIDER HIM ARMED AND HIGHLY DANGEROUS.
IF HE WON'T COME QUIET--

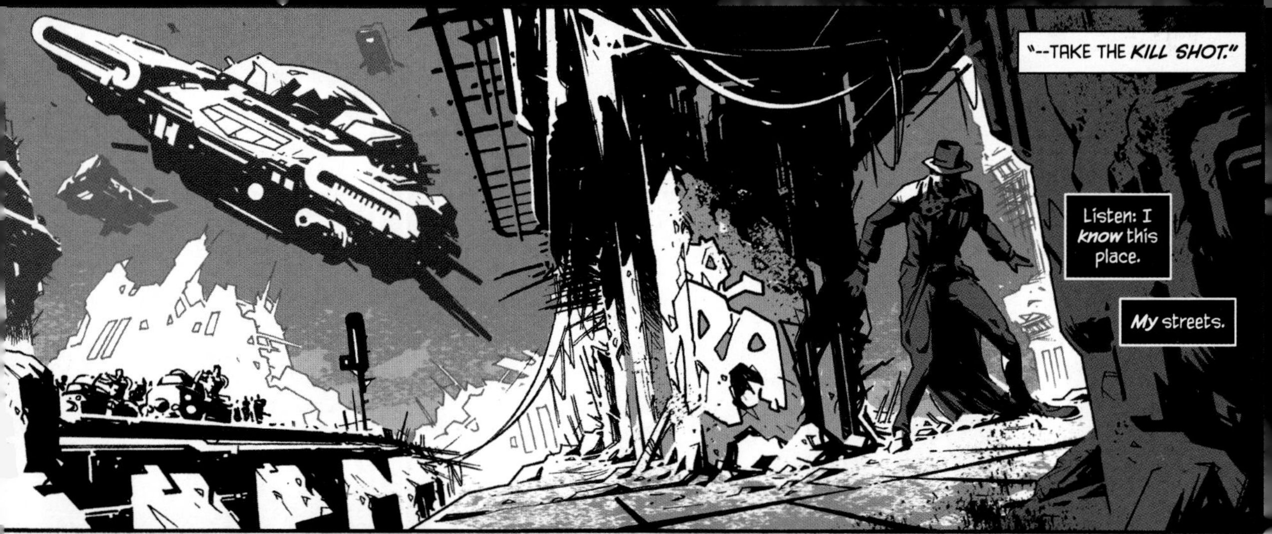
"--TAKE THE *KILL SHOT.*"
Listen: I *know* this place.
My streets.

On a ***good day*** even a sat-nav ***Psihound*** couldn't find me, I didn't want it to. All these ***leather lovelies*** and ***badge-bastards*** ain't gotta ***hope.***

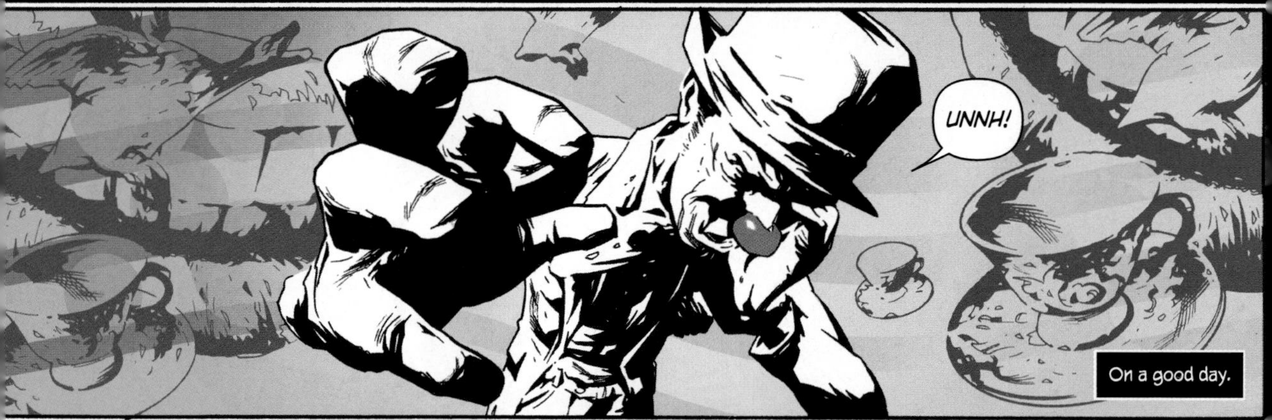
UNNH!
On a good day.

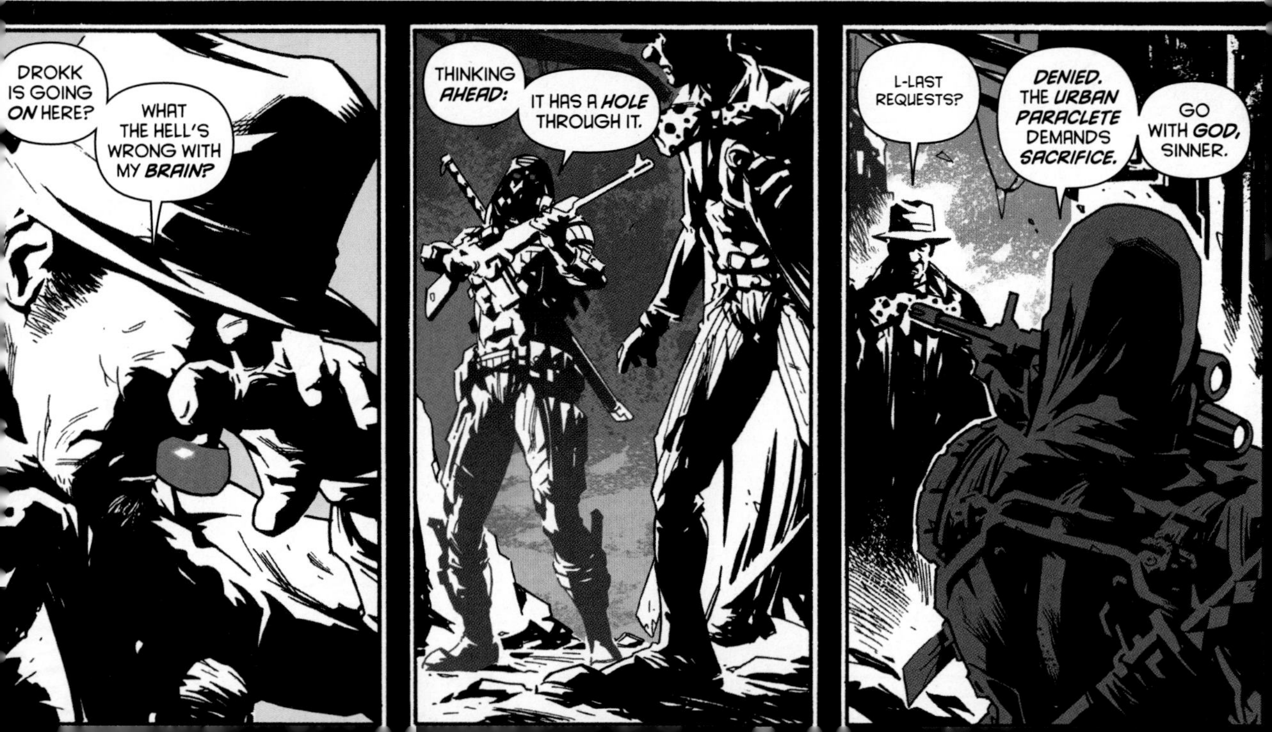
DROKK IS GOING *ON* HERE?
WHAT THE HELL'S WRONG WITH MY *BRAIN?*
THINKING *AHEAD:*
IT HAS A *HOLE* THROUGH IT.
L-LAST REQUESTS?
DENIED. THE *URBAN PARACLETE* DEMANDS *SACRIFICE.*
GO WITH *GOD,* SINNER.

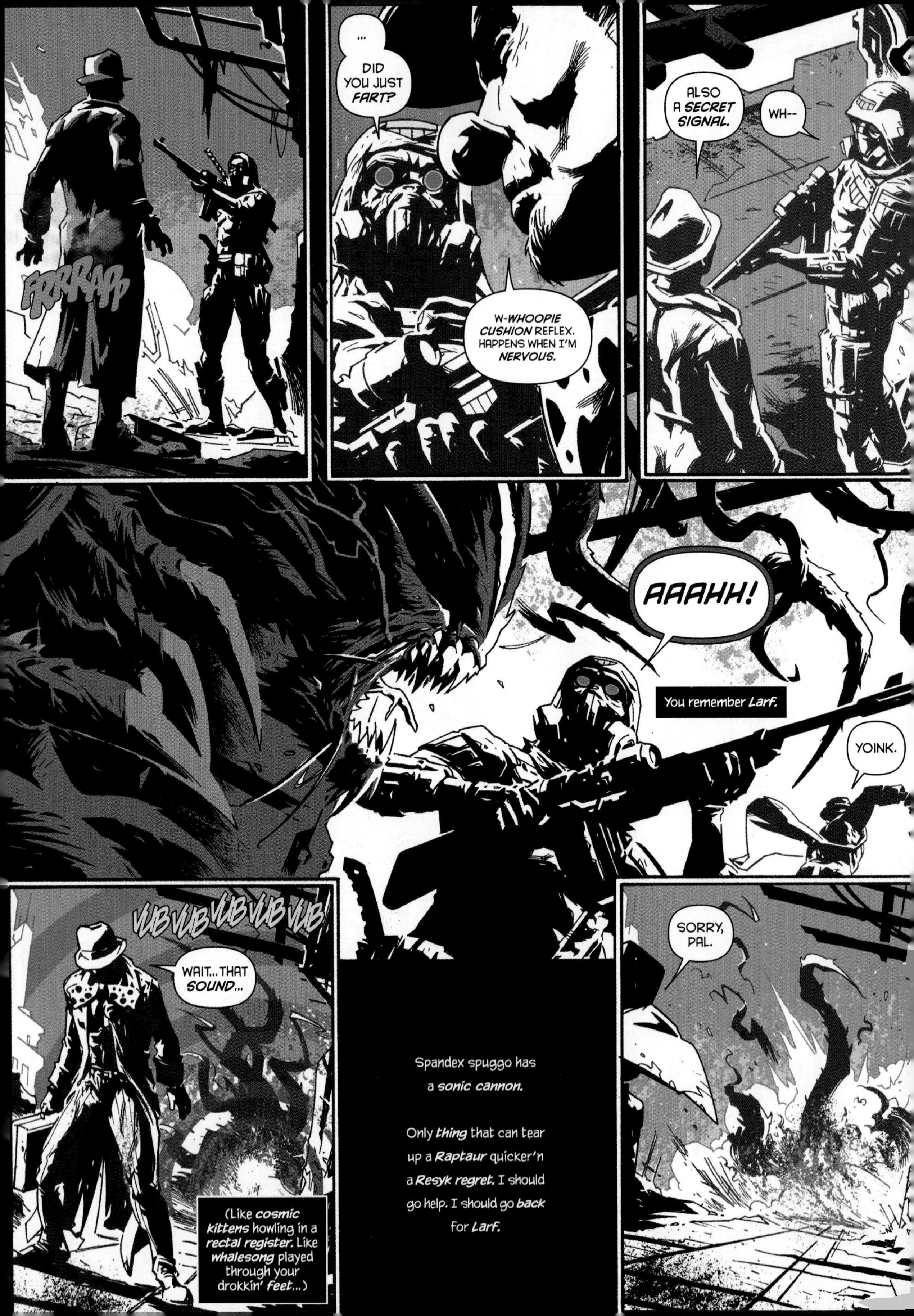
FRRRRAPP
...
DID YOU JUST FART?
W-WHOOPIE CUSHION REFLEX. HAPPENS WHEN I'M NERVOUS.
ALSO A SECRET SIGNAL.
WH--
AAAHH!
You remember Larf.
YOINK.
VUB VUB VUB VUB VUB
WAIT... THAT SOUND...
(Like cosmic kittens howling in a rectal register. Like whalesong played through your drokkin' feet...)
Spandex spuggo has a sonic cannon.
Only thing that can tear up a Raptaur quicker'n a Resyk regret. I should go help. I should go back for Larf.
SORRY, PAL.

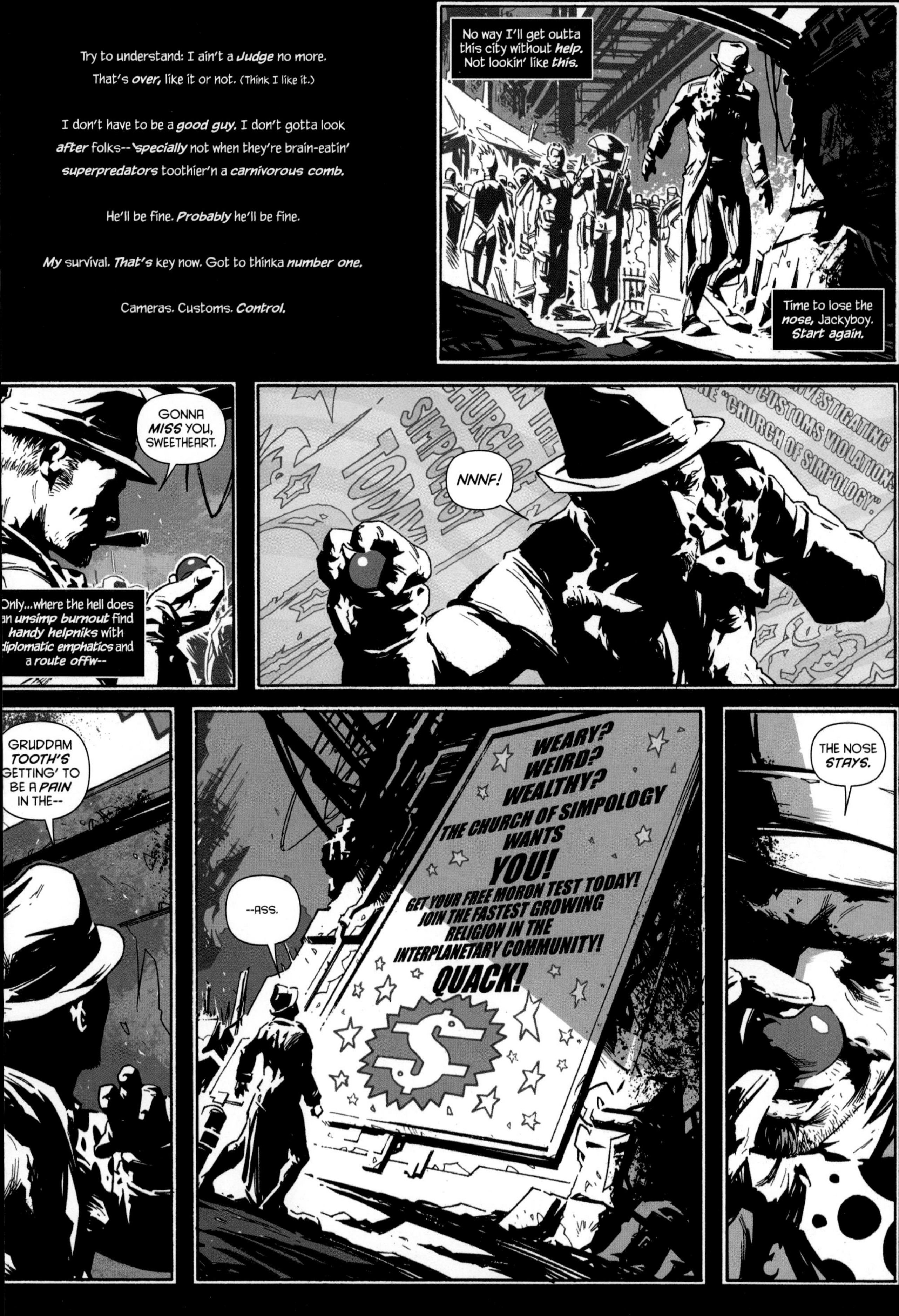
Try to understand: I ain't a Judge no more.
That's over, like it or not. (Think I like it.)
I don't have to be a good guy. I don't gotta look after folks--'specially not when they're brain-eatin' superpredators toothier'n a carnivorous comb.
He'll be fine. Probably he'll be fine.
My survival. That's key now. Got to thinka number one.
Cameras. Customs. Control.
No way I'll get outta this city without help. Not lookin' like this.
Time to lose the nose, Jackyboy. Start again.
GONNA MISS YOU, SWEETHEART.
Only...where the hell does an unsimp burnout find handy helpniks with diplomatic emphatics and a route offw--
NNNF!
GRUDDAM TOOTH'S GETTING' TO BE A PAIN IN THE--
--ASS.
WEARY? WEIRD? WEALTHY?
THE CHURCH OF SIMPOLOGY WANTS YOU!
GET YOUR FREE MORON TEST TODAY!
JOIN THE FASTEST GROWING RELIGION IN THE INTERPLANETARY COMMUNITY!
QUACK!
$
THE NOSE STAYS.

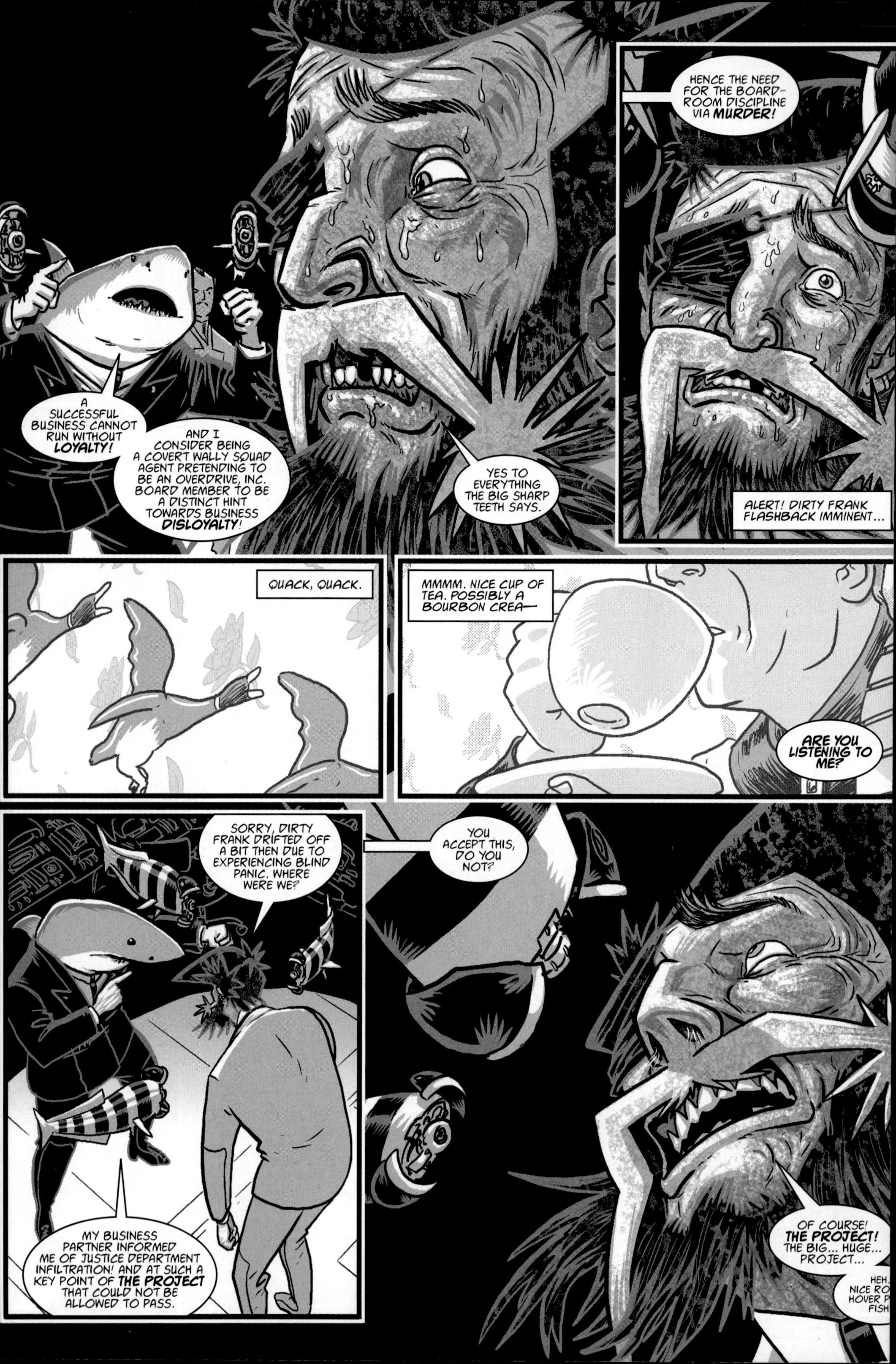
A SUCCESSFUL BUSINESS CANNOT RUN WITHOUT LOYALTY!
AND I CONSIDER BEING A COVERT WALLY SQUAD AGENT PRETENDING TO BE AN OVERDRIVE, INC. BOARD MEMBER TO BE A DISTINCT HINT TOWARDS BUSINESS DISLOYALTY!
YES TO EVERYTHING THE BIG SHARP TEETH SAYS.
HENCE THE NEED FOR THE BOARD-ROOM DISCIPLINE VIA MURDER!
ALERT! DIRTY FRANK FLASHBACK IMMINENT...
QUACK, QUACK.
MMMM. NICE CUP OF TEA. POSSIBLY A BOURBON CREA—
ARE YOU LISTENING TO ME?
SORRY, DIRTY FRANK DRIFTED OFF A BIT THEN DUE TO EXPERIENCING BLIND PANIC. WHERE WERE WE?
YOU ACCEPT THIS, DO YOU NOT?
MY BUSINESS PARTNER INFORMED ME OF JUSTICE DEPARTMENT INFILTRATION! AND AT SUCH A KEY POINT OF THE PROJECT THAT COULD NOT BE ALLOWED TO PASS.
OF COURSE! THE PROJECT! THE BIG... HUGE... PROJECT...
HEH. NICE RO HOVER P FISH

Panel 1:
ALL HAIL THE PROJECT!

ALL HAIL OVERDRIVE, INC.!

ALLE HAGEL DAS PROJEKT!

Panel 2:
GO ON...

Panel 3:

ALLE... HAGEL DAS... PROJEKT!

Panel 4:
LIKE THE CUT F YOUR JIB, RANK!

YOU WILL CUT OFF DIRTY FRANK'S JIB?

WHAT? NO! NOT UNLESS YOU'RE ALSO AN UNDERCOVER WALLY SQUAD JUDGE! **HA HA!**

HA. HA. ALSO: HA.

I WOULD **KNOW** IF YOU WERE, FRANK. MY BUSINESS PARTNER IS **VERY** HIGH UP WITHIN JUSTICE DEPARTMENT.

Panel 5:
HANDY. WHO'S THAT, THEN?

I HAD YOU THOROUGHLY CHECKED OUT BEFORE ARRIVAL HERE, OF COURSE.

AND I DIDN'T TELL YOU ABOUT MY PLANS FOR LOM BECAUSE I WANTED TO SEE IF YOU WERE WILLING TO ACCEPT MURDER AS STANDARD BUSINESS PRACTICE.

Panel 6:
ONE HUMAN LIFE MEANS SO LITTLE COMPARED TO THE **SCALE** OF WHAT WE'RE DOING HERE, FRANK. I'M GLAD YOU SEE THAT.

I'M SHOCKED TO HEAR MYSELF SAY IT BUT THIS... IT ALMOST **TRANSCENDS** BUSINESS ITSELF.

BOTH MEIN GOTT AND BLIMEY!

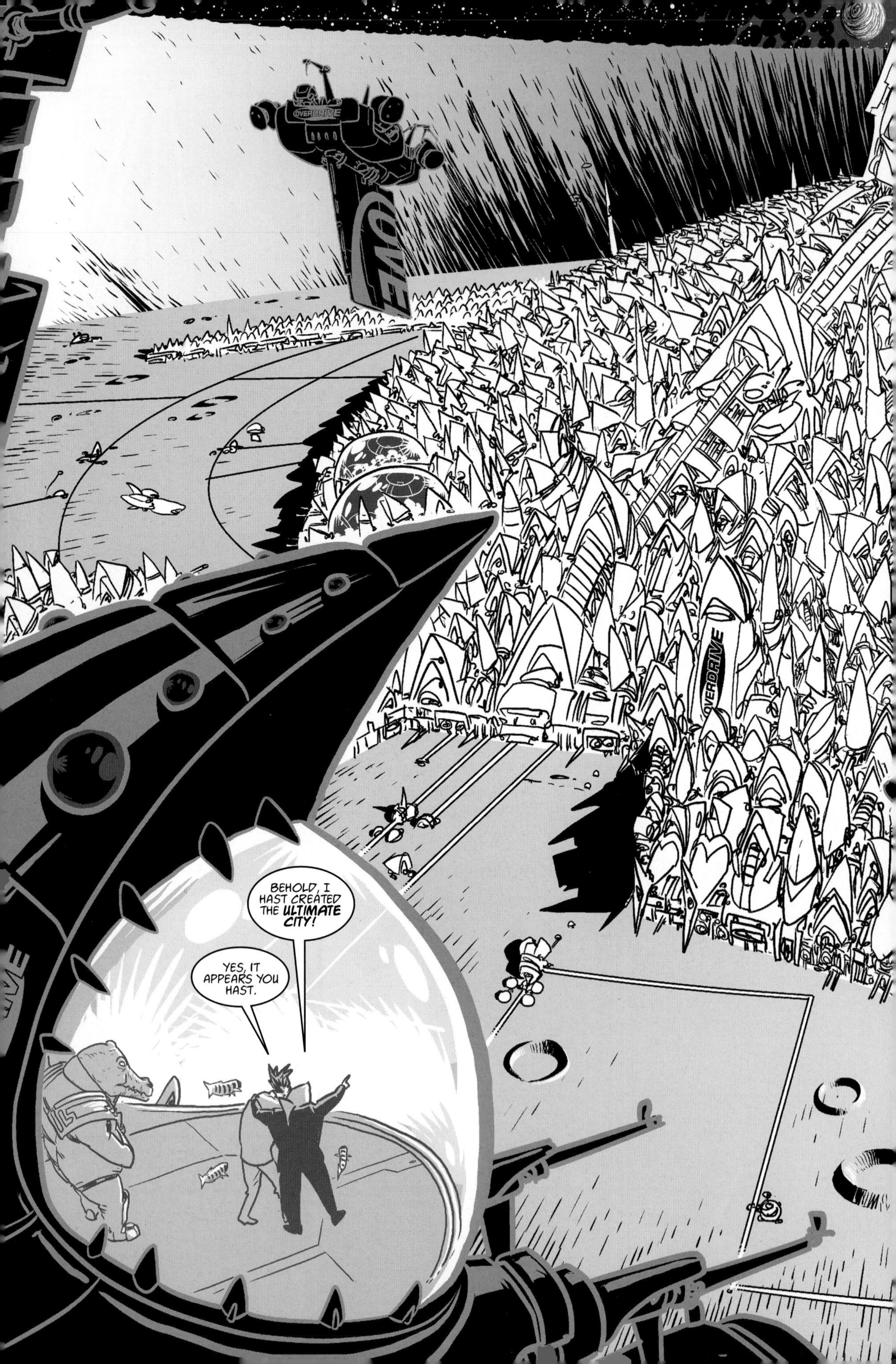
OVERDRIVE
BEHOLD, I HAST CREATED THE **ULTIMATE CITY!**
YES, IT APPEARS YOU HAST.
OVERDRIVE

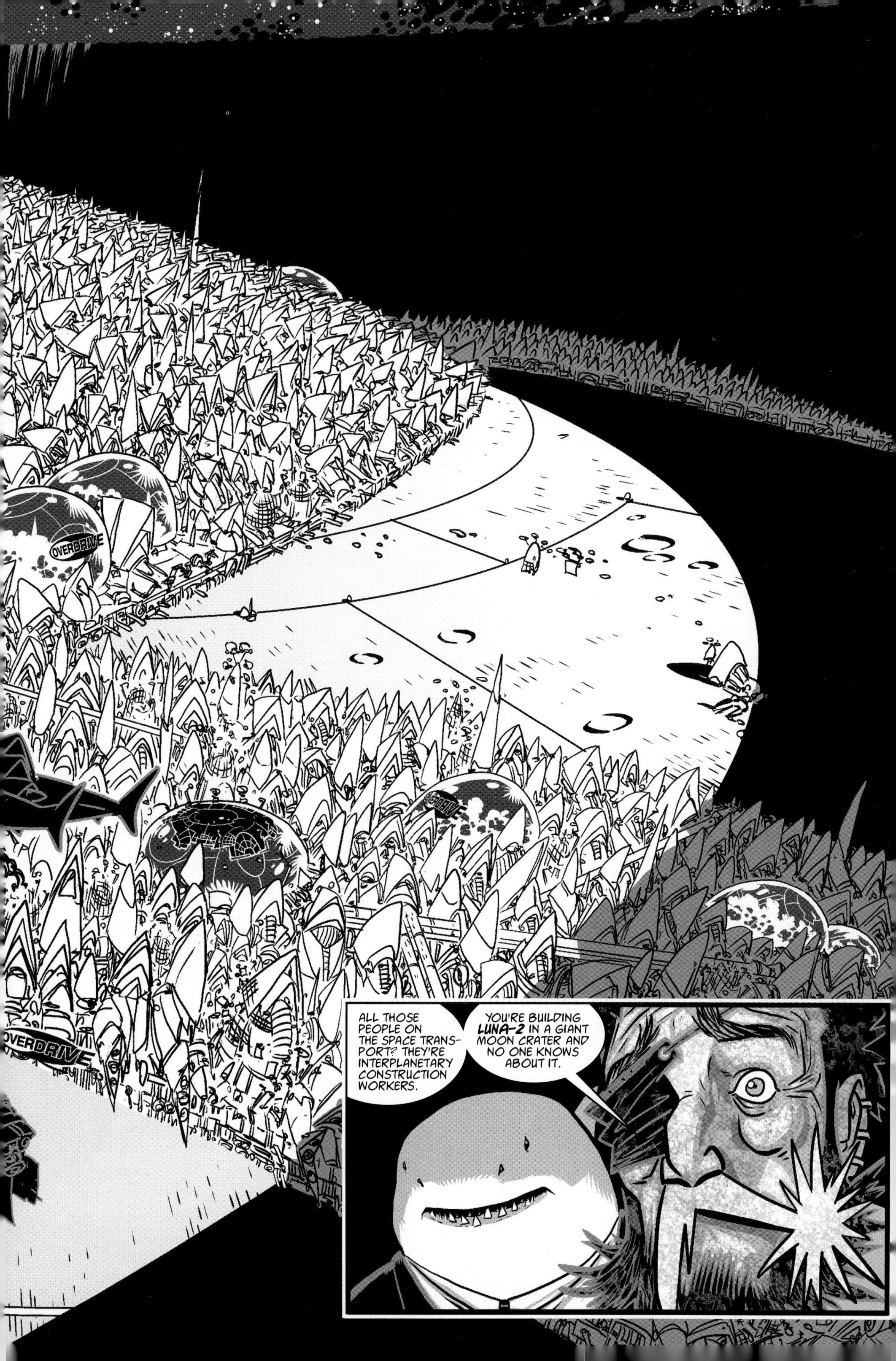
OVERDRIVE
OVERDRIVE
OVERDRIVE
ALL THOSE PEOPLE ON THE SPACE TRANSPORT? THEY'RE INTERPLANETARY CONSTRUCTION WORKERS.
YOU'RE BUILDING LUNA-2 IN A GIANT MOON CRATER AND NO ONE KNOWS ABOUT IT.

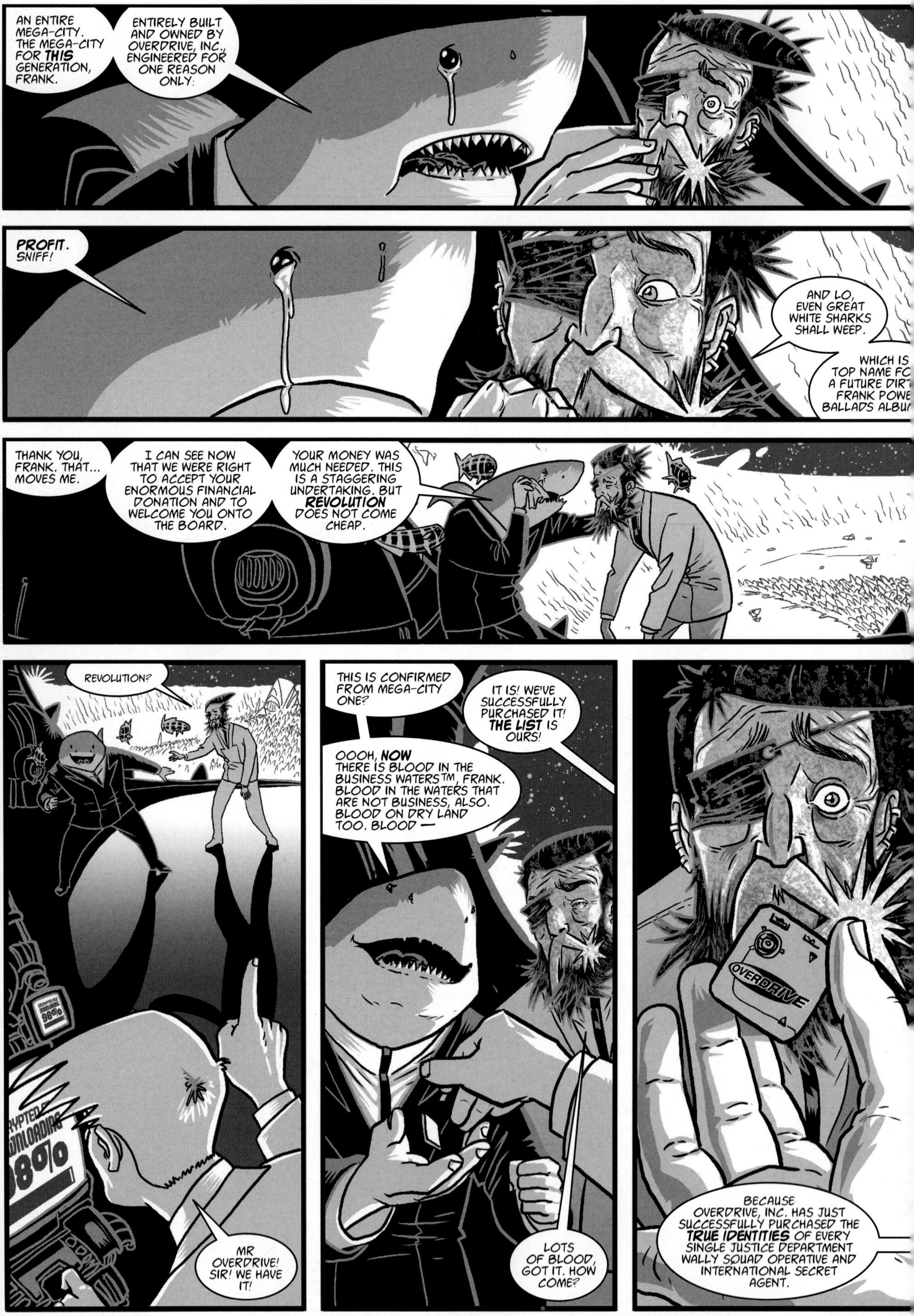
AN ENTIRE MEGA-CITY. THE MEGA-CITY FOR **THIS** GENERATION, FRANK.
ENTIRELY BUILT AND OWNED BY OVERDRIVE, INC., ENGINEERED FOR ONE REASON ONLY:
PROFIT. SNIFF!
AND LO, EVEN GREAT WHITE SHARKS SHALL WEEP.
WHICH IS TOP NAME FO A FUTURE DIRT FRANK POWE BALLADS ALBU
THANK YOU, FRANK. THAT... MOVES ME.
I CAN SEE NOW THAT WE WERE RIGHT TO ACCEPT YOUR ENORMOUS FINANCIAL DONATION AND TO WELCOME YOU ONTO THE BOARD.
YOUR MONEY WAS MUCH NEEDED. THIS IS A STAGGERING UNDERTAKING. BUT **REVOLUTION** DOES NOT COME CHEAP.
REVOLUTION?
MR OVERDRIVE! SIR! WE HAVE IT!
THIS IS CONFIRMED FROM MEGA-CITY ONE?
IT IS! WE'VE SUCCESSFULLY PURCHASED IT! **THE LIST** IS OURS!
OOOH, **NOW** THERE IS BLOOD IN THE BUSINESS WATERS™, FRANK. BLOOD IN THE WATERS THAT ARE NOT BUSINESS, ALSO. BLOOD ON DRY LAND TOO. BLOOD —
LOTS OF BLOOD, GOT IT. HOW COME?
OVERDRIVE
BECAUSE OVERDRIVE, INC. HAS JUST SUCCESSFULLY PURCHASED THE **TRUE IDENTITIES** OF EVERY SINGLE JUSTICE DEPARTMENT WALLY SQUAD OPERATIVE AND INTERNATIONAL SECRET AGENT.

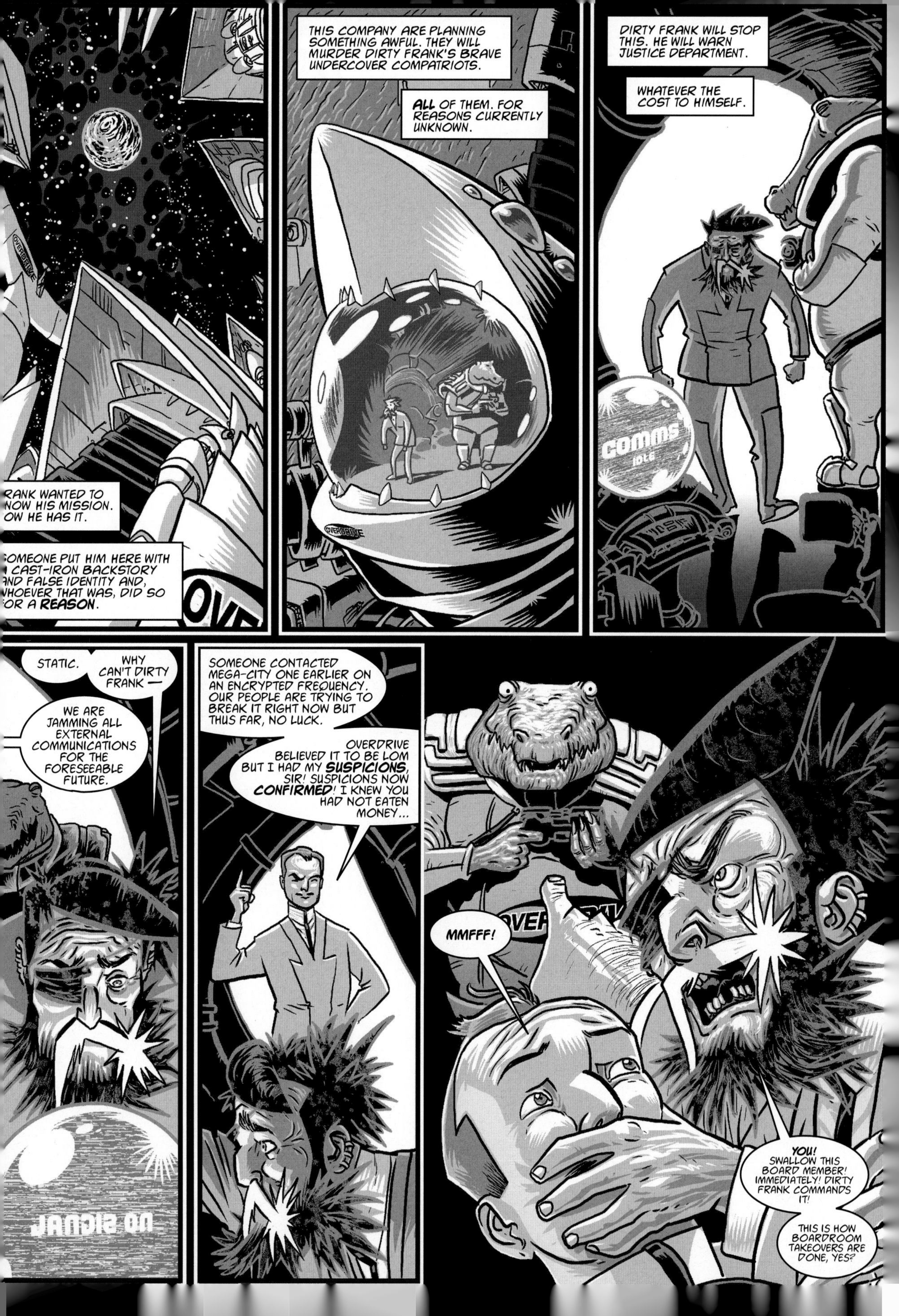
RANK WANTED TO NOW HIS MISSION. OW HE HAS IT.
SOMEONE PUT HIM HERE WITH CAST-IRON BACKSTORY AND FALSE IDENTITY AND, WHOEVER THAT WAS, DID SO FOR A **REASON**.
THIS COMPANY ARE PLANNING SOMETHING AWFUL. THEY WILL MURDER DIRTY FRANK'S BRAVE UNDERCOVER COMPATRIOTS.
ALL OF THEM. FOR REASONS CURRENTLY UNKNOWN.
OVERDRIVE
DIRTY FRANK WILL STOP THIS. HE WILL WARN JUSTICE DEPARTMENT.
WHATEVER THE COST TO HIMSELF.
COMMS IDLE
STATIC.
WHY CAN'T DIRTY FRANK —
WE ARE JAMMING ALL EXTERNAL COMMUNICATIONS FOR THE FORESEEABLE FUTURE.
SOMEONE CONTACTED MEGA-CITY ONE EARLIER ON AN ENCRYPTED FREQUENCY. OUR PEOPLE ARE TRYING TO BREAK IT RIGHT NOW BUT THUS FAR, NO LUCK.
OVERDRIVE BELIEVED IT TO BE LOM BUT I HAD MY **SUSPICIONS**, SIR! SUSPICIONS NOW **CONFIRMED**! I KNEW YOU HAD NOT EATEN MONEY...
MMFFF!
YOU! SWALLOW THIS BOARD MEMBER! IMMEDIATELY! DIRTY FRANK COMMANDS IT!
THIS IS HOW BOARDROOM TAKEOVERS ARE DONE, YES?

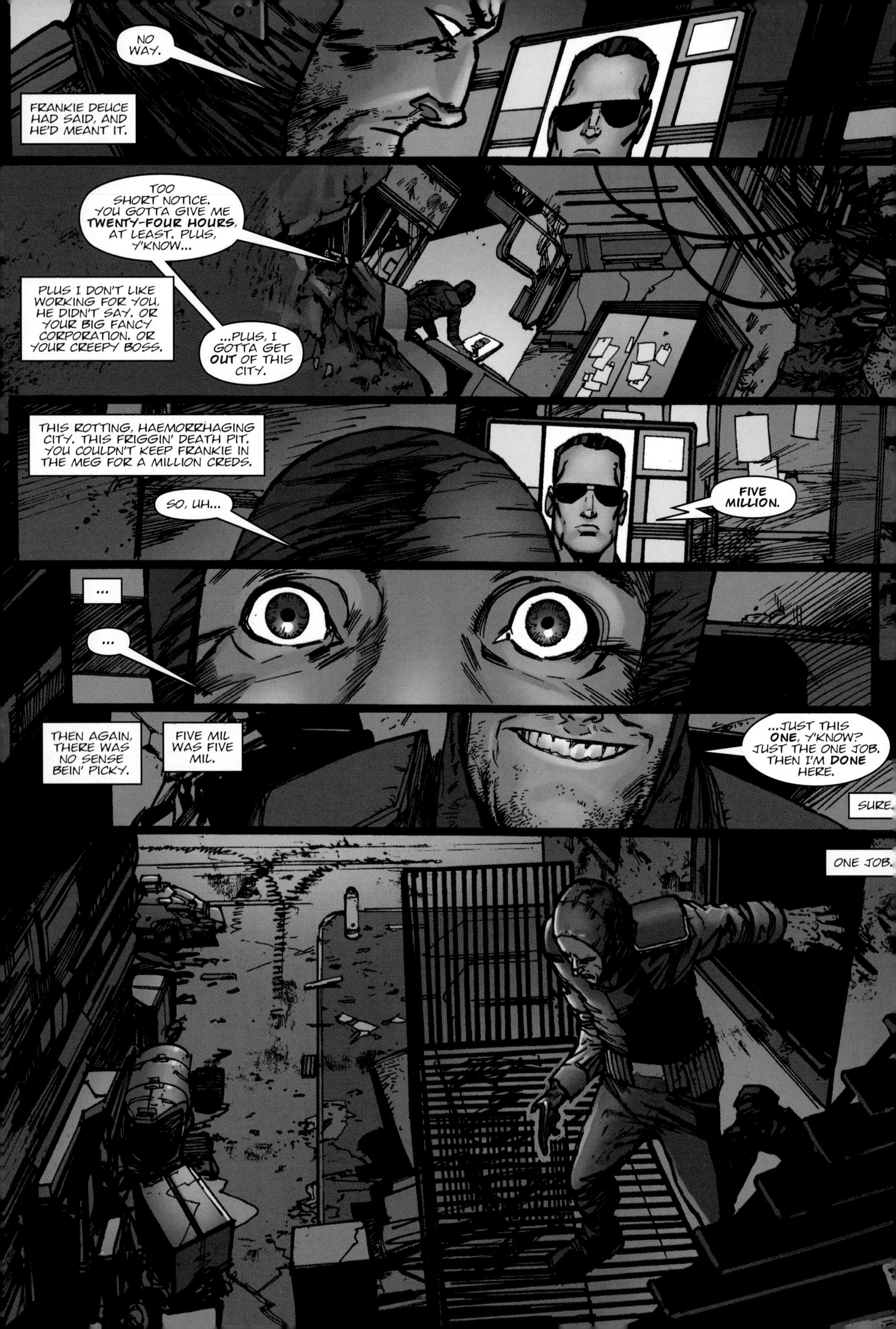
NO WAY.
FRANKIE DEUCE HAD SAID, AND HE'D MEANT IT.
TOO SHORT NOTICE. YOU GOTTA GIVE ME **TWENTY-FOUR HOURS**, AT LEAST. PLUS, Y'KNOW...
PLUS I DON'T LIKE WORKING FOR YOU, HE DIDN'T SAY. OR YOUR BIG FANCY CORPORATION. OR YOUR CREEPY BOSS.
...PLUS, I GOTTA GET **OUT** OF THIS CITY.
THIS ROTTING, HAEMORRHAGING CITY. THIS FRIGGIN' DEATH PIT. YOU COULDN'T KEEP FRANKIE IN THE MEG FOR A MILLION CREDS.
SO, UH...
FIVE MILLION.
...
...
THEN AGAIN, THERE WAS NO SENSE BEIN' PICKY.
FIVE MIL WAS FIVE MIL.
...JUST THIS **ONE**, Y'KNOW? JUST THE ONE JOB. THEN I'M **DONE** HERE.
SURE.
ONE JOB.

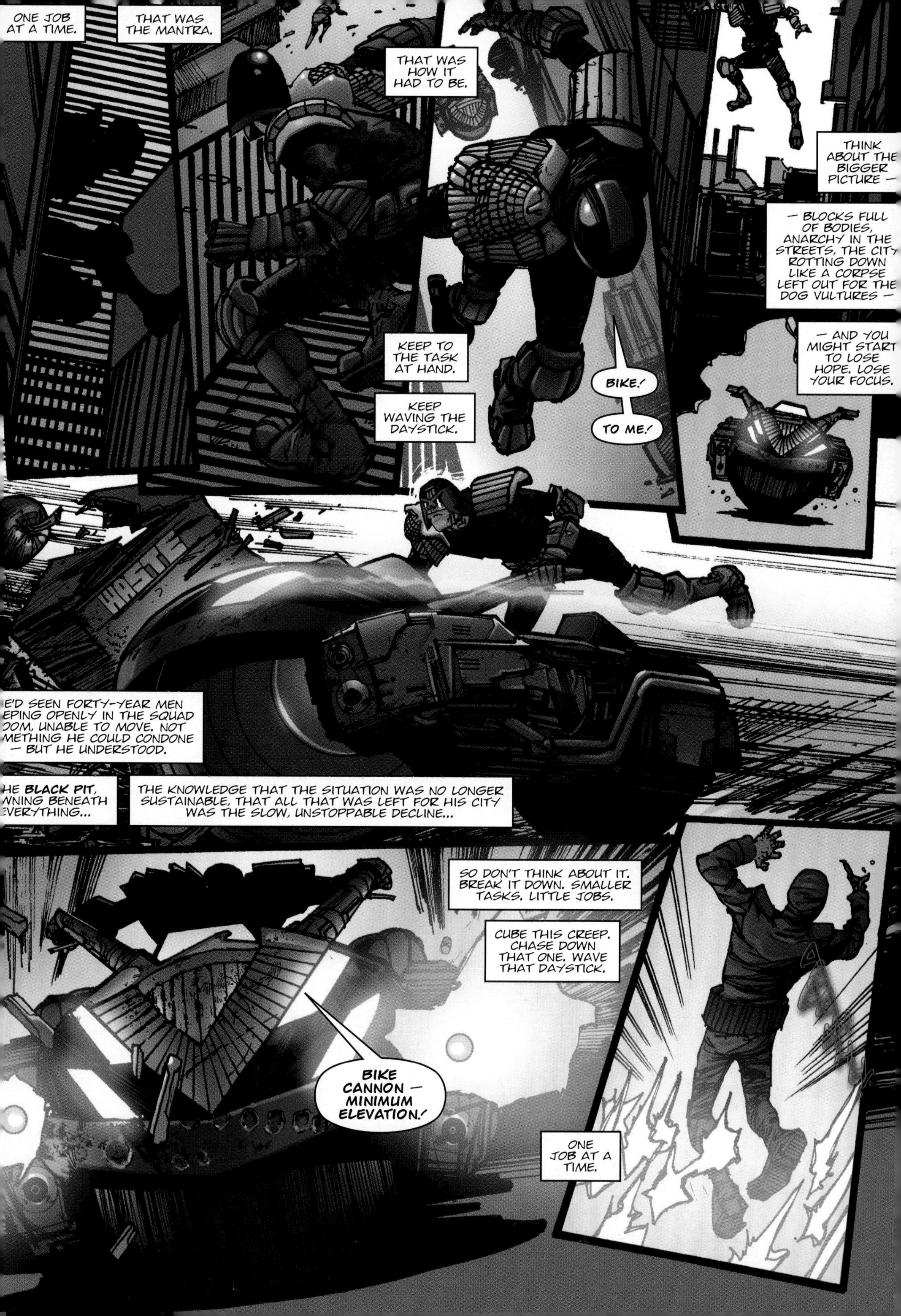
ONE JOB AT A TIME.
THAT WAS THE MANTRA.
THAT WAS HOW IT HAD TO BE.
KEEP TO THE TASK AT HAND.
KEEP WAVING THE DAYSTICK.
BIKE!
TO ME!
THINK ABOUT THE BIGGER PICTURE —
— BLOCKS FULL OF BODIES, ANARCHY IN THE STREETS, THE CITY ROTTING DOWN LIKE A CORPSE LEFT OUT FOR THE DOG VULTURES —
— AND YOU MIGHT START TO LOSE HOPE. LOSE YOUR FOCUS.
HASTE
'D SEEN FORTY-YEAR MEN EPING OPENLY IN THE SQUAD OOM, UNABLE TO MOVE. NOT METHING HE COULD CONDONE — BUT HE UNDERSTOOD.
HE BLACK PIT, WNING BENEATH EVERYTHING...
THE KNOWLEDGE THAT THE SITUATION WAS NO LONGER SUSTAINABLE, THAT ALL THAT WAS LEFT FOR HIS CITY WAS THE SLOW, UNSTOPPABLE DECLINE...
BIKE CANNON — MINIMUM ELEVATION!
SO DON'T THINK ABOUT IT. BREAK IT DOWN. SMALLER TASKS. LITTLE JOBS.
CUBE THIS CREEP. CHASE DOWN THAT ONE. WAVE THAT DAYSTICK.
ONE JOB AT A TIME.

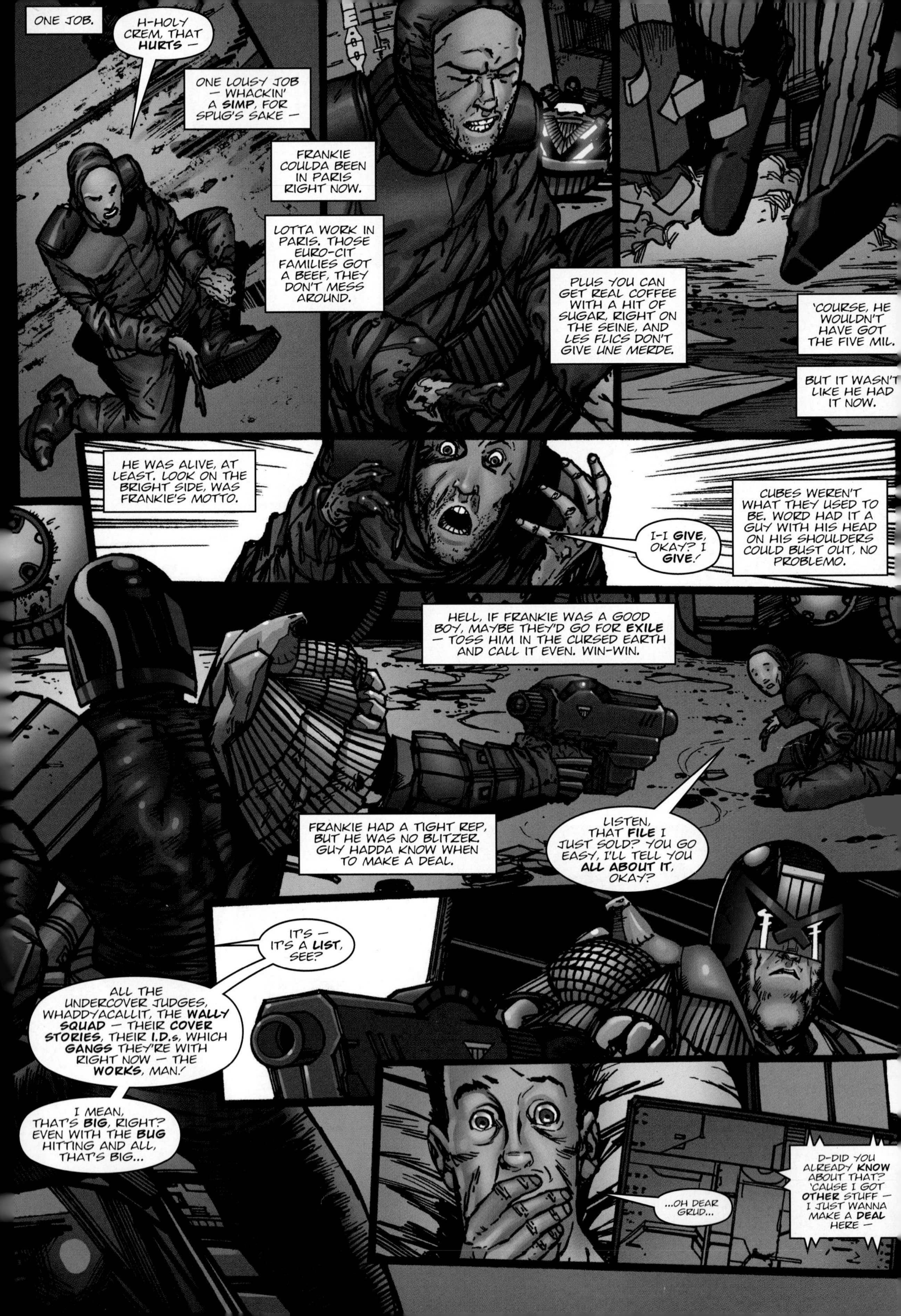
ONE JOB.
H-HOLY CREM, THAT **HURTS** —
ONE LOUSY JOB — WHACKIN' A **SIMP**, FOR SPUG'S SAKE —
FRANKIE COULDA BEEN IN PARIS RIGHT NOW.
LOTTA WORK IN PARIS. THOSE EURO-CIT FAMILIES GOT A BEEF, THEY DON'T MESS AROUND.
PLUS YOU CAN GET REAL COFFEE WITH A HIT OF SUGAR, RIGHT ON THE SEINE, AND *LES FLICS* DON'T GIVE *UNE MERDE*.
'COURSE, HE WOULDN'T HAVE GOT THE FIVE MIL.
BUT IT WASN'T LIKE HE HAD IT NOW.
HE WAS ALIVE, AT LEAST. LOOK ON THE BRIGHT SIDE, WAS FRANKIE'S MOTTO.
I-I **GIVE**, OKAY? I **GIVE**!
CUBES WEREN'T WHAT THEY USED TO BE. WORD HAD IT A GUY WITH HIS HEAD ON HIS SHOULDERS COULD BUST OUT, NO PROBLEMO.
HELL, IF FRANKIE WAS A GOOD BOY, MAYBE THEY'D GO FOR **EXILE** — TOSS HIM IN THE CURSED EARTH AND CALL IT EVEN. WIN-WIN.
FRANKIE HAD A TIGHT REP, BUT HE WAS NO BLITZER. GUY HADDA KNOW WHEN TO MAKE A DEAL.
LISTEN, THAT **FILE** I JUST SOLD? YOU GO EASY, I'LL TELL YOU **ALL ABOUT IT**, OKAY?
IT'S — IT'S A **LIST**, SEE?
ALL THE UNDERCOVER JUDGES, WHADDYACALLIT, THE **WALLY SQUAD** — THEIR **COVER STORIES**, THEIR **I.D.s**, WHICH **GANGS** THEY'RE WITH RIGHT NOW — THE **WORKS**, MAN!
I MEAN, THAT'S **BIG**, RIGHT? EVEN WITH THE **BUG** HITTING AND ALL, THAT'S BIG...
...OH DEAR GRUD...
D-DID YOU ALREADY **KNOW** ABOUT THAT? 'CAUSE I GOT **OTHER** STUFF — I JUST WANNA MAKE A **DEAL** HERE —

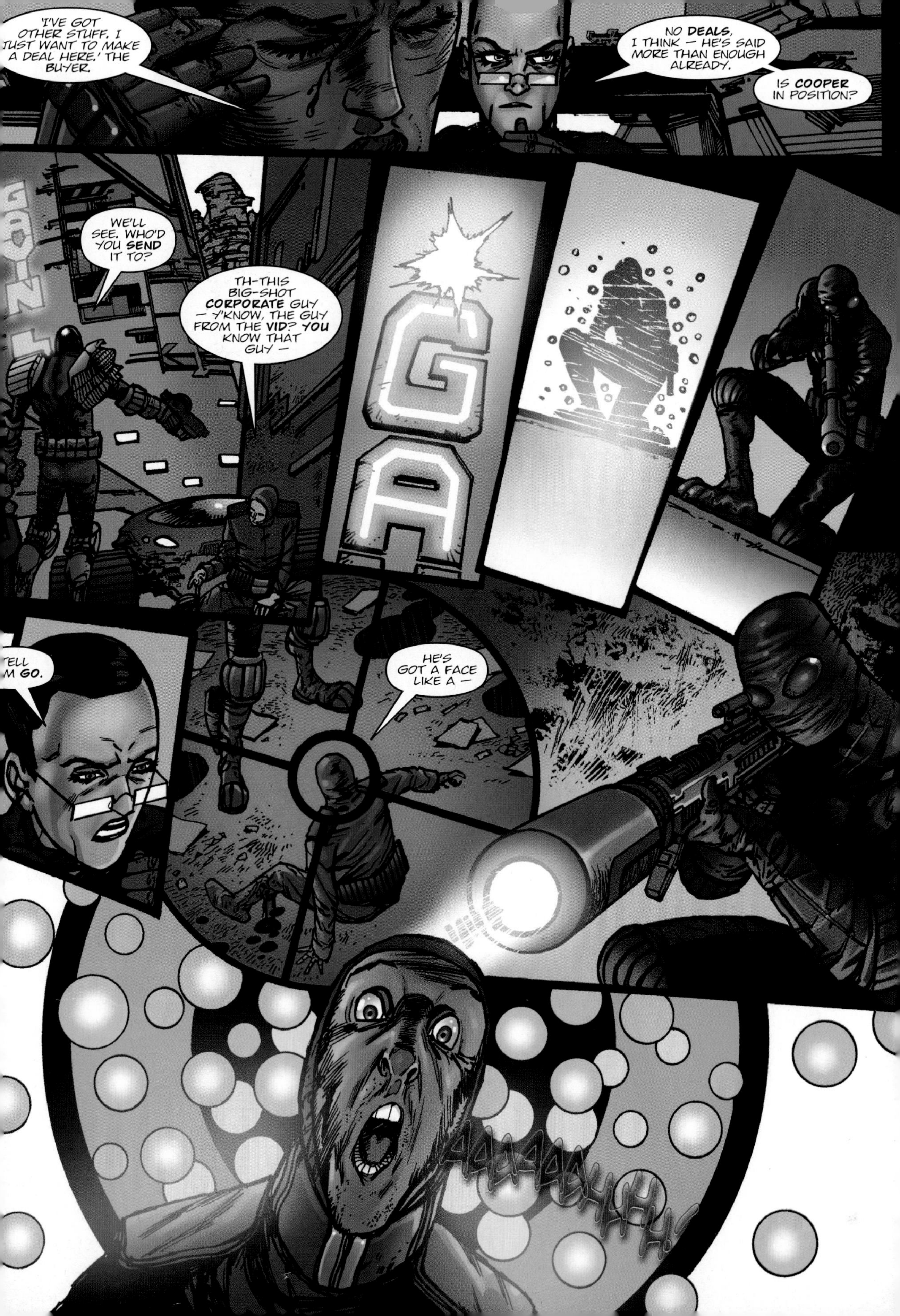

'I'VE GOT OTHER STUFF. I JUST WANT TO MAKE A DEAL HERE.' THE BUYER.
NO DEALS, I THINK — HE'S SAID MORE THAN ENOUGH ALREADY.
IS COOPER IN POSITION?
WE'LL SEE. WHO'D YOU SEND IT TO?
TH-THIS BIG-SHOT CORPORATE GUY — Y'KNOW, THE GUY FROM THE VID? YOU KNOW THAT GUY —
GA
TELL M GO.
HE'S GOT A FACE LIKE A —
AAAAAAAHHH!

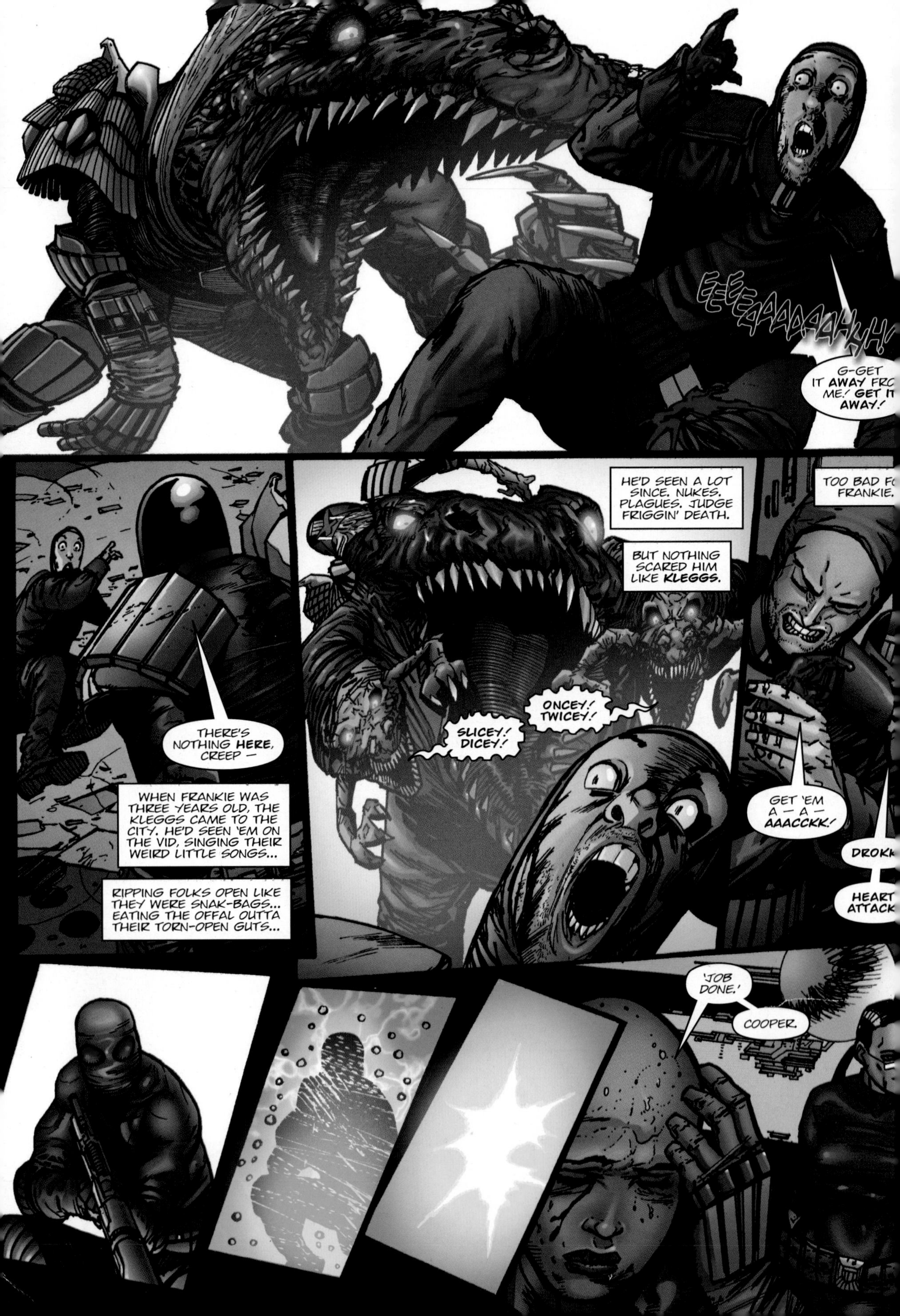

EEEEAAAAAAAHHH!
G-GET IT AWAY FRO ME! GET IT AWAY!
THERE'S NOTHING HERE, CREEP —
WHEN FRANKIE WAS THREE YEARS OLD, THE KLEGGS CAME TO THE CITY. HE'D SEEN 'EM ON THE VID, SINGING THEIR WEIRD LITTLE SONGS...
RIPPING FOLKS OPEN LIKE THEY WERE SNAK-BAGS... EATING THE OFFAL OUTTA THEIR TORN-OPEN GUTS...
HE'D SEEN A LOT SINCE. NUKES. PLAGUES. JUDGE FRIGGIN' DEATH.
BUT NOTHING SCARED HIM LIKE KLEGGS.
ONCEY! TWICEY!
SLICEY! DICEY!
TOO BAD FO FRANKIE.
GET 'EM A — A — AAACCKK!
DROKK
HEART ATTACK
'JOB DONE.'
COOPER.

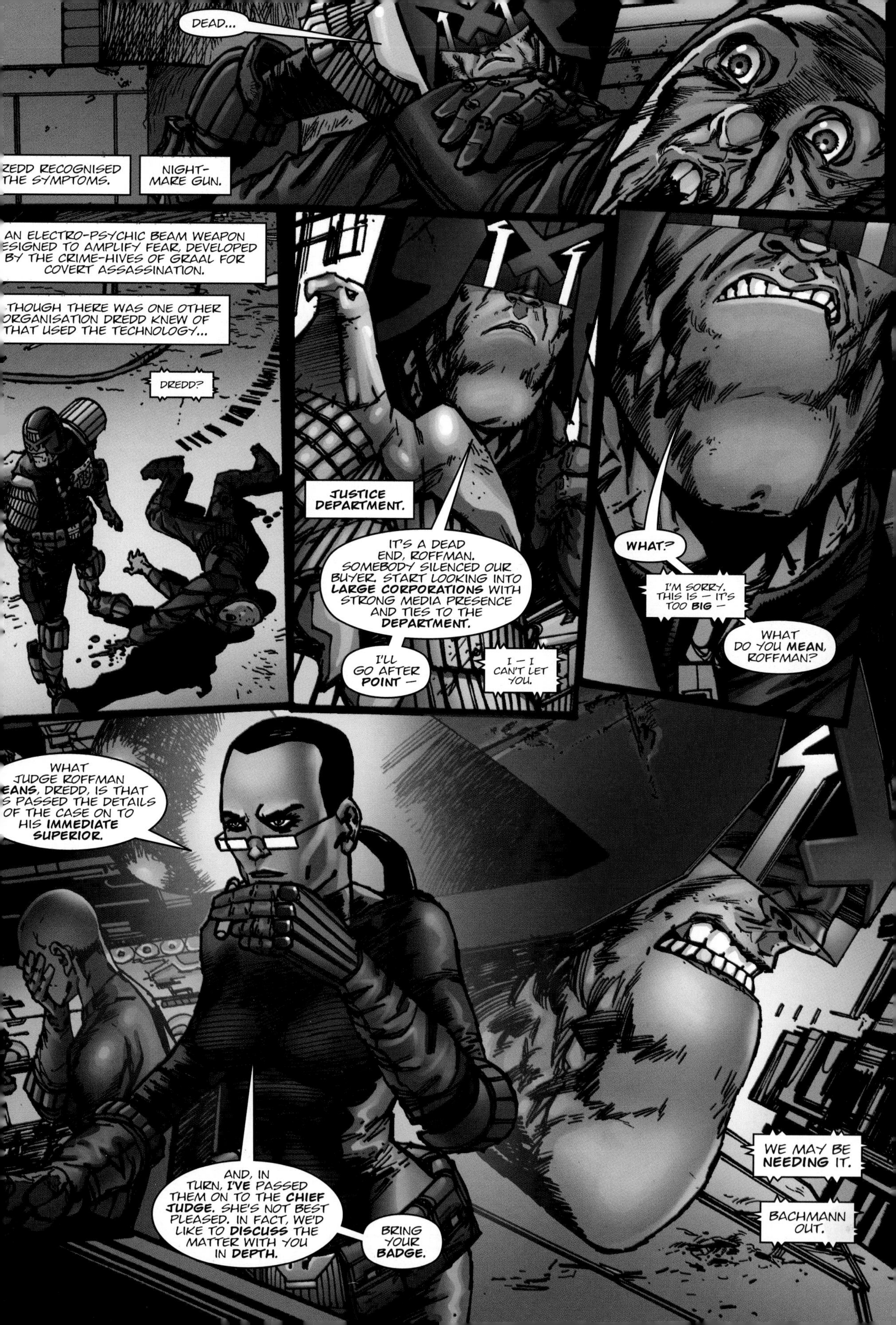
DEAD...
ZEDD RECOGNISED THE SYMPTOMS.
NIGHT-MARE GUN.
AN ELECTRO-PSYCHIC BEAM WEAPON ESIGNED TO AMPLIFY FEAR, DEVELOPED BY THE CRIME-HIVES OF GRAAL FOR COVERT ASSASSINATION.
THOUGH THERE WAS ONE OTHER ORGANISATION DREDD KNEW OF THAT USED THE TECHNOLOGY...
DREDD?
JUSTICE DEPARTMENT.
IT'S A DEAD END, ROFFMAN. SOMEBODY SILENCED OUR BUYER. START LOOKING INTO LARGE CORPORATIONS WITH STRONG MEDIA PRESENCE AND TIES TO THE DEPARTMENT.
I'LL GO AFTER POINT —
I — I CAN'T LET YOU.
WHAT?
I'M SORRY. THIS IS — IT'S TOO BIG —
WHAT DO YOU MEAN, ROFFMAN?
WHAT JUDGE ROFFMAN EANS, DREDD, IS THAT S PASSED THE DETAILS OF THE CASE ON TO HIS IMMEDIATE SUPERIOR.
AND, IN TURN, I'VE PASSED THEM ON TO THE CHIEF JUDGE. SHE'S NOT BEST PLEASED. IN FACT, WE'D LIKE TO DISCUSS THE MATTER WITH YOU IN DEPTH.
BRING YOUR BADGE.
WE MAY BE NEEDING IT.
BACHMANN OUT.

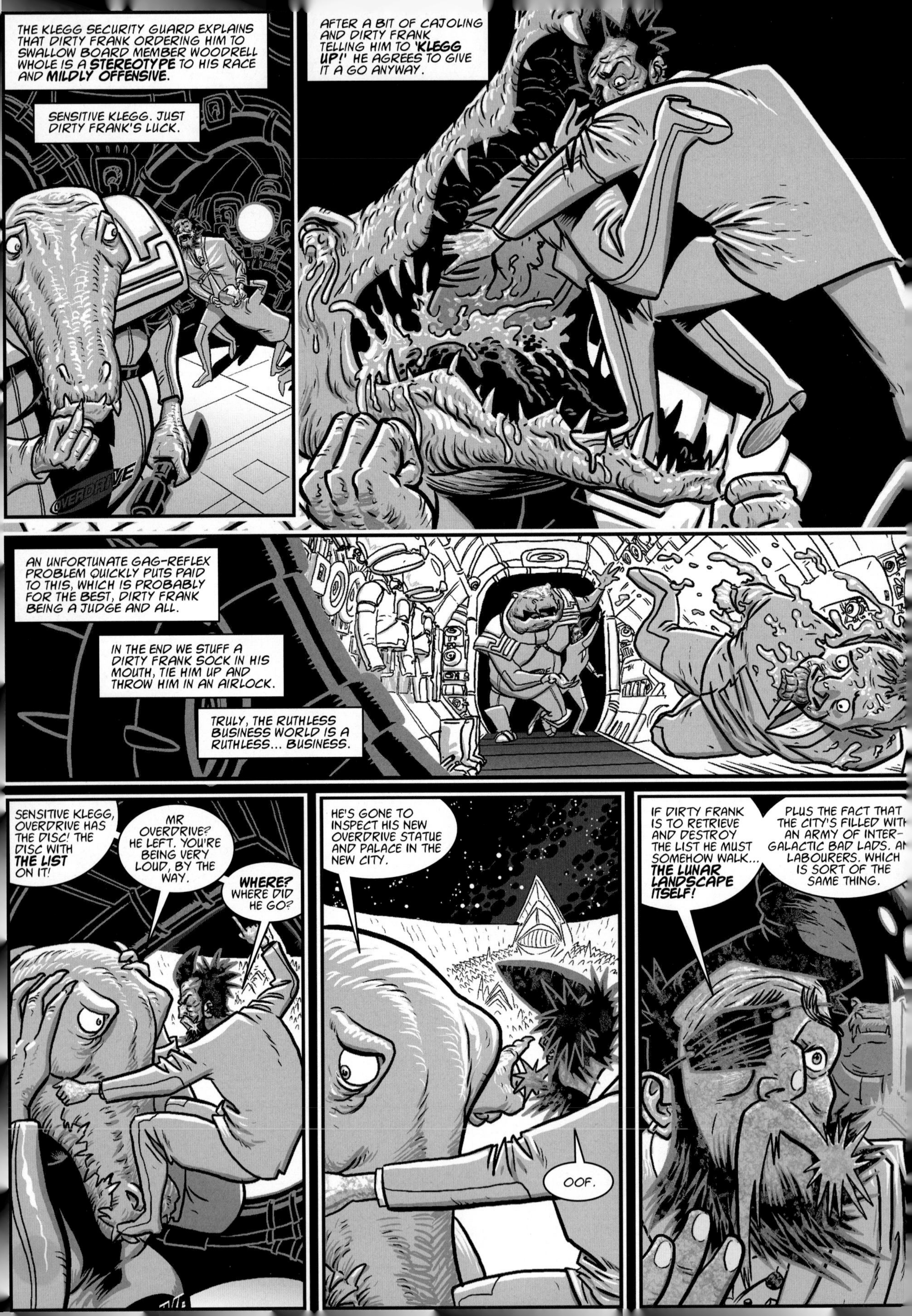
THE KLEGG SECURITY GUARD EXPLAINS THAT DIRTY FRANK ORDERING HIM TO SWALLOW BOARD MEMBER WOODRELL WHOLE IS A STEREOTYPE TO HIS RACE AND MILDLY OFFENSIVE.
SENSITIVE KLEGG. JUST DIRTY FRANK'S LUCK.
OVERDRIVE
AFTER A BIT OF CAJOLING AND DIRTY FRANK TELLING HIM TO 'KLEGG UP!' HE AGREES TO GIVE IT A GO ANYWAY.
AN UNFORTUNATE GAG-REFLEX PROBLEM QUICKLY PUTS PAID TO THIS, WHICH IS PROBABLY FOR THE BEST, DIRTY FRANK BEING A JUDGE AND ALL.
IN THE END WE STUFF A DIRTY FRANK SOCK IN HIS MOUTH, TIE HIM UP AND THROW HIM IN AN AIRLOCK.
TRULY, THE RUTHLESS BUSINESS WORLD IS A RUTHLESS... BUSINESS.
SENSITIVE KLEGG, OVERDRIVE HAS THE DISC! THE DISC WITH THE LIST ON IT!
MR OVERDRIVE? HE LEFT. YOU'RE BEING VERY LOUD, BY THE WAY.
WHERE? WHERE DID HE GO?
HE'S GONE TO INSPECT HIS NEW OVERDRIVE STATUE AND PALACE IN THE NEW CITY.
OOF.
IF DIRTY FRANK IS TO RETRIEVE AND DESTROY THE LIST HE MUST SOMEHOW WALK... THE LUNAR LANDSCAPE ITSELF!
PLUS THE FACT THAT THE CITY'S FILLED WITH AN ARMY OF INTER-GALACTIC BAD LADS. A LABOURERS. WHICH IS SORT OF THE SAME THING.

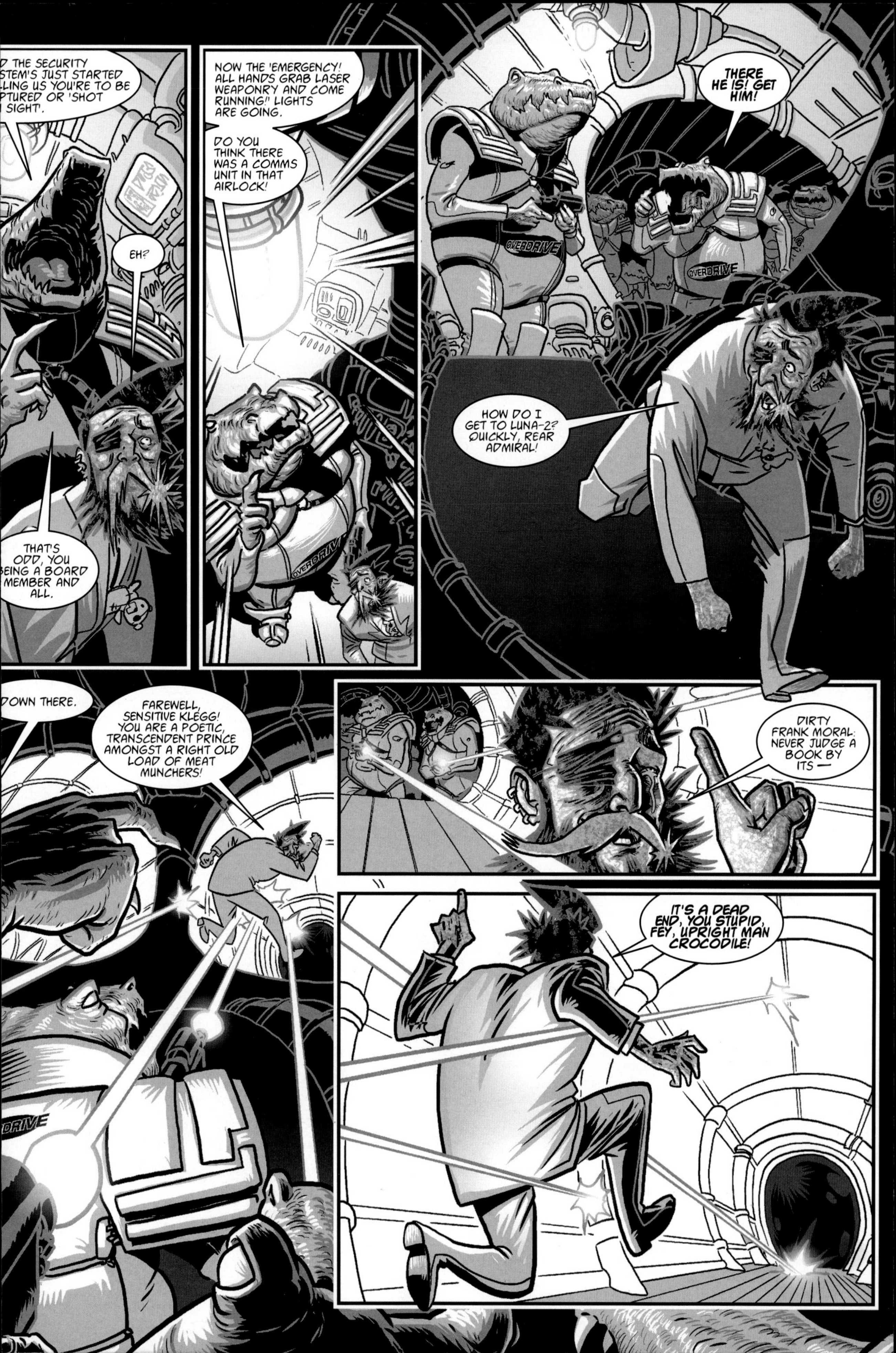
D THE SECURITY STEM'S JUST STARTED LLING US YOU'RE TO BE PTURED OR 'SHOT N SIGHT'.
EH?
THAT'S ODD, YOU BEING A BOARD MEMBER AND ALL.
NOW THE 'EMERGENCY! ALL HANDS GRAB LASER WEAPONRY AND COME RUNNING!' LIGHTS ARE GOING.
DO YOU THINK THERE WAS A COMMS UNIT IN THAT AIRLOCK!
THERE HE IS! GET HIM!
OVERDRIVE
HOW DO I GET TO LUNA-2? QUICKLY, REAR ADMIRAL!
DOWN THERE.
FAREWELL, SENSITIVE KLEGG! YOU ARE A POETIC, TRANSCENDENT PRINCE AMONGST A RIGHT OLD LOAD OF MEAT MUNCHERS!
DIRTY FRANK MORAL: NEVER JUDGE A BOOK BY ITS —
IT'S A DEAD END, YOU STUPID, FEY, UPRIGHT MAN CROCODILE!

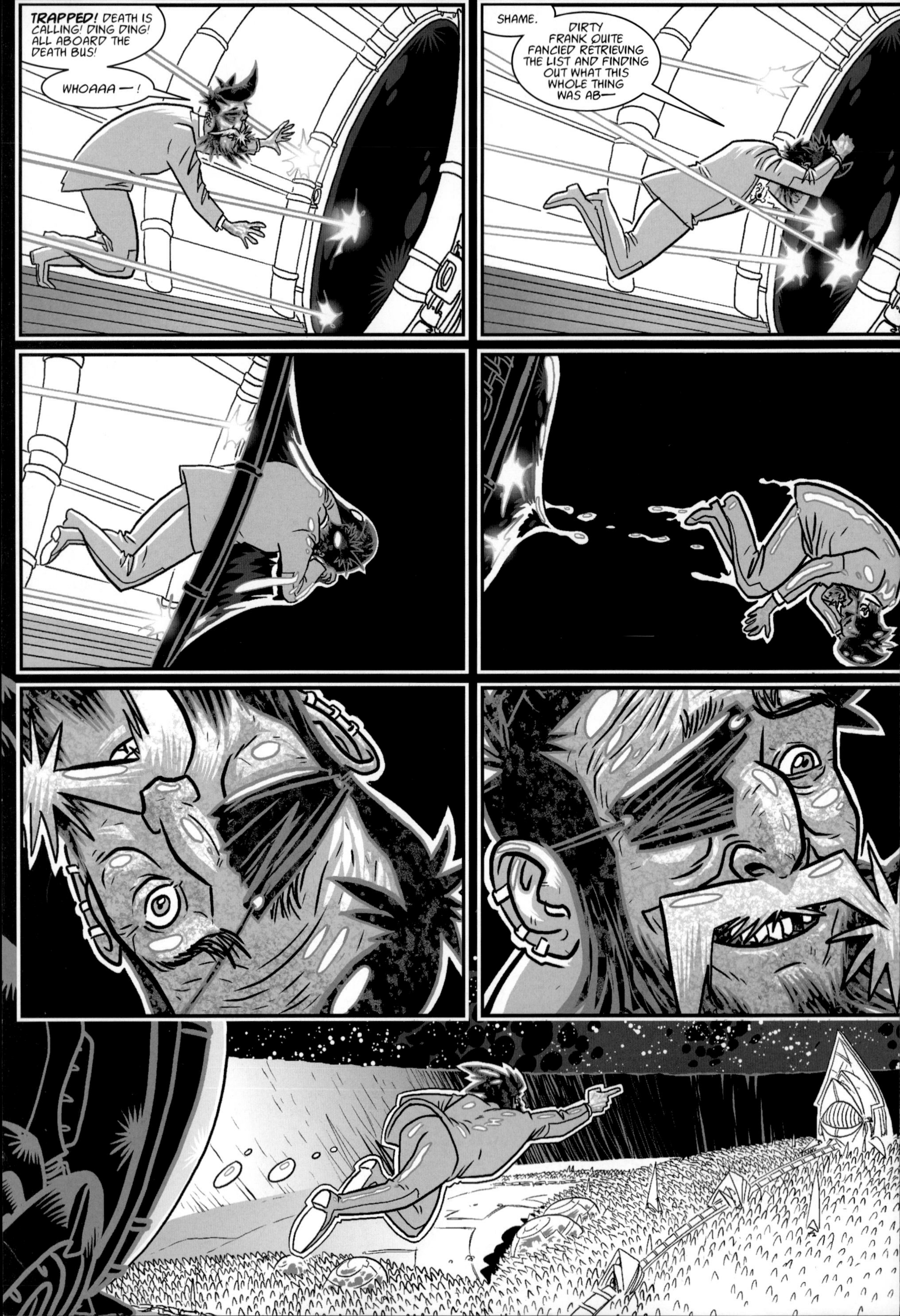
TRAPPED! DEATH IS CALLING! DING DING! ALL ABOARD THE DEATH BUS!
WHOAAA—!
SHAME.
DIRTY FRANK QUITE FANCIED RETRIEVING THE LIST AND FINDING OUT WHAT THIS WHOLE THING WAS AB—

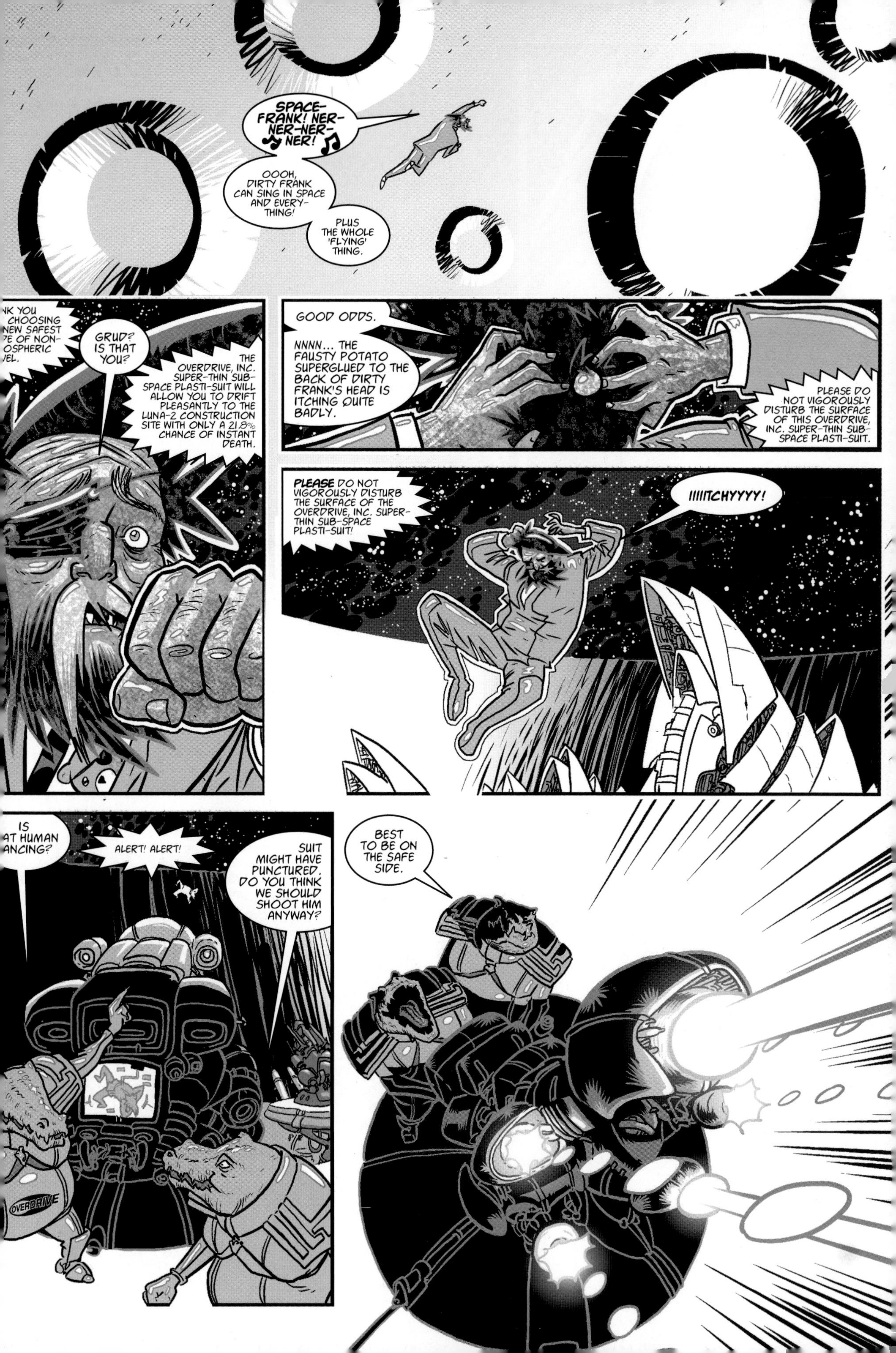
SPACE-FRANK! NER-NER-NER-NER!
OOOH, DIRTY FRANK CAN SING IN SPACE AND EVERY-THING!
PLUS THE WHOLE 'FLYING' THING.
NK YOU CHOOSING NEW SAFEST E OF NON-OSPHERIC VEL.
GRUD? IS THAT YOU?
THE OVERDRIVE, INC. SUPER-THIN SUB-SPACE PLASTI-SUIT WILL ALLOW YOU TO DRIFT PLEASANTLY TO THE LUNA-2 CONSTRUCTION SITE WITH ONLY A 21.8% CHANCE OF INSTANT DEATH.
GOOD ODDS.
NNNN... THE FAUSTY POTATO SUPERGLUED TO THE BACK OF DIRTY FRANK'S HEAD IS ITCHING QUITE BADLY.
PLEASE DO NOT VIGOROUSLY DISTURB THE SURFACE OF THIS OVERDRIVE, INC. SUPER-THIN SUB-SPACE PLASTI-SUIT.
PLEASE DO NOT VIGOROUSLY DISTURB THE SURFACE OF THE OVERDRIVE, INC. SUPER-THIN SUB-SPACE PLASTI-SUIT!
IIIIIITCHYYYY!
IS AT HUMAN ANCING?
ALERT! ALERT!
SUIT MIGHT HAVE PUNCTURED. DO YOU THINK WE SHOULD SHOOT HIM ANYWAY?
OVERDRIVE
BEST TO BE ON THE SAFE SIDE.

OHHH, FIREWORKS.

STOP SCRATCHING ME!

KLIK

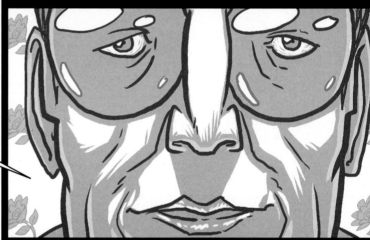

I'VE GOT A TINY JOB FOR YOU, JUDGE FRANK...

WHOEVER THAT IS, DIRTY FRANK WOULD LIKE TO GIVE HIM A RIGHT SLAP.

ALERT! ALERT!

YOU'VE ALREADY SAID THAT!

LEAVING SAFE LUNAR PARAMETERS! HEADING INTO OPEN SPACE! CHANCE OF DEATH 86.7% AND RISING!

BAD ODDS! BAD ODDS!

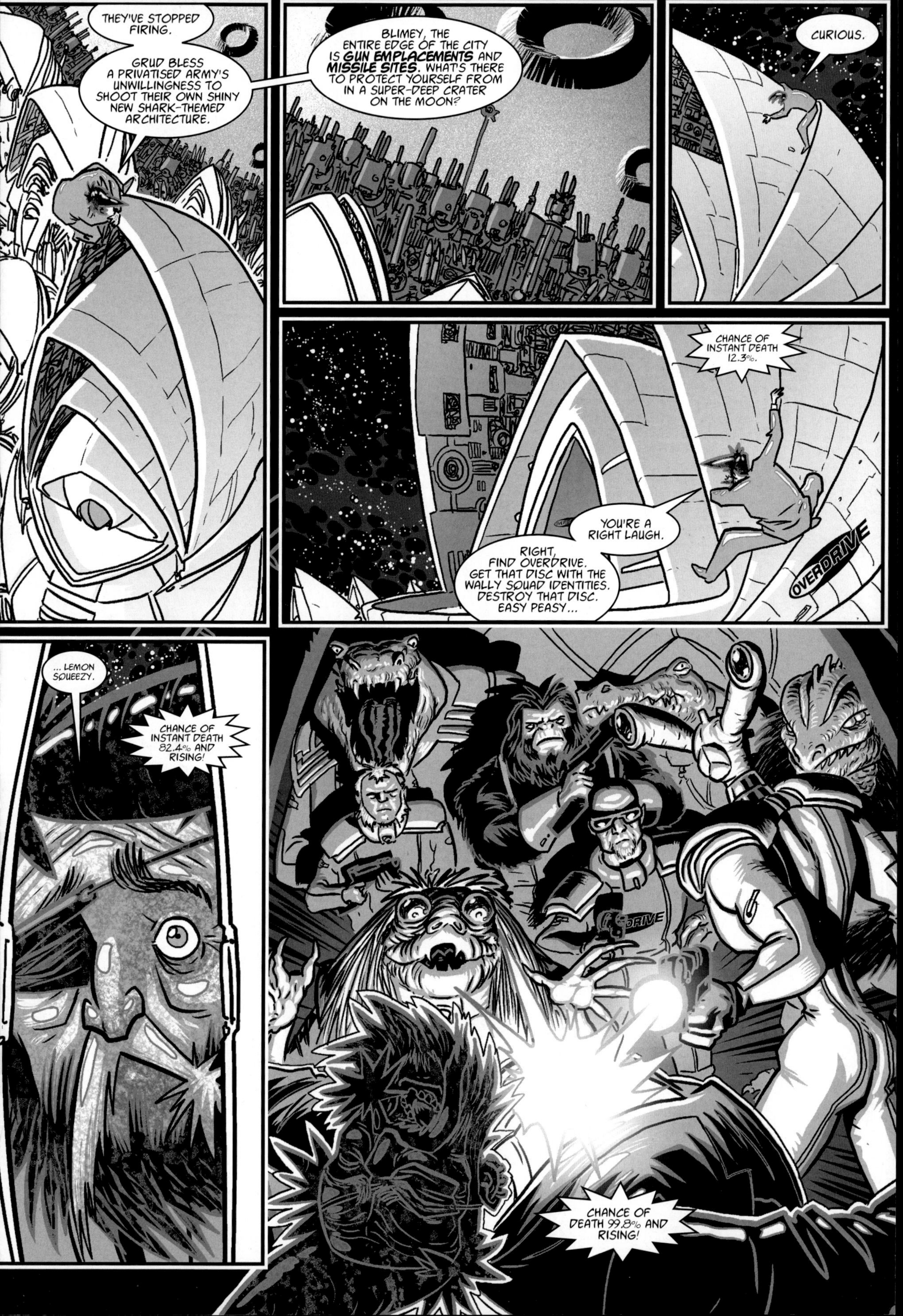
THEY'VE STOPPED FIRING.
GRUD BLESS A PRIVATISED ARMY'S UNWILLINGNESS TO SHOOT THEIR OWN SHINY NEW SHARK-THEMED ARCHITECTURE.
BLIMEY, THE ENTIRE EDGE OF THE CITY IS **GUN EMPLACEMENTS** AND **MISSILE SITES**. WHAT'S THERE TO PROTECT YOURSELF FROM IN A SUPER-DEEP CRATER ON THE MOON?
CURIOUS.
CHANCE OF INSTANT DEATH 12.3%.
YOU'RE A RIGHT LAUGH.
RIGHT, FIND OVERDRIVE. GET THAT DISC WITH THE WALLY SQUAD IDENTITIES. DESTROY THAT DISC. EASY PEASY...
OVERDRIVE
... LEMON SQUEEZY.
CHANCE OF INSTANT DEATH 82.4% AND RISING!
CHANCE OF DEATH 99.8% AND RISING!

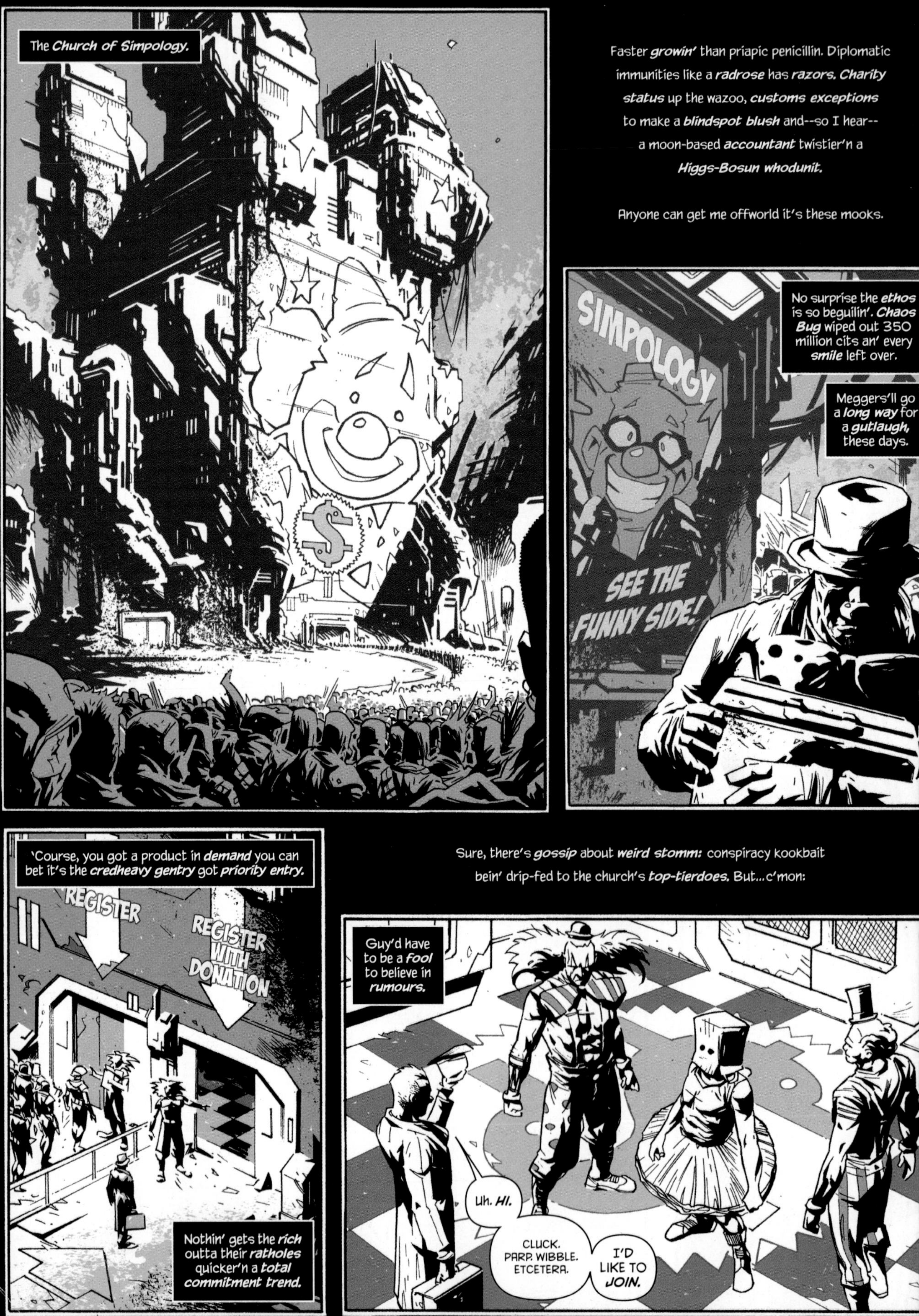
The Church of Simpology.
Faster growin' than priapic penicillin. Diplomatic immunities like a radrose has razors. Charity status up the wazoo, customs exceptions to make a blindspot blush and--so I hear--a moon-based accountant twistier'n a Higgs-Bosun whodunit.
Anyone can get me offworld it's these mooks.
SIMPOLOGY
SEE THE FUNNY SIDE!
No surprise the ethos is so beguilin'. Chaos Bug wiped out 350 million cits an' every smile left over.
Meggers'll go a long way for a gutlaugh, these days.
'Course, you got a product in demand you can bet it's the credheavy gentry got priority entry.
REGISTER
REGISTER WITH DONATION
Nothin' gets the rich outta their ratholes quicker'n a total commitment trend.
Sure, there's gossip about weird stomm: conspiracy kookbait bein' drip-fed to the church's top-tierdoes. But...c'mon:
Guy'd have to be a fool to believe in rumours.
Uh. HI.
CLUCK. PARP. WIBBLE. ETCETERA.
I'D LIKE TO JOIN.

YOU GOTTA SUBMIT TO A *QUACK QUACK* INITIAL *SECURITY CHECK.* SIGN HERE.

UH, SURE.

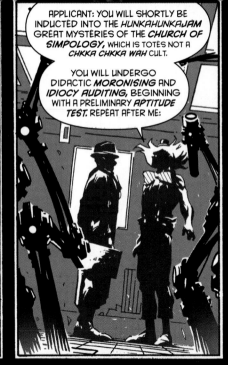

APPLICANT: YOU WILL SHORTLY BE INDUCTED INTO THE *HUNKAHUNKAJAM* GREAT MYSTERIES OF THE *CHURCH OF SIMPOLOGY,* WHICH IS TOTES NOT A *CHKKA CHKKA WAH* CULT.

YOU WILL UNDERGO DIDACTIC *MORONISING* AND *IDIOCY AUDITING,* BEGINNING WITH A PRELIMINARY *APTITUDE TEST.* REPEAT AFTER ME:

PARP.

AAA! P-PARP!

FNEG.

FNEG!

BOOBIES, TEE HEE HEE.

BOOBIES, TEE HEE HEE.

SECURITY ALERT!

"S-SECURITY ALERT."

YOU DON'T GOTTA REPEAT *THAT* BIT. JIZZPOOP WEEVILNUT.

HUH. YOU GOT A *BUGBOT* IN YOUR *TOOTH,* PAL.

I...I GOT NO IDEA WHERE THAT *CAME* FROOOOOAAAAAA!

HE'S TELLING THE *TRUTH.* PROB'LY ANOTHER *JOURNO-STING PATSY.* HE'S *CLUELESS.*

AND HIS *AUDITING ASSETS?*

ALPHA PLUS-PLUS. HE'S WELCOME.

EXTREMELY, *EXTREMELY* WELCOME.

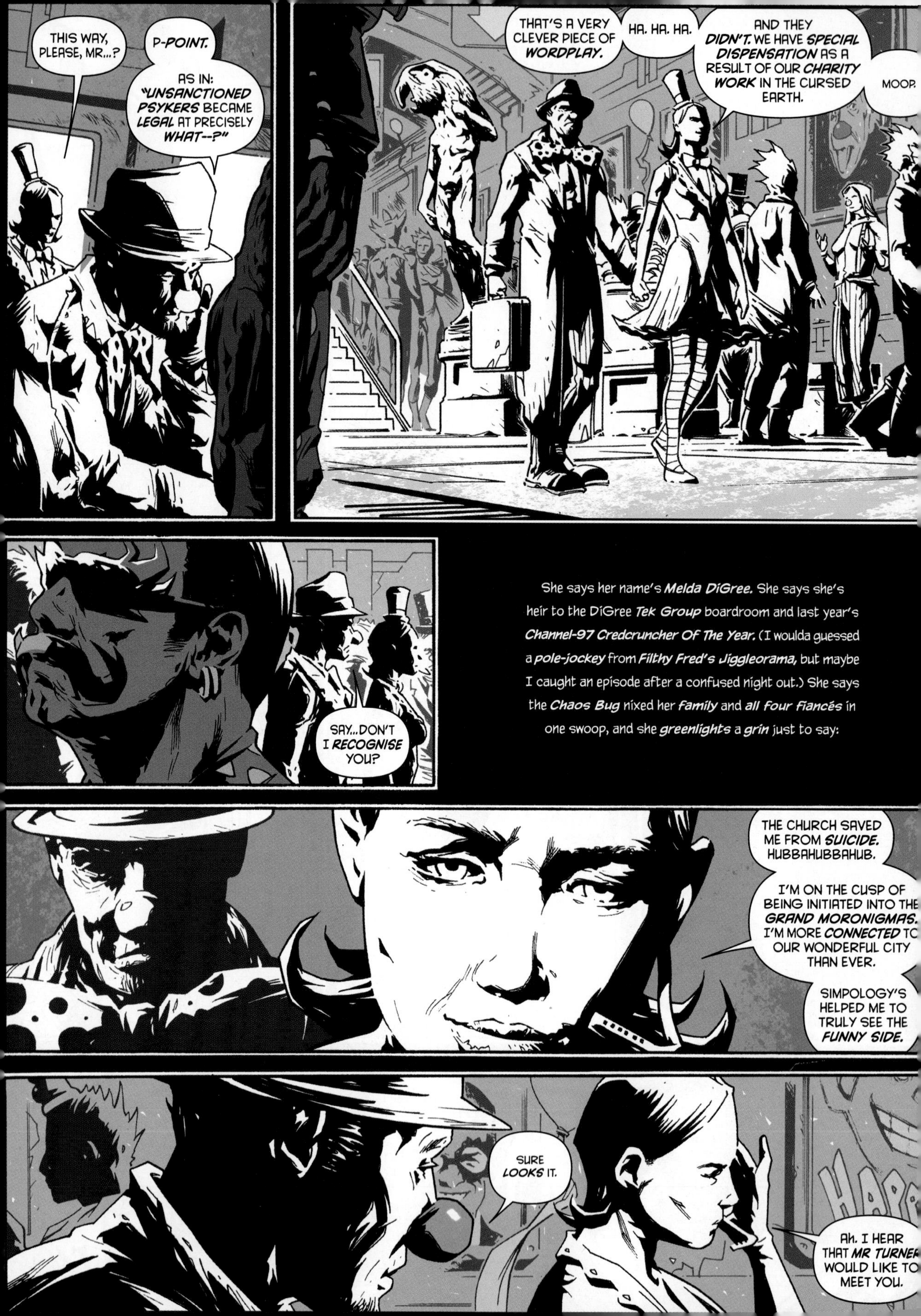
THIS WAY, PLEASE, MR...?
P-POINT.
AS IN: "UNSANCTIONED PSYKERS BECAME LEGAL AT PRECISELY WHAT--?"
THAT'S A VERY CLEVER PIECE OF WORDPLAY.
HA. HA. HA.
AND THEY DIDN'T. WE HAVE SPECIAL DISPENSATION AS A RESULT OF OUR CHARITY WORK IN THE CURSED EARTH.
MOOP.
SAY...DON'T I RECOGNISE YOU?
She says her name's Melda DiGree. She says she's heir to the DiGree Tek Group boardroom and last year's Channel-97 Credcruncher Of The Year. (I woulda guessed a pole-jockey from Filthy Fred's Jiggleorama, but maybe I caught an episode after a confused night out.) She says the Chaos Bug nixed her family and all four fiancés in one swoop, and she greenlights a grin just to say:
THE CHURCH SAVED ME FROM SUICIDE. HUBBAHUBBAHUB.
I'M ON THE CUSP OF BEING INITIATED INTO THE GRAND MORONIGMAS. I'M MORE CONNECTED TO OUR WONDERFUL CITY THAN EVER.
SIMPOLOGY'S HELPED ME TO TRULY SEE THE FUNNY SIDE.
SURE LOOKS IT.
AH. I HEAR THAT MR TURNER WOULD LIKE TO MEET YOU.

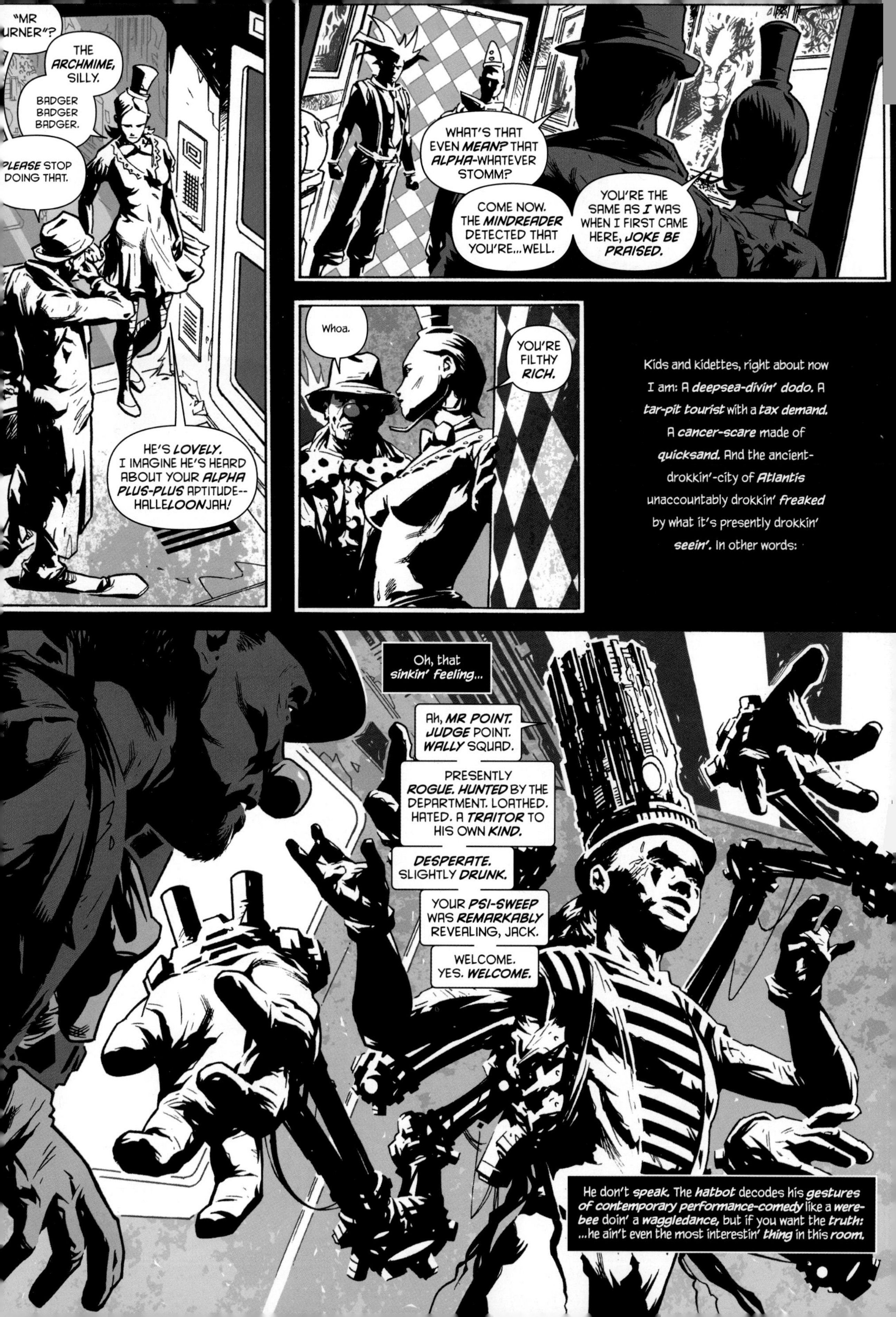
"MR
URNER"?
THE ARCHMIME, SILLY.
BADGER BADGER BADGER.
PLEASE STOP DOING THAT.
HE'S LOVELY. I IMAGINE HE'S HEARD ABOUT YOUR ALPHA PLUS-PLUS APTITUDE-- HALLELOONJAH!
WHAT'S THAT EVEN MEAN? THAT ALPHA-WHATEVER STOMM?
COME NOW. THE MINDREADER DETECTED THAT YOU'RE...WELL.
YOU'RE THE SAME AS I WAS WHEN I FIRST CAME HERE, JOKE BE PRAISED.
Whoa.
YOU'RE FILTHY RICH.
Kids and kidettes, right about now I am: A deepsea-divin' dodo. A tar-pit tourist with a tax demand. A cancer-scare made of quicksand. And the ancient-drokkin'-city of Atlantis unaccountably drokkin' freaked by what it's presently drokkin' seein'. In other words:
Oh, that sinkin' feeling...
Ah, MR POINT. JUDGE POINT. WALLY SQUAD.
PRESENTLY ROGUE. HUNTED BY THE DEPARTMENT. LOATHED. HATED. A TRAITOR TO HIS OWN KIND.
DESPERATE. SLIGHTLY DRUNK.
YOUR PSI-SWEEP WAS REMARKABLY REVEALING, JACK.
WELCOME. YES. WELCOME.
He don't speak. The hatbot decodes his gestures of contemporary performance-comedy like a were-bee doin' a waggledance, but if you want the truth: ...he ain't even the most interestin' thing in this room.

Y-YOU, UH, YOU GOT A LOT OF EXCITIN' ILLEGAL *DRUGS*, SIR.

ALSO: *GUNS.* UH, *QUACK.*

MM. CONSIDER ME A *FLAUNTER* OF *SMUGNESS*, MR POINT.

AS A DEPARTMENTALLY RECOGNISED *RELIGION*, IN MANY WAYS MY ORGANISATION OPERATES *OUTSIDE* THE LAW. THE TEMPTATION TO *EXPLOIT* SUCH LICENSE IS...*INTOXICATING.*

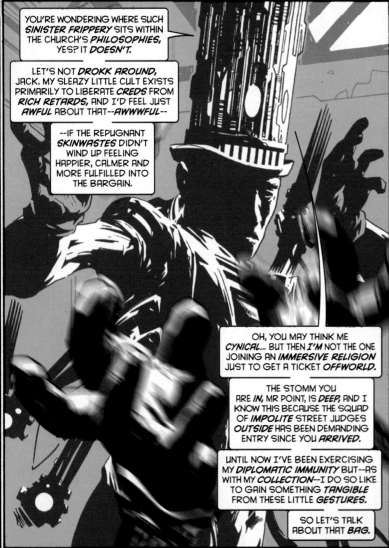

YOU'RE WONDERING WHERE SUCH *SINISTER FRIPPERY* SITS WITHIN THE CHURCH'S *PHILOSOPHIES*, YES? IT *DOESN'T.*

LET'S NOT *DROKK AROUND,* JACK. MY SLEAZY LITTLE CULT EXISTS PRIMARILY TO LIBERATE *CREDS* FROM *RICH RETARDS,* AND I'D FEEL JUST *AWFUL* ABOUT THAT--*AWWWFUL*--

--IF THE REPUGNANT *SKINWASTES* DIDN'T WIND UP FEELING *HAPPIER, CALMER* AND MORE *FULFILLED* INTO THE BARGAIN.

OH, YOU MAY THINK ME *CYNICAL...* BUT THEN *I'M* NOT THE ONE JOINING AN *IMMERSIVE RELIGION* JUST TO GET A TICKET *OFFWORLD.*

THE STOMM YOU ARE *IN,* MR POINT, IS *DEEP,* AND I KNOW THIS BECAUSE THE SQUAD OF *IMPOLITE* STREET JUDGES *OUTSIDE* HAS BEEN DEMANDING ENTRY SINCE YOU *ARRIVED.*

UNTIL NOW I'VE BEEN EXERCISING MY *DIPLOMATIC IMMUNITY* BUT--AS WITH MY *COLLECTION*--I DO SO LIKE TO GAIN SOMETHING *TANGIBLE* FROM THESE LITTLE *GESTURES.*

SO LET'S TALK ABOUT THAT *BAG.*

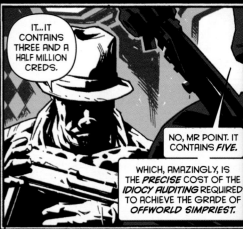

IT...IT CONTAINS THREE AND A HALF MILLION CREDS.

NO, MR POINT. IT CONTAINS *FIVE.*

WHICH, AMAZINGLY, IS THE *PRECISE* COST OF THE *IDIOCY AUDITING* REQUIRED TO ACHIEVE THE GRADE OF *OFFWORLD SIMPRIEST.*

WHAT A *FUNNY* COINCIDENCE.

HA.

HA.

HA.

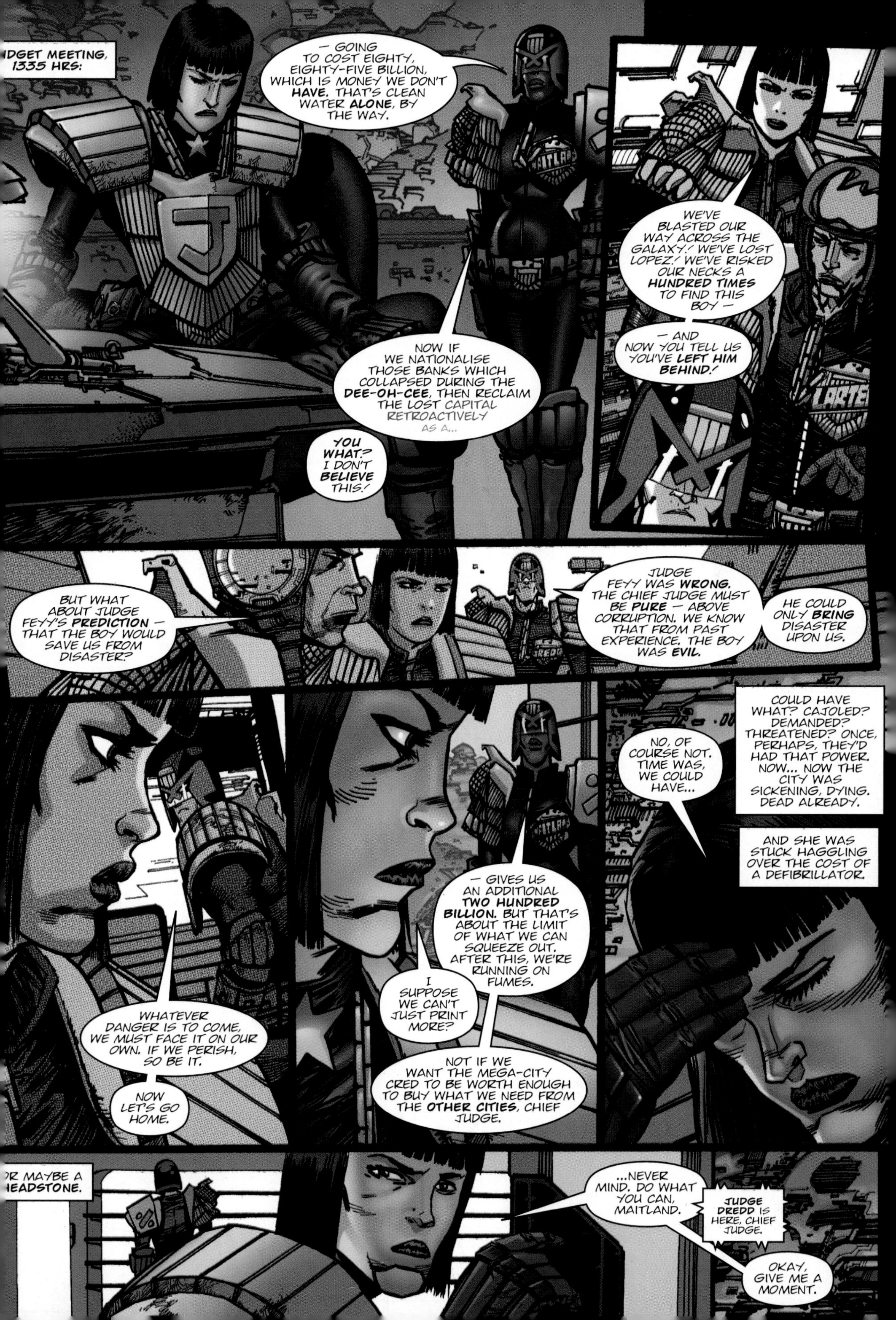

IDGET MEETING, 1335 HRS:
— GOING TO COST EIGHTY, EIGHTY-FIVE BILLION, WHICH IS MONEY WE DON'T HAVE. THAT'S CLEAN WATER ALONE, BY THE WAY.
NOW IF WE NATIONALISE THOSE BANKS WHICH COLLAPSED DURING THE DEE-OH-CEE, THEN RECLAIM THE LOST CAPITAL RETROACTIVELY AS A...
YOU WHAT? I DON'T BELIEVE THIS!
WE'VE BLASTED OUR WAY ACROSS THE GALAXY! WE'VE LOST LOPEZ! WE'VE RISKED OUR NECKS A HUNDRED TIMES TO FIND THIS BOY —
— AND NOW YOU TELL US YOU'VE LEFT HIM BEHIND!
BUT WHAT ABOUT JUDGE FEYY'S PREDICTION — THAT THE BOY WOULD SAVE US FROM DISASTER?
JUDGE FEYY WAS WRONG. THE CHIEF JUDGE MUST BE PURE — ABOVE CORRUPTION. WE KNOW THAT FROM PAST EXPERIENCE. THE BOY WAS EVIL.
HE COULD ONLY BRING DISASTER UPON US.
WHATEVER DANGER IS TO COME, WE MUST FACE IT ON OUR OWN. IF WE PERISH, SO BE IT.
NOW LET'S GO HOME.
— GIVES US AN ADDITIONAL TWO HUNDRED BILLION. BUT THAT'S ABOUT THE LIMIT OF WHAT WE CAN SQUEEZE OUT. AFTER THIS, WE'RE RUNNING ON FUMES.
I SUPPOSE WE CAN'T JUST PRINT MORE?
NOT IF WE WANT THE MEGA-CITY CRED TO BE WORTH ENOUGH TO BUY WHAT WE NEED FROM THE OTHER CITIES, CHIEF JUDGE.
NO, OF COURSE NOT. TIME WAS, WE COULD HAVE...
COULD HAVE WHAT? CAJOLED? DEMANDED? THREATENED? ONCE, PERHAPS, THEY'D HAD THAT POWER. NOW... NOW THE CITY WAS SICKENING, DYING. DEAD ALREADY.
AND SHE WAS STUCK HAGGLING OVER THE COST OF A DEFIBRILLATOR.
OR MAYBE A HEADSTONE.
...NEVER MIND. DO WHAT YOU CAN, MAITLAND.
JUDGE DREDD IS HERE, CHIEF JUDGE.
OKAY, GIVE ME A MOMENT.

SOMETHING **WRONG?**

MAITLAND.

...DREDD.

...NO, IT'S JUST... DEJA VU, OR...

...DID A LITTLE **DIGGING** — FOUND SOME FIGURES FOR BLACK OPS OVERSPEND OVER THE LAST SIX YEARS. OBVIOUSLY THIS IS **BLACK BUDGET** STUFF — IMPOSSIBLE TO PROVE.

ANYWAY, I RAN THOSE FIGURES THROUGH THE **COMPUTER** — CROSS-MATCHED AGAINST ANY UNEXPLAINED **ADDITIONAL INCOME** FROM PRIVATE COMPANIES.

SIX YEARS RUNNING, THE **SAME** OFF-WORLD COMPANY SCORED A **PERFECT MATCH.**

MY, MY. I CAN SEE I WAS **WRONG** ABOUT YOU, JUDGE MAITLAND. YOU'RE VERY MUCH AN ASSET TO THE **TEAM.**

NOW, WHAT WAS THIS COMPANY'S **NAME...?**

...NO. NO, IT'S GONE.

MAYBE I **DREAMT** IT...

MAYBE **YOU** DID.

JUDGE DREDD? THE **CHIEF JUDGE** WILL SEE YOU NOW.

...I'LL KEEP THIS BRIEF. THANKS TO YOU, THE WALLY LIST IS OUT IN THE **WILD.** A LIST OF **EVERY** UNDERCOVER OPERATIVE WE HAVE.

WALLY SQUAD BEING THE ONE ARM OF JUSTICE DEPARTMENT THAT SUFFERED LESS THAN **TEN PER CENT** CASUALTIES ON CHAOS DAY.

THEY'RE **GOOD** AT SURVIVING IN EXTREME SITUATIONS.

I JUST HOPE THEY CAN SURVIVE **THIS.**

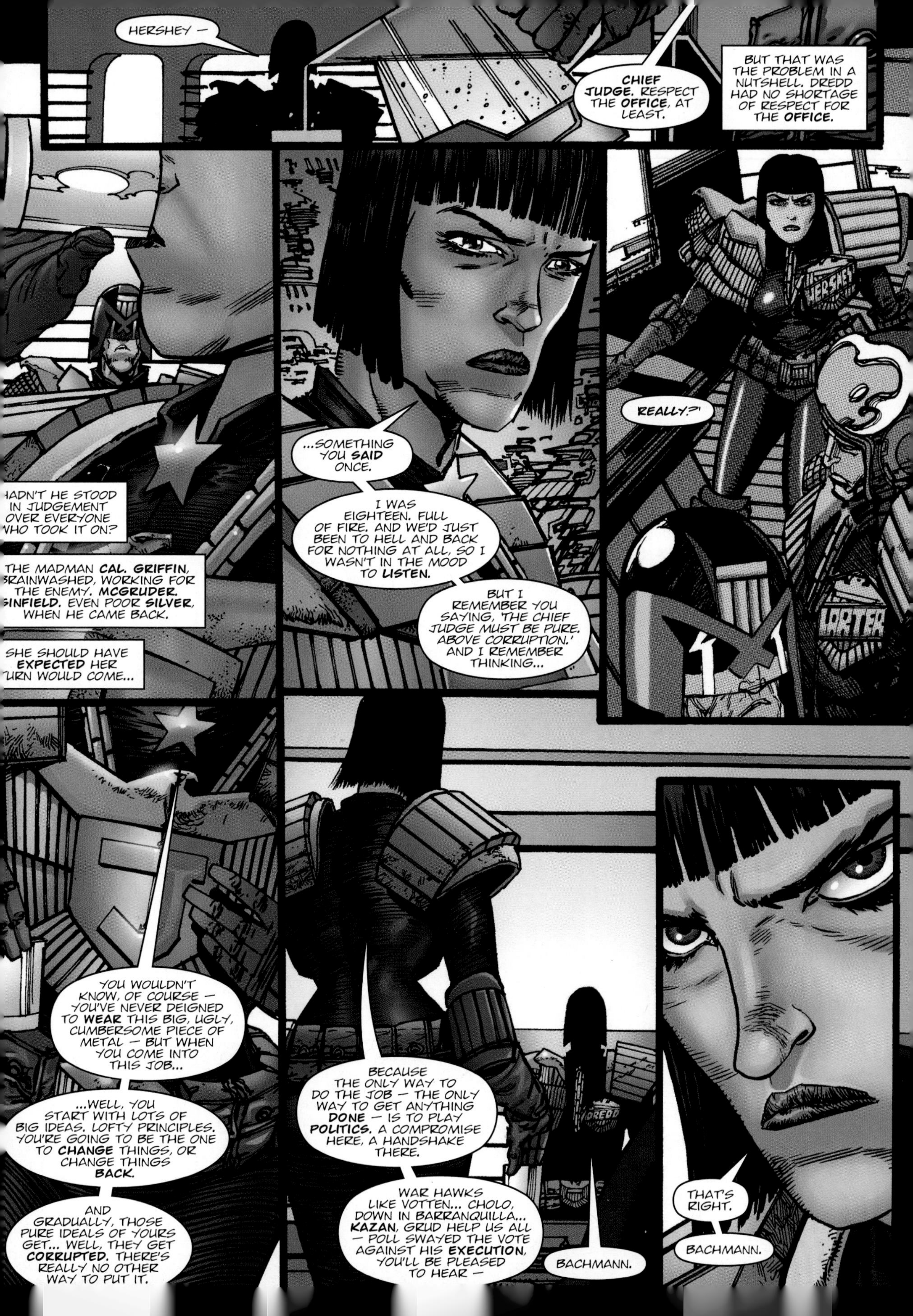

HERSHEY —
CHIEF JUDGE. RESPECT THE OFFICE, AT LEAST.
BUT THAT WAS THE PROBLEM IN A NUTSHELL. DREDD HAD NO SHORTAGE OF RESPECT FOR THE OFFICE.
HADN'T HE STOOD IN JUDGEMENT OVER EVERYONE WHO TOOK IT ON?
THE MADMAN CAL. GRIFFIN, BRAINWASHED, WORKING FOR THE ENEMY. MCGRUDER. SINFIELD. EVEN POOR SILVER, WHEN HE CAME BACK.
SHE SHOULD HAVE EXPECTED HER TURN WOULD COME...
...SOMETHING YOU SAID ONCE.
I WAS EIGHTEEN. FULL OF FIRE. AND WE'D JUST BEEN TO HELL AND BACK FOR NOTHING AT ALL, SO I WASN'T IN THE MOOD TO LISTEN.
BUT I REMEMBER YOU SAYING, 'THE CHIEF JUDGE MUST BE PURE. ABOVE CORRUPTION.' AND I REMEMBER THINKING...
REALLY?!
HERSHEY
CARTER
YOU WOULDN'T KNOW, OF COURSE — YOU'VE NEVER DEIGNED TO WEAR THIS BIG, UGLY, CUMBERSOME PIECE OF METAL — BUT WHEN YOU COME INTO THIS JOB...
...WELL, YOU START WITH LOTS OF BIG IDEAS. LOFTY PRINCIPLES. YOU'RE GOING TO BE THE ONE TO CHANGE THINGS, OR CHANGE THINGS BACK.
AND GRADUALLY, THOSE PURE IDEALS OF YOURS GET... WELL, THEY GET CORRUPTED. THERE'S REALLY NO OTHER WAY TO PUT IT.
BECAUSE THE ONLY WAY TO DO THE JOB — THE ONLY WAY TO GET ANYTHING DONE — IS TO PLAY POLITICS. A COMPROMISE HERE, A HANDSHAKE THERE.
WAR HAWKS LIKE VOTTEN... CHOLO, DOWN IN BARRANQUILLA... KAZAN, GRUD HELP US ALL — POLL SWAYED THE VOTE AGAINST HIS EXECUTION, YOU'LL BE PLEASED TO HEAR —
DREDD
BACHMANN.
THAT'S RIGHT.
BACHMANN.

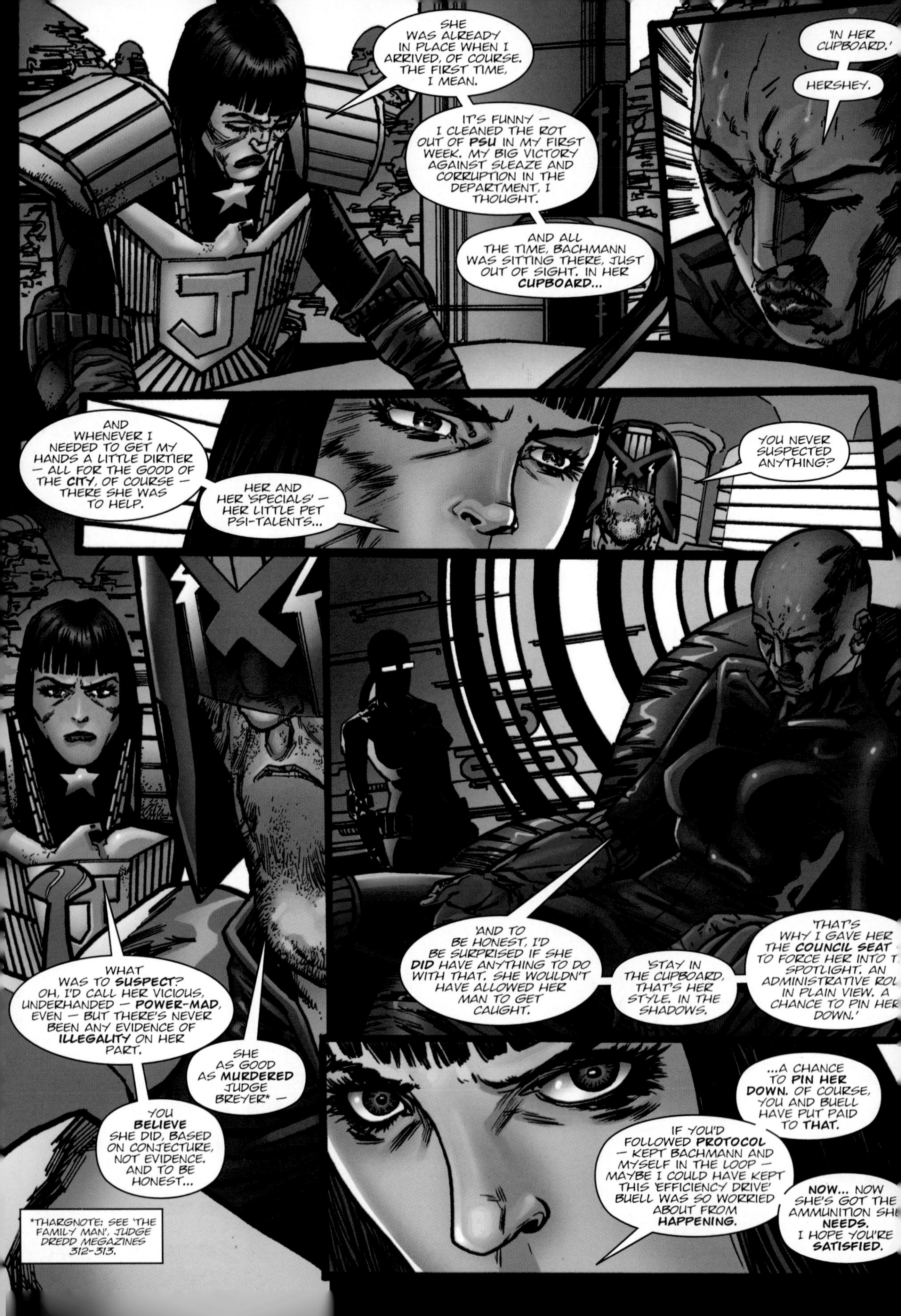

SHE WAS ALREADY IN PLACE WHEN I ARRIVED, OF COURSE. THE FIRST TIME, I MEAN.
IT'S FUNNY — I CLEANED THE ROT OUT OF **PSU** IN MY FIRST WEEK. MY BIG VICTORY AGAINST SLEAZE AND CORRUPTION IN THE DEPARTMENT, I THOUGHT.
AND ALL THE TIME, BACHMANN WAS SITTING THERE, JUST OUT OF SIGHT. IN HER **CUPBOARD...**
'IN HER CUPBOARD.'
HERSHEY.
AND WHENEVER I NEEDED TO GET MY HANDS A LITTLE DIRTIER — ALL FOR THE GOOD OF THE **CITY**, OF COURSE — THERE SHE WAS TO HELP.
HER AND HER 'SPECIALS' — HER LITTLE PET PSI-TALENTS...
YOU NEVER SUSPECTED ANYTHING?
WHAT WAS TO **SUSPECT**? OH, I'D CALL HER VICIOUS, UNDERHANDED — **POWER-MAD**, EVEN — BUT THERE'S NEVER BEEN ANY EVIDENCE OF **ILLEGALITY** ON HER PART.
SHE AS GOOD AS **MURDERED** JUDGE BREYER* —
YOU **BELIEVE** SHE DID, BASED ON CONJECTURE, NOT EVIDENCE. AND TO BE HONEST...
*THARGNOTE: SEE 'THE FAMILY MAN', JUDGE DREDD MEGAZINES 312-313.
'AND TO BE HONEST, I'D BE SURPRISED IF SHE **DID** HAVE ANYTHING TO DO WITH THAT. SHE WOULDN'T HAVE ALLOWED HER MAN TO GET CAUGHT.
'STAY IN THE CUPBOARD, THAT'S HER STYLE. IN THE SHADOWS.
'THAT'S WHY I GAVE HER THE **COUNCIL SEAT** TO FORCE HER INTO THE SPOTLIGHT. AN ADMINISTRATIVE ROLE IN PLAIN VIEW. A CHANCE TO PIN HER DOWN.'
...A CHANCE TO **PIN HER DOWN.** OF COURSE, YOU AND BUELL HAVE PUT PAID TO **THAT.**
IF YOU'D FOLLOWED **PROTOCOL** — KEPT BACHMANN AND MYSELF IN THE LOOP — MAYBE I COULD HAVE KEPT THIS 'EFFICIENCY DRIVE' BUELL WAS SO WORRIED ABOUT FROM **HAPPENING.**
NOW... NOW SHE'S GOT THE AMMUNITION SHE **NEEDS.** I HOPE YOU'RE **SATISFIED.**

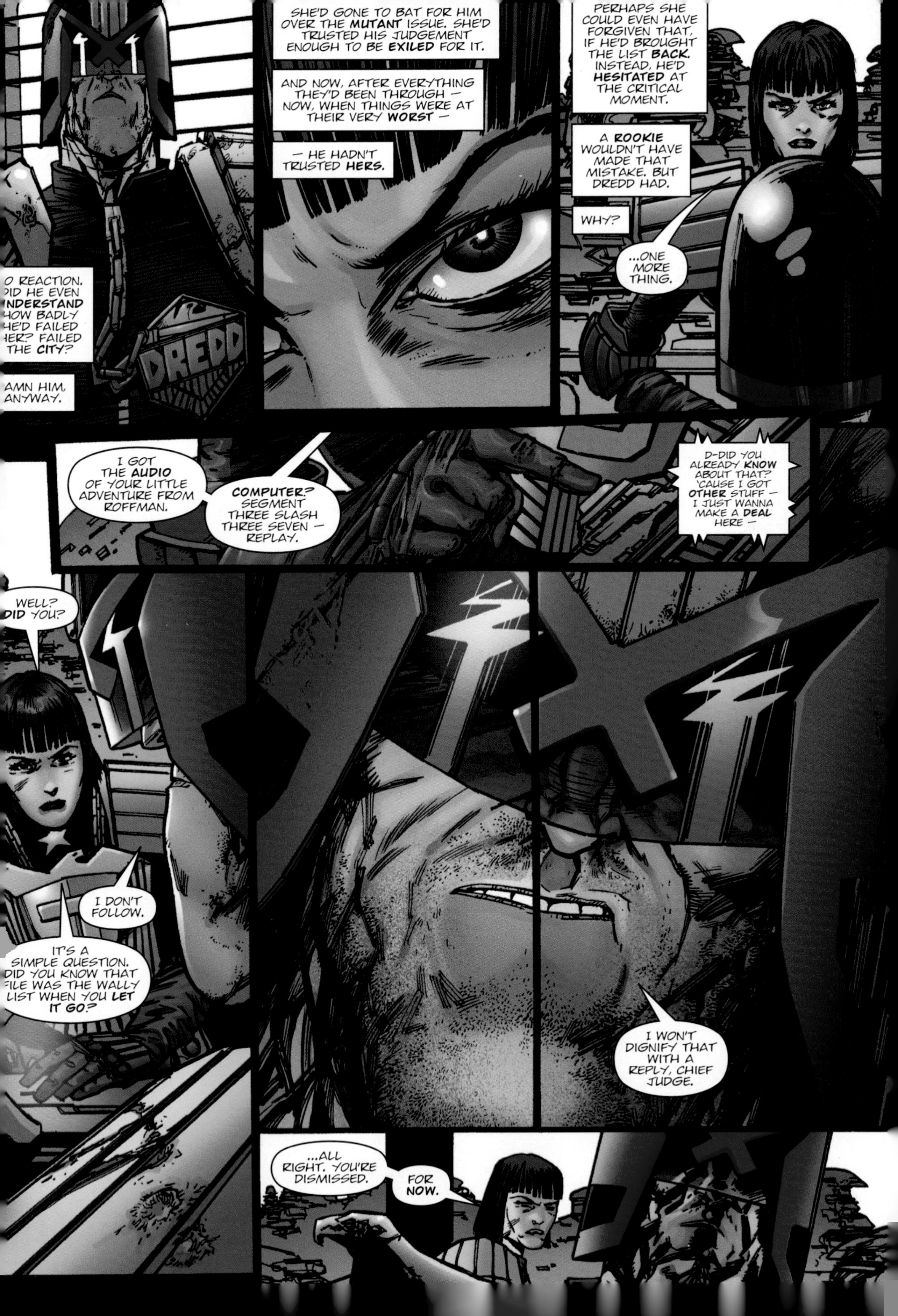

SHE'D GONE TO BAT FOR HIM OVER THE MUTANT ISSUE. SHE'D TRUSTED HIS JUDGEMENT ENOUGH TO BE EXILED FOR IT.
AND NOW, AFTER EVERYTHING THEY'D BEEN THROUGH — NOW, WHEN THINGS WERE AT THEIR VERY WORST —
— HE HADN'T TRUSTED HERS.
PERHAPS SHE COULD EVEN HAVE FORGIVEN THAT, IF HE'D BROUGHT THE LIST BACK. INSTEAD, HE'D HESITATED AT THE CRITICAL MOMENT.
A ROOKIE WOULDN'T HAVE MADE THAT MISTAKE. BUT DREDD HAD.
WHY?
...ONE MORE THING.
O REACTION. ID HE EVEN NDERSTAND HOW BADLY HE'D FAILED HER? FAILED THE CITY?
AMN HIM, ANYWAY.
DREDD
I GOT THE AUDIO OF YOUR LITTLE ADVENTURE FROM ROFFMAN.
COMPUTER? SEGMENT THREE SLASH THREE SEVEN — REPLAY.
D-DID YOU ALREADY KNOW ABOUT THAT? 'CAUSE I GOT OTHER STUFF — I JUST WANNA MAKE A DEAL HERE —
WELL? DID YOU?
I DON'T FOLLOW.
IT'S A SIMPLE QUESTION. DID YOU KNOW THAT FILE WAS THE WALLY LIST WHEN YOU LET IT GO?
I WON'T DIGNIFY THAT WITH A REPLY, CHIEF JUDGE.
...ALL RIGHT. YOU'RE DISMISSED.
FOR NOW.

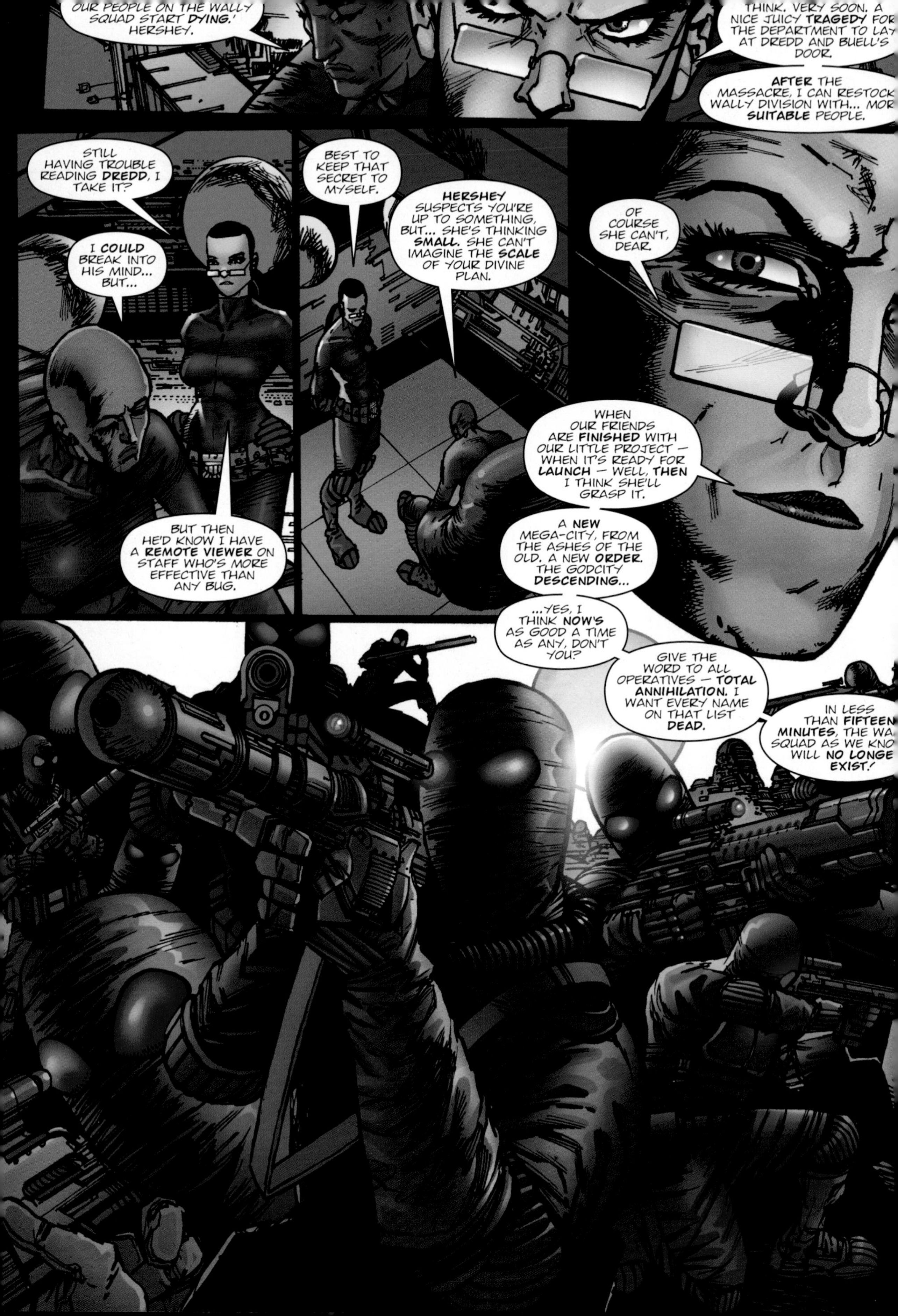
OUR PEOPLE ON THE WALLY SQUAD START DYING.' HERSHEY.
THINK. VERY SOON. A NICE JUICY TRAGEDY FOR THE DEPARTMENT TO LAY AT DREDD AND BUELL'S DOOR.
AFTER THE MASSACRE, I CAN RESTOCK WALLY DIVISION WITH... MORE SUITABLE PEOPLE.
STILL HAVING TROUBLE READING DREDD, I TAKE IT?
I COULD BREAK INTO HIS MIND... BUT...
BUT THEN HE'D KNOW I HAVE A REMOTE VIEWER ON STAFF WHO'S MORE EFFECTIVE THAN ANY BUG.
BEST TO KEEP THAT SECRET TO MYSELF.
HERSHEY SUSPECTS YOU'RE UP TO SOMETHING, BUT... SHE'S THINKING SMALL. SHE CAN'T IMAGINE THE SCALE OF YOUR DIVINE PLAN.
OF COURSE SHE CAN'T, DEAR.
WHEN OUR FRIENDS ARE FINISHED WITH OUR LITTLE PROJECT — WHEN IT'S READY FOR LAUNCH — WELL, THEN I THINK SHE'LL GRASP IT.
A NEW MEGA-CITY, FROM THE ASHES OF THE OLD. A NEW ORDER. THE GODCITY DESCENDING...
...YES, I THINK NOW'S AS GOOD A TIME AS ANY, DON'T YOU?
GIVE THE WORD TO ALL OPERATIVES — TOTAL ANNIHILATION. I WANT EVERY NAME ON THAT LIST DEAD.
IN LESS THAN FIFTEEN MINUTES, THE WALLY SQUAD AS WE KNOW IT WILL NO LONGER EXIST!

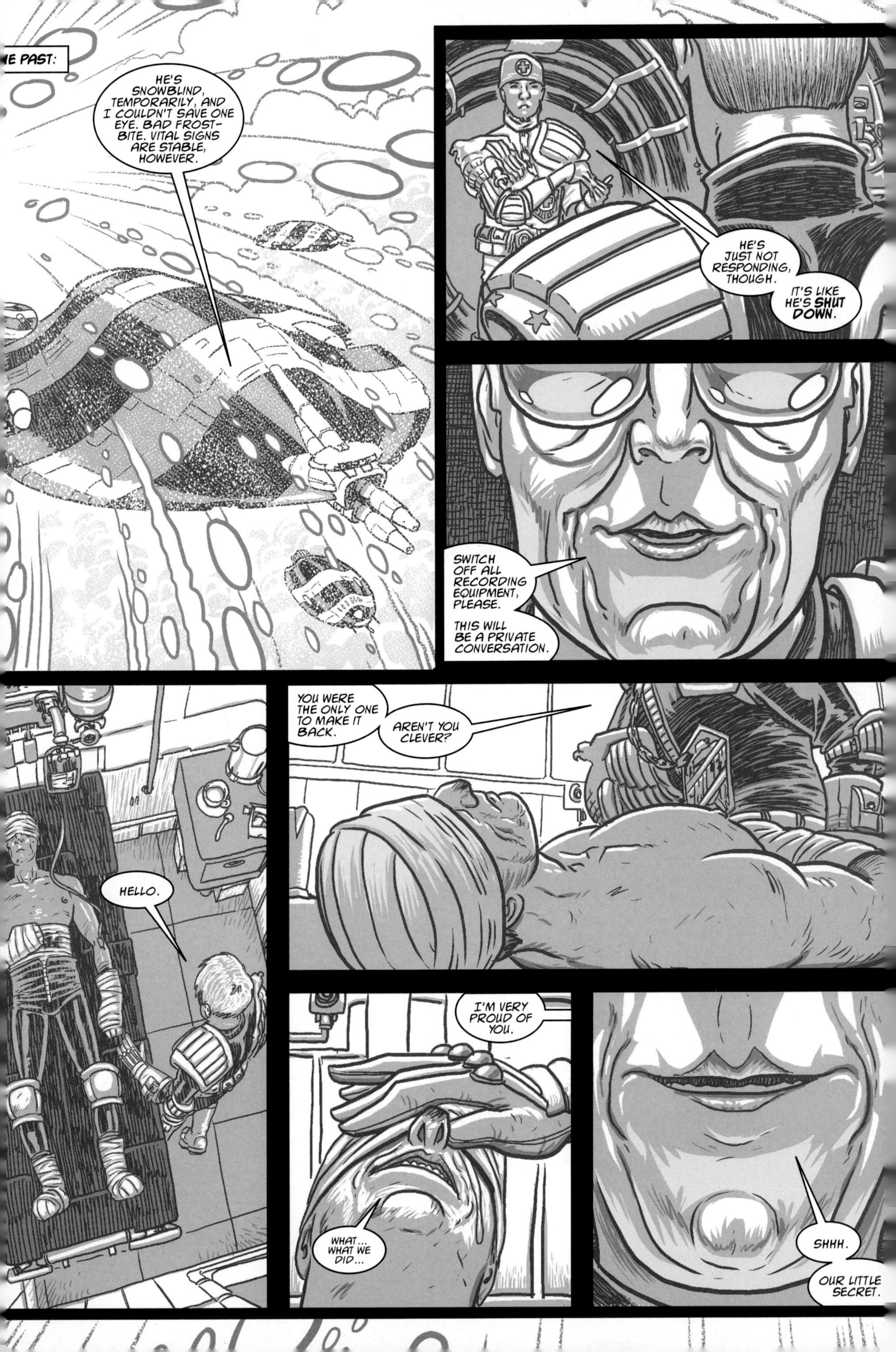
E PAST:
HE'S SNOWBLIND, TEMPORARILY, AND I COULDN'T SAVE ONE EYE. BAD FROST-BITE. VITAL SIGNS ARE STABLE, HOWEVER.
HE'S JUST NOT RESPONDING, THOUGH.
IT'S LIKE HE'S SHUT DOWN.
SWITCH OFF ALL RECORDING EQUIPMENT, PLEASE.
THIS WILL BE A PRIVATE CONVERSATION.
HELLO.
YOU WERE THE ONLY ONE TO MAKE IT BACK.
AREN'T YOU CLEVER?
I'M VERY PROUD OF YOU.
WHAT... WHAT WE DID...
SHHH.
OUR LITTLE SECRET.

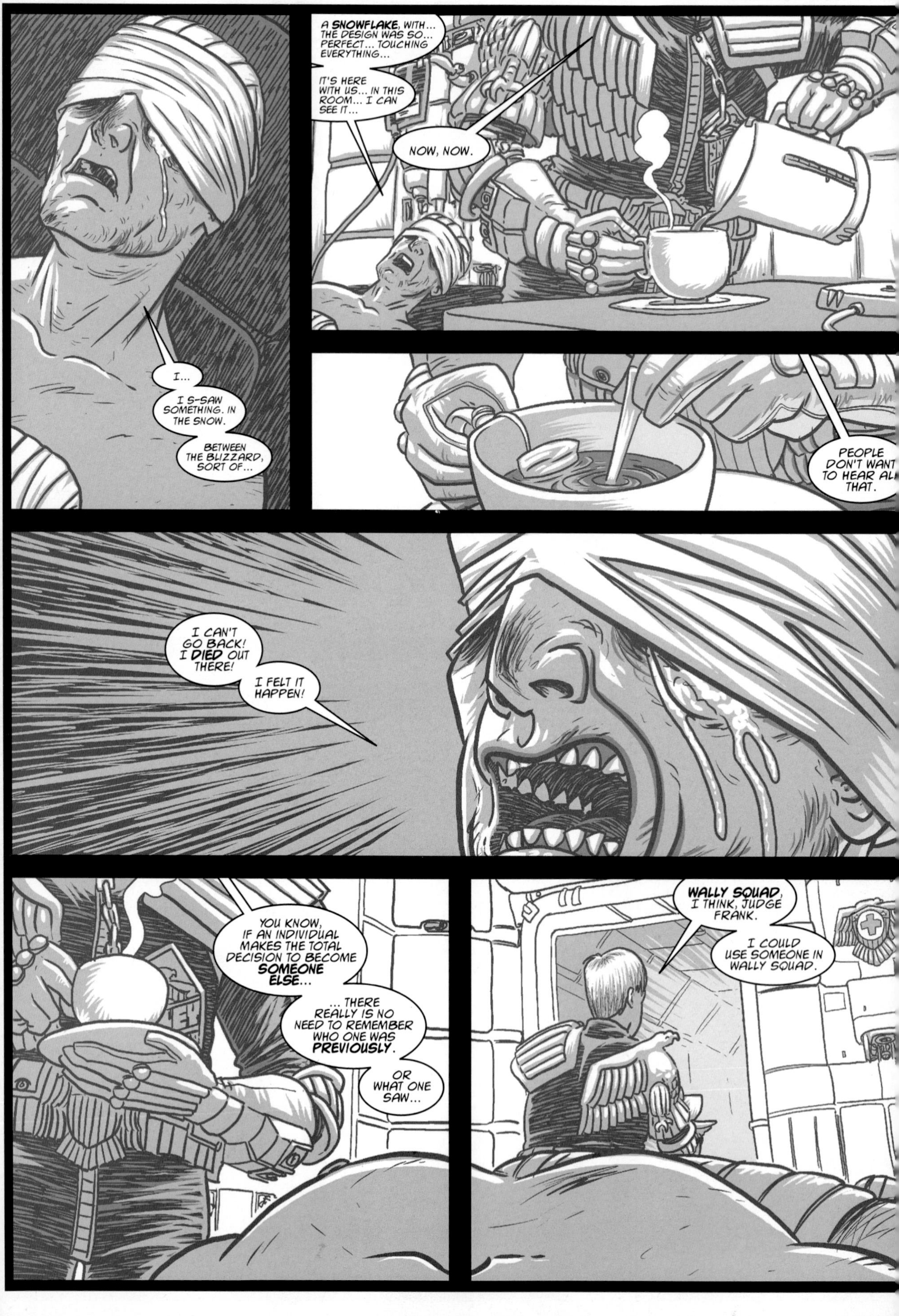

A **SNOWFLAKE**, WITH... THE DESIGN WAS SO... PERFECT... TOUCHING EVERYTHING...
IT'S HERE WITH US... IN THIS ROOM... I CAN SEE IT...
NOW, NOW.
I...
I S-SAW SOMETHING. IN THE SNOW.
BETWEEN THE BLIZZARD, SORT OF...
PEOPLE DON'T WANT TO HEAR AL THAT.
I CAN'T GO BACK! I **DIED** OUT THERE!
I FELT IT HAPPEN!
YOU KNOW, IF AN INDIVIDUAL MAKES THE TOTAL DECISION TO BECOME **SOMEONE ELSE**...
... THERE REALLY IS NO NEED TO REMEMBER WHO ONE WAS **PREVIOUSLY**.
OR WHAT ONE SAW...
WALLY SQUAD, I THINK, JUDGE FRANK.
I COULD USE SOMEONE IN WALLY SQUAD.

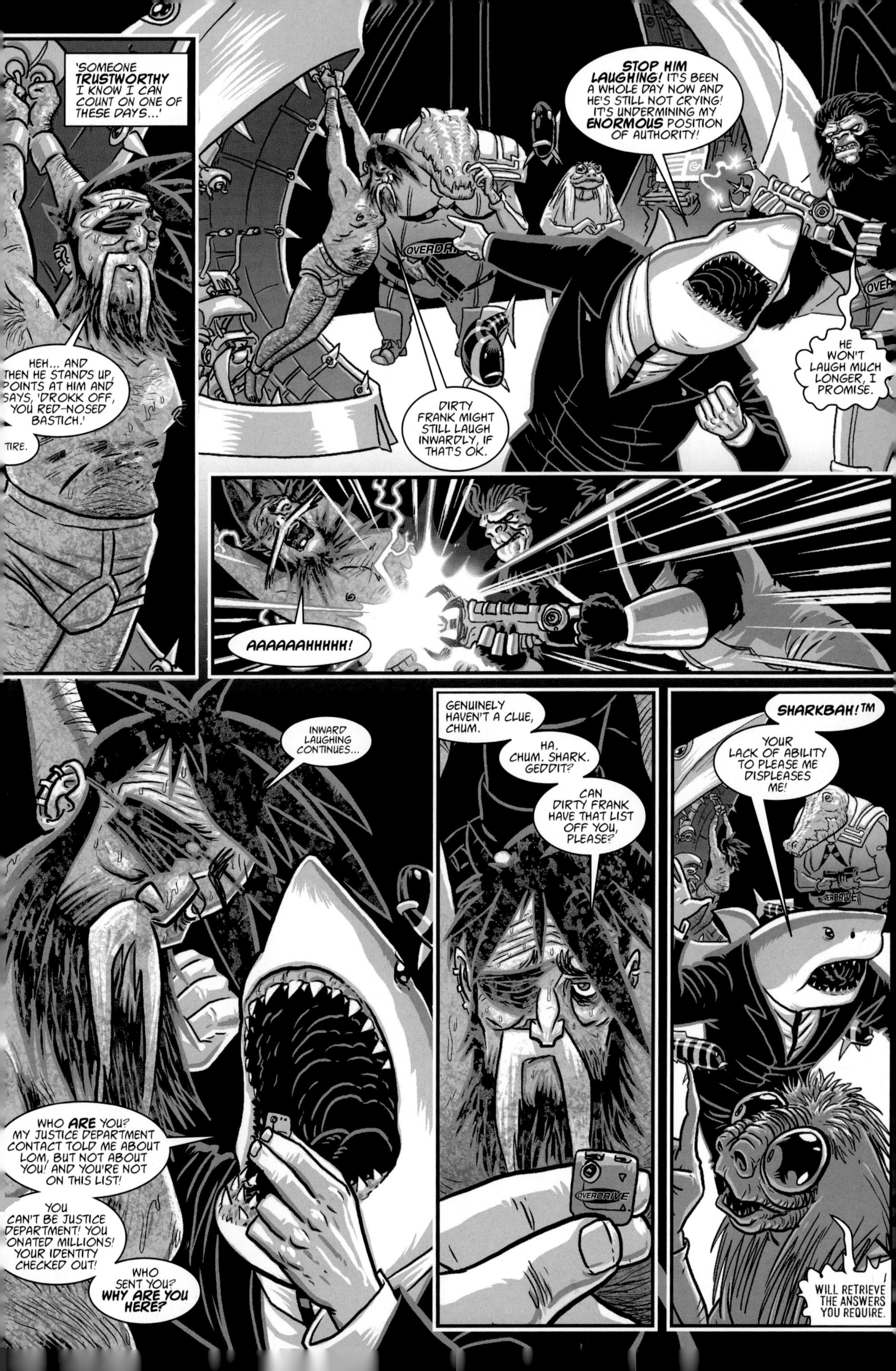
'SOMEONE TRUSTWORTHY I KNOW I CAN COUNT ON ONE OF THESE DAYS...'
HEH... AND THEN HE STANDS UP, POINTS AT HIM AND SAYS, 'DROKK OFF, YOU RED-NOSED BASTICH.'
TIRE.
STOP HIM LAUGHING! IT'S BEEN A WHOLE DAY NOW AND HE'S STILL NOT CRYING! IT'S UNDERMINING MY ENORMOUS POSITION OF AUTHORITY!
DIRTY FRANK MIGHT STILL LAUGH INWARDLY, IF THAT'S OK.
HE WON'T LAUGH MUCH LONGER, I PROMISE.
OVERDRIVE
AAAAAAHHHHH!
INWARD LAUGHING CONTINUES...
WHO ARE YOU? MY JUSTICE DEPARTMENT CONTACT TOLD ME ABOUT LOM, BUT NOT ABOUT YOU! AND YOU'RE NOT ON THIS LIST!
YOU CAN'T BE JUSTICE DEPARTMENT! YOU DONATED MILLIONS! YOUR IDENTITY CHECKED OUT!
WHO SENT YOU? WHY ARE YOU HERE?
GENUINELY HAVEN'T A CLUE, CHUM.
HA. CHUM. SHARK. GEDDIT?
CAN DIRTY FRANK HAVE THAT LIST OFF YOU, PLEASE?
OVERDRIVE
SHARKBAH!™
YOUR LACK OF ABILITY TO PLEASE ME DISPLEASES ME!
I WILL RETRIEVE THE ANSWERS YOU REQUIRE.

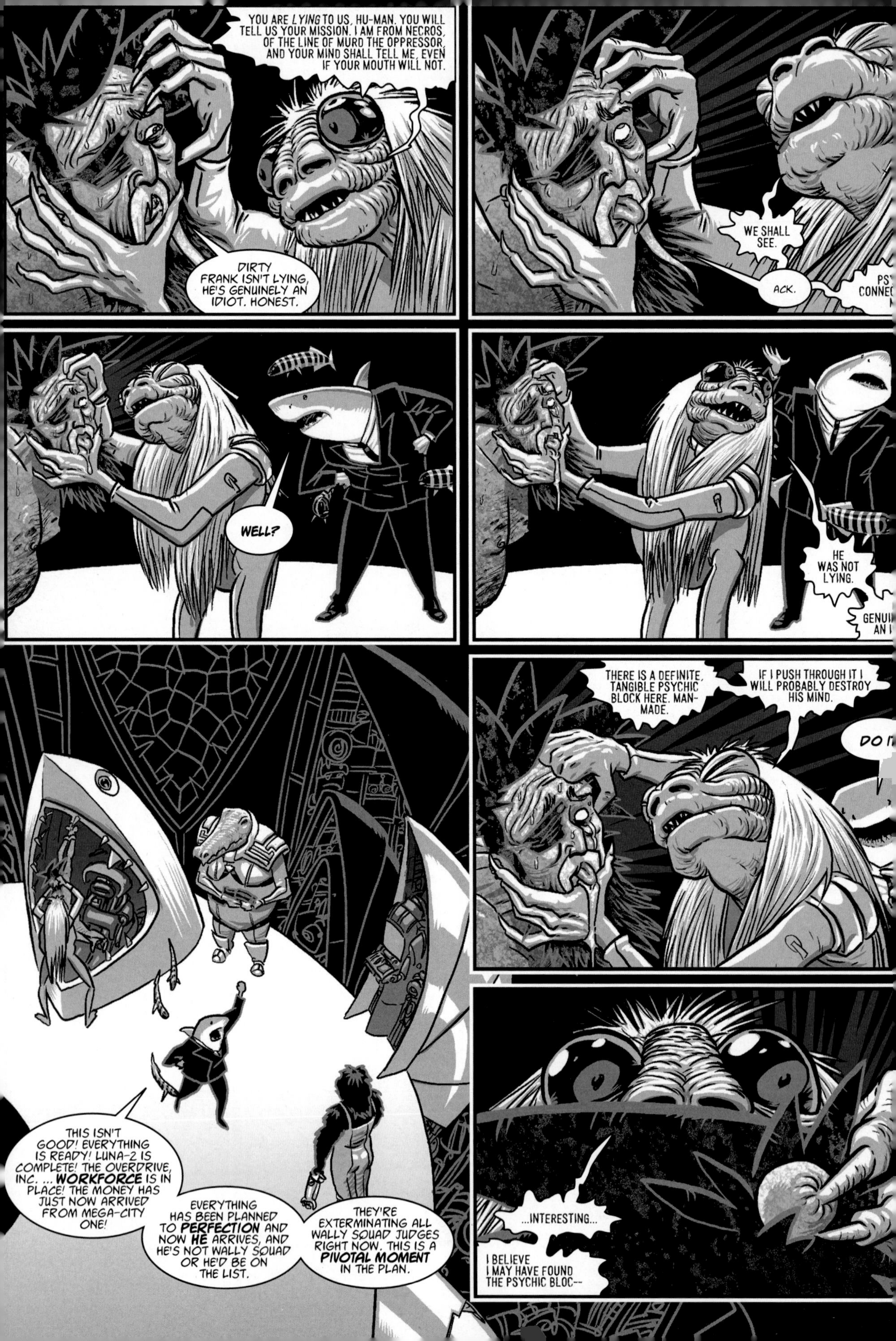

YOU ARE *LYING* TO US, HU-MAN. YOU WILL TELL US YOUR MISSION. I AM FROM NECROS, OF THE LINE OF MURD THE OPPRESSOR, AND YOUR MIND SHALL TELL ME, EVEN IF YOUR MOUTH WILL NOT.
DIRTY FRANK ISN'T LYING, HE'S GENUINELY AN IDIOT. HONEST.
WE SHALL SEE.
ACK.
WELL?
HE WAS NOT LYING.
THIS ISN'T GOOD! EVERYTHING IS READY! LUNA-2 IS COMPLETE! THE OVERDRIVE, INC. ... **WORKFORCE** IS IN PLACE! THE MONEY HAS JUST NOW ARRIVED FROM MEGA-CITY ONE!
EVERYTHING HAS BEEN PLANNED TO **PERFECTION** AND NOW **HE** ARRIVES, AND HE'S NOT WALLY SQUAD OR HE'D BE ON THE LIST.
THEY'RE EXTERMINATING ALL WALLY SQUAD JUDGES RIGHT NOW. THIS IS A **PIVOTAL MOMENT** IN THE PLAN.
THERE IS A DEFINITE, TANGIBLE PSYCHIC BLOCK HERE. MAN-MADE.
IF I PUSH THROUGH IT I WILL PROBABLY DESTROY HIS MIND.
...INTERESTING...
I BELIEVE I MAY HAVE FOUND THE PSYCHIC BLOC--

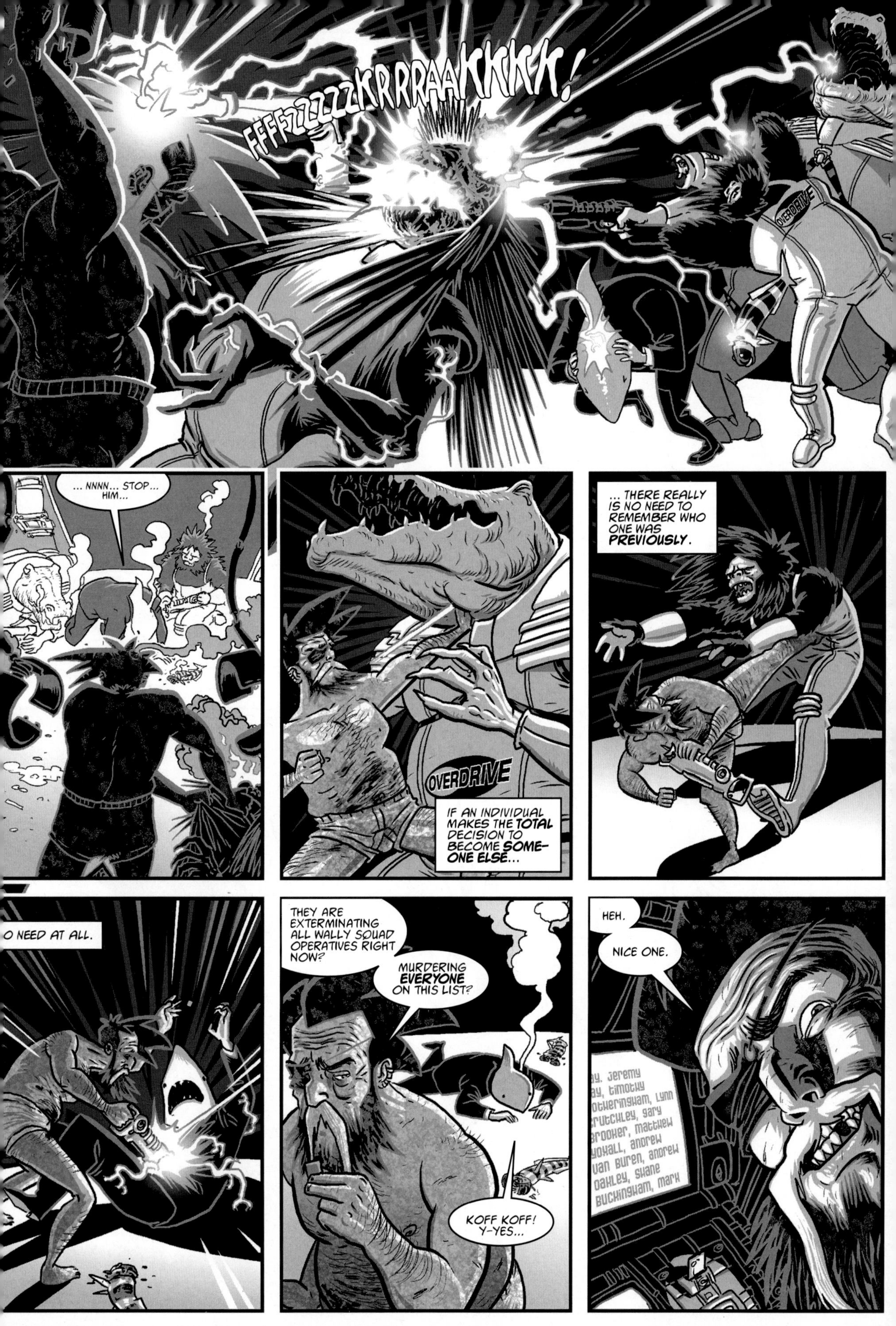

FFFFZZZZZZKRRRAAKKKKK!
... NNNN... STOP... HIM...
IF AN INDIVIDUAL MAKES THE **TOTAL** DECISION TO BECOME **SOME-ONE ELSE**...
... THERE REALLY IS NO NEED TO REMEMBER WHO ONE WAS **PREVIOUSLY**.
O NEED AT ALL.
THEY ARE EXTERMINATING ALL WALLY SQUAD OPERATIVES RIGHT NOW?
MURDERING **EVERYONE** ON THIS LIST?
KOFF KOFF! Y-YES...
HEH.
NICE ONE.
ay. Jeremy
ay, timothy
otheringham, Lynn
rutchley, gary
Brooker, matthew
yoxall, andrew
van Buren, andrew
oakley, shane
Buckingham, mark

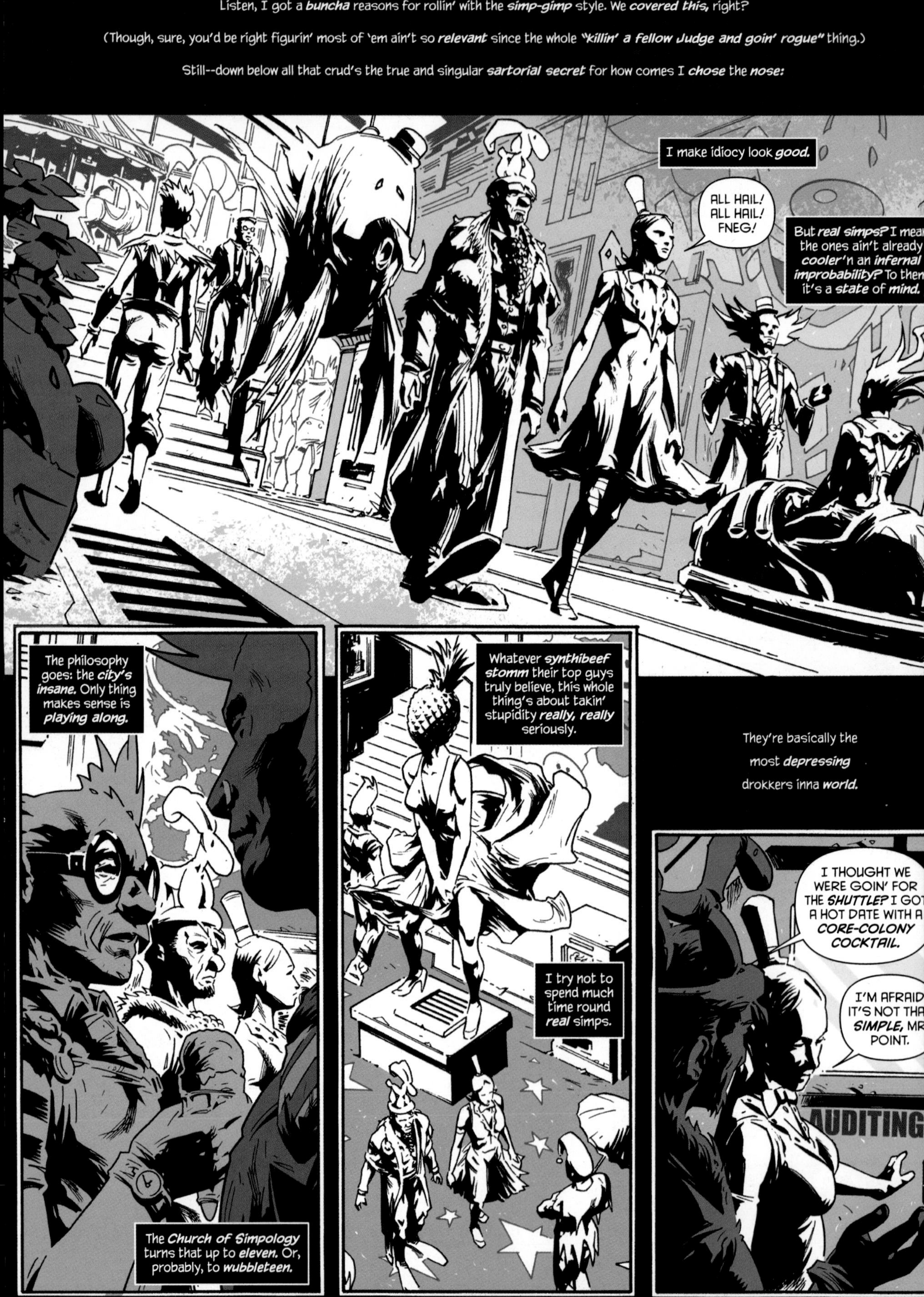
Listen, I got a buncha reasons for rollin' with the simp-gimp style. We covered this, right?
(Though, sure, you'd be right figurin' most of 'em ain't so relevant since the whole "killin' a fellow Judge and goin' rogue" thing.)
Still--down below all that crud's the true and singular sartorial secret for how comes I chose the nose:
I make idiocy look good.
ALL HAIL! ALL HAIL! FNEG!
But real simps? I mea the ones ain't already cooler'n an infernal improbability? To then it's a state of mind.
The philosophy goes: the city's insane. Only thing makes sense is playing along.
The Church of Simpology turns that up to eleven. Or, probably, to wubbleteen.
Whatever synthibeef stomm their top guys truly believe, this whole thing's about takin' stupidity really, really seriously.
I try not to spend much time round real simps.
They're basically the most depressing drokkers inna world.
I THOUGHT WE WERE GOIN' FOR THE SHUTTLE? I GOT A HOT DATE WITH A CORE-COLONY COCKTAIL.
I'M AFRAID IT'S NOT THA SIMPLE, MR POINT.
AUDITING

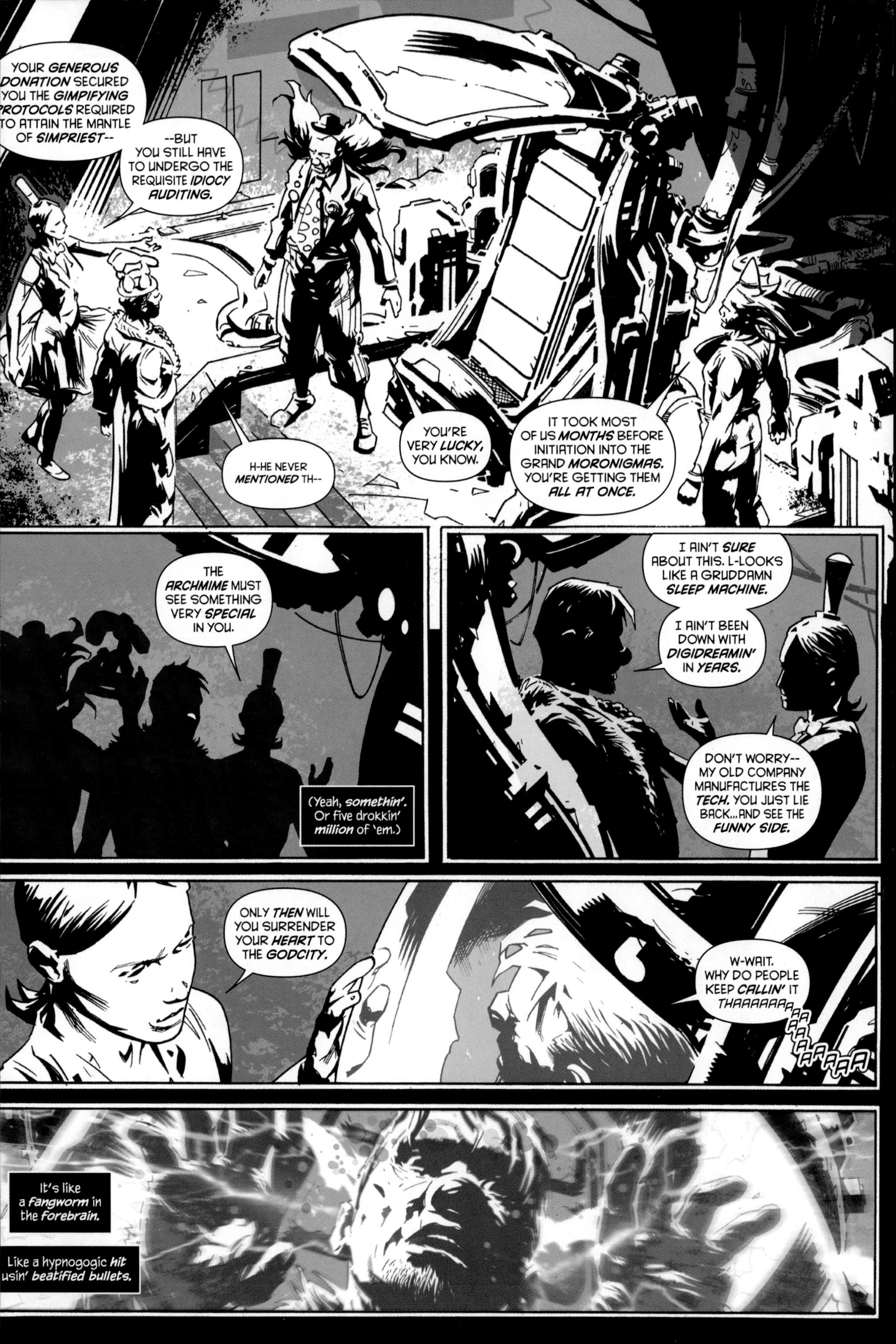
YOUR GENEROUS DONATION SECURED YOU THE GIMPIFYING PROTOCOLS REQUIRED TO ATTAIN THE MANTLE OF SIMPRIEST--
--BUT YOU STILL HAVE TO UNDERGO THE REQUISITE IDIOCY AUDITING.
H-HE NEVER MENTIONED TH--
YOU'RE VERY LUCKY, YOU KNOW.
IT TOOK MOST OF US MONTHS BEFORE INITIATION INTO THE GRAND MORONIGMAS. YOU'RE GETTING THEM ALL AT ONCE.
THE ARCHMIME MUST SEE SOMETHING VERY SPECIAL IN YOU.
(Yeah, somethin'. Or five drokkin' million of 'em.)
I AIN'T SURE ABOUT THIS. L-LOOKS LIKE A GRUDDAMN SLEEP MACHINE.
I AIN'T BEEN DOWN WITH DIGIDREAMIN' IN YEARS.
DON'T WORRY-- MY OLD COMPANY MANUFACTURES THE TECH. YOU JUST LIE BACK...AND SEE THE FUNNY SIDE.
ONLY THEN WILL YOU SURRENDER YOUR HEART TO THE GODCITY.
W-WAIT. WHY DO PEOPLE KEEP CALLIN' IT THAAAAAAAAAAAAAAAAAA
It's like a fangworm in the forebrain.
Like a hypnogogic hit usin' beatified bullets.

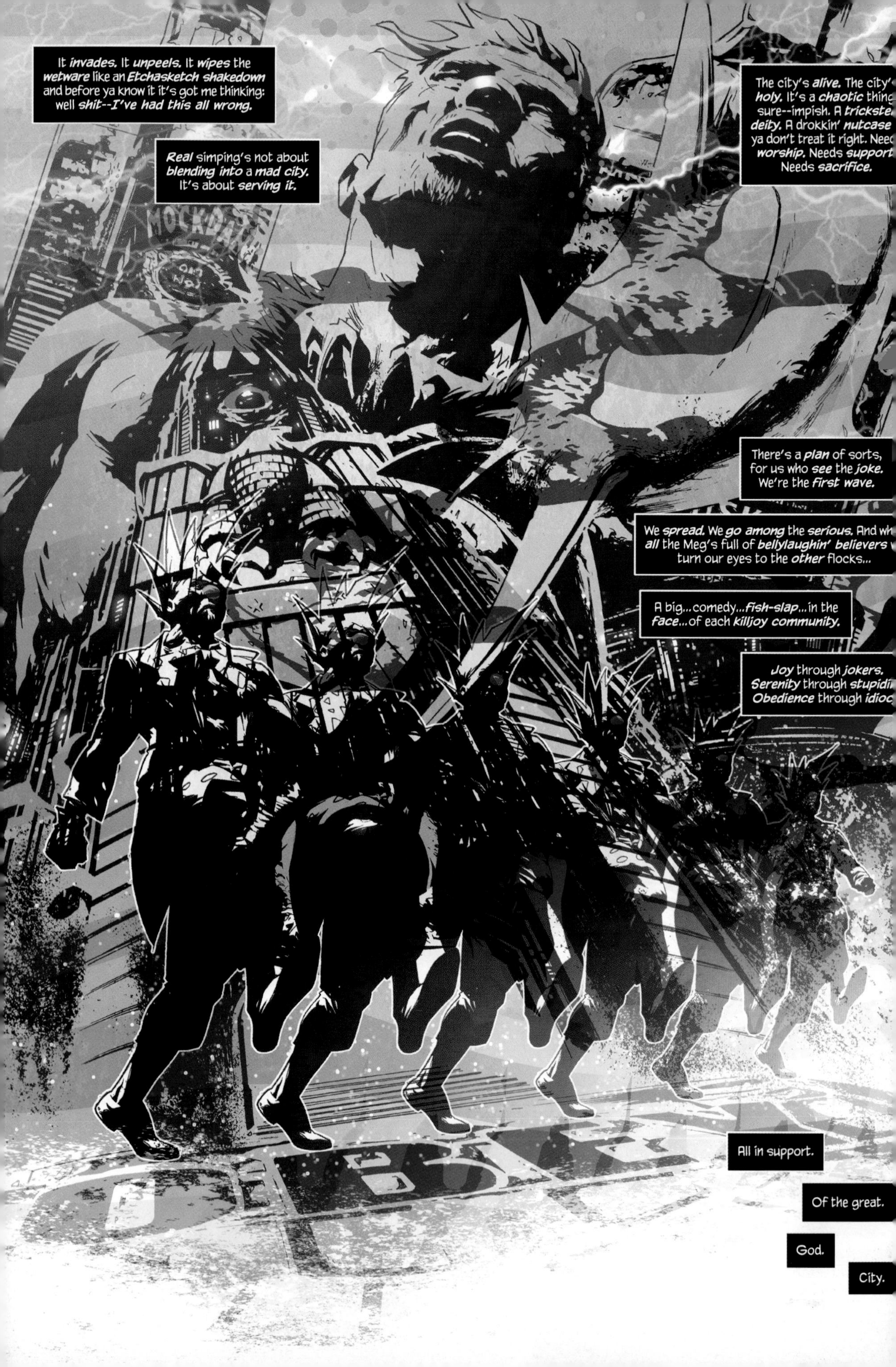
It invades. It unpeels. It wipes the wetware like an Etchasketch shakedown and before ya know it it's got me thinking: well shit--I've had this all wrong.
Real simping's not about blending into a mad city. It's about serving it.
The city's alive. The city' holy. It's a chaotic thing sure--impish. A trickste deity. A drokkin' nutcase ya don't treat it right. Need worship. Needs support Needs sacrifice.
MOCKDA
There's a plan of sorts, for us who see the joke. We're the first wave.
We spread. We go among the serious. And wh all the Meg's full of bellylaughin' believers turn our eyes to the other flocks...
A big...comedy...fish-slap...in the face...of each killjoy community.
Joy through jokers. Serenity through stupidi Obedience through idioc
All in support.
Of the great.
God.
City.

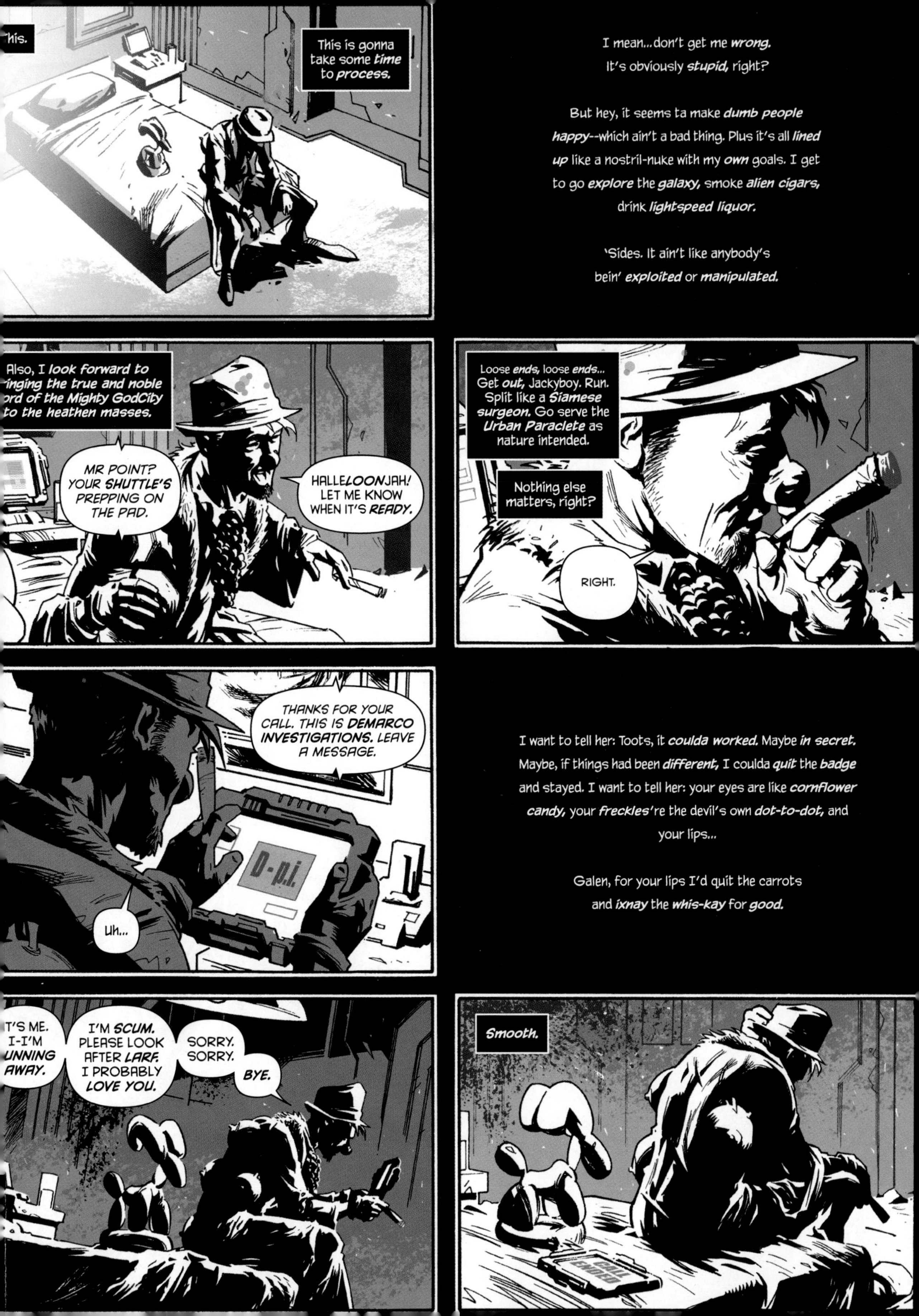
his.
This is gonna take some time to process.
I mean...don't get me wrong. It's obviously stupid, right?
But hey, it seems ta make dumb people happy--which ain't a bad thing. Plus it's all lined up like a nostril-nuke with my own goals. I get to go explore the galaxy, smoke alien cigars, drink lightspeed liquor.
'Sides. It ain't like anybody's bein' exploited or manipulated.
Also, I look forward to -inging the true and noble ord of the Mighty GodCity to the heathen masses.
MR POINT? YOUR SHUTTLE'S PREPPING ON THE PAD.
HALLELOONJAH! LET ME KNOW WHEN IT'S READY.
Loose ends, loose ends... Get out, Jackyboy. Run. Split like a Siamese surgeon. Go serve the Urban Paraclete as nature intended.
Nothing else matters, right?
RIGHT.
THANKS FOR YOUR CALL. THIS IS DEMARCO INVESTIGATIONS. LEAVE A MESSAGE.
D-p.i.
Uh...
I want to tell her: Toots, it coulda worked. Maybe in secret. Maybe, if things had been different, I coulda quit the badge and stayed. I want to tell her: your eyes are like cornflower candy, your freckles're the devil's own dot-to-dot, and your lips...
Galen, for your lips I'd quit the carrots and ixnay the whis-kay for good.
T'S ME. I-I'M UNNING AWAY.
I'M SCUM. PLEASE LOOK AFTER LARF. I PROBABLY LOVE YOU.
SORRY. SORRY.
BYE.
Smooth.
CALL ENDED

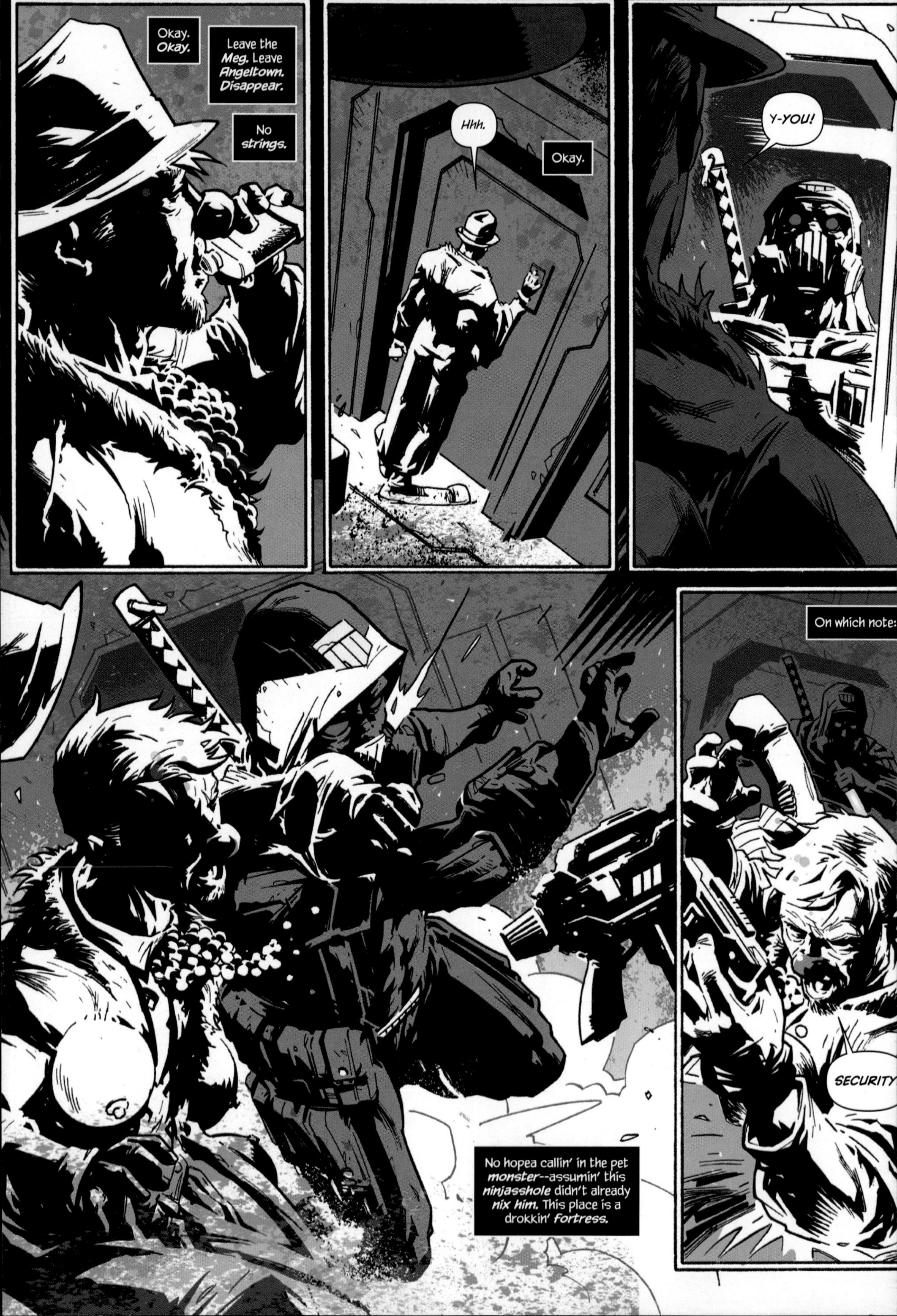

Okay. *Okay.*
Leave the *Meg.* Leave *Angeltown. Disappear.*
No *strings.*
Hhh.
Okay.
Y-YOU!
No hopea callin' in the pet *monster*--assumin' this *ninjasshole* didn't already *nix him.* This place is a drokkin' *fortress.*
On which note:
SECURITY

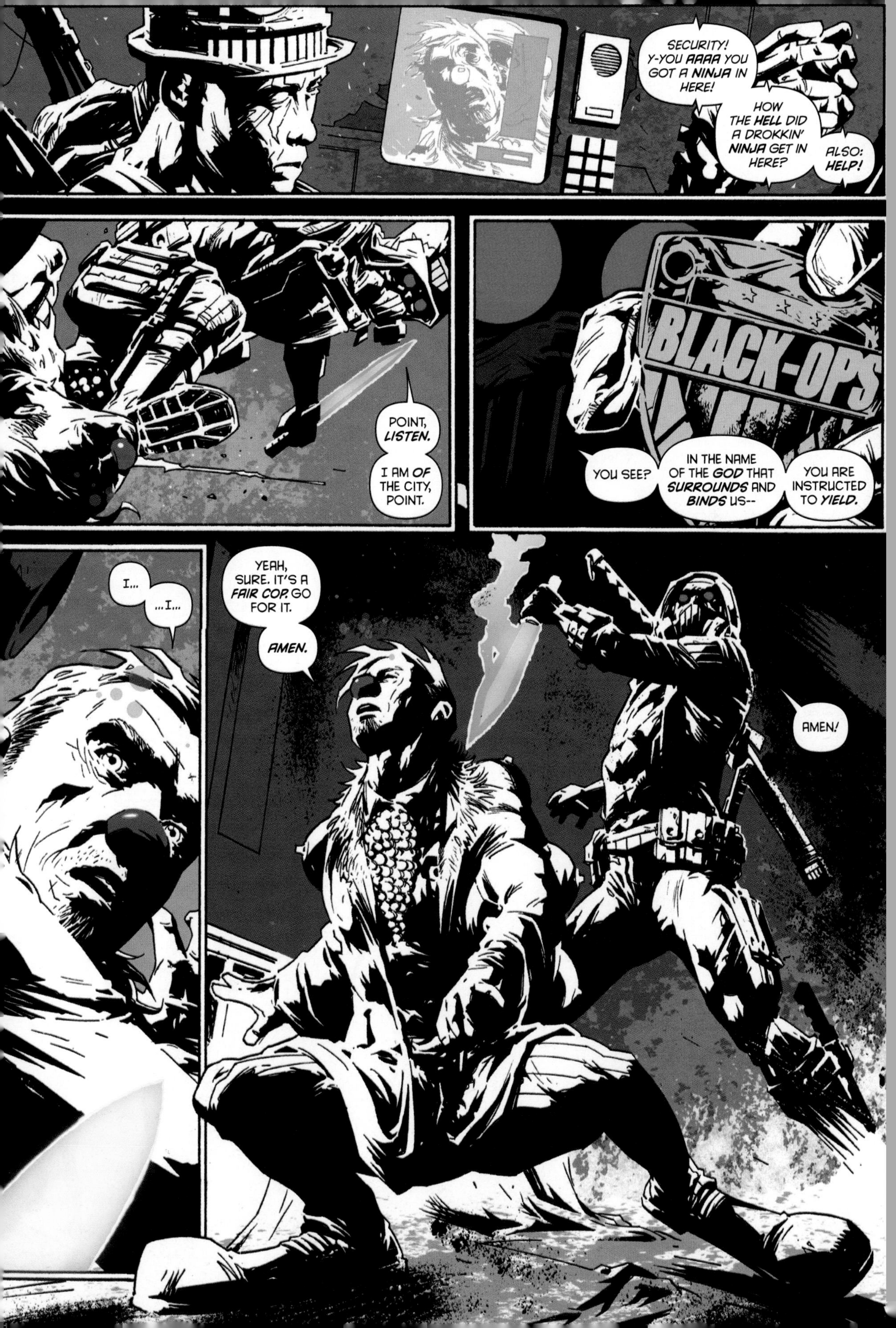
SECURITY! Y-YOU AAAA YOU GOT A NINJA IN HERE!
HOW THE HELL DID A DROKKIN' NINJA GET IN HERE?
ALSO: HELP!
POINT, LISTEN.
I AM OF THE CITY, POINT.
BLACK-OPS
YOU SEE?
IN THE NAME OF THE GOD THAT SURROUNDS AND BINDS US--
YOU ARE INSTRUCTED TO YIELD.
I...
...I...
YEAH, SURE. IT'S A FAIR COP. GO FOR IT.
AMEN.
AMEN!

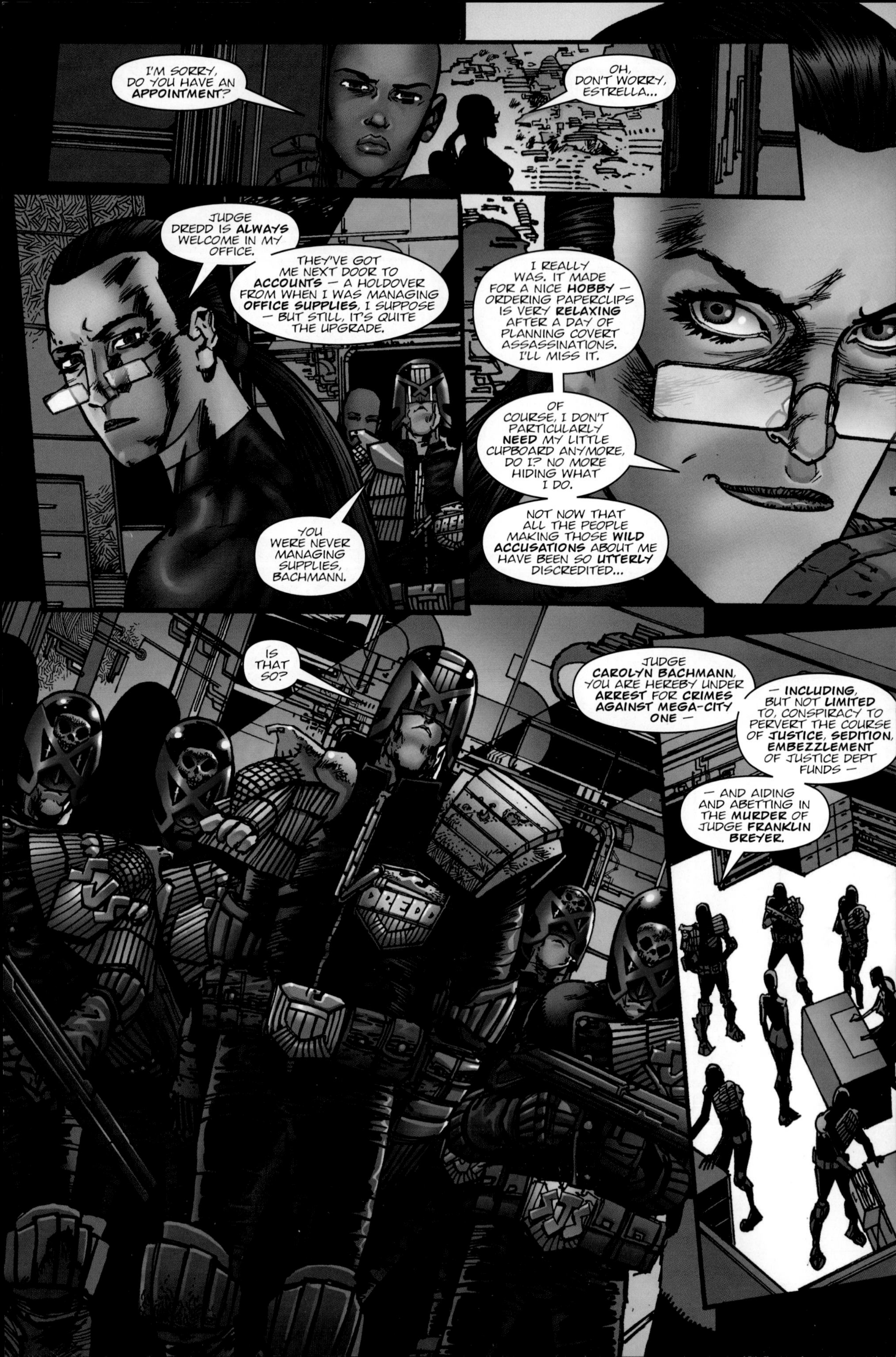
I'M SORRY, DO YOU HAVE AN APPOINTMENT?
OH, DON'T WORRY, ESTRELLA...
JUDGE DREDD IS ALWAYS WELCOME IN MY OFFICE.
THEY'VE GOT ME NEXT DOOR TO ACCOUNTS — A HOLDOVER FROM WHEN I WAS MANAGING OFFICE SUPPLIES, I SUPPOSE — BUT STILL, IT'S QUITE THE UPGRADE.
YOU WERE NEVER MANAGING SUPPLIES, BACHMANN.
I REALLY WAS. IT MADE FOR A NICE HOBBY — ORDERING PAPERCLIPS IS VERY RELAXING AFTER A DAY OF PLANNING COVERT ASSASSINATIONS. I'LL MISS IT.
OF COURSE, I DON'T PARTICULARLY NEED MY LITTLE CUPBOARD ANYMORE, DO I? NO MORE HIDING WHAT I DO.
NOT NOW THAT ALL THE PEOPLE MAKING THOSE WILD ACCUSATIONS ABOUT ME HAVE BEEN SO UTTERLY DISCREDITED...
IS THAT SO?
JUDGE CAROLYN BACHMANN, YOU ARE HEREBY UNDER ARREST FOR CRIMES AGAINST MEGA-CITY ONE —
— INCLUDING, BUT NOT LIMITED TO, CONSPIRACY TO PERVERT THE COURSE OF JUSTICE, SEDITION, EMBEZZLEMENT OF JUSTICE DEPT FUNDS —
— AND AIDING AND ABETTING IN THE MURDER OF JUDGE FRANKLIN BREYER.

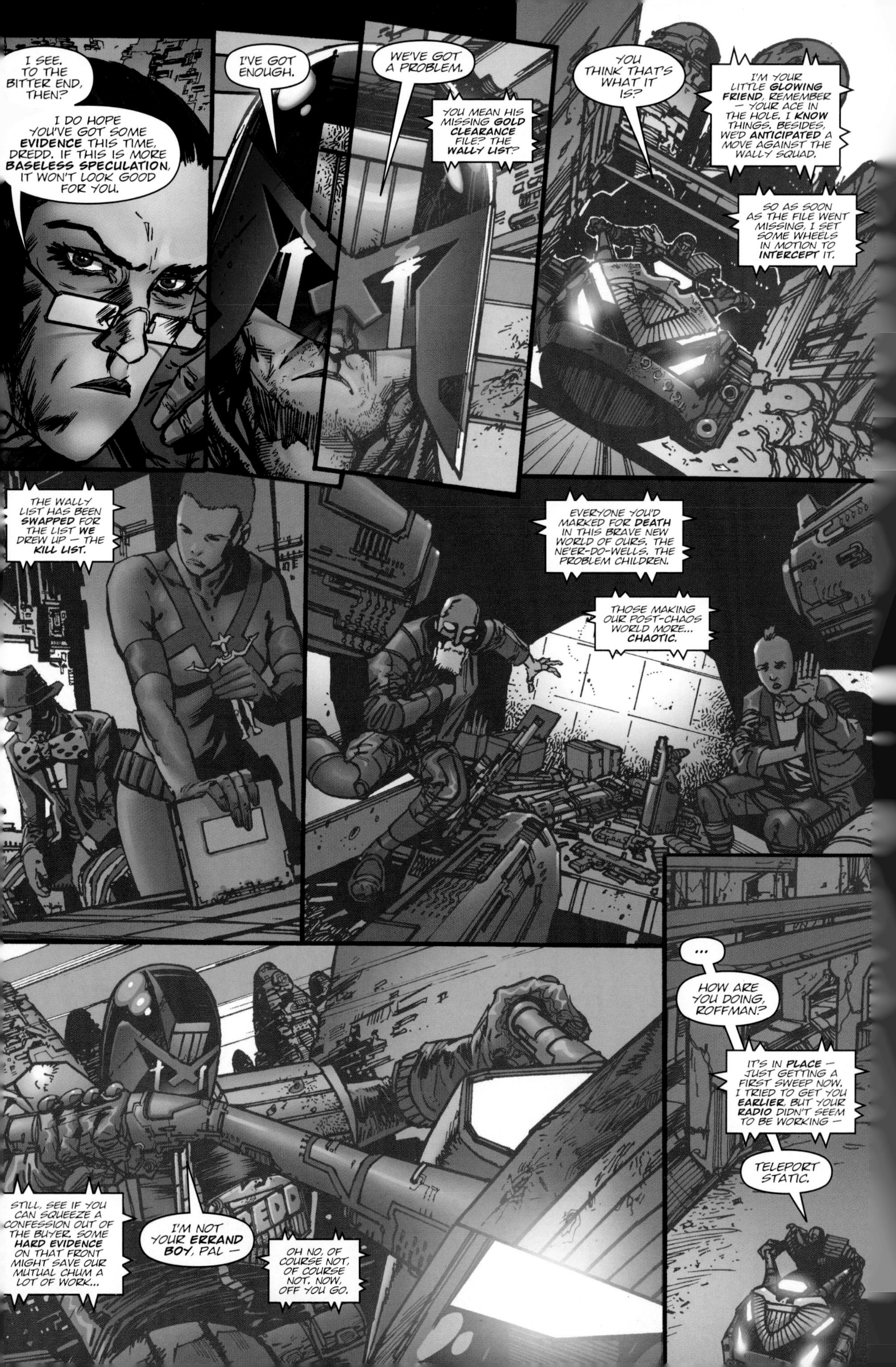

I SEE. TO THE BITTER END, THEN?
I DO HOPE YOU'VE GOT SOME EVIDENCE THIS TIME, DREDD. IF THIS IS MORE BASELESS SPECULATION, IT WON'T LOOK GOOD FOR YOU.
I'VE GOT ENOUGH.
WE'VE GOT A PROBLEM.
YOU MEAN HIS MISSING GOLD CLEARANCE FILE? THE WALLY LIST?
YOU THINK THAT'S WHAT IT IS?
I'M YOUR LITTLE GLOWING FRIEND, REMEMBER — YOUR ACE IN THE HOLE. I KNOW THINGS. BESIDES, WE'D ANTICIPATED A MOVE AGAINST THE WALLY SQUAD.
SO AS SOON AS THE FILE WENT MISSING, I SET SOME WHEELS IN MOTION TO INTERCEPT IT.
THE WALLY LIST HAS BEEN SWAPPED FOR THE LIST WE DREW UP — THE KILL LIST.
EVERYONE YOU'D MARKED FOR DEATH IN THIS BRAVE NEW WORLD OF OURS. THE NE'ER-DO-WELLS. THE PROBLEM CHILDREN.
THOSE MAKING OUR POST-CHAOS WORLD MORE... CHAOTIC.
STILL, SEE IF YOU CAN SQUEEZE A CONFESSION OUT OF THE BUYER. SOME HARD EVIDENCE ON THAT FRONT MIGHT SAVE OUR MUTUAL CHUM A LOT OF WORK...
I'M NOT YOUR ERRAND BOY, PAL —
OH NO, OF COURSE NOT, OF COURSE NOT. NOW, OFF YOU GO.
...
HOW ARE YOU DOING, ROFFMAN?
IT'S IN PLACE — JUST GETTING A FIRST SWEEP NOW. I TRIED TO GET YOU EARLIER, BUT YOUR RADIO DIDN'T SEEM TO BE WORKING —
TELEPORT STATIC.

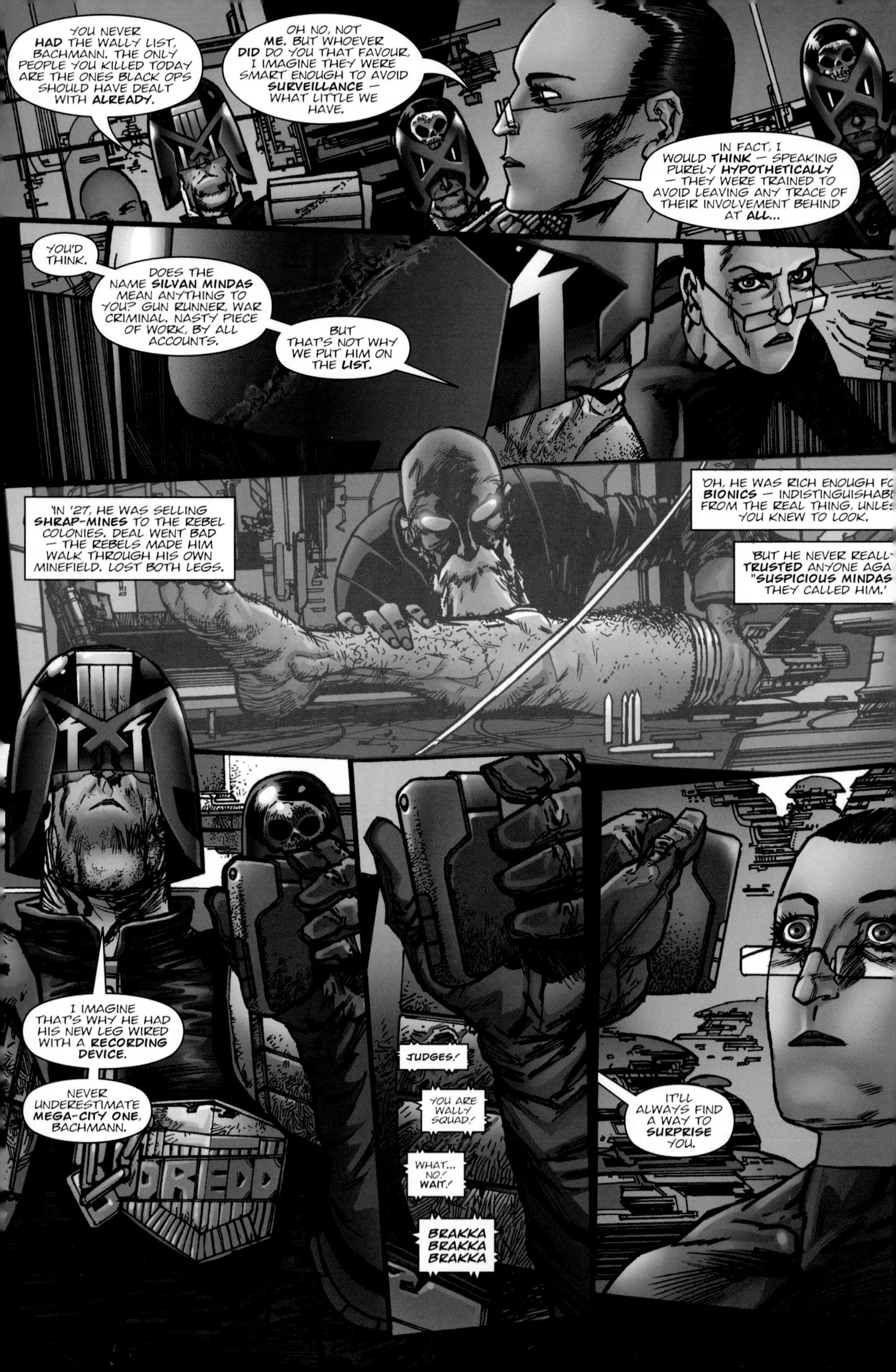
YOU NEVER HAD THE WALLY LIST, BACHMANN. THE ONLY PEOPLE YOU KILLED TODAY ARE THE ONES BLACK OPS SHOULD HAVE DEALT WITH ALREADY.
OH NO, NOT ME. BUT WHOEVER DID DO YOU THAT FAVOUR, I IMAGINE THEY WERE SMART ENOUGH TO AVOID SURVEILLANCE — WHAT LITTLE WE HAVE.
IN FACT, I WOULD THINK — SPEAKING PURELY HYPOTHETICALLY — THEY WERE TRAINED TO AVOID LEAVING ANY TRACE OF THEIR INVOLVEMENT BEHIND AT ALL...
YOU'D THINK.
DOES THE NAME SILVAN MINDAS MEAN ANYTHING TO YOU? GUN RUNNER, WAR CRIMINAL. NASTY PIECE OF WORK, BY ALL ACCOUNTS.
BUT THAT'S NOT WHY WE PUT HIM ON THE LIST.
'IN '27, HE WAS SELLING SHRAP-MINES TO THE REBEL COLONIES. DEAL WENT BAD — THE REBELS MADE HIM WALK THROUGH HIS OWN MINEFIELD. LOST BOTH LEGS.
'OH, HE WAS RICH ENOUGH FO BIONICS — INDISTINGUISHAB FROM THE REAL THING, UNLES YOU KNEW TO LOOK.
'BUT HE NEVER REALL TRUSTED ANYONE AGA "SUSPICIOUS MINDAS" THEY CALLED HIM.'
I IMAGINE THAT'S WHY HE HAD HIS NEW LEG WIRED WITH A RECORDING DEVICE.
NEVER UNDERESTIMATE MEGA-CITY ONE, BACHMANN.
DREDD
JUDGES!
YOU ARE WALLY SQUAD!
WHAT... NO! WAIT!
BRAKKA BRAKKA BRAKKA
IT'LL ALWAYS FIND A WAY TO SURPRISE YOU.

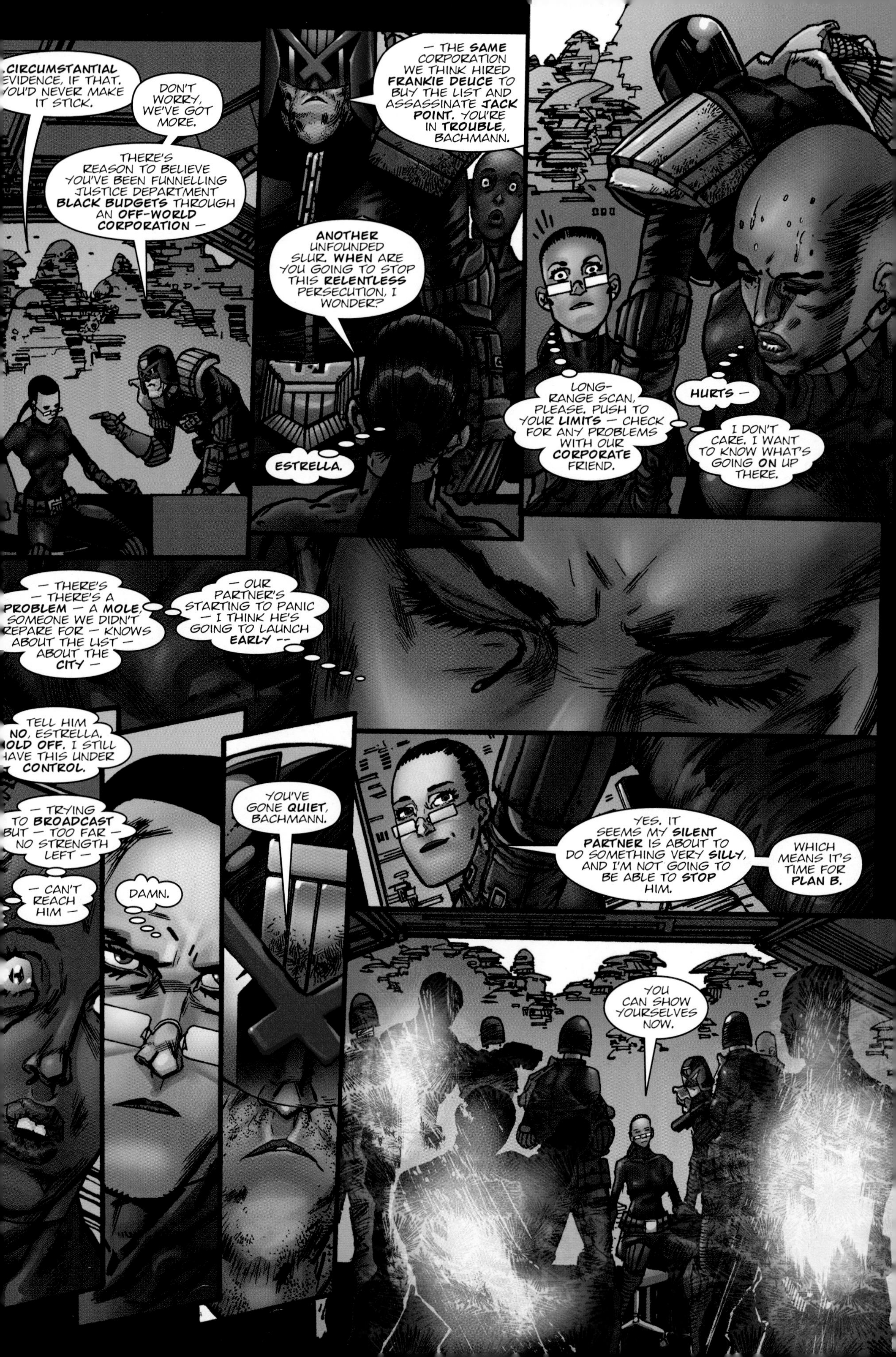
CIRCUMSTANTIAL EVIDENCE, IF THAT. YOU'D NEVER MAKE IT STICK.
DON'T WORRY, WE'VE GOT MORE.
THERE'S REASON TO BELIEVE YOU'VE BEEN FUNNELLING JUSTICE DEPARTMENT BLACK BUDGETS THROUGH AN OFF-WORLD CORPORATION —
— THE SAME CORPORATION WE THINK HIRED FRANKIE DEUCE TO BUY THE LIST AND ASSASSINATE JACK POINT. YOU'RE IN TROUBLE, BACHMANN.
ANOTHER UNFOUNDED SLUR. WHEN ARE YOU GOING TO STOP THIS RELENTLESS PERSECUTION, I WONDER?
ESTRELLA.
LONG-RANGE SCAN, PLEASE. PUSH TO YOUR LIMITS — CHECK FOR ANY PROBLEMS WITH OUR CORPORATE FRIEND.
HURTS —
I DON'T CARE. I WANT TO KNOW WHAT'S GOING ON UP THERE.
— THERE'S — THERE'S A PROBLEM — A MOLE, SOMEONE WE DIDN'T PREPARE FOR — KNOWS ABOUT THE LIST — ABOUT THE CITY —
— OUR PARTNER'S STARTING TO PANIC — I THINK HE'S GOING TO LAUNCH EARLY --
TELL HIM NO, ESTRELLA. HOLD OFF. I STILL HAVE THIS UNDER CONTROL.
— TRYING TO BROADCAST BUT — TOO FAR — NO STRENGTH LEFT —
— CAN'T REACH HIM —
DAMN.
YOU'VE GONE QUIET, BACHMANN.
YES. IT SEEMS MY SILENT PARTNER IS ABOUT TO DO SOMETHING VERY SILLY, AND I'M NOT GOING TO BE ABLE TO STOP HIM.
WHICH MEANS IT'S TIME FOR PLAN B.
YOU CAN SHOW YOURSELVES NOW.

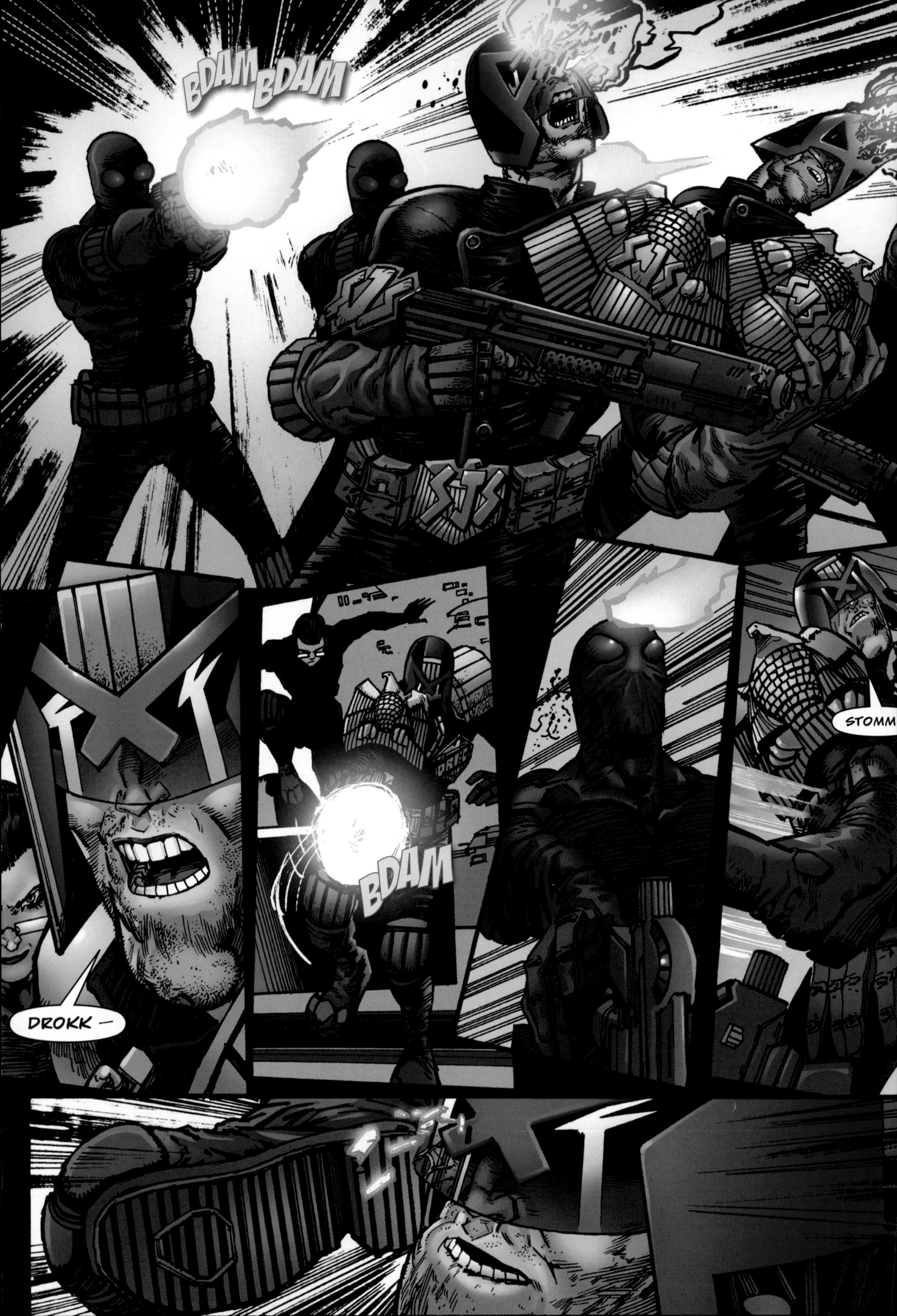
BDAM BDAM
DROKK —
BDAM
STOMM

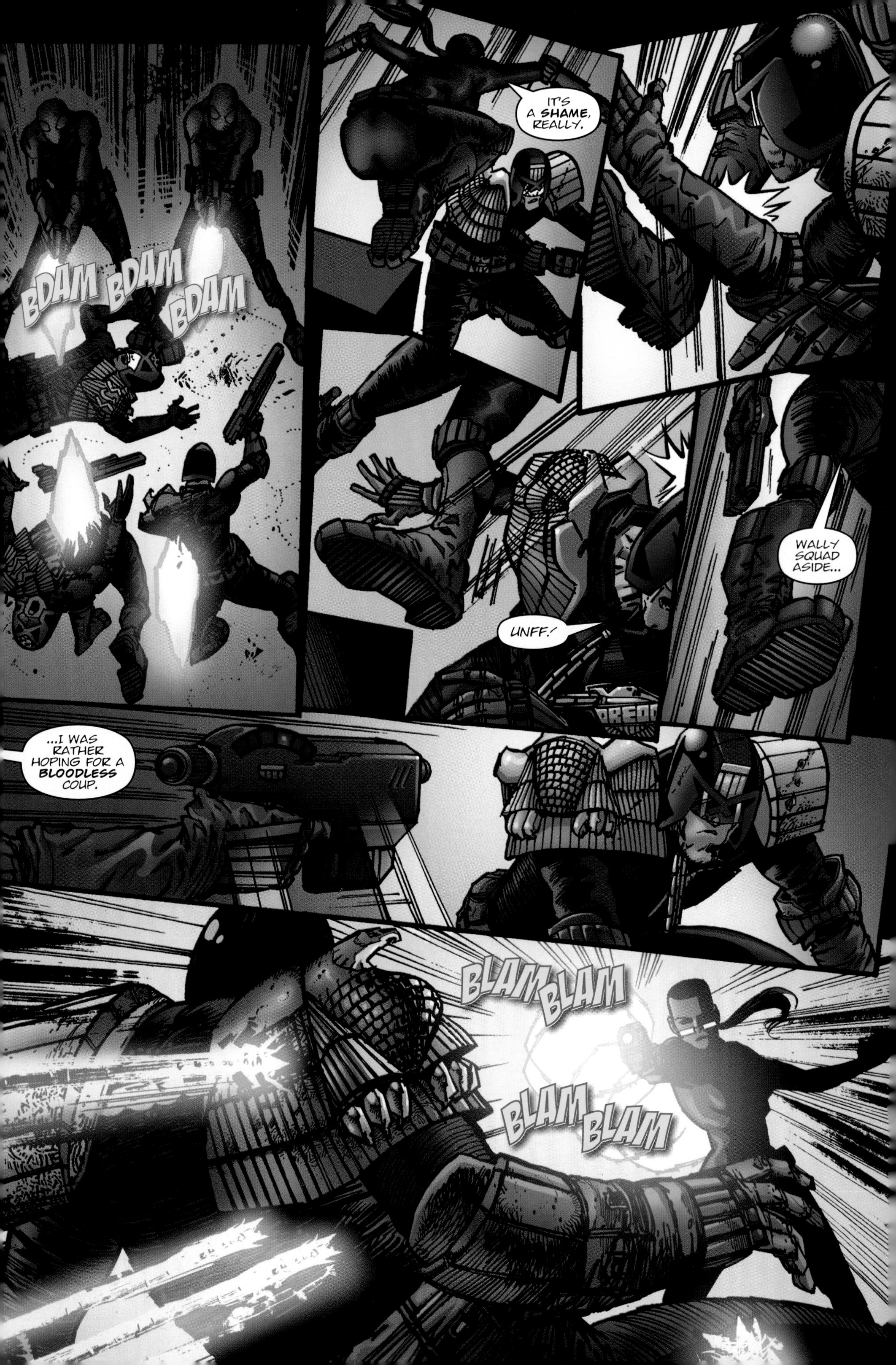
BDAM BDAM BDAM
IT'S A SHAME, REALLY.
WALLY SQUAD ASIDE...
UNFF!
...I WAS RATHER HOPING FOR A BLOODLESS COUP.
BLAM BLAM
BLAM BLAM

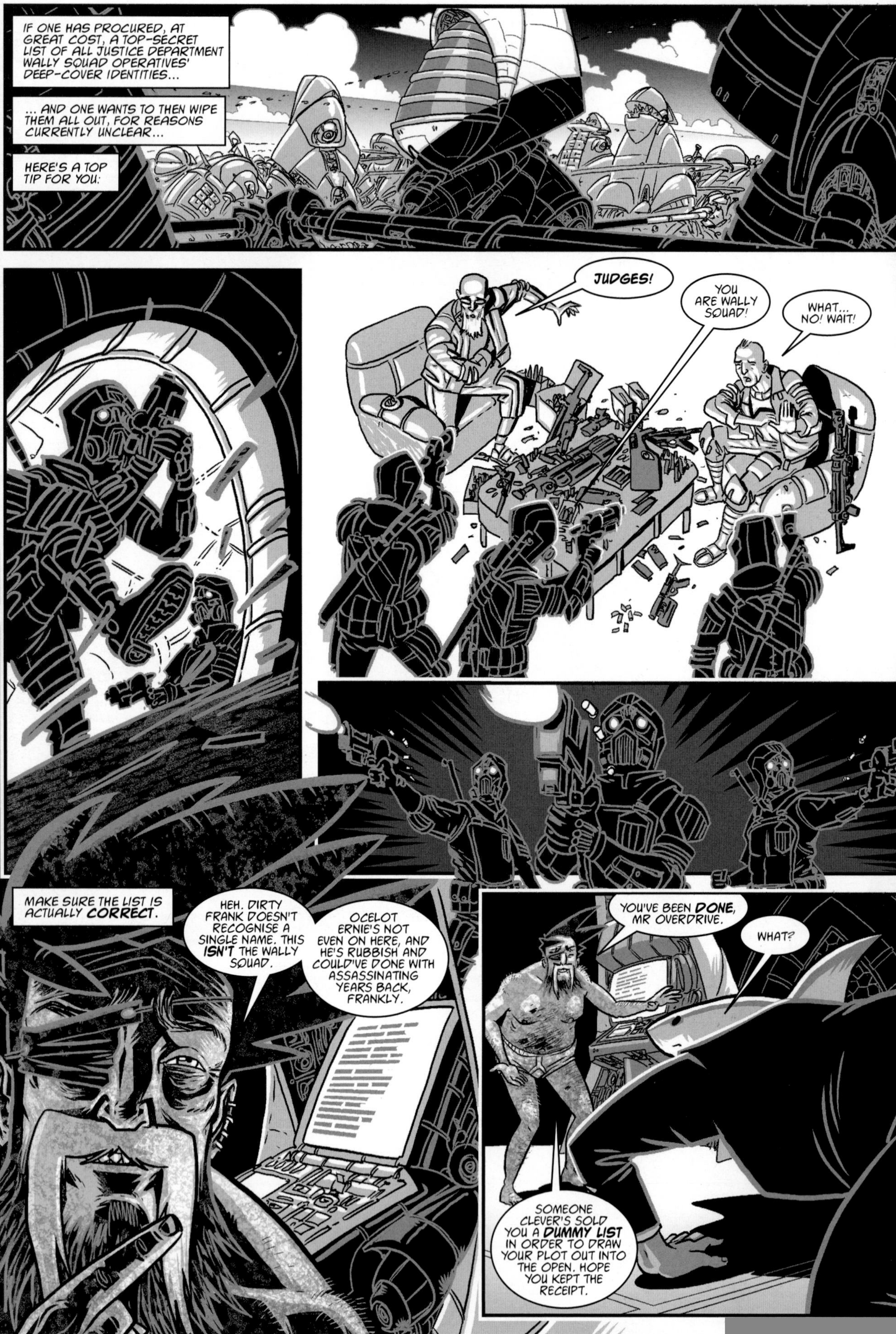
IF ONE HAS PROCURED, AT GREAT COST, A TOP-SECRET LIST OF ALL JUSTICE DEPARTMENT WALLY SQUAD OPERATIVES' DEEP-COVER IDENTITIES...
... AND ONE WANTS TO THEN WIPE THEM ALL OUT, FOR REASONS CURRENTLY UNCLEAR...
HERE'S A TOP TIP FOR YOU:
JUDGES!
YOU ARE WALLY SQUAD!
WHAT... NO! WAIT!
MAKE SURE THE LIST IS ACTUALLY CORRECT.
HEH. DIRTY FRANK DOESN'T RECOGNISE A SINGLE NAME. THIS ISN'T THE WALLY SQUAD.
OCELOT ERNIE'S NOT EVEN ON HERE, AND HE'S RUBBISH AND COULD'VE DONE WITH ASSASSINATING YEARS BACK, FRANKLY.
YOU'VE BEEN DONE, MR OVERDRIVE.
WHAT?
SOMEONE CLEVER'S SOLD YOU A DUMMY LIST IN ORDER TO DRAW YOUR PLOT OUT INTO THE OPEN. HOPE YOU KEPT THE RECEIPT.

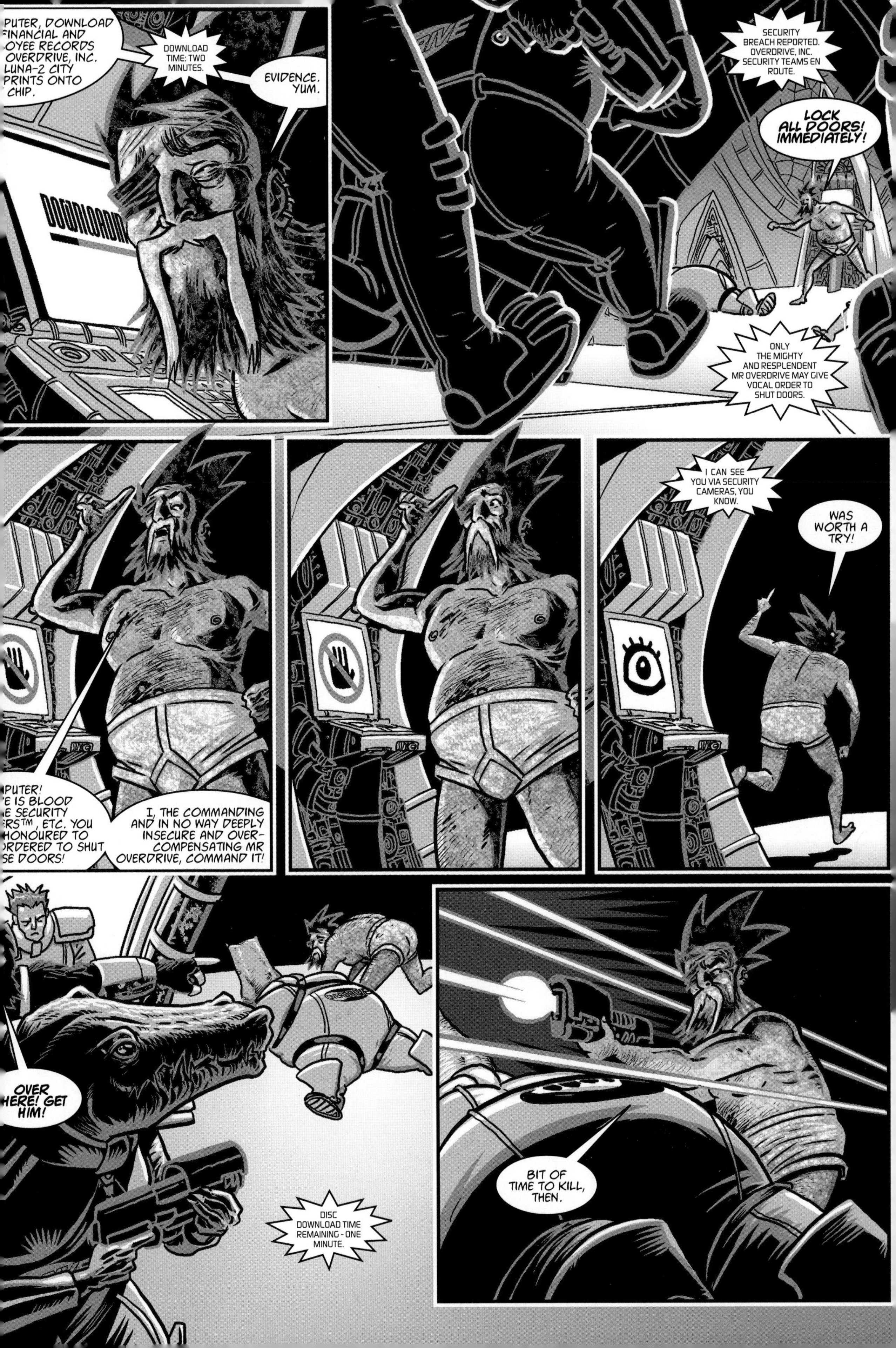

PUTER, DOWNLOAD FINANCIAL AND OYEE RECORDS OVERDRIVE, INC. LUNA-2 CITY PRINTS ONTO CHIP.
DOWNLOAD TIME: TWO MINUTES.
EVIDENCE. YUM.
SECURITY BREACH REPORTED. OVERDRIVE, INC. SECURITY TEAMS EN ROUTE.
LOCK ALL DOORS! IMMEDIATELY!
ONLY THE MIGHTY AND RESPLENDENT MR OVERDRIVE MAY GIVE VOCAL ORDER TO SHUT DOORS.
PUTER! E IS BLOOD E SECURITY ERS™, ETC. YOU HONOURED TO ORDERED TO SHUT SE DOORS!
I, THE COMMANDING AND IN NO WAY DEEPLY INSECURE AND OVER-COMPENSATING MR OVERDRIVE, COMMAND IT!
I CAN SEE YOU VIA SECURITY CAMERAS, YOU KNOW.
WAS WORTH A TRY!
OVER HERE! GET HIM!
DISC DOWNLOAD TIME REMAINING - ONE MINUTE.
BIT OF TIME TO KILL, THEN.

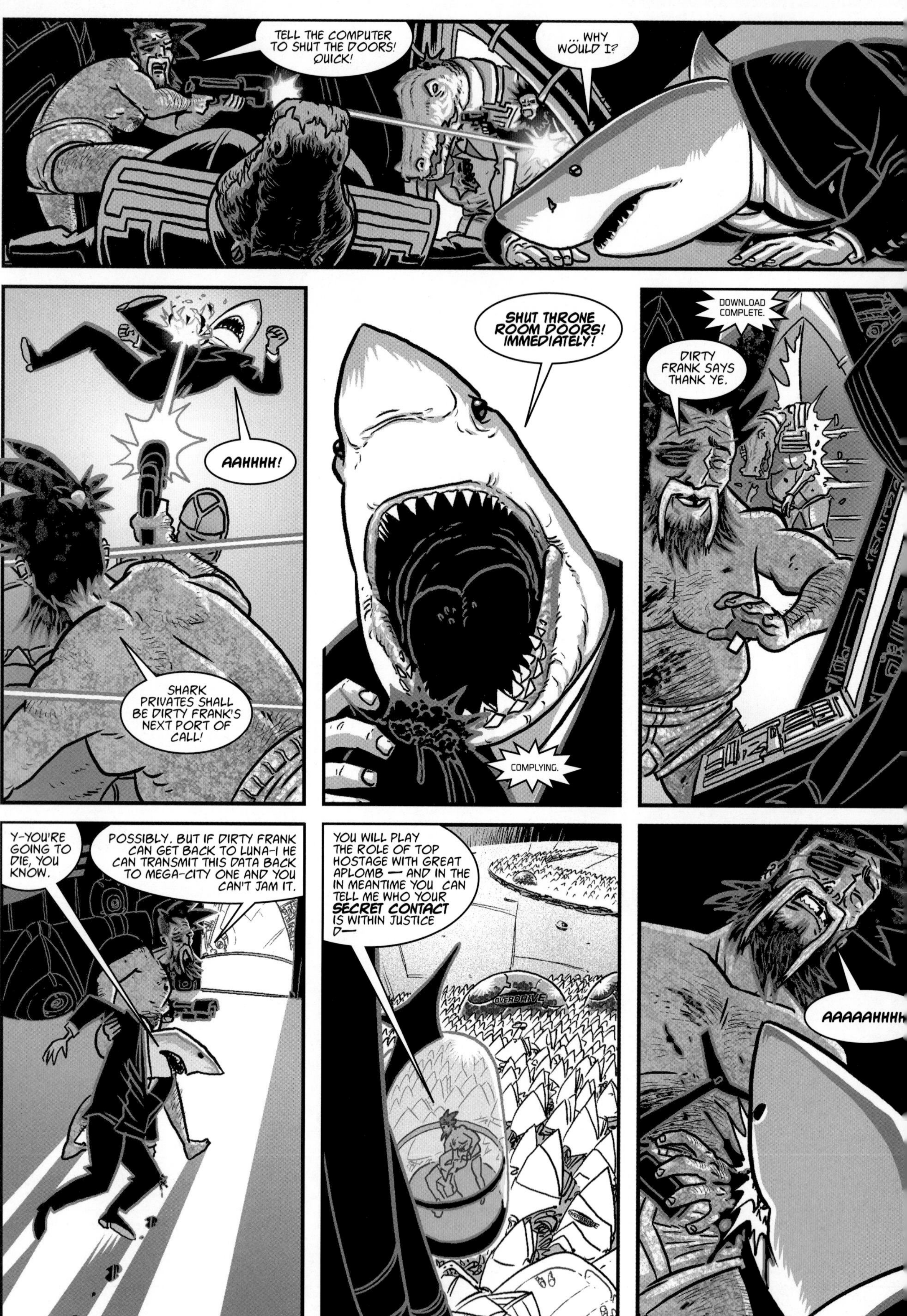
TELL THE COMPUTER TO SHUT THE DOORS! QUICK!
... WHY WOULD I?
AAHHHH!
SHARK PRIVATES SHALL BE DIRTY FRANK'S NEXT PORT OF CALL!
SHUT THRONE ROOM DOORS! IMMEDIATELY!
COMPLYING.
DOWNLOAD COMPLETE.
DIRTY FRANK SAYS THANK YE.
Y-YOU'RE GOING TO DIE, YOU KNOW.
POSSIBLY. BUT IF DIRTY FRANK CAN GET BACK TO LUNA-I HE CAN TRANSMIT THIS DATA BACK TO MEGA-CITY ONE AND YOU CAN'T JAM IT.
YOU WILL PLAY THE ROLE OF TOP HOSTAGE WITH GREAT APLOMB — AND IN THE IN MEANTIME YOU CAN TELL ME WHO YOUR SECRET CONTACT IS WITHIN JUSTICE D—
OVERDRIVE
AAAAAHHH

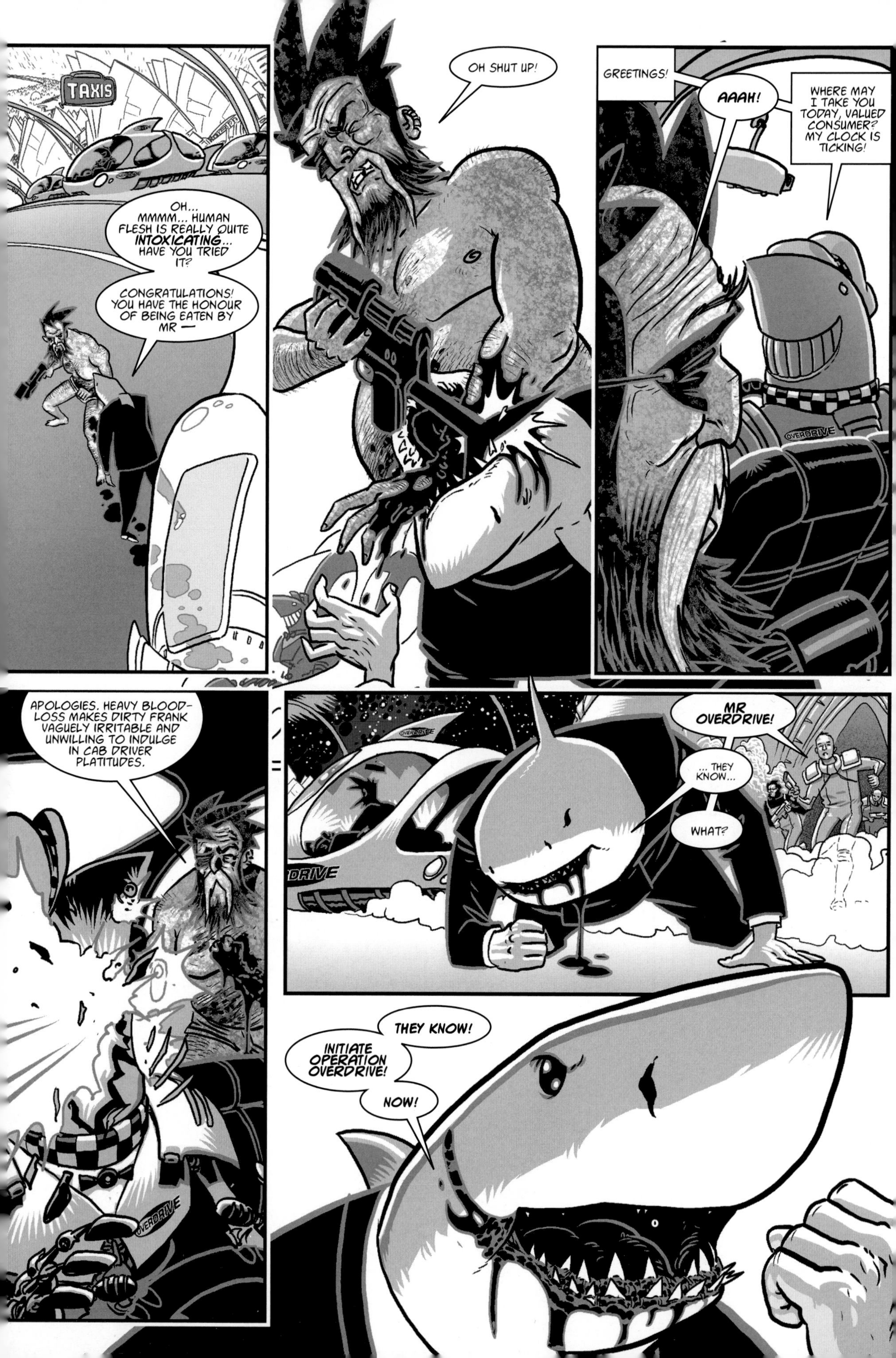
TAXIS
OH... MMMM... HUMAN FLESH IS REALLY QUITE INTOXICATING... HAVE YOU TRIED IT?
CONGRATULATIONS! YOU HAVE THE HONOUR OF BEING EATEN BY MR —
OH SHUT UP!
GREETINGS!
AAAH!
WHERE MAY I TAKE YOU TODAY, VALUED CONSUMER? MY CLOCK IS TICKING!
OVERDRIVE
APOLOGIES. HEAVY BLOOD-LOSS MAKES DIRTY FRANK VAGUELY IRRITABLE AND UNWILLING TO INDULGE IN CAB DRIVER PLATITUDES.
OVERDRIVE
MR OVERDRIVE!
... THEY KNOW...
WHAT?
THEY KNOW!
INITIATE OPERATION OVERDRIVE!
NOW!

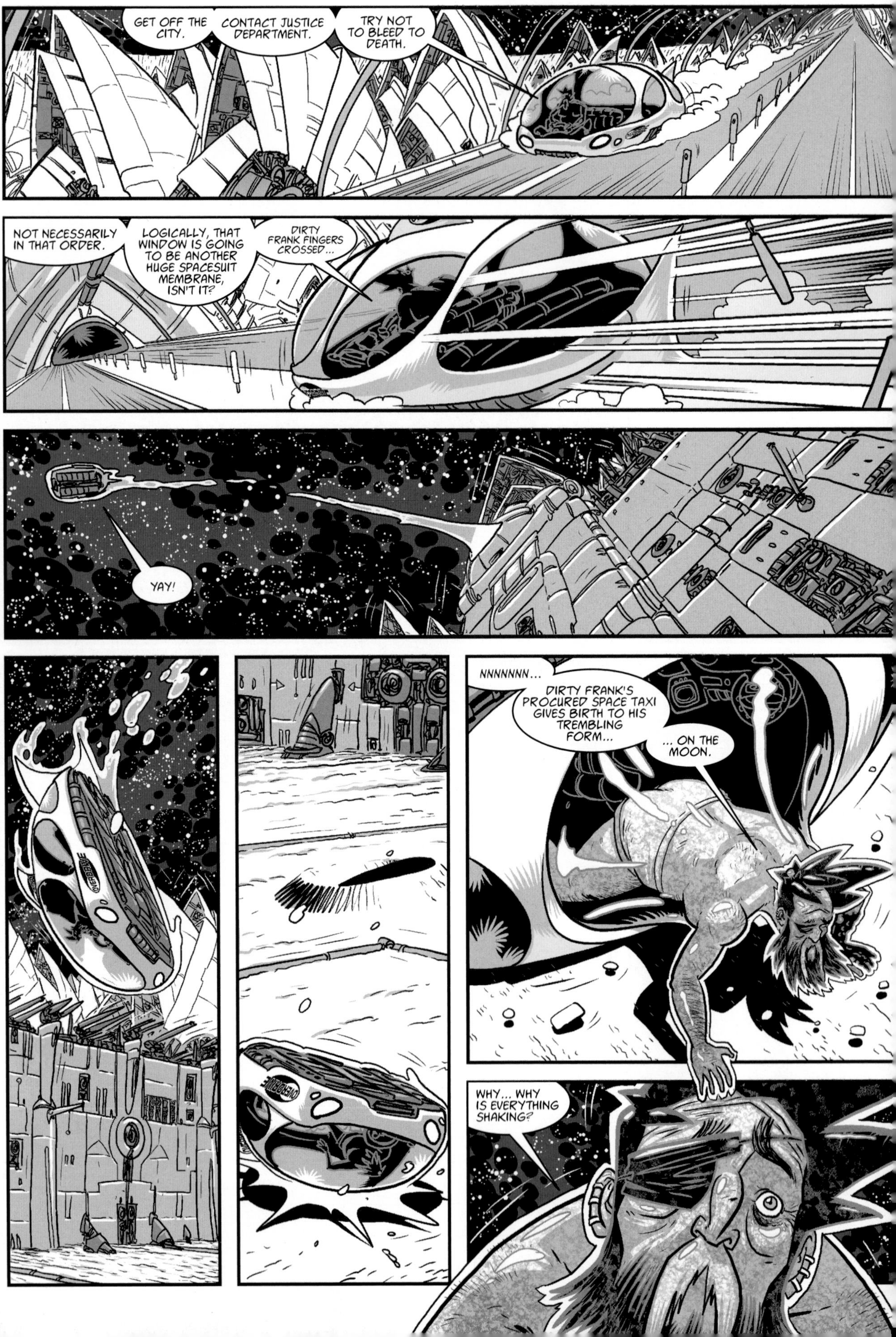
GET OFF THE CITY.
CONTACT JUSTICE DEPARTMENT.
TRY NOT TO BLEED TO DEATH.
NOT NECESSARILY IN THAT ORDER.
LOGICALLY, THAT WINDOW IS GOING TO BE ANOTHER HUGE SPACESUIT MEMBRANE, ISN'T IT?
DIRTY FRANK FINGERS CROSSED...
YAY!
OVERDRIVE
OVERDRIVE
NNNNNNN...
DIRTY FRANK'S PROCURED SPACE TAXI GIVES BIRTH TO HIS TREMBLING FORM...
... ON THE MOON.
WHY... WHY IS EVERYTHING SHAKING?

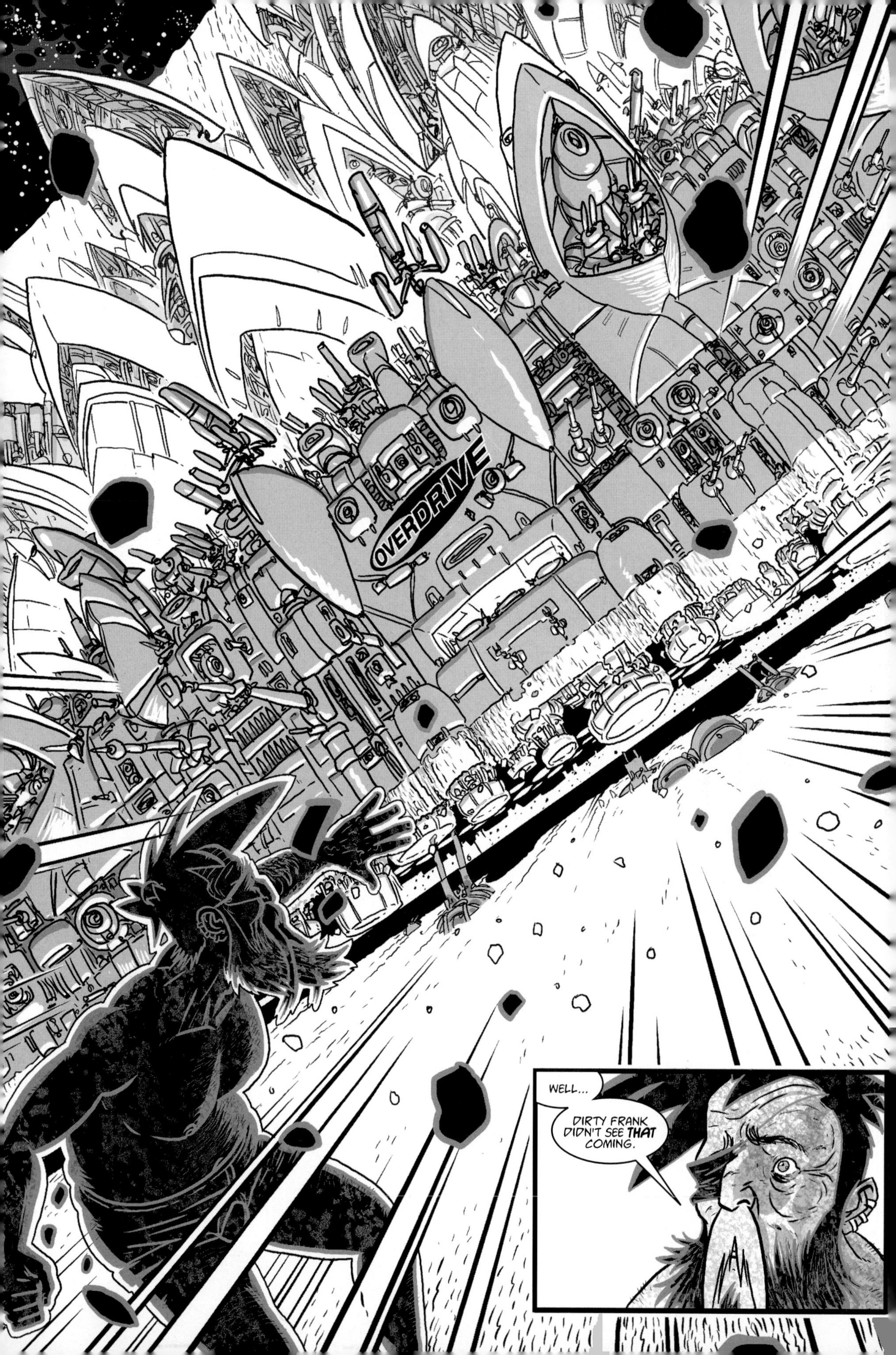
OVERDRIVE
WELL...
DIRTY FRANK DIDN'T SEE **THAT** COMING.

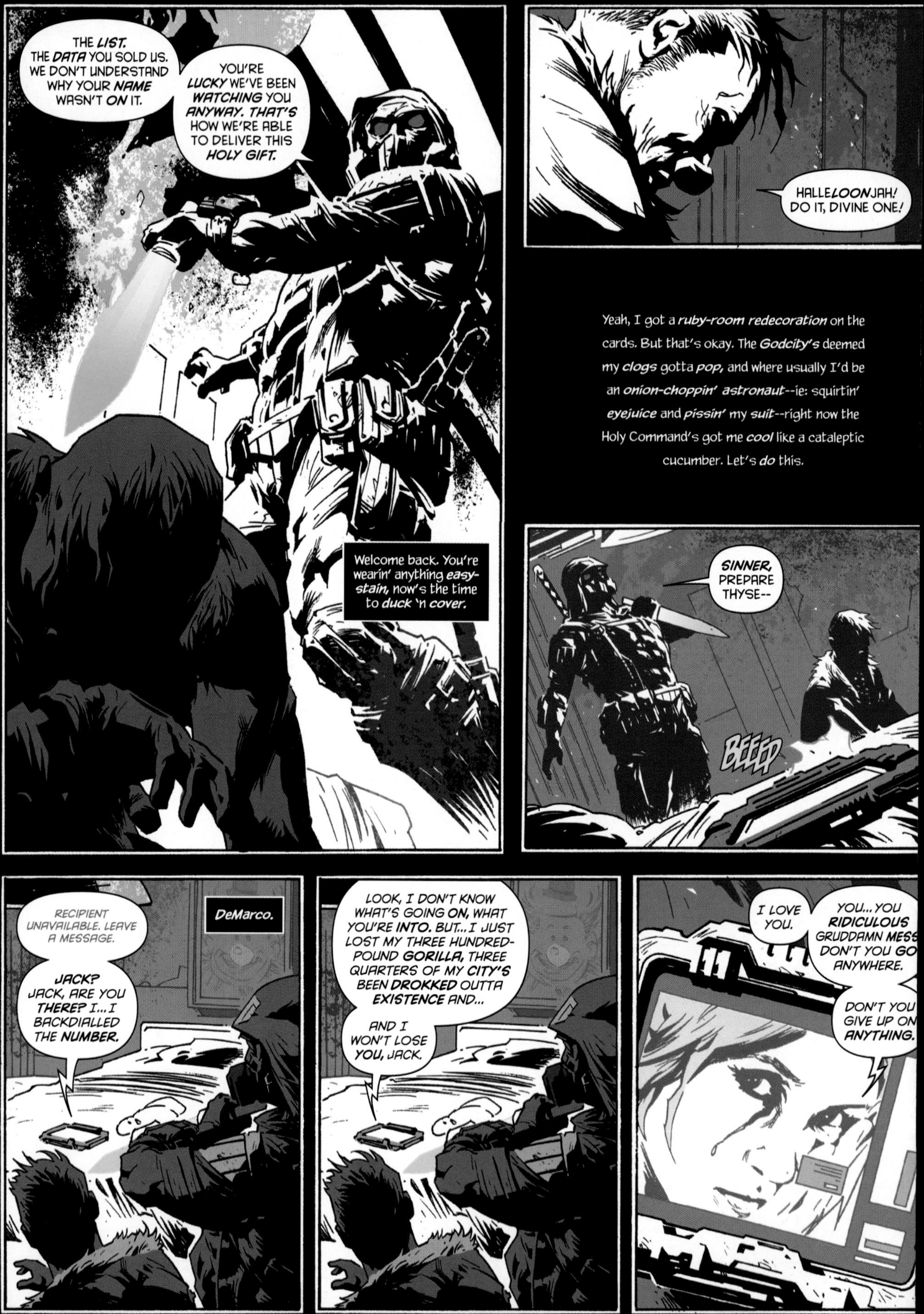

THE *LIST.* THE *DATA* YOU SOLD US. WE DON'T UNDERSTAND WHY YOUR *NAME* WASN'T *ON* IT.
YOU'RE *LUCKY* WE'VE BEEN *WATCHING* YOU *ANYWAY. THAT'S* HOW WE'RE ABLE TO DELIVER THIS *HOLY GIFT.*
Welcome back. You're wearin' anything *easy-stain,* now's the time to *duck 'n cover.*
HALLE*LOON*JAH! DO IT, DIVINE ONE!
Yeah, I got a *ruby-room redecoration* on the cards. But that's okay. The *Godcity's* deemed my *clogs* gotta *pop,* and where usually I'd be an *onion-choppin' astronaut*--ie: squirtin' *eyejuice* and *pissin'* my *suit*--right now the Holy Command's got me *cool* like a cataleptic cucumber. Let's *do* this.
SINNER, PREPARE THYSE--
BEEEP
RECIPIENT UNAVAILABLE. LEAVE A MESSAGE.
DeMarco.
JACK? JACK, ARE YOU *THERE?* I... I BACKDIALLED THE *NUMBER.*
LOOK, I DON'T KNOW WHAT'S GOING *ON,* WHAT YOU'RE *INTO.* BUT... I JUST LOST MY THREE HUNDRED-POUND *GORILLA,* THREE QUARTERS OF MY *CITY'S* BEEN *DROKKED* OUTTA *EXISTENCE* AND...
AND I WON'T LOSE *YOU,* JACK.
I LOVE YOU.
YOU... YOU *RIDICULOUS* GRUDDAMN *MESS* DON'T YOU *GO* ANYWHERE.
DON'T YOU GIVE UP ON *ANYTHING.*

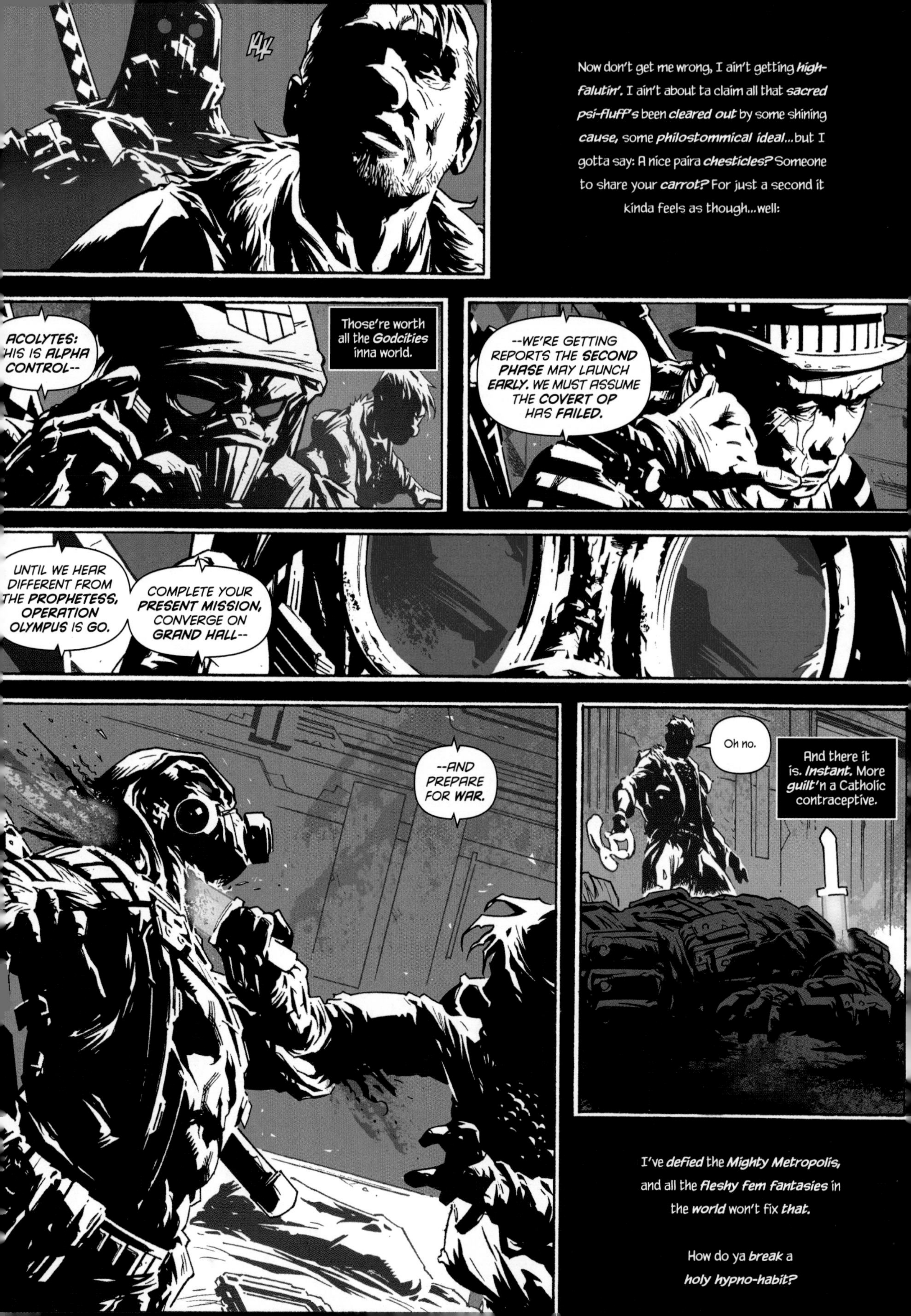
Now don't get me wrong, I ain't getting *high-falutin'*. I ain't about ta claim all that *sacred psi-fluff's* been *cleared out* by some shining *cause*, some *philostommical ideal*...but I gotta say: A nice paira *chesticles?* Someone to share your *carrot?* For just a second it kinda feels as though...well:
ACOLYTES: THIS IS ALPHA CONTROL--
Those're worth all the *Godcities* inna world.
--WE'RE GETTING REPORTS THE SECOND PHASE MAY LAUNCH EARLY. WE MUST ASSUME THE COVERT OP HAS FAILED.
UNTIL WE HEAR DIFFERENT FROM THE PROPHETESS, OPERATION OLYMPUS IS GO.
COMPLETE YOUR PRESENT MISSION, CONVERGE ON GRAND HALL--
--AND PREPARE FOR WAR.
Oh no.
And there it is. *Instant.* More *guilt*'n a Catholic contraceptive.
I've *defied* the *Mighty Metropolis*, and all the *fleshy fem fantasies* in the *world* won't fix *that.*
How do ya *break* a *holy hypno-habit?*

Huh. Judge *Folger*-- all done up with *fake flabbon,* if only I'd known. *She* was waxin' wide with the faith-fandango *too*...

WHAT'S HAPPENIN' IS: A FREAKY *XT NARCOTOXIN'S* SEEPIN' THROUGH YOUR *BODY*...

Drugs. Psychotropic skulldrokk. That was the only thing *strong enough* to set her *free* from the *conditioning.*

Worth a *squirt,* right

Guilt's almost *too much,* all the same. Dread to *think* what'd happen if this *moronising mojo* ever fell into the *wrong h*--

SHE... SHE MADE ME *STEAL IT!* Y-YOU C-CAN'T...

YOU CAN'T LLLET HER HHHAHVE *IT.*

Wrong hands. *Ah crap.*

Ah crap*crapcrap.*

PREP THE *BOOTHS.*

WE DO THINGS THE *BLUNT* WAY NOW. ACCELERATED *REVELATION* FOR *ALL MEMBERS.* YOU TWO INCLUDED.

HER MAJESTY'S GOING TO NEED A LITTLE *CANNON FODDER* ON THE *STREETS*--AT LEAST UNTIL THE *SLEEP CYCLE* CONVERTS A FEW *HELMETS.*

I have no idea what the *freakoid's* talkin' about--

--but it's got him *worked up* enough to leave his *office* unlocked.

Psychotropic skulldrokk, huh

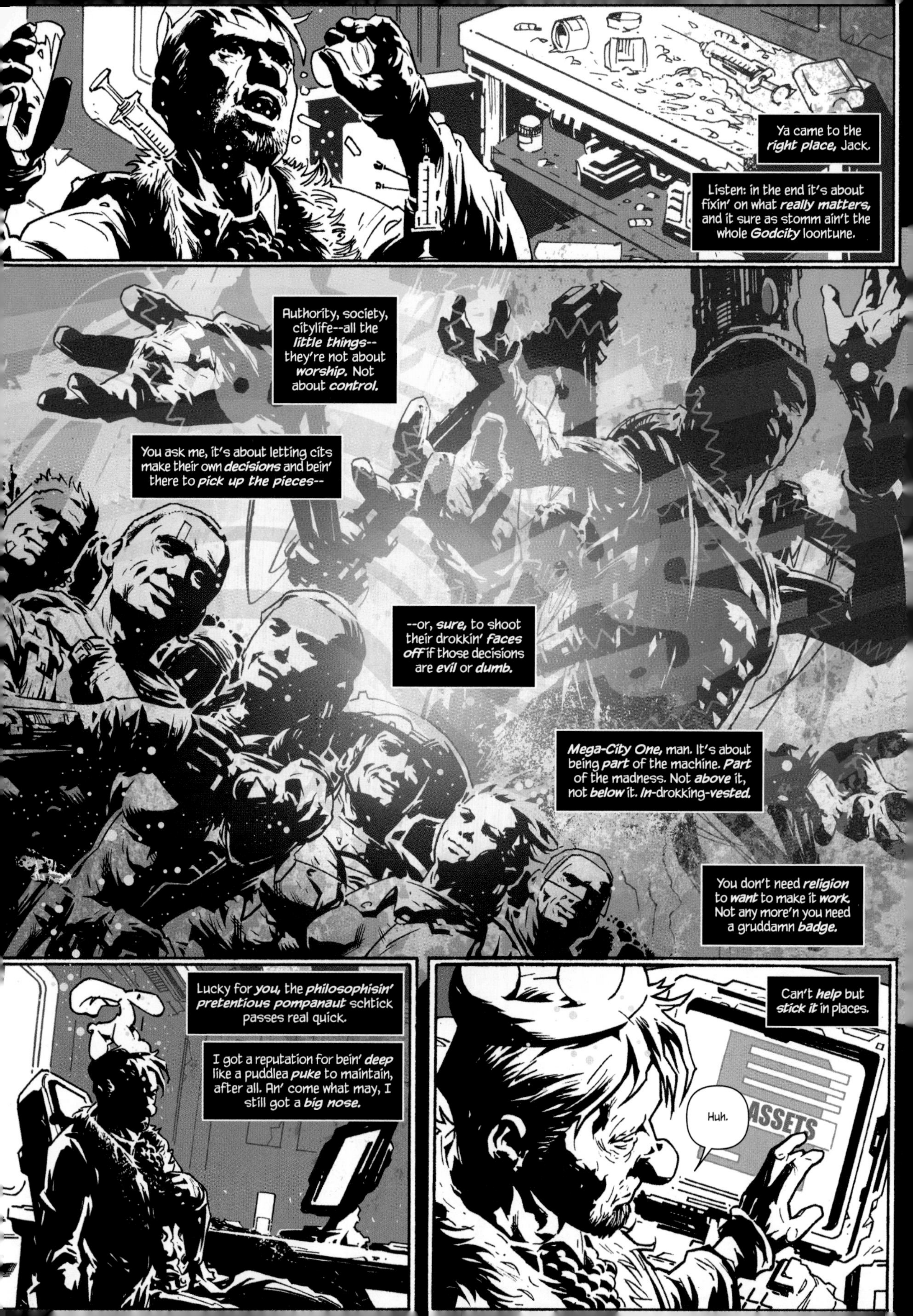

Ya came to the *right place,* Jack.
Listen: in the end it's about fixin' on what *really matters,* and it sure as stomm ain't the whole *Godcity* loontune.
Authority, society, citylife--all the *little things*--they're not about *worship.* Not about *control.*
You ask me, it's about letting cits make their own *decisions* and bein' there to *pick up the pieces*--
--or, *sure,* to shoot their drokkin' *faces off* if those decisions are *evil* or *dumb.*
Mega-City One, man. It's about being *part* of the machine. *Part* of the madness. Not *above* it, not *below* it. *In*-drokking-*vested.*
You don't need *religion* to *want* to make it *work.* Not any more'n you need a gruddamn *badge.*
Lucky for *you,* the *philosophisin' pretentious pompanaut* schtick passes real quick.
I got a reputation for bein' *deep* like a puddlea *puke* to maintain, after all. An' come what may, I still got a *big nose.*
Can't *help* but *stick it* in places.
Huh.
ASSETS

"*Masterz DiGree™*", it says. That's the *tek firm* my sadsack pal *Melda* ran before *fallin'* for *Foolin'*. And *boy* did she *fall*...

Says *here* she handed over the *whole firm* to the *Church*--lock, stock and *checkbook*--to cover her *gimpifying fees*.

And ol' *Turner?* That whitefaced mo'dro's got *plans*.

New sorta *Tri-D chip*, it says, for every *gogglebox* in town. "*Impro Your Viewing Experience By DiGree's* They ain't *rolled out* yet, on accou of the firm's got a *higher priorit*

Ohhhhh *STOMM.*

Which is ta *say:*

...supplyin' *Sleep Machines* to *every Sector House* in the Meg.

And *those?* Those left the warehouse *two months ago.*

FULL REVELATION PROTOCOLS INITIATED

VIEW BOOTH CHAMBER? IY / NI

?

♪ ALL CLOWNS DUMB AND DU-TI-FUL, ASS-ES ON WHICH TO FAAALL. GUNS BOTH HUGE AND KILL-ING-FUL, THE GODTOWN LOVES THEM ALL. ♪

♪ BUT IT HATES THE SNEERING TRAII-TORS, WHO WON'T ACCEPT ITS YOKE. WITH CUSTARD PIES OF NAA-PALM, WE'LL HELP THEM SEE THE JOKE! ♪

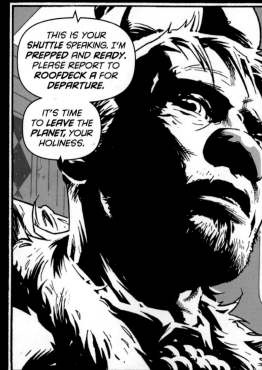

SLEEP MACHINES. Aw *CRAP.*

SIMPRIEST JACK POINT?

THIS IS YOUR *SHUTTLE* SPEAKING. I'M *PREPPED* AND *READY.* PLEASE REPORT TO *ROOFDECK A* FOR *DEPARTURE.*

IT'S TIME TO *LEAVE THE PLANET, YOUR HOLINESS.*

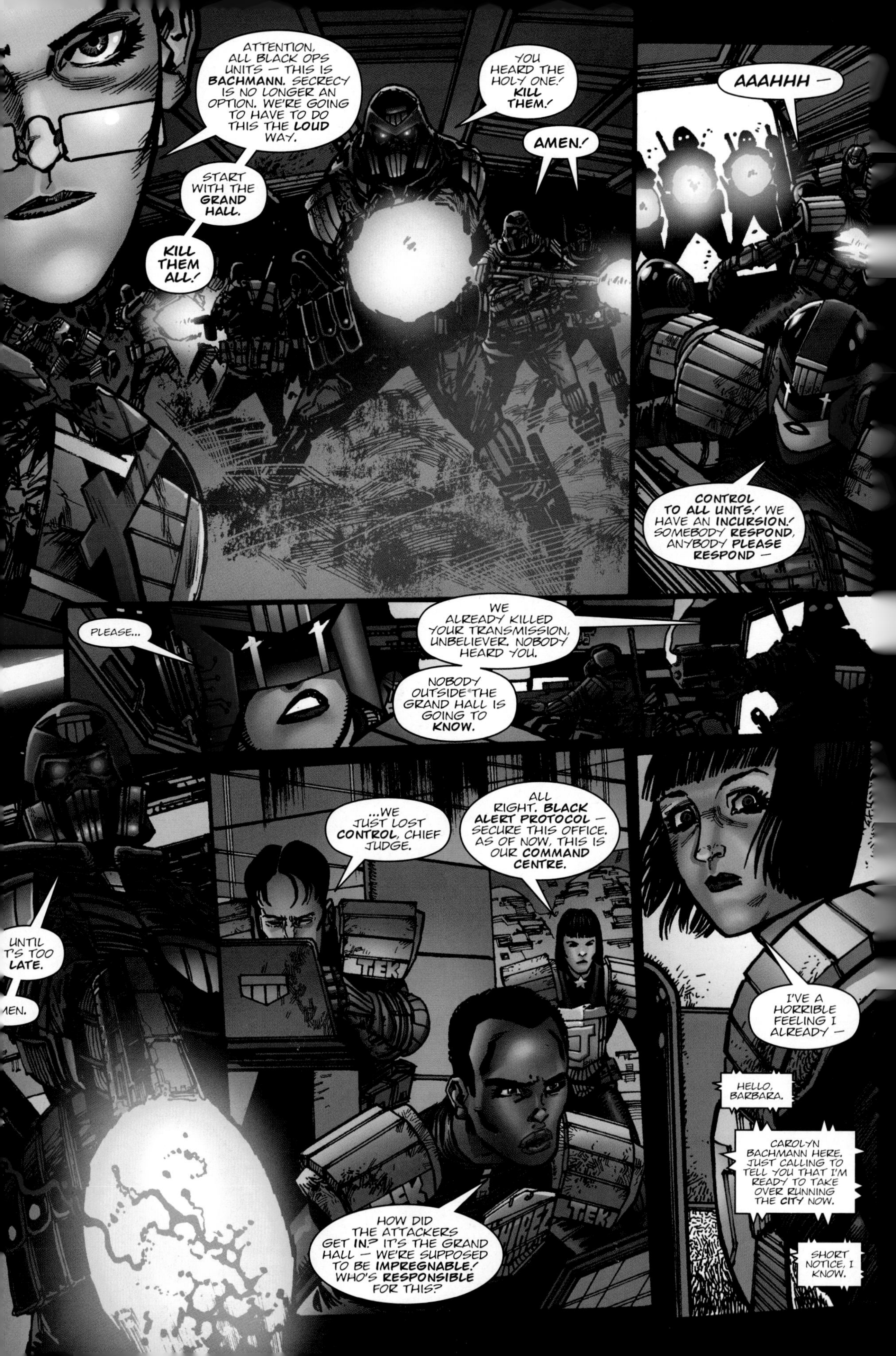

ATTENTION, ALL BLACK OPS UNITS — THIS IS BACHMANN. SECRECY IS NO LONGER AN OPTION. WE'RE GOING TO HAVE TO DO THIS THE LOUD WAY.
START WITH THE GRAND HALL.
KILL THEM ALL!
YOU HEARD THE HOLY ONE! KILL THEM!
AMEN!
AAAHHH —
CONTROL TO ALL UNITS! WE HAVE AN INCURSION! SOMEBODY RESPOND, ANYBODY PLEASE RESPOND —
PLEASE...
WE ALREADY KILLED YOUR TRANSMISSION, UNBELIEVER. NOBODY HEARD YOU.
NOBODY OUTSIDE THE GRAND HALL IS GOING TO KNOW.
UNTIL T'S TOO LATE.
MEN.
...WE JUST LOST CONTROL, CHIEF JUDGE.
ALL RIGHT. BLACK ALERT PROTOCOL — SECURE THIS OFFICE. AS OF NOW, THIS IS OUR COMMAND CENTRE.
HOW DID THE ATTACKERS GET IN? IT'S THE GRAND HALL — WE'RE SUPPOSED TO BE IMPREGNABLE! WHO'S RESPONSIBLE FOR THIS?
I'VE A HORRIBLE FEELING I ALREADY —
HELLO, BARBARA.
CAROLYN BACHMANN HERE. JUST CALLING TO TELL YOU THAT I'M READY TO TAKE OVER RUNNING THE CITY NOW.
SHORT NOTICE, I KNOW.

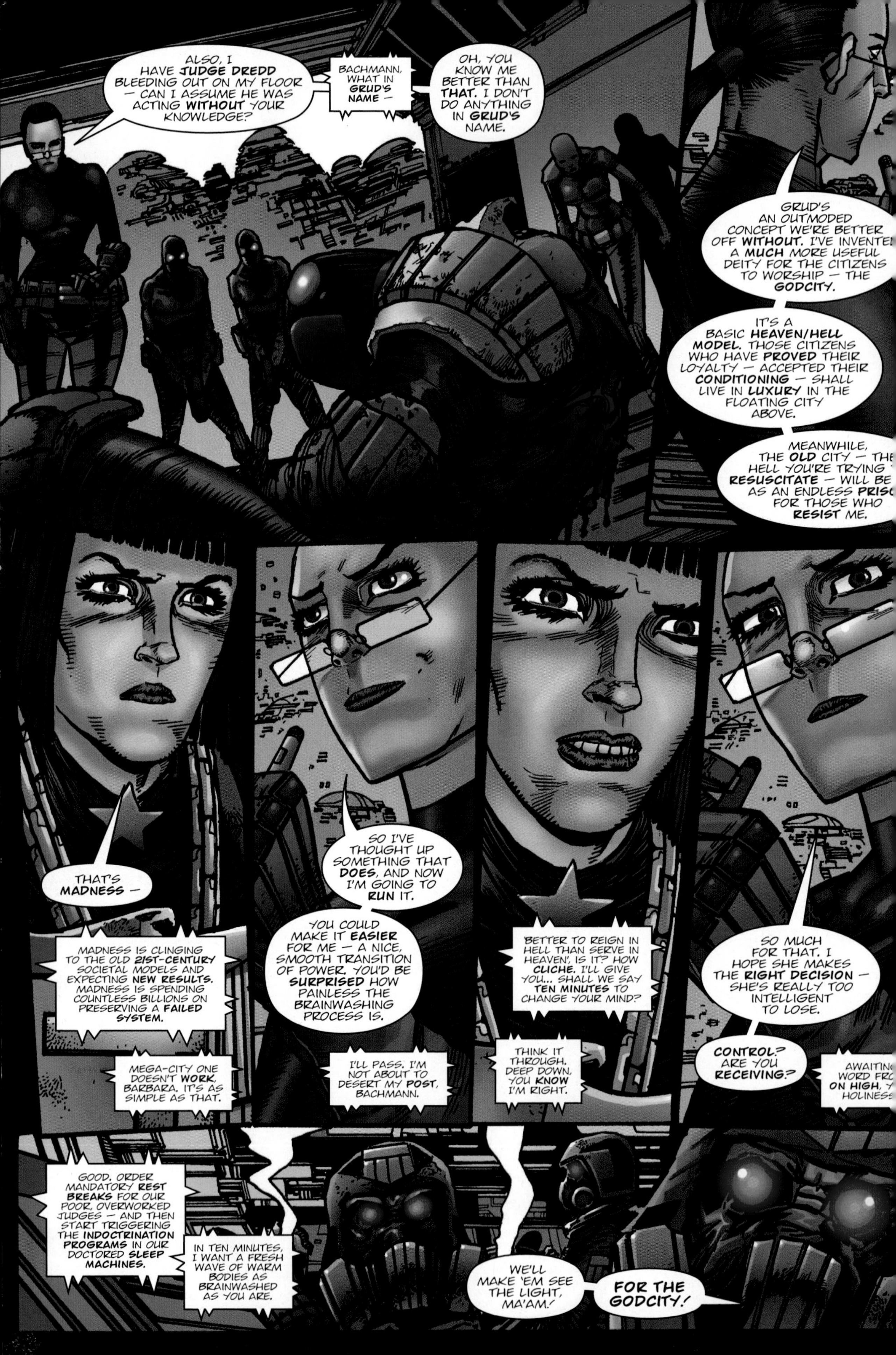
ALSO, I HAVE JUDGE DREDD BLEEDING OUT ON MY FLOOR — CAN I ASSUME HE WAS ACTING WITHOUT YOUR KNOWLEDGE?
BACHMANN, WHAT IN GRUD'S NAME —
OH, YOU KNOW ME BETTER THAN THAT. I DON'T DO ANYTHING IN GRUD'S NAME.
GRUD'S AN OUTMODED CONCEPT WE'RE BETTER OFF WITHOUT. I'VE INVENTE A MUCH MORE USEFUL DEITY FOR THE CITIZENS TO WORSHIP — THE GODCITY.
IT'S A BASIC HEAVEN/HELL MODEL. THOSE CITIZENS WHO HAVE PROVED THEIR LOYALTY — ACCEPTED THEIR CONDITIONING — SHALL LIVE IN LUXURY IN THE FLOATING CITY ABOVE.
MEANWHILE, THE OLD CITY — TH HELL YOU'RE TRYING RESUSCITATE — WILL BE AS AN ENDLESS PRIS FOR THOSE WHO RESIST ME.
THAT'S MADNESS —
MADNESS IS CLINGING TO THE OLD 21ST-CENTURY SOCIETAL MODELS AND EXPECTING NEW RESULTS. MADNESS IS SPENDING COUNTLESS BILLIONS ON PRESERVING A FAILED SYSTEM.
MEGA-CITY ONE DOESN'T WORK, BARBARA. IT'S AS SIMPLE AS THAT.
SO I'VE THOUGHT UP SOMETHING THAT DOES, AND NOW I'M GOING TO RUN IT.
YOU COULD MAKE IT EASIER FOR ME — A NICE, SMOOTH TRANSITION OF POWER. YOU'D BE SURPRISED HOW PAINLESS THE BRAINWASHING PROCESS IS.
I'LL PASS. I'M NOT ABOUT TO DESERT MY POST, BACHMANN.
'BETTER TO REIGN IN HELL THAN SERVE IN HEAVEN', IS IT? HOW CLICHE. I'LL GIVE YOU... SHALL WE SAY TEN MINUTES TO CHANGE YOUR MIND?
THINK IT THROUGH. DEEP DOWN, YOU KNOW I'M RIGHT.
SO MUCH FOR THAT. I HOPE SHE MAKES THE RIGHT DECISION — SHE'S REALLY TOO INTELLIGENT TO LOSE.
CONTROL? ARE YOU RECEIVING?
AWAITIN WORD FR ON HIGH, HOLINES
GOOD. ORDER MANDATORY REST BREAKS FOR OUR POOR, OVERWORKED JUDGES — AND THEN START TRIGGERING THE INDOCTRINATION PROGRAMS IN OUR DOCTORED SLEEP MACHINES.
IN TEN MINUTES, I WANT A FRESH WAVE OF WARM BODIES AS BRAINWASHED AS YOU ARE.
WE'LL MAKE 'EM SEE THE LIGHT, MA'AM!
FOR THE GODCITY!

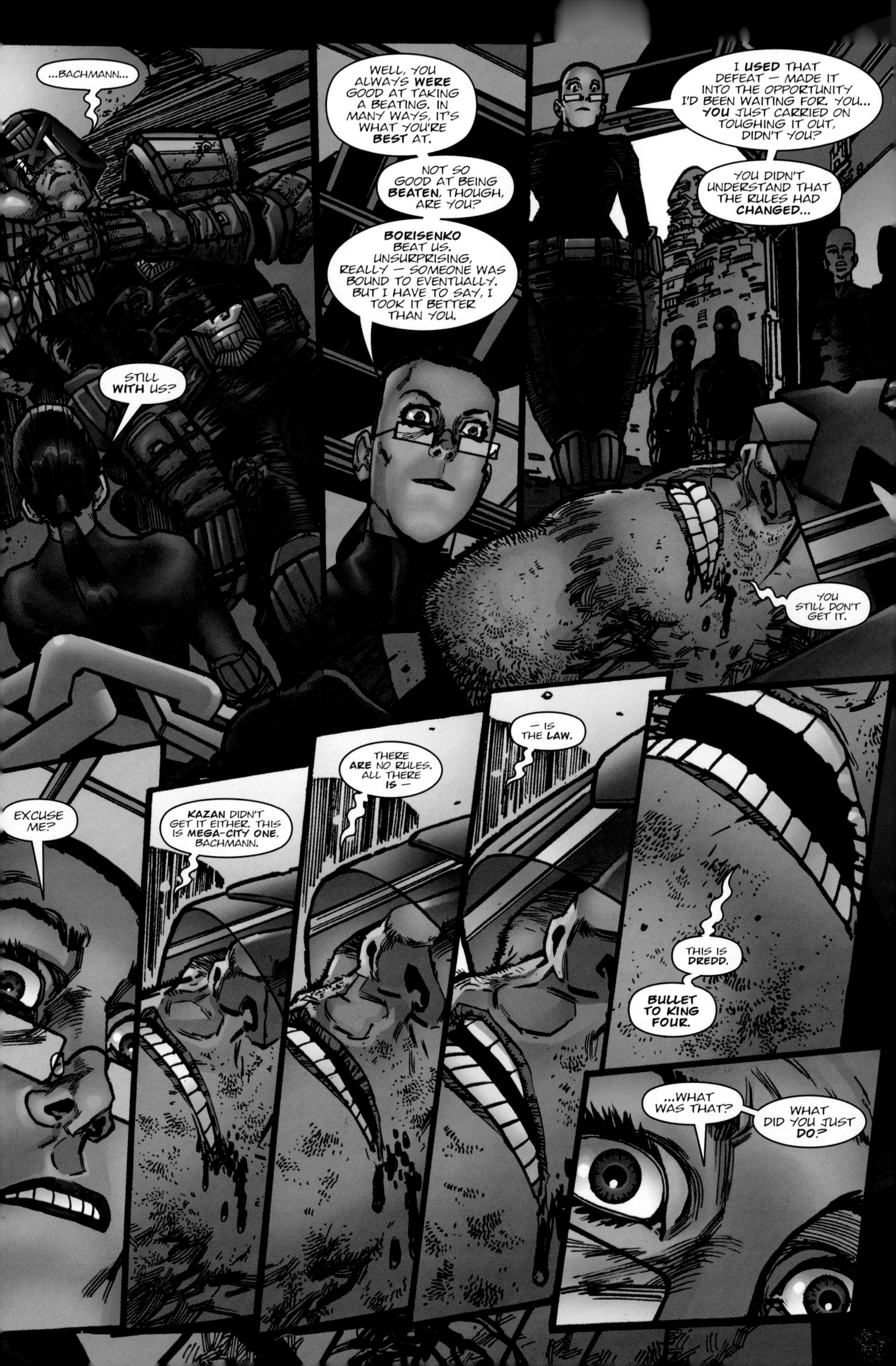
...BACHMANN...
STILL WITH US?
WELL, YOU ALWAYS WERE GOOD AT TAKING A BEATING. IN MANY WAYS, IT'S WHAT YOU'RE BEST AT.
NOT SO GOOD AT BEING BEATEN, THOUGH, ARE YOU?
BORISENKO BEAT US. UNSURPRISING, REALLY — SOMEONE WAS BOUND TO EVENTUALLY. BUT I HAVE TO SAY, I TOOK IT BETTER THAN YOU.
I USED THAT DEFEAT — MADE IT INTO THE OPPORTUNITY I'D BEEN WAITING FOR. YOU... YOU JUST CARRIED ON TOUGHING IT OUT, DIDN'T YOU?
YOU DIDN'T UNDERSTAND THAT THE RULES HAD CHANGED...
YOU STILL DON'T GET IT.
EXCUSE ME?
KAZAN DIDN'T GET IT EITHER. THIS IS MEGA-CITY ONE, BACHMANN.
THERE ARE NO RULES. ALL THERE IS —
— IS THE LAW.
THIS IS DREDD.
BULLET TO KING FOUR.
...WHAT WAS THAT?
WHAT DID YOU JUST DO?

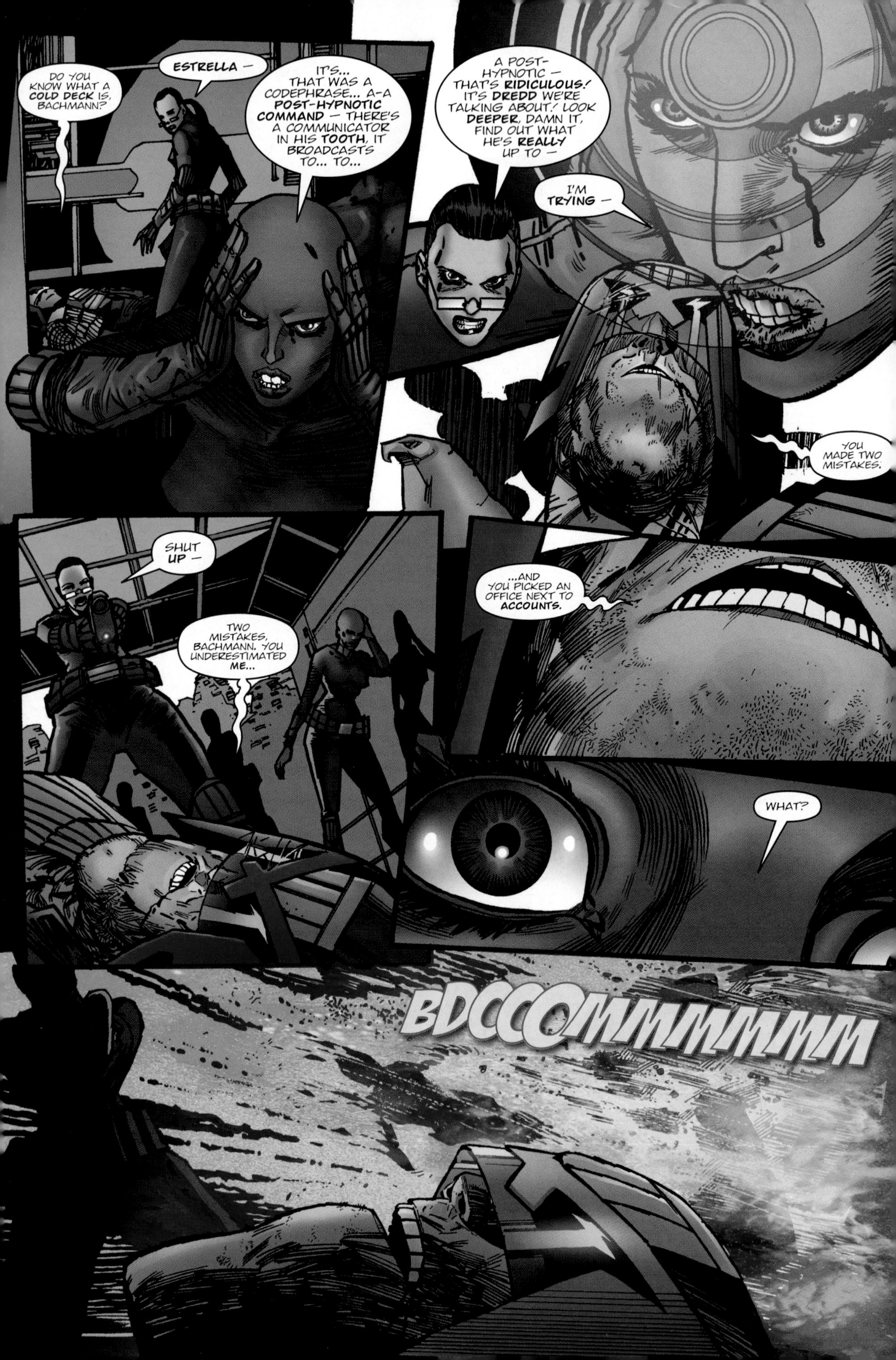
DO YOU KNOW WHAT A COLD DECK IS, BACHMANN?
ESTRELLA —
IT'S... THAT WAS A CODEPHRASE... A-A POST-HYPNOTIC COMMAND — THERE'S A COMMUNICATOR IN HIS TOOTH, IT BROADCASTS TO... TO...
A POST-HYPNOTIC — THAT'S RIDICULOUS! IT'S DREDD WE'RE TALKING ABOUT! LOOK DEEPER, DAMN IT, FIND OUT WHAT HE'S REALLY UP TO —
I'M TRYING —
YOU MADE TWO MISTAKES.
SHUT UP —
TWO MISTAKES, BACHMANN. YOU UNDERESTIMATED ME...
...AND YOU PICKED AN OFFICE NEXT TO ACCOUNTS.
WHAT?
BDCCOMMMMMMM

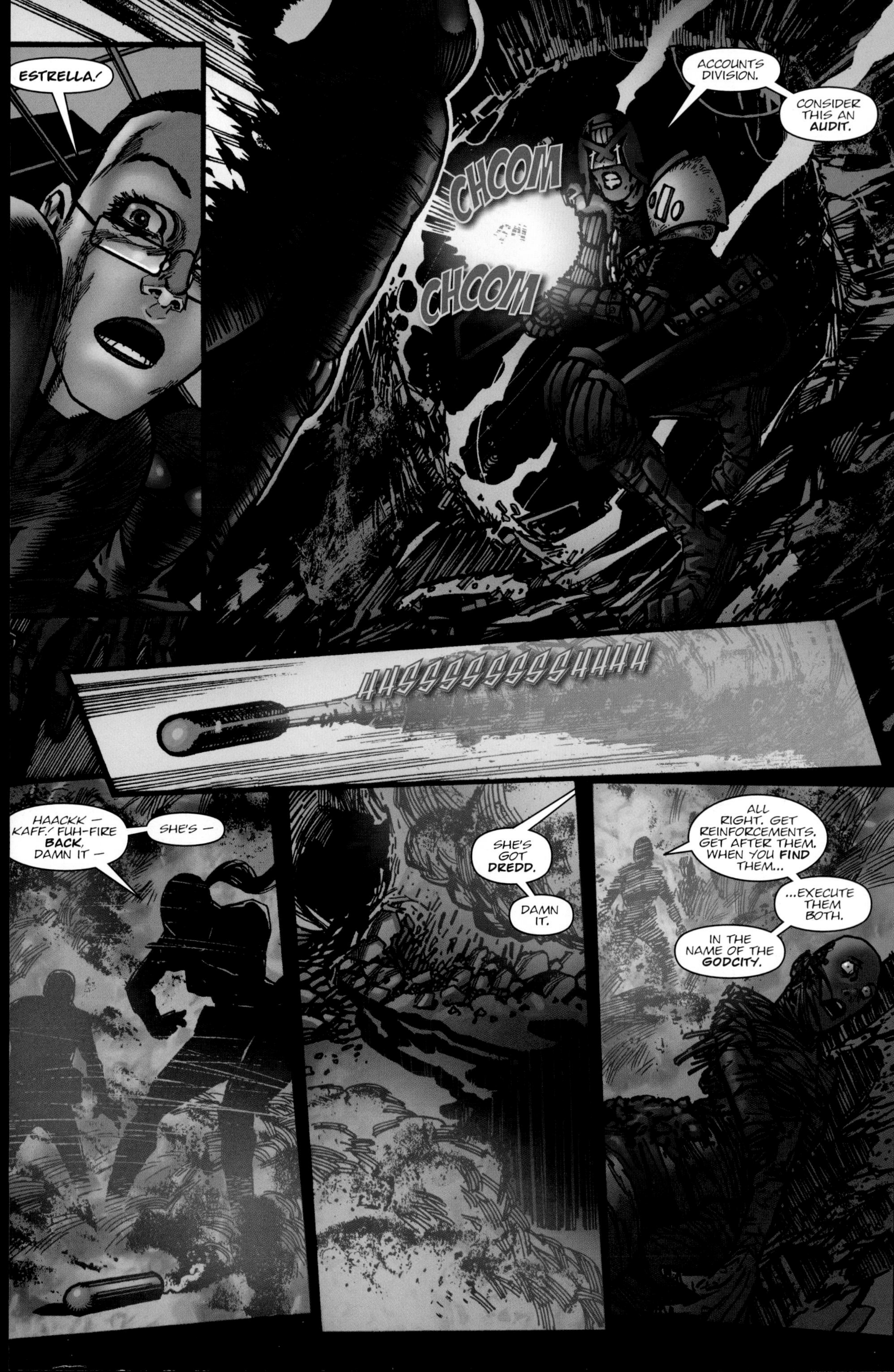
ESTRELLA!
ACCOUNTS DIVISION.
CONSIDER THIS AN AUDIT.
CHCOM
CHCOM
HHSSSSSSSSHHHH
HAACKK — KAFF! FUH-FIRE BACK, DAMN IT —
SHE'S —
SHE'S GOT DREDD.
DAMN IT.
ALL RIGHT. GET REINFORCEMENTS. GET AFTER THEM. WHEN YOU FIND THEM...
...EXECUTE THEM BOTH.
IN THE NAME OF THE GODCITY.

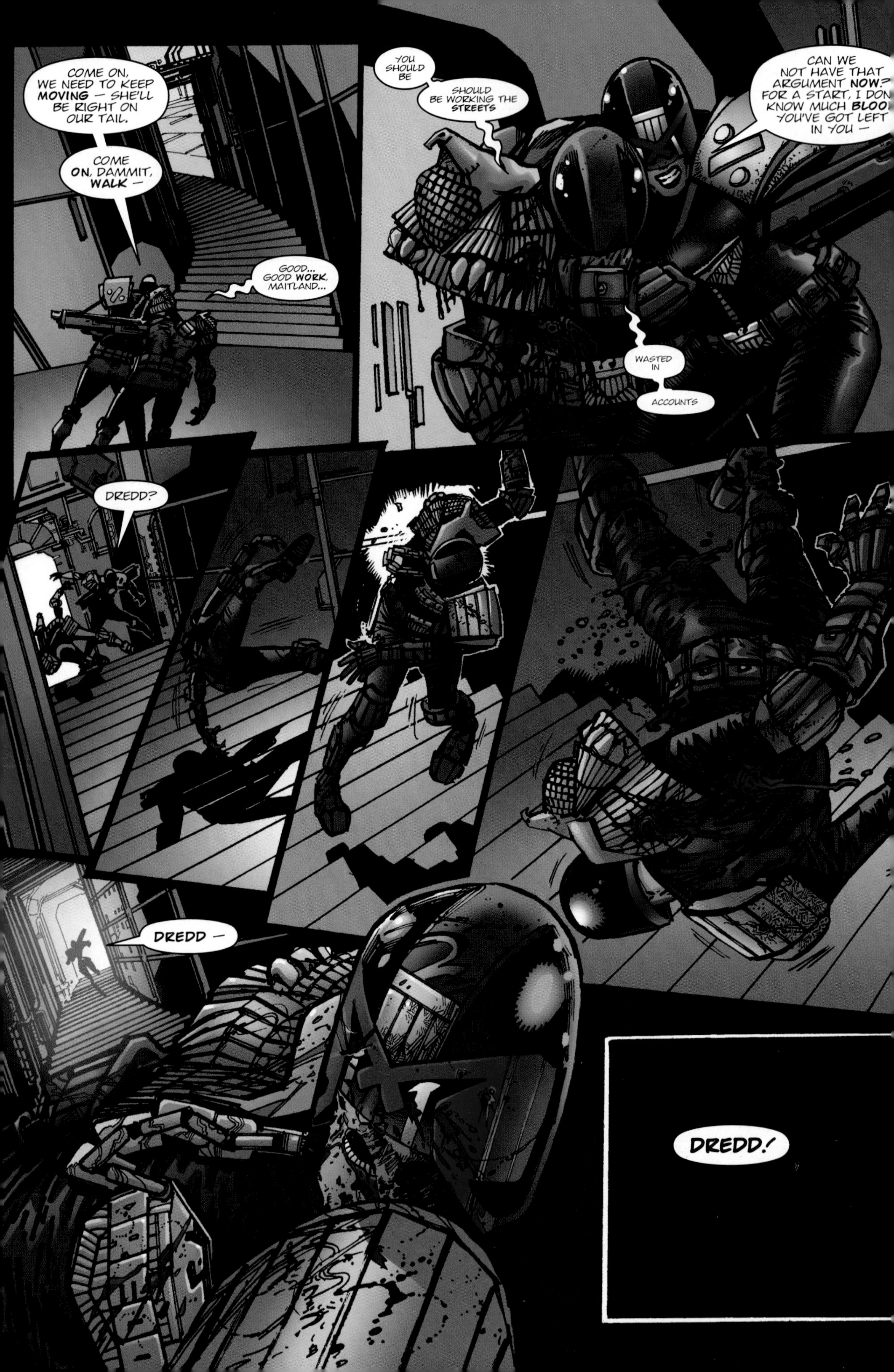
COME ON, WE NEED TO KEEP MOVING — SHE'LL BE RIGHT ON OUR TAIL.
COME ON, DAMMIT, WALK —
GOOD... GOOD WORK, MAITLAND...
YOU SHOULD BE
SHOULD BE WORKING THE STREETS
WASTED IN
ACCOUNTS
CAN WE NOT HAVE THAT ARGUMENT NOW? FOR A START, I DON KNOW MUCH BLOO YOU'VE GOT LEFT IN YOU —
DREDD?
DREDD —
DREDD!

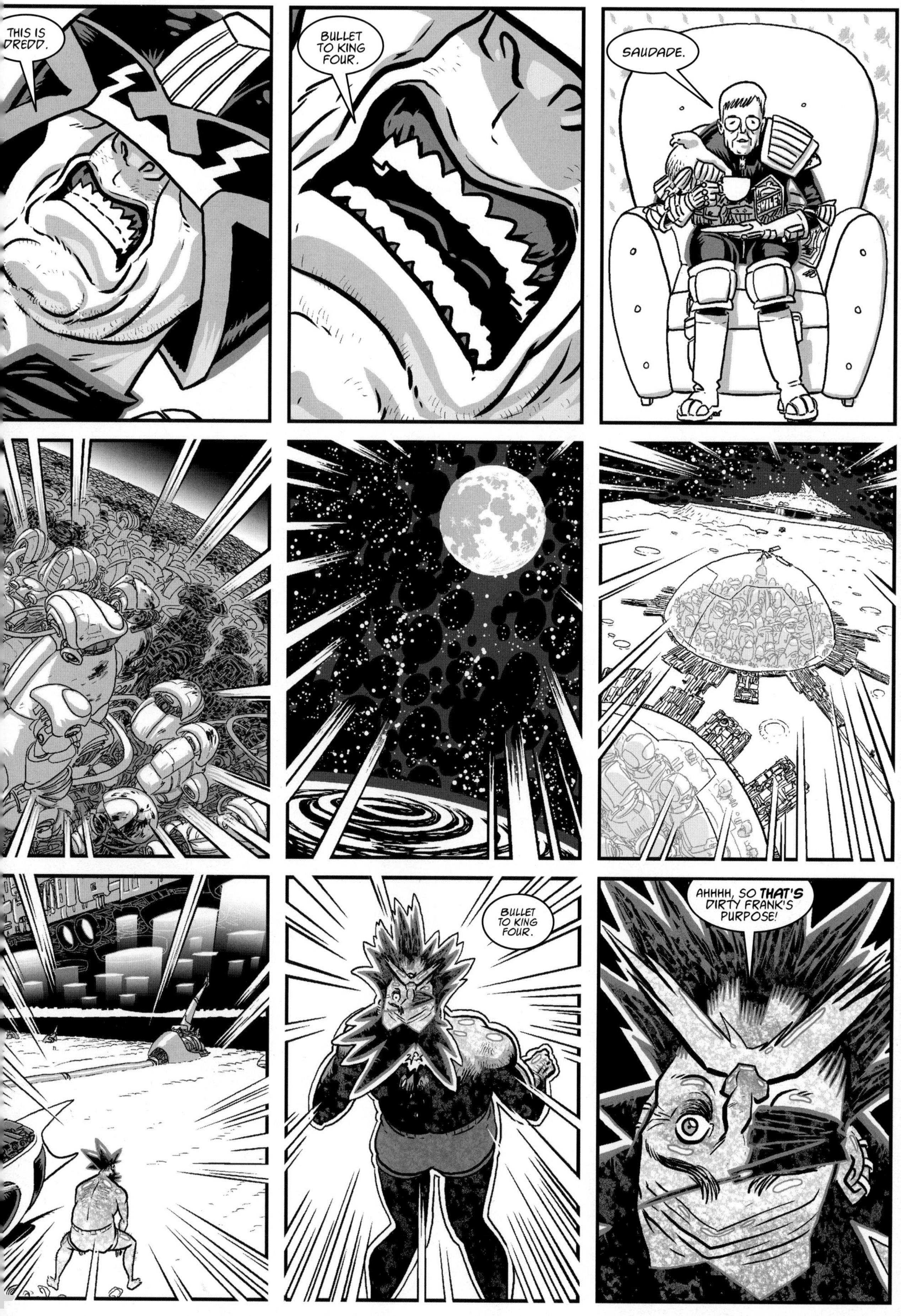
THIS IS DREDD.
BULLET TO KING FOUR.
SAUDADE.
BULLET TO KING FOUR.
AHHHH, SO **THAT'S** DIRTY FRANK'S PURPOSE!

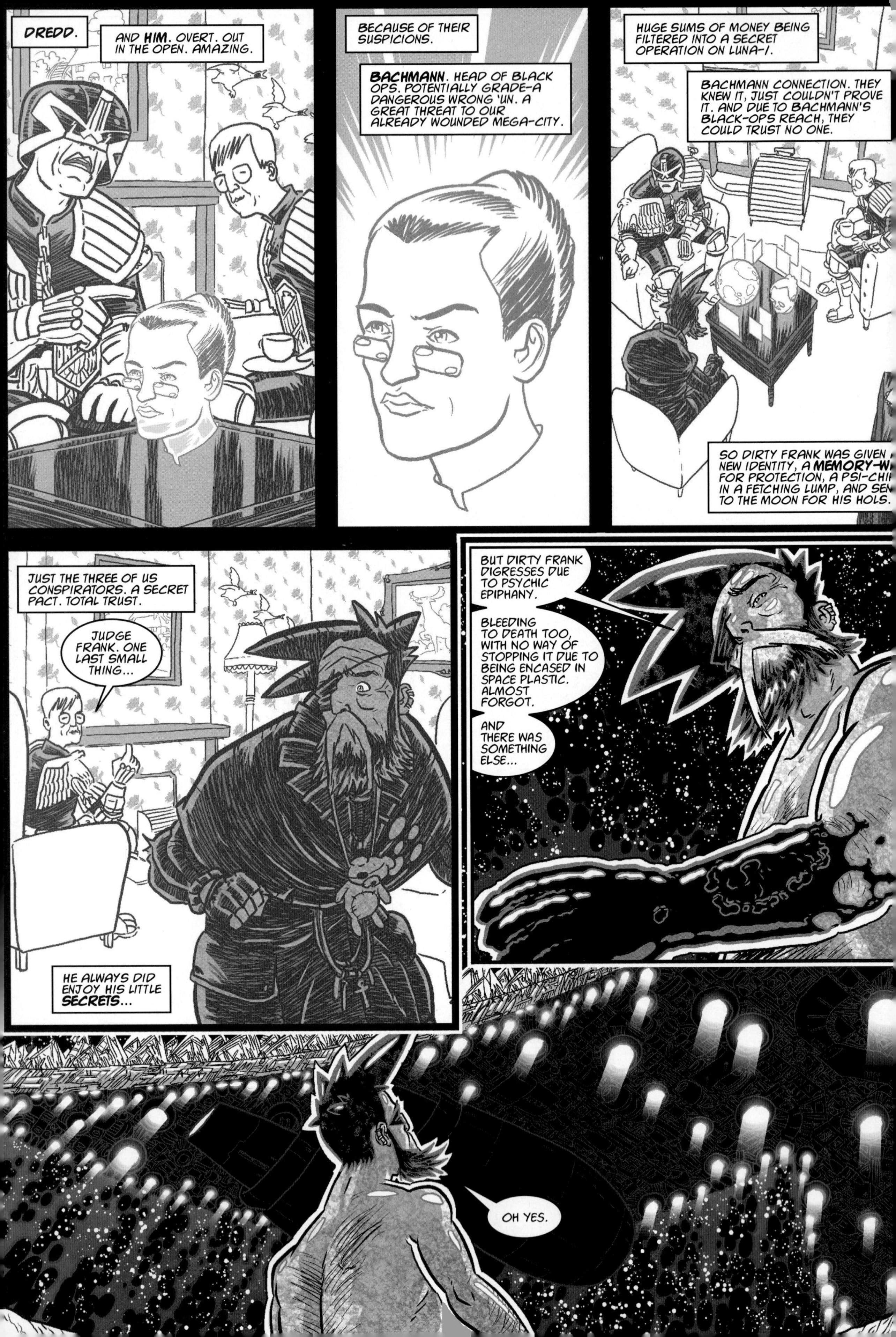
DREDD.
AND HIM. OVERT. OUT IN THE OPEN. AMAZING.
BECAUSE OF THEIR SUSPICIONS.
BACHMANN. HEAD OF BLACK OPS. POTENTIALLY GRADE-A DANGEROUS WRONG 'UN. A GREAT THREAT TO OUR ALREADY WOUNDED MEGA-CITY.
HUGE SUMS OF MONEY BEING FILTERED INTO A SECRET OPERATION ON LUNA-1.
BACHMANN CONNECTION. THEY KNEW IT, JUST COULDN'T PROVE IT. AND DUE TO BACHMANN'S BLACK-OPS REACH, THEY COULD TRUST NO ONE.
SO DIRTY FRANK WAS GIVEN NEW IDENTITY, A MEMORY-W FOR PROTECTION, A PSI-CHI IN A FETCHING LUMP, AND SEN TO THE MOON FOR HIS HOLS.
JUST THE THREE OF US CONSPIRATORS. A SECRET PACT. TOTAL TRUST.
JUDGE FRANK. ONE LAST SMALL THING...
HE ALWAYS DID ENJOY HIS LITTLE SECRETS...
BUT DIRTY FRANK DIGRESSES DUE TO PSYCHIC EPIPHANY.
BLEEDING TO DEATH TOO, WITH NO WAY OF STOPPING IT DUE TO BEING ENCASED IN SPACE PLASTIC. ALMOST FORGOT.
AND THERE WAS SOMETHING ELSE...
OH YES.

WHERE DO YOU THINK THEY'RE OFF TO, THEN?

WITH THEIR GUNS AND THEIR MISSILES AND THEIR BIG ARMY WITH THEIR GUNS AND MISSILES...

DEAR GRUD...

DIDN'T ENOUGH PEOPLE DIE FROM THE CHAOS BUG?

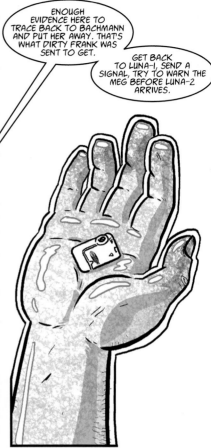

ENOUGH EVIDENCE HERE TO TRACE BACK TO BACHMANN AND PUT HER AWAY. THAT'S WHAT DIRTY FRANK WAS SENT TO GET.

GET BACK TO LUNA-1, SEND A SIGNAL, TRY TO WARN THE MEG BEFORE LUNA-2 ARRIVES.

'WARN' WON'T STOP MISSILES...

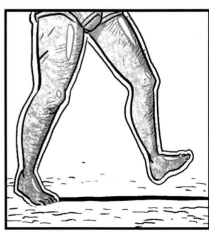

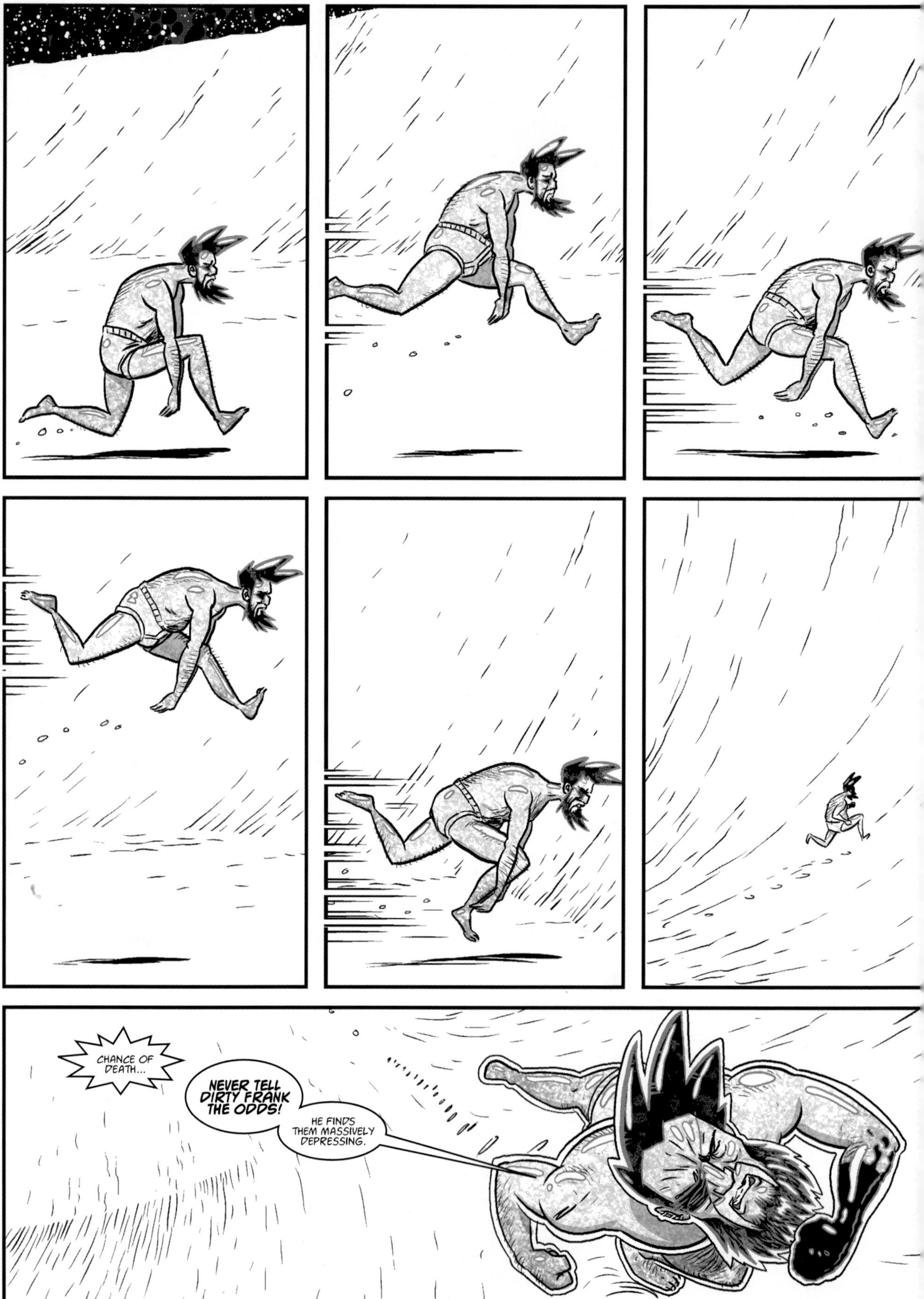
CHANCE OF DEATH...
NEVER TELL DIRTY FRANK THE ODDS!
HE FINDS THEM MASSIVELY DEPRESSING.

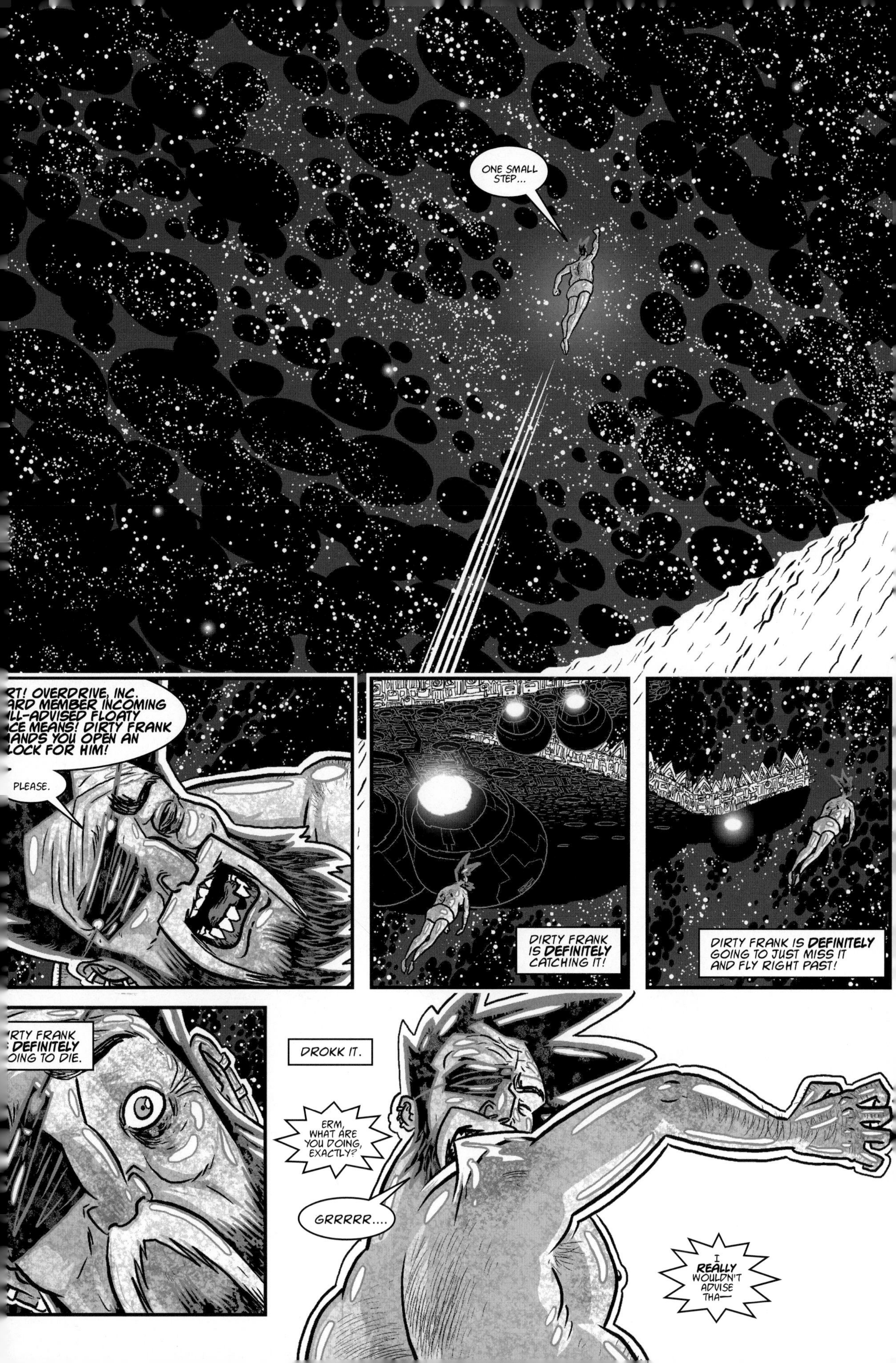

ONE SMALL STEP...
RT! OVERDRIVE, INC. ARD MEMBER INCOMING ILL-ADVISED FLOATY CE MEANS! DIRTY FRANK ANDS YOU OPEN AN LOCK FOR HIM!
PLEASE.
DIRTY FRANK IS DEFINITELY CATCHING IT!
DIRTY FRANK IS DEFINITELY GOING TO JUST MISS IT AND FLY RIGHT PAST!
IRTY FRANK DEFINITELY OING TO DIE.
DROKK IT.
ERM, WHAT ARE YOU DOING, EXACTLY?
GRRRRR....
I REALLY WOULDN'T ADVISE THA—

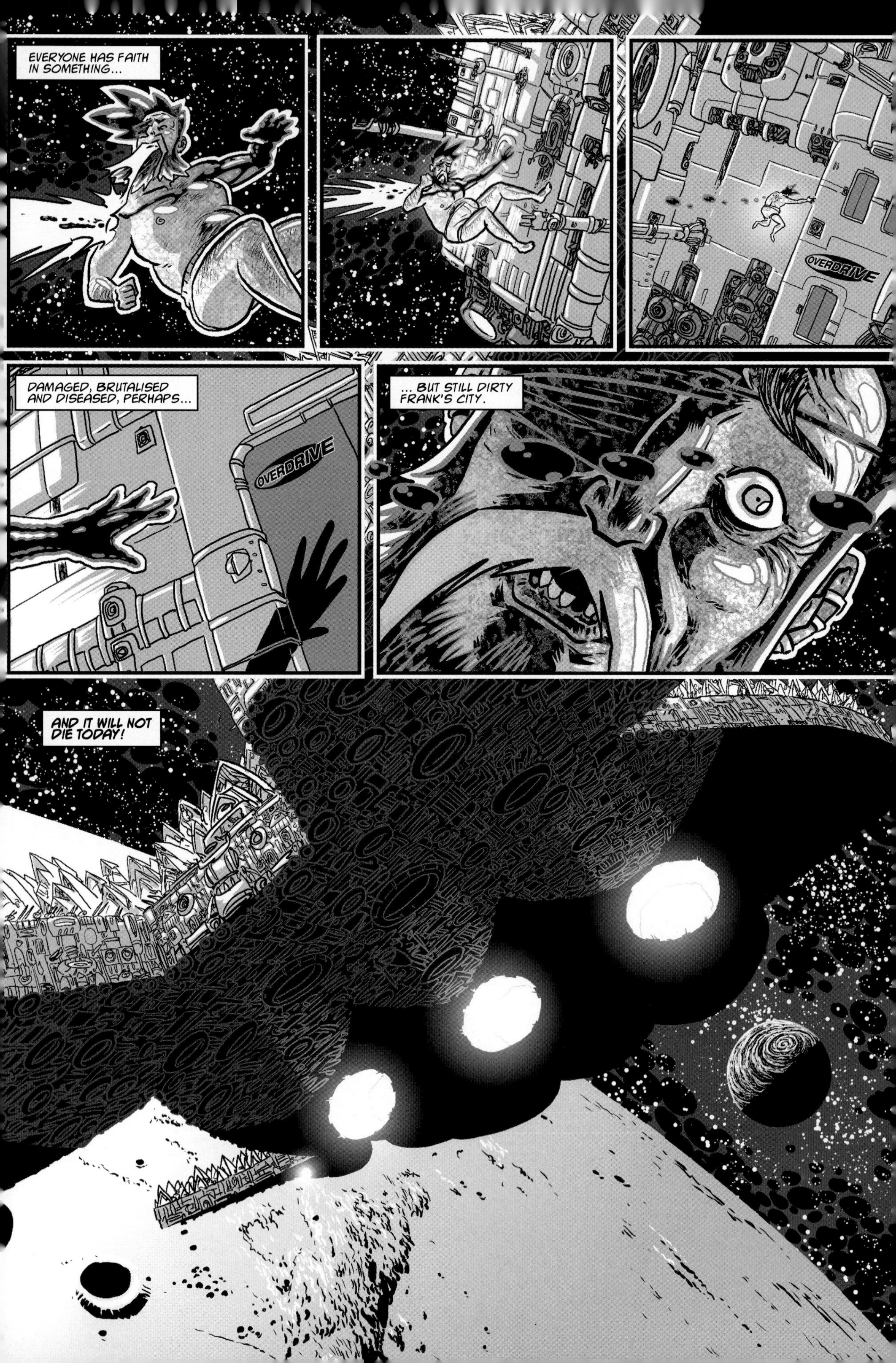
EVERYONE HAS FAITH IN SOMETHING...
OVERDRIVE
DAMAGED, BRUTALISED AND DISEASED, PERHAPS...
OVERDRIVE
... BUT STILL DIRTY FRANK'S CITY.
AND IT WILL NOT DIE TODAY!

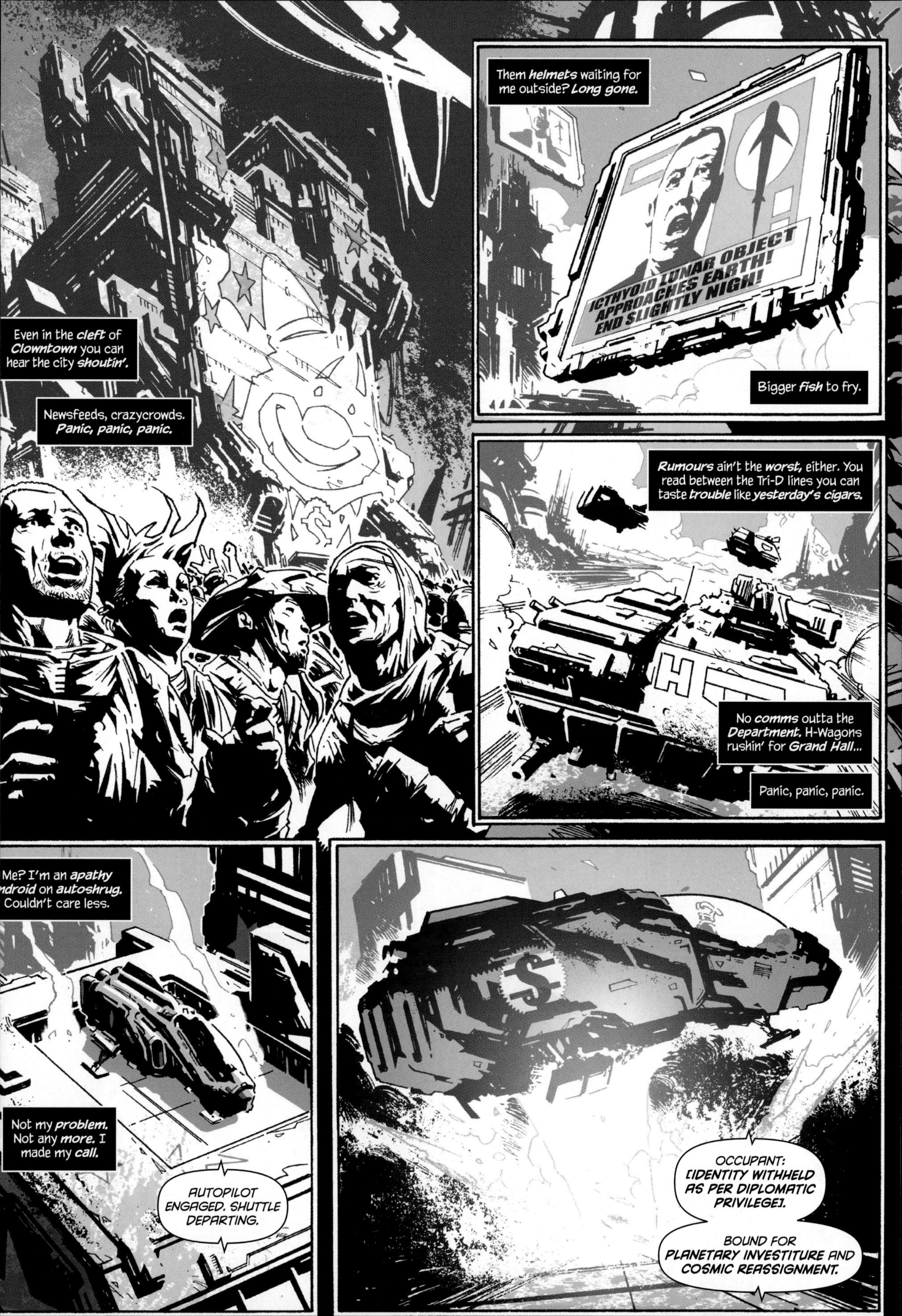
Even in the cleft of Clowntown you can hear the city shoutin'.
Newsfeeds, crazycrowds. Panic, panic, panic.
Them helmets waiting for me outside? Long gone.
ICTHYOID LUNAR OBJECT APPROACHES EARTH! END SLIGHTLY NIGH!
Bigger fish to fry.
Rumours ain't the worst, either. You read between the Tri-D lines you can taste trouble like yesterday's cigars.
No comms outta the Department. H-Wagons rushin' for Grand Hall...
Panic, panic, panic.
Me? I'm an apathy android on autoshrug. Couldn't care less.
Not my problem. Not any more. I made my call.
AUTOPILOT ENGAGED. SHUTTLE DEPARTING.
OCCUPANT: [IDENTITY WITHHELD AS PER DIPLOMATIC PRIVILEGE].
BOUND FOR PLANETARY INVESTITURE AND COSMIC REASSIGNMENT.

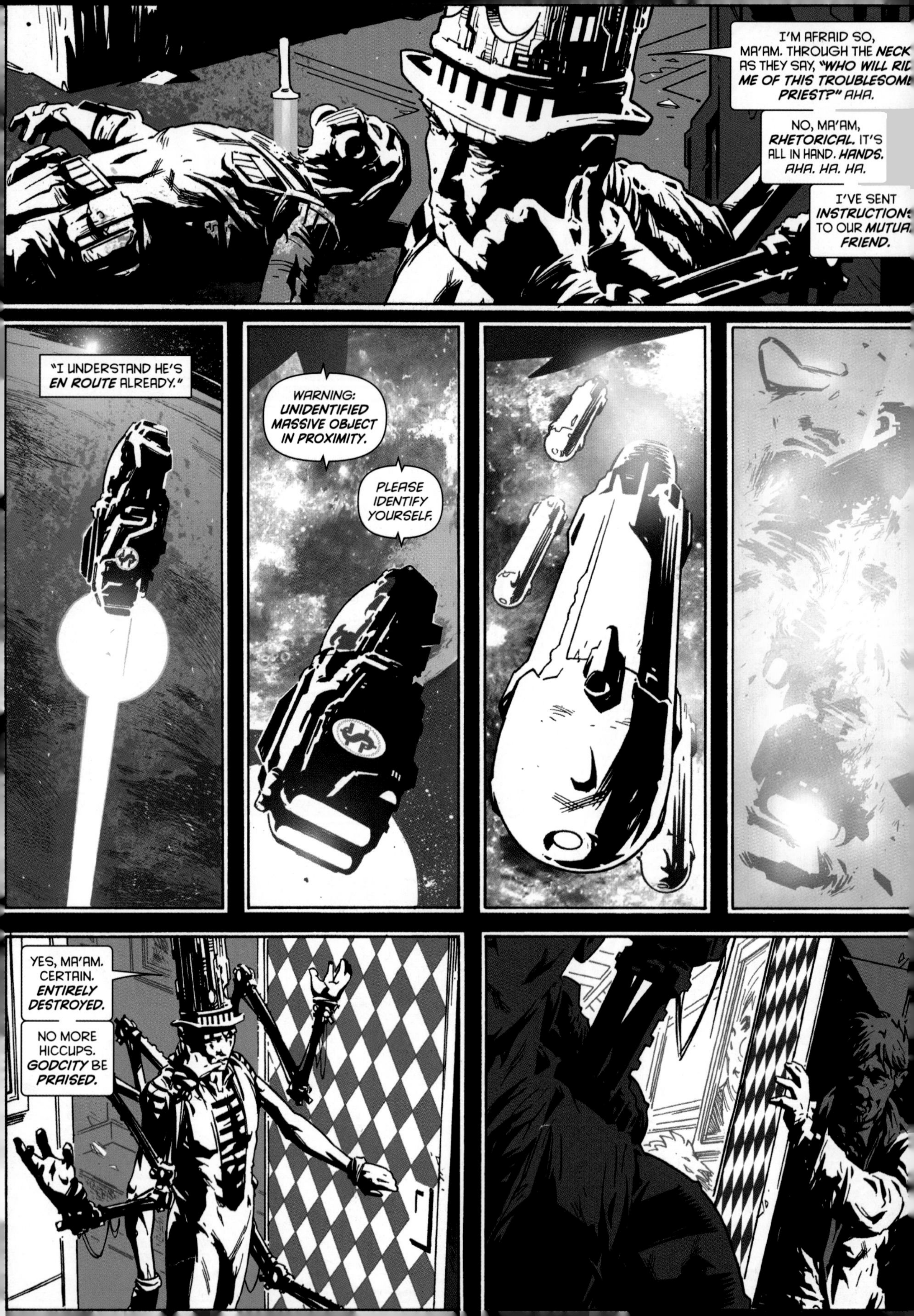

I'M AFRAID SO, MA'AM. THROUGH THE *NECK*. AS THEY SAY, *"WHO WILL RID ME OF THIS TROUBLESOME PRIEST?"* AHA.
NO, MA'AM, *RHETORICAL*. IT'S ALL IN HAND. *HANDS*. AHA. HA. HA.
I'VE SENT *INSTRUCTIONS* TO OUR *MUTUAL FRIEND*.
"I UNDERSTAND HE'S *EN ROUTE* ALREADY."
WARNING: UNIDENTIFIED MASSIVE OBJECT IN PROXIMITY.
PLEASE IDENTIFY YOURSELF.
YES, MA'AM. CERTAIN. *ENTIRELY DESTROYED*.
NO MORE HICCUPS. *GODCITY* BE *PRAISED*.

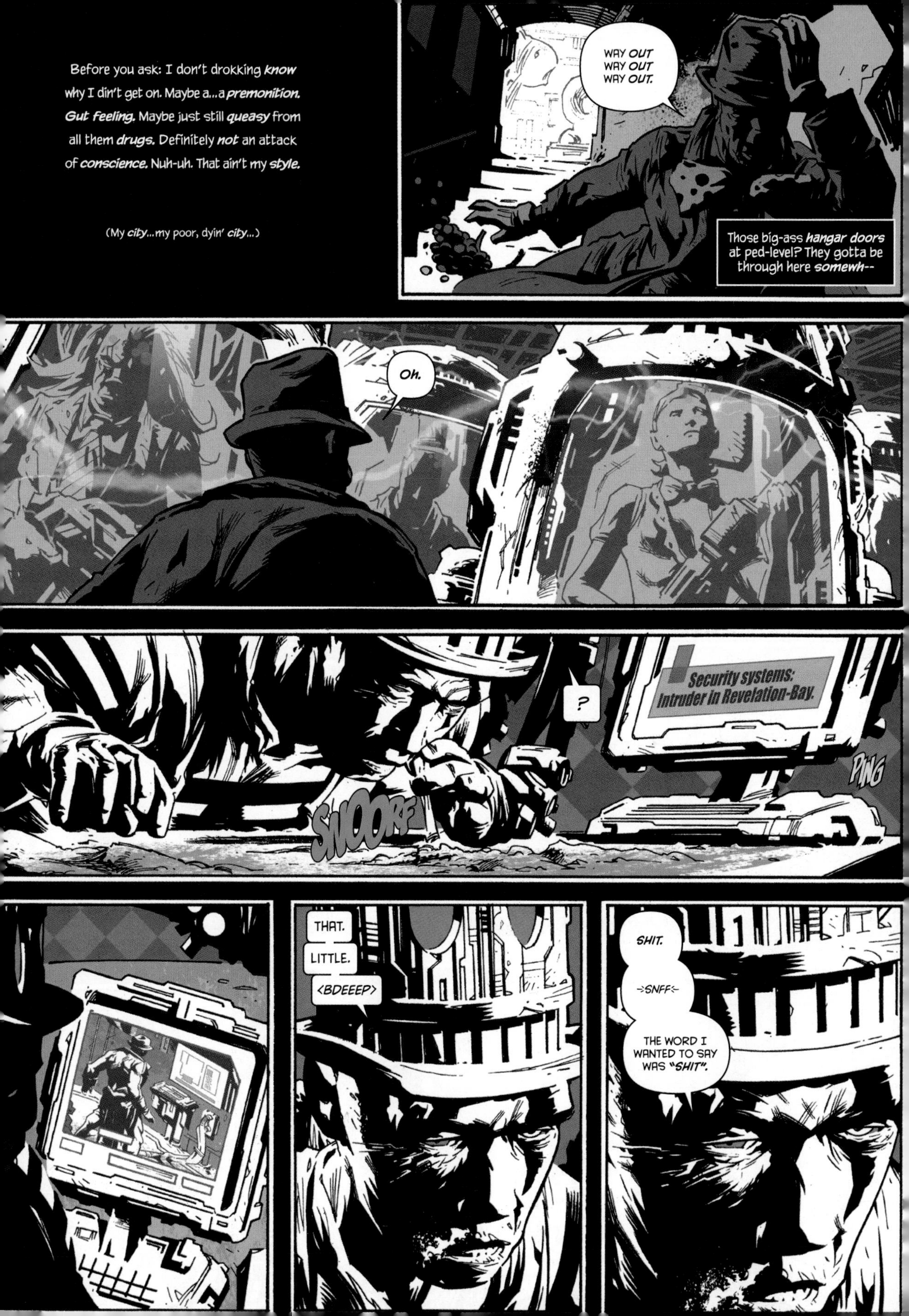
Before you ask: I don't drokking know why I din't get on. Maybe a...a premonition. Gut feeling. Maybe just still queasy from all them drugs. Definitely not an attack of conscience. Nuh-uh. That ain't my style.
(My city...my poor, dyin' city...)
WAY OUT WAY OUT WAY OUT.
Those big-ass hangar doors at ped-level? They gotta be through here somewh--
Oh.
?
Security systems: Intruder in Revelation-Bay.
PING
SNOORF
THAT.
LITTLE.
<BDEEEP>
SHIT.
SNFF
THE WORD I WANTED TO SAY WAS "SHIT".

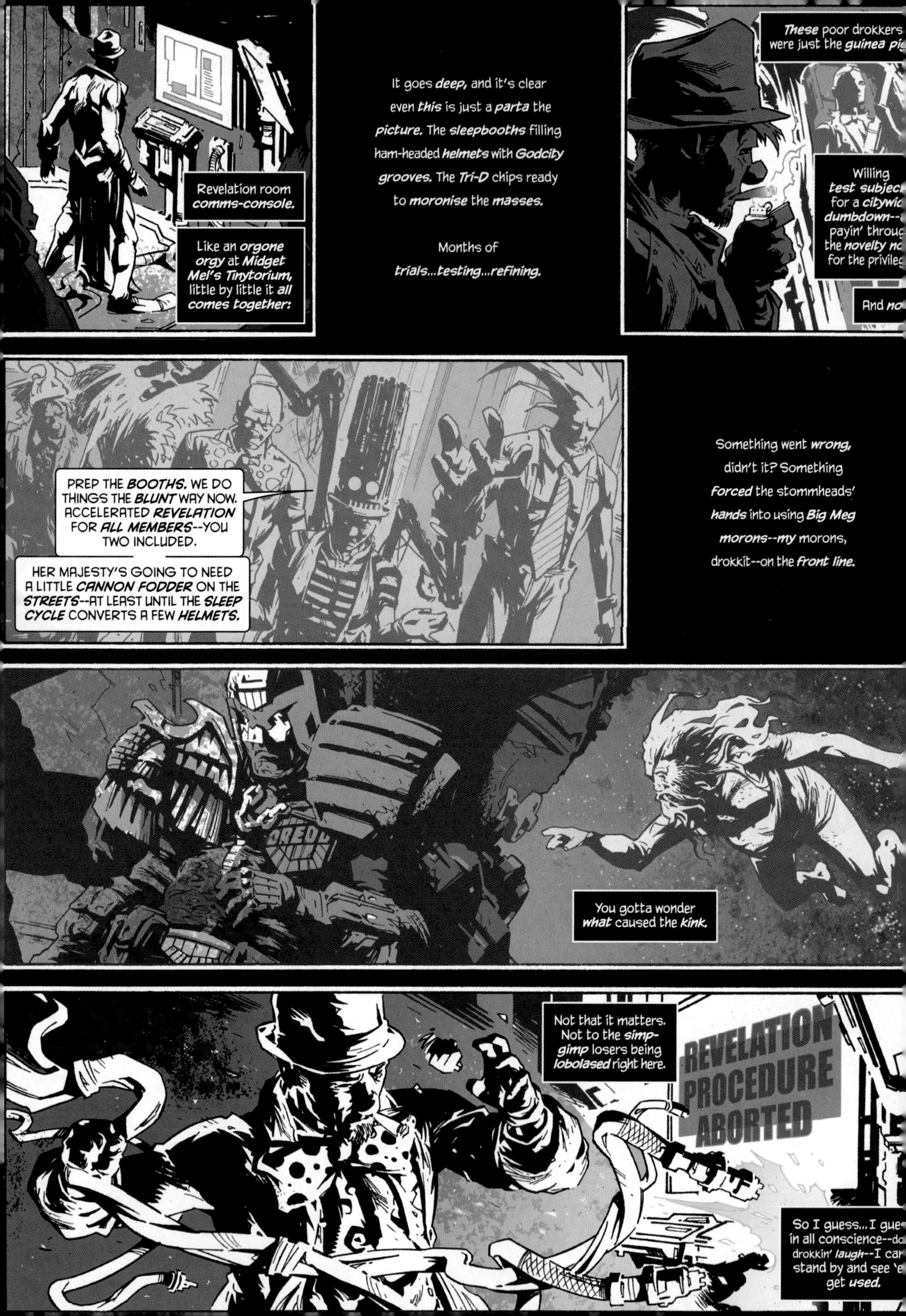

Revelation room comms-console.
Like an orgone orgy at Midget Mel's Tinytorium, little by little it all comes together:
It goes deep, and it's clear even this is just a parta the picture. The sleepbooths filling ham-headed helmets with Godcity grooves. The Tri-D chips ready to moronise the masses.
Months of trials...testing...refining.
These poor drokkers were just the guinea pi
Willing test subjec for a citywi dumbdown-- payin' throug the novelty n for the privileg
And no
PREP THE BOOTHS. WE DO THINGS THE BLUNT WAY NOW. ACCELERATED REVELATION FOR ALL MEMBERS--YOU TWO INCLUDED.
HER MAJESTY'S GOING TO NEED A LITTLE CANNON FODDER ON THE STREETS--AT LEAST UNTIL THE SLEEP CYCLE CONVERTS A FEW HELMETS.
Something went wrong, didn't it? Something forced the stommheads' hands into using Big Meg morons--my morons, drokkit--on the front line.
DREDD
You gotta wonder what caused the kink.
Not that it matters. Not to the simp-gimp losers being lobolased right here.
REVELATION PROCEDURE ABORTED
So I guess...I gue in all conscience--d drokkin' laugh--I ca stand by and see 'e get used.

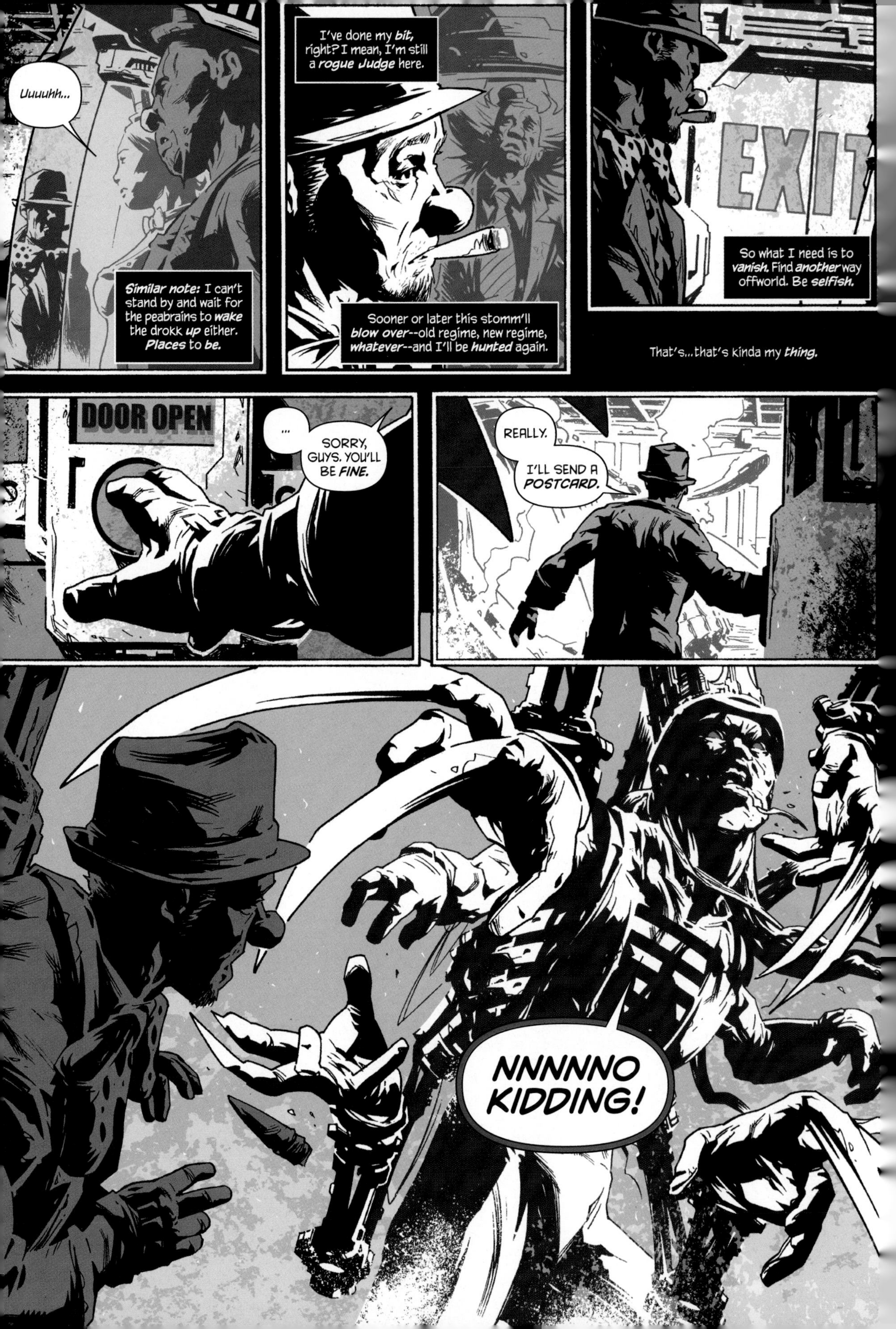
Uuuuhh...
Similar note: I can't stand by and wait for the peabrains to wake the drokk up either. Places to be.
I've done my bit, right? I mean, I'm still a rogue Judge here.
Sooner or later this storm'll blow over--old regime, new regime, whatever--and I'll be hunted again.
EXIT
So what I need is to vanish. Find another way offworld. Be selfish.
That's...that's kinda my thing.
DOOR OPEN
...
SORRY, GUYS. YOU'LL BE FINE.
REALLY.
I'LL SEND A POSTCARD.
NNNNNO KIDDING!

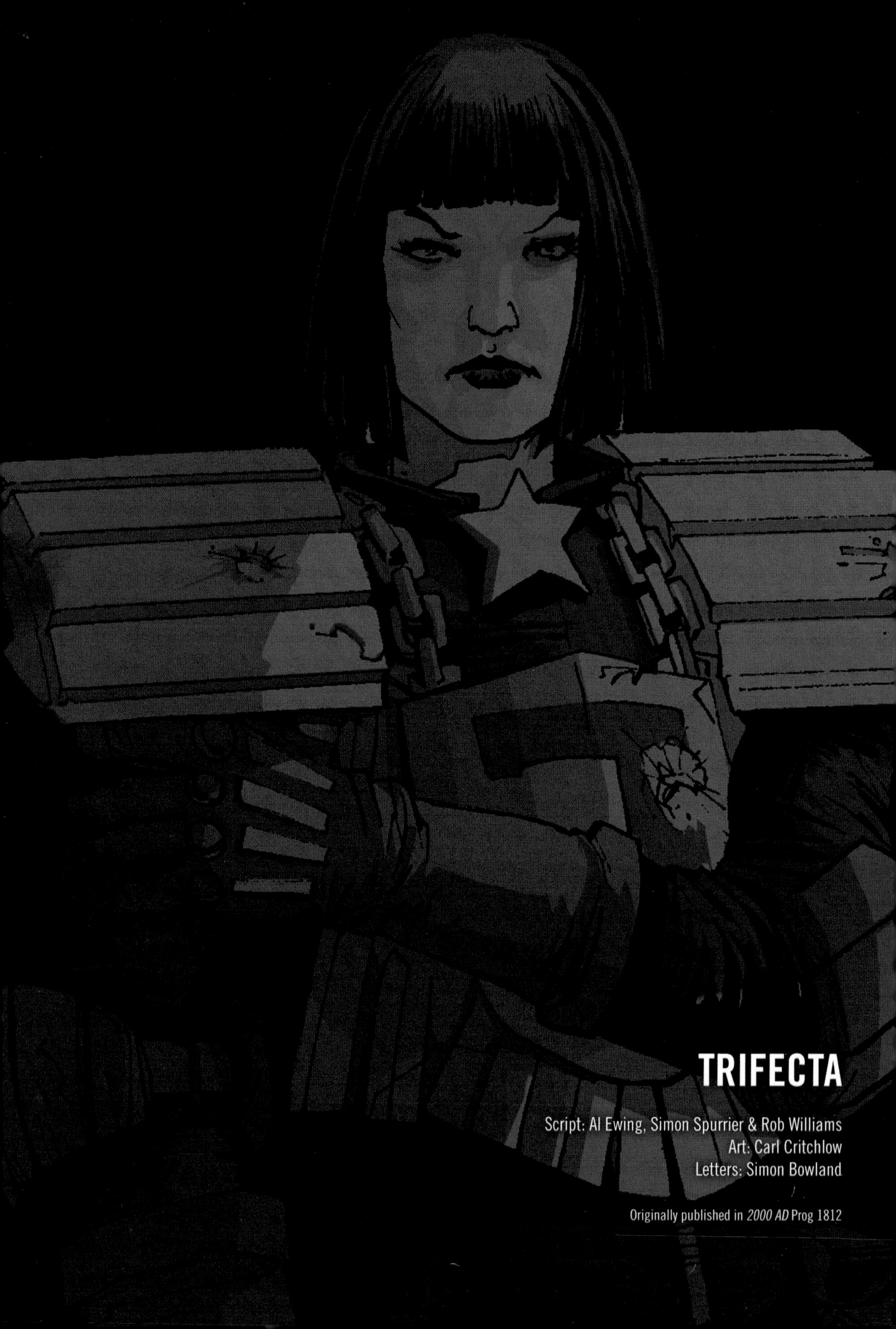

TRIFECTA

Script: Al Ewing, Simon Spurrier & Rob Williams
Art: Carl Critchlow
Letters: Simon Bowland

Originally published in *2000 AD* Prog 1812

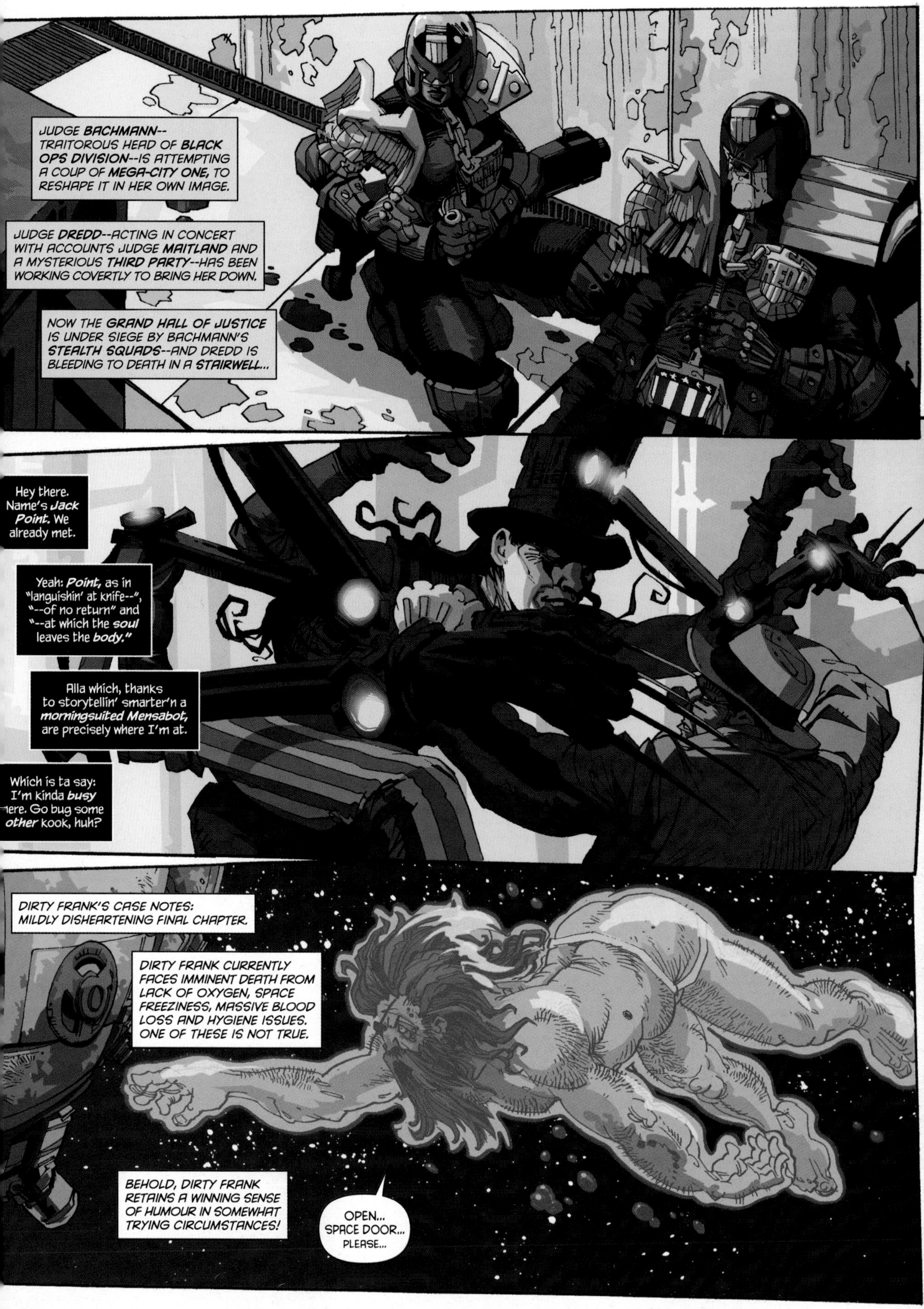

JUDGE BACHMANN--TRAITOROUS HEAD OF BLACK OPS DIVISION--IS ATTEMPTING A COUP OF MEGA-CITY ONE, TO RESHAPE IT IN HER OWN IMAGE.
JUDGE DREDD--ACTING IN CONCERT WITH ACCOUNTS JUDGE MAITLAND AND A MYSTERIOUS THIRD PARTY--HAS BEEN WORKING COVERTLY TO BRING HER DOWN.
NOW THE GRAND HALL OF JUSTICE IS UNDER SIEGE BY BACHMANN'S STEALTH SQUADS--AND DREDD IS BLEEDING TO DEATH IN A STAIRWELL...
Hey there. Name's Jack Point. We already met.
Yeah: Point, as in "languishin' at knife--", "--of no return" and "--at which the soul leaves the body."
Alla which, thanks to storytellin' smarter'n a morningsuited Mensabot, are precisely where I'm at.
Which is ta say: I'm kinda busy here. Go bug some other kook, huh?
DIRTY FRANK'S CASE NOTES: MILDLY DISHEARTENING FINAL CHAPTER.
DIRTY FRANK CURRENTLY FACES IMMINENT DEATH FROM LACK OF OXYGEN, SPACE FREEZINESS, MASSIVE BLOOD LOSS AND HYGIENE ISSUES. ONE OF THESE IS NOT TRUE.
BEHOLD, DIRTY FRANK RETAINS A WINNING SENSE OF HUMOUR IN SOMEWHAT TRYING CIRCUMSTANCES!
OPEN... SPACE DOOR... PLEASE...

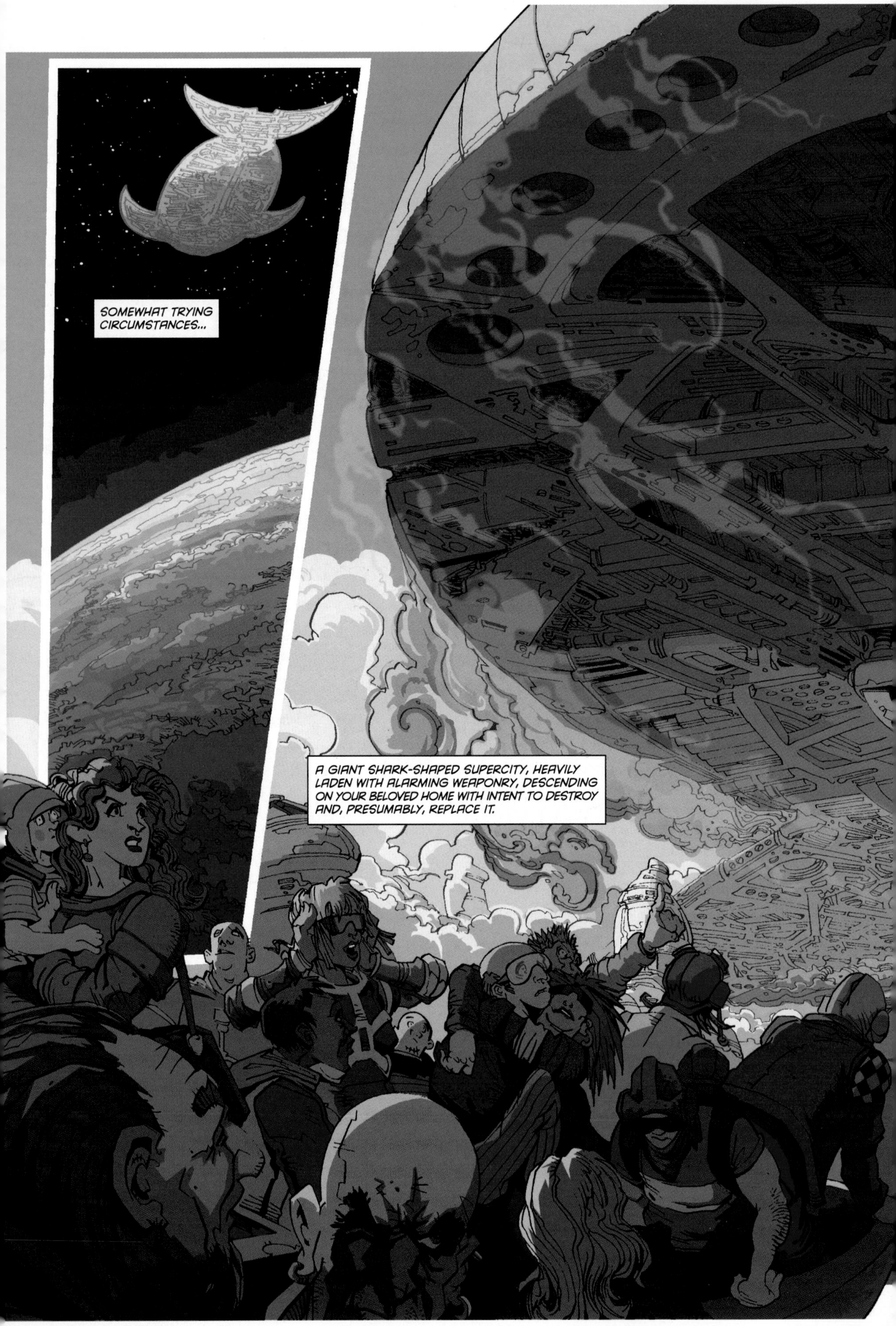
SOMEWHAT TRYING CIRCUMSTANCES...
A GIANT SHARK-SHAPED SUPERCITY, HEAVILY LADEN WITH ALARMING WEAPONRY, DESCENDING ON YOUR BELOVED HOME WITH INTENT TO DESTROY AND, PRESUMABLY, REPLACE IT.

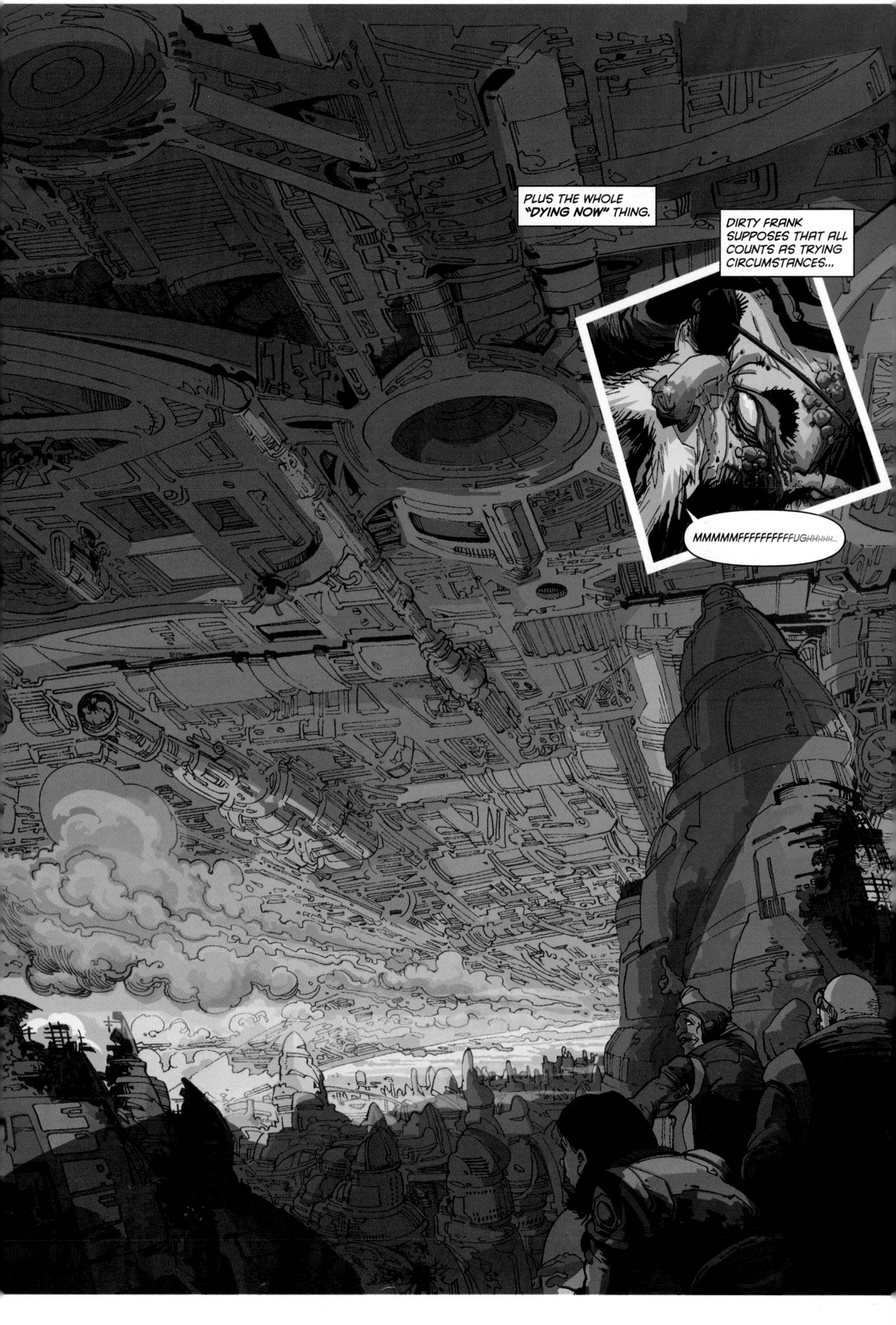
PLUS THE WHOLE "DYING NOW" THING.
DIRTY FRANK SUPPOSES THAT ALL COUNTS AS TRYING CIRCUMSTANCES...
MMMMMFFFFFFFFFFUGHHHHH...

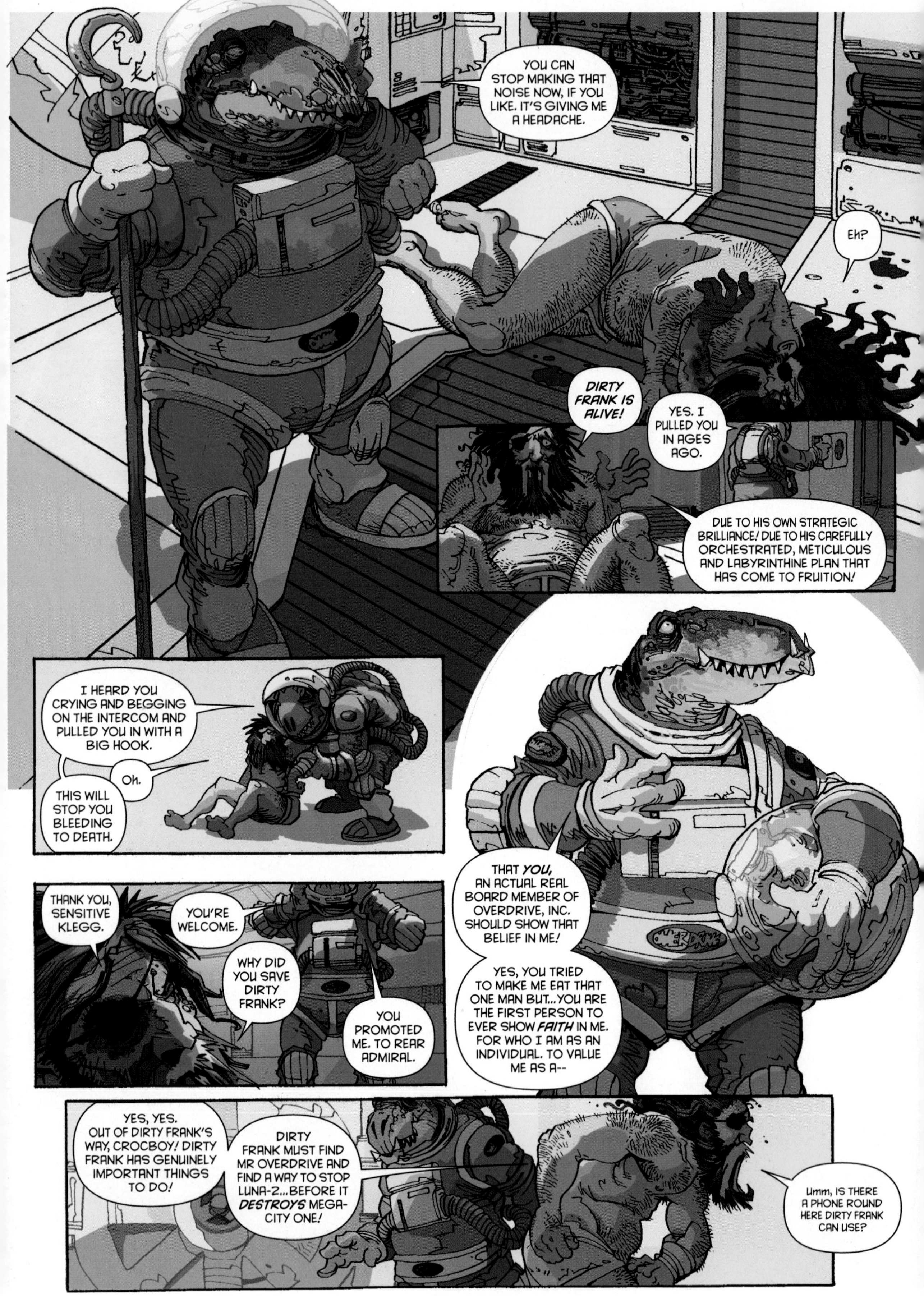
YOU CAN STOP MAKING THAT NOISE NOW, IF YOU LIKE. IT'S GIVING ME A HEADACHE.
Eh?
DIRTY FRANK IS ALIVE!
YES. I PULLED YOU IN AGES AGO.
DUE TO HIS OWN STRATEGIC BRILLIANCE! DUE TO HIS CAREFULLY ORCHESTRATED, METICULOUS AND LABYRINTHINE PLAN THAT HAS COME TO FRUITION!
I HEARD YOU CRYING AND BEGGING ON THE INTERCOM AND PULLED YOU IN WITH A BIG HOOK.
Oh.
THIS WILL STOP YOU BLEEDING TO DEATH.
THANK YOU, SENSITIVE KLEGG.
YOU'RE WELCOME.
WHY DID YOU SAVE DIRTY FRANK?
YOU PROMOTED ME. TO REAR ADMIRAL.
THAT YOU, AN ACTUAL REAL BOARD MEMBER OF OVERDRIVE, INC. SHOULD SHOW THAT BELIEF IN ME!
YES, YOU TRIED TO MAKE ME EAT THAT ONE MAN BUT...YOU ARE THE FIRST PERSON TO EVER SHOW FAITH IN ME. FOR WHO I AM AS AN INDIVIDUAL. TO VALUE ME AS A--
YES, YES. OUT OF DIRTY FRANK'S WAY, CROCBOY! DIRTY FRANK HAS GENUINELY IMPORTANT THINGS TO DO!
DIRTY FRANK MUST FIND MR OVERDRIVE AND FIND A WAY TO STOP LUNA-2...BEFORE IT DESTROYS MEGA-CITY ONE!
Umm, IS THERE A PHONE ROUND HERE DIRTY FRANK CAN USE?

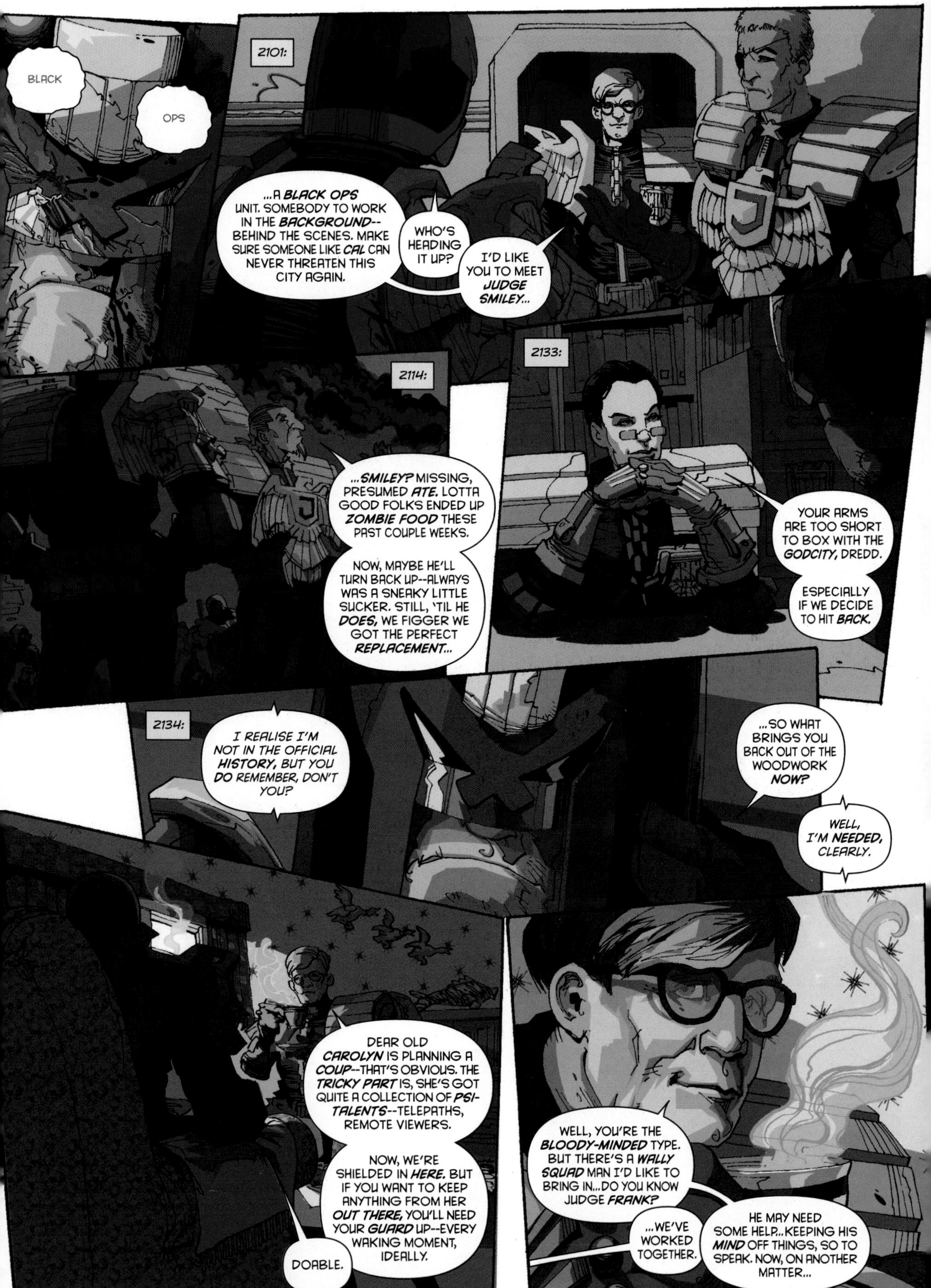
BLACK
OPS
2101:
...A BLACK OPS UNIT. SOMEBODY TO WORK IN THE BACKGROUND-- BEHIND THE SCENES. MAKE SURE SOMEONE LIKE CAL CAN NEVER THREATEN THIS CITY AGAIN.
WHO'S HEADING IT UP?
I'D LIKE YOU TO MEET JUDGE SMILEY...
2114:
...SMILEY? MISSING, PRESUMED ATE. LOTTA GOOD FOLKS ENDED UP ZOMBIE FOOD THESE PAST COUPLE WEEKS.
NOW, MAYBE HE'LL TURN BACK UP--ALWAYS WAS A SNEAKY LITTLE SUCKER. STILL, 'TIL HE DOES, WE FIGGER WE GOT THE PERFECT REPLACEMENT...
2133:
YOUR ARMS ARE TOO SHORT TO BOX WITH THE GODCITY, DREDD.
ESPECIALLY IF WE DECIDE TO HIT BACK.
2134:
I REALISE I'M NOT IN THE OFFICIAL HISTORY, BUT YOU DO REMEMBER, DON'T YOU?
...SO WHAT BRINGS YOU BACK OUT OF THE WOODWORK NOW?
WELL, I'M NEEDED, CLEARLY.
DEAR OLD CAROLYN IS PLANNING A COUP--THAT'S OBVIOUS. THE TRICKY PART IS, SHE'S GOT QUITE A COLLECTION OF PSI-TALENTS--TELEPATHS, REMOTE VIEWERS.
NOW, WE'RE SHIELDED IN HERE. BUT IF YOU WANT TO KEEP ANYTHING FROM HER OUT THERE, YOU'LL NEED YOUR GUARD UP--EVERY WAKING MOMENT, IDEALLY.
DOABLE.
WELL, YOU'RE THE BLOODY-MINDED TYPE. BUT THERE'S A WALLY SQUAD MAN I'D LIKE TO BRING IN...DO YOU KNOW JUDGE FRANK?
...WE'VE WORKED TOGETHER.
HE MAY NEED SOME HELP...KEEPING HIS MIND OFF THINGS, SO TO SPEAK. NOW, ON ANOTHER MATTER...

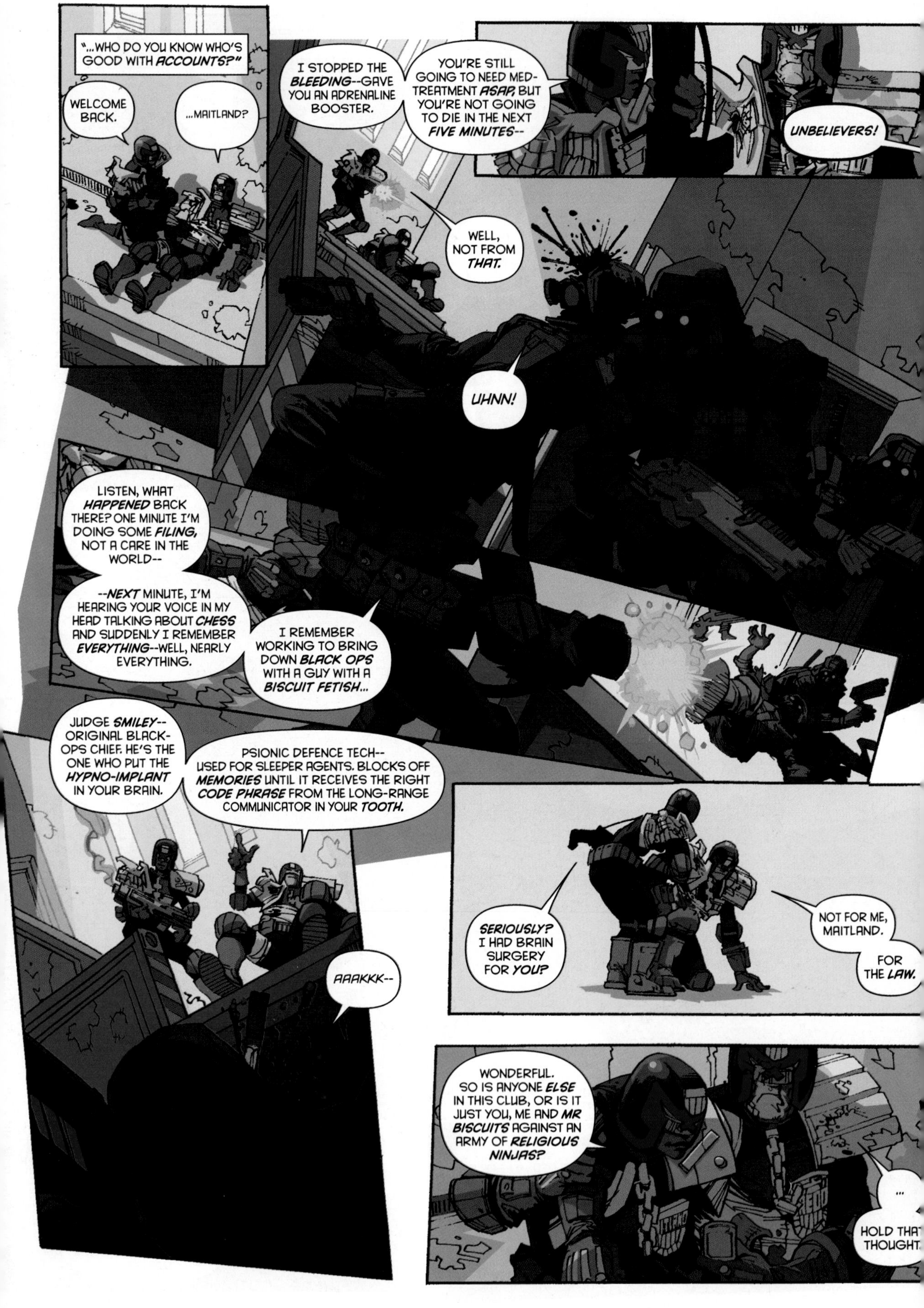
"...WHO DO YOU KNOW WHO'S GOOD WITH ACCOUNTS?"
WELCOME BACK.
...MAITLAND?
I STOPPED THE BLEEDING--GAVE YOU AN ADRENALINE BOOSTER.
YOU'RE STILL GOING TO NEED MED-TREATMENT ASAP, BUT YOU'RE NOT GOING TO DIE IN THE NEXT FIVE MINUTES--
UNBELIEVERS!
WELL, NOT FROM THAT.
UHNN!
LISTEN, WHAT HAPPENED BACK THERE? ONE MINUTE I'M DOING SOME FILING, NOT A CARE IN THE WORLD--
--NEXT MINUTE, I'M HEARING YOUR VOICE IN MY HEAD TALKING ABOUT CHESS AND SUDDENLY I REMEMBER EVERYTHING--WELL, NEARLY EVERYTHING.
I REMEMBER WORKING TO BRING DOWN BLACK OPS WITH A GUY WITH A BISCUIT FETISH...
JUDGE SMILEY--ORIGINAL BLACK-OPS CHIEF. HE'S THE ONE WHO PUT THE HYPNO-IMPLANT IN YOUR BRAIN.
PSIONIC DEFENCE TECH--USED FOR SLEEPER AGENTS. BLOCKS OFF MEMORIES UNTIL IT RECEIVES THE RIGHT CODE PHRASE FROM THE LONG-RANGE COMMUNICATOR IN YOUR TOOTH.
AAAKKK--
SERIOUSLY? I HAD BRAIN SURGERY FOR YOU?
NOT FOR ME, MAITLAND.
FOR THE LAW.
WONDERFUL. SO IS ANYONE ELSE IN THIS CLUB, OR IS IT JUST YOU, ME AND MR BISCUITS AGAINST AN ARMY OF RELIGIOUS NINJAS?
...
HOLD THAT THOUGHT.

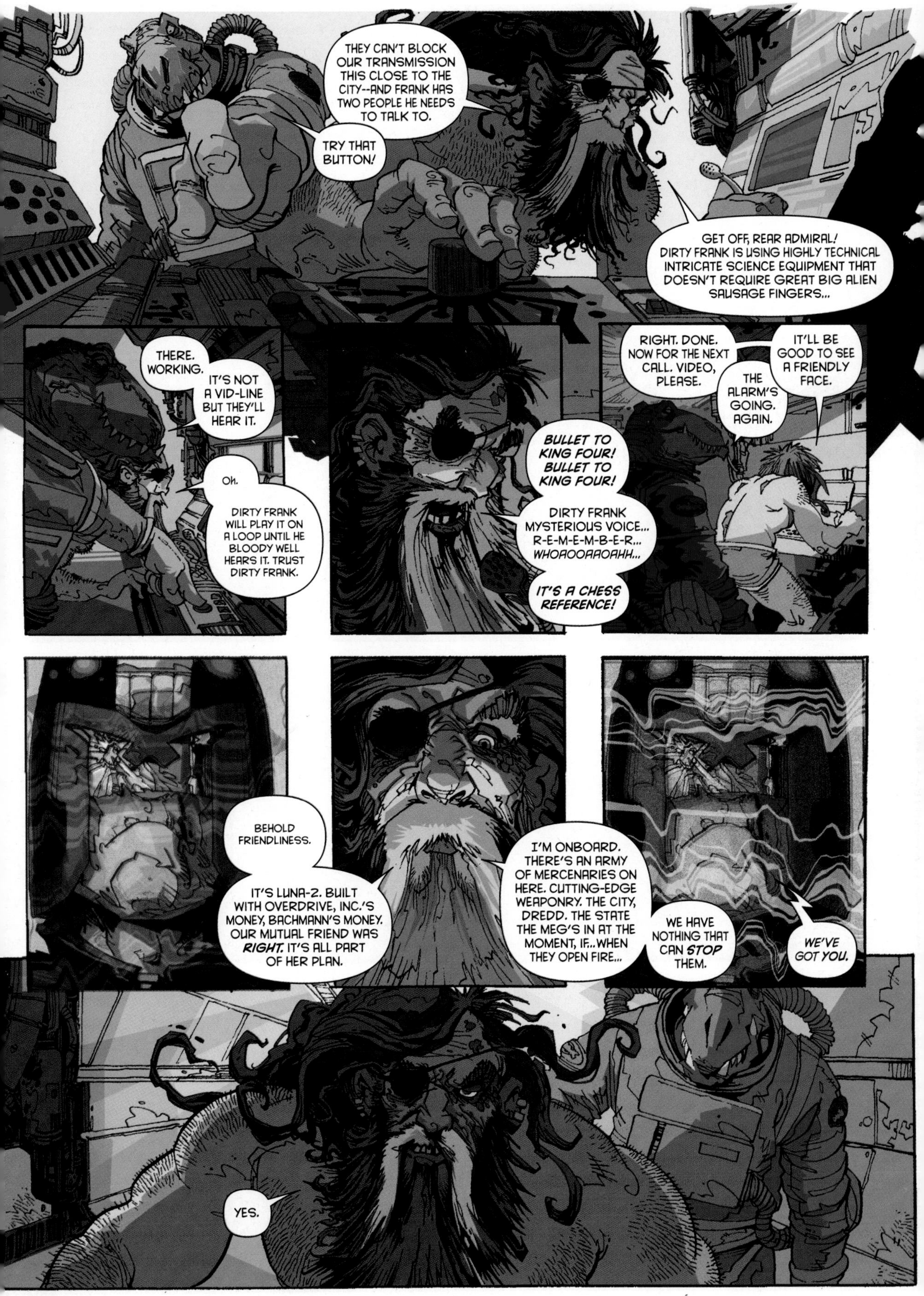
THEY CAN'T BLOCK OUR TRANSMISSION THIS CLOSE TO THE CITY--AND FRANK HAS TWO PEOPLE HE NEEDS TO TALK TO.
TRY THAT BUTTON!
GET OFF, REAR ADMIRAL! DIRTY FRANK IS USING HIGHLY TECHNICAL INTRICATE SCIENCE EQUIPMENT THAT DOESN'T REQUIRE GREAT BIG ALIEN SAUSAGE FINGERS...
THERE. WORKING.
IT'S NOT A VID-LINE BUT THEY'LL HEAR IT.
Oh.
DIRTY FRANK WILL PLAY IT ON A LOOP UNTIL HE BLOODY WELL HEARS IT. TRUST DIRTY FRANK.
BULLET TO KING FOUR! BULLET TO KING FOUR!
DIRTY FRANK MYSTERIOUS VOICE... R-E-M-E-M-B-E-R... WHOAOORAOAHH...
IT'S A CHESS REFERENCE!
RIGHT. DONE. NOW FOR THE NEXT CALL. VIDEO, PLEASE.
IT'LL BE GOOD TO SEE A FRIENDLY FACE.
THE ALARM'S GOING. AGAIN.
BEHOLD FRIENDLINESS.
IT'S LUNA-2. BUILT WITH OVERDRIVE, INC.'S MONEY, BACHMANN'S MONEY. OUR MUTUAL FRIEND WAS RIGHT. IT'S ALL PART OF HER PLAN.
I'M ONBOARD. THERE'S AN ARMY OF MERCENARIES ON HERE. CUTTING-EDGE WEAPONRY. THE CITY, DREDD. THE STATE THE MEG'S IN AT THE MOMENT, IF...WHEN THEY OPEN FIRE...
WE HAVE NOTHING THAT CAN STOP THEM.
WE'VE GOT YOU.
YES.

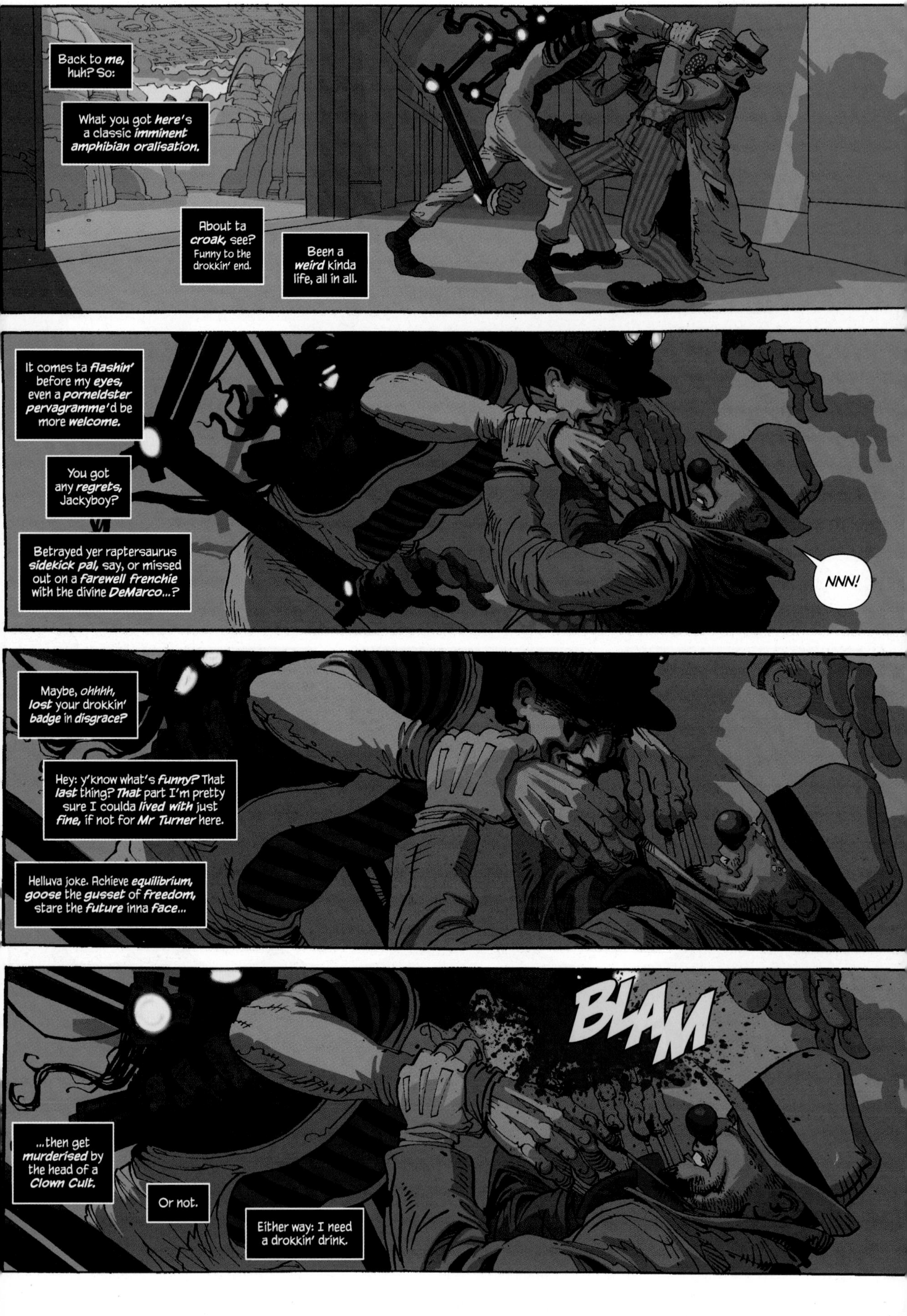
Back to *me*, huh? So:
What you got *here*'s a classic *imminent amphibian oralisation.*
About ta *croak*, see? Funny to the drokkin' end.
Been a *weird* kinda life, all in all.
It comes ta *flashin'* before my *eyes*, even a *porneldster pervagramme'*d be more *welcome.*
You got any *regrets*, Jackyboy?
Betrayed yer raptersaurus *sidekick pal*, say, or missed out on a *farewell frenchie* with the divine *DeMarco*...?
NNN!
Maybe, *ohhhh*, *lost* your drokkin' *badge* in *disgrace?*
Hey: y'know what's *funny?* That *last* thing? *That* part I'm pretty sure I coulda *lived with* just *fine*, if not for *Mr Turner* here.
Helluva joke. Achieve *equilibrium*, *goose* the *gusset* of *freedom*, stare the *future* inna *face*...
BLAM
...then get *murderised* by the head of a *Clown Cult.*
Or not.
Either way: I need a drokkin' drink.

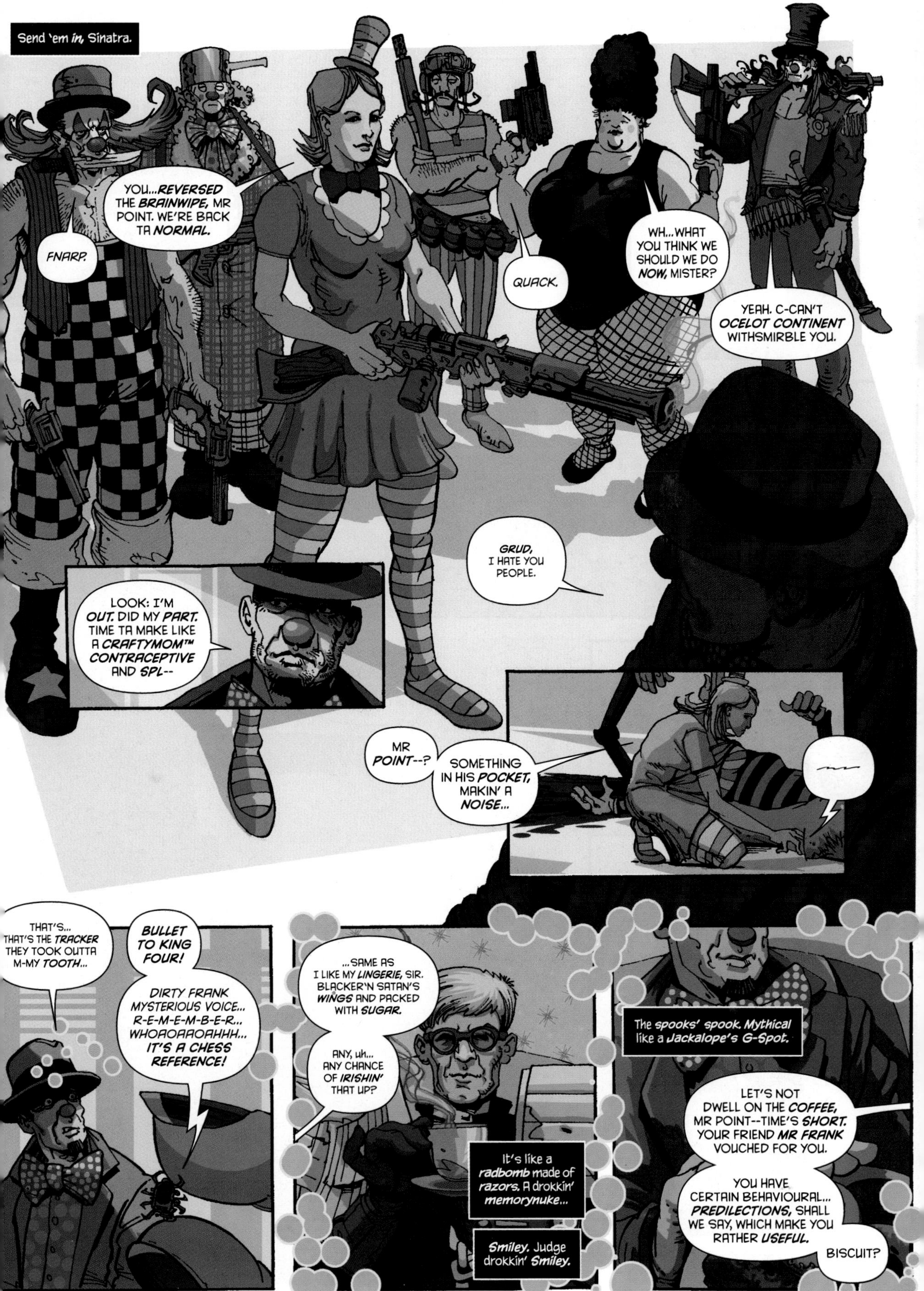
Send 'em in, Sinatra.
FNARP.
YOU...REVERSED THE BRAINWIPE, MR POINT. WE'RE BACK TA NORMAL.
QUACK.
WH...WHAT YOU THINK WE SHOULD WE DO NOW, MISTER?
YEAH. C-CAN'T OCELOT CONTINENT WITHSMIRBLE YOU.
GRUD, I HATE YOU PEOPLE.
LOOK: I'M OUT. DID MY PART. TIME TA MAKE LIKE A CRAFTYMOM™ CONTRACEPTIVE AND SPL--
MR POINT--?
SOMETHING IN HIS POCKET, MAKIN' A NOISE...
THAT'S... THAT'S THE TRACKER THEY TOOK OUTTA M-MY TOOTH...
BULLET TO KING FOUR!
DIRTY FRANK MYSTERIOUS VOICE... R-E-M-E-M-B-E-R... WHOAOAAOAHHH... IT'S A CHESS REFERENCE!
...SAME AS I LIKE MY LINGERIE, SIR. BLACKER'N SATAN'S WINGS AND PACKED WITH SUGAR.
ANY, uh... ANY CHANCE OF IRISHIN' THAT UP?
It's like a radbomb made of razors. A drokkin' memorynuke...
Smiley. Judge drokkin' Smiley.
The spooks' spook. Mythical like a Jackalope's G-Spot.
LET'S NOT DWELL ON THE COFFEE, MR POINT--TIME'S SHORT. YOUR FRIEND MR FRANK VOUCHED FOR YOU.
YOU HAVE CERTAIN BEHAVIOURAL... PREDILECTIONS, SHALL WE SAY, WHICH MAKE YOU RATHER USEFUL.
BISCUIT?

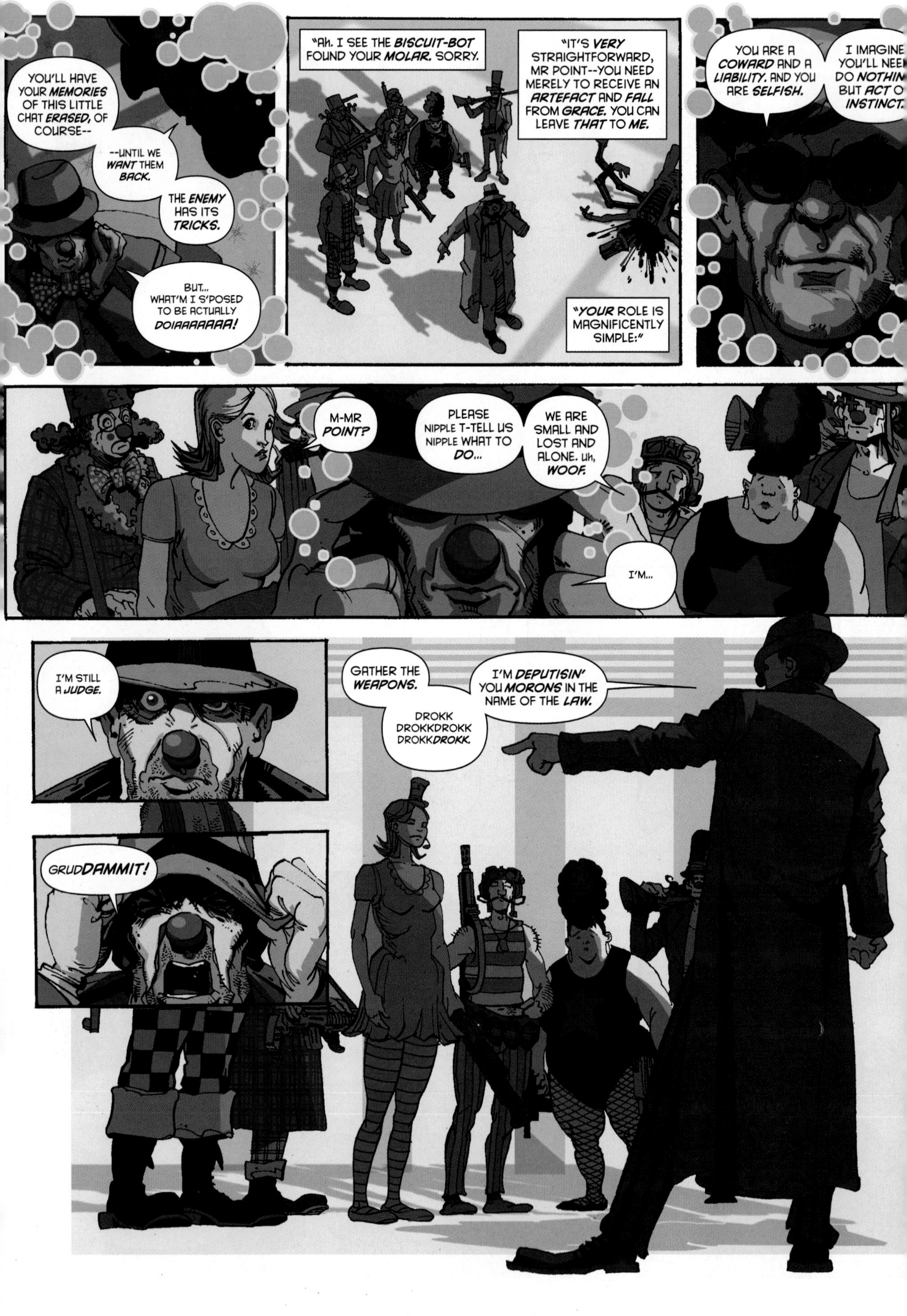

YOU'LL HAVE YOUR MEMORIES OF THIS LITTLE CHAT ERASED, OF COURSE--
--UNTIL WE WANT THEM BACK.
THE ENEMY HAS ITS TRICKS.
BUT... WHAT'M I S'POSED TO BE ACTUALLY DOIAAAAAAAA!
"AH. I SEE THE BISCUIT-BOT FOUND YOUR MOLAR. SORRY.
"IT'S VERY STRAIGHTFORWARD, MR POINT--YOU NEED MERELY TO RECEIVE AN ARTEFACT AND FALL FROM GRACE. YOU CAN LEAVE THAT TO ME.
"YOUR ROLE IS MAGNIFICENTLY SIMPLE:"
YOU ARE A COWARD AND A LIABILITY. AND YOU ARE SELFISH.
I IMAGINE YOU'LL NEE DO NOTHIN BUT ACT O INSTINCT.
M-MR POINT?
PLEASE NIPPLE T-TELL US NIPPLE WHAT TO DO...
WE ARE SMALL AND LOST AND ALONE. UH, WOOF.
I'M...
I'M STILL A JUDGE.
GRUDDAMMIT!
GATHER THE WEAPONS.
I'M DEPUTISIN' YOU MORONS IN THE NAME OF THE LAW.
DROKK DROKKDROKK DROKKDROKK.

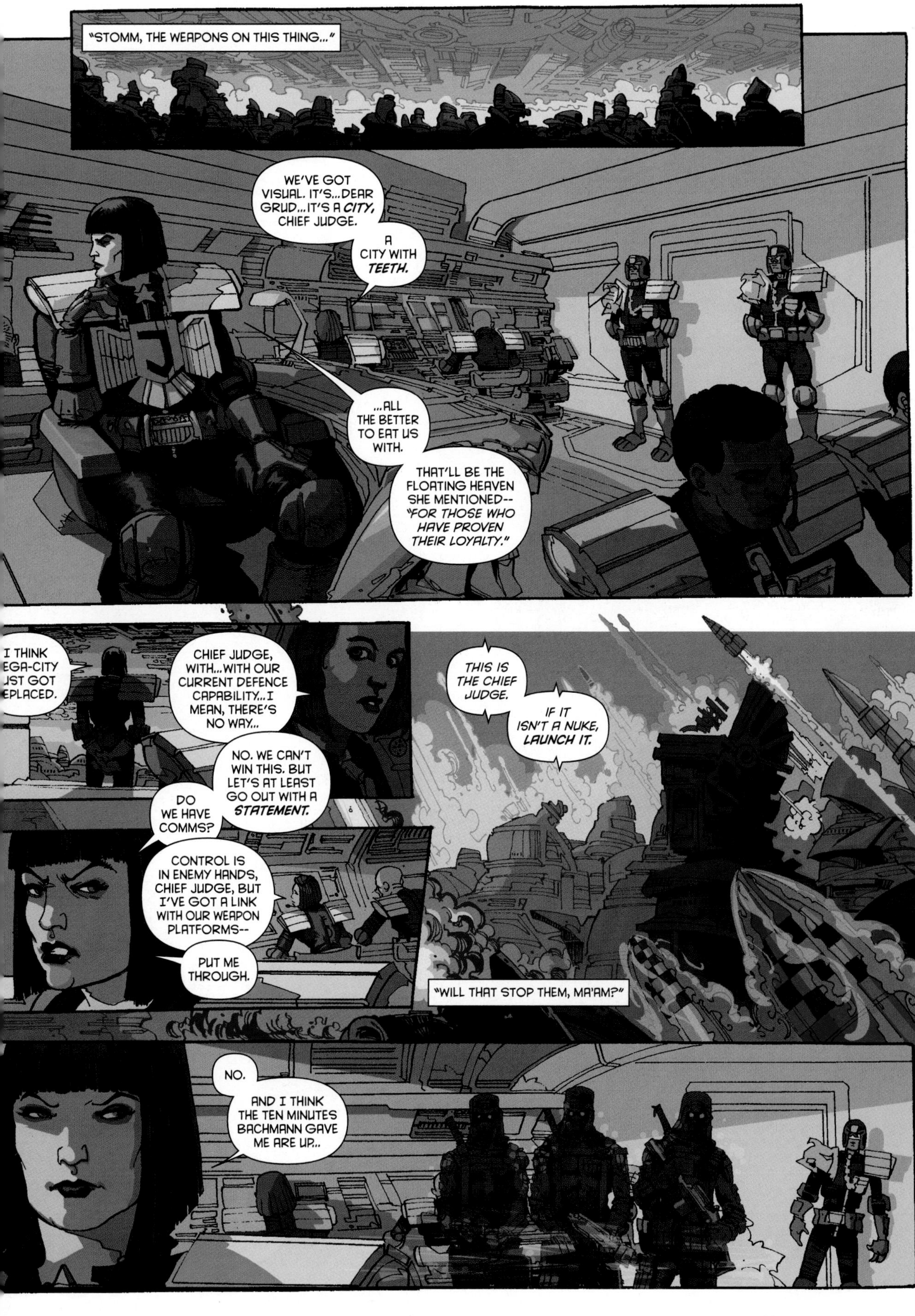
"STOMM, THE WEAPONS ON THIS THING..."
WE'VE GOT VISUAL. IT'S...DEAR GRUD...IT'S A *CITY,* CHIEF JUDGE.
A CITY WITH ***TEETH.***
...ALL THE BETTER TO EAT US WITH.
THAT'LL BE THE FLOATING HEAVEN SHE MENTIONED-- *"FOR THOSE WHO HAVE PROVEN THEIR LOYALTY."*
I THINK EGA-CITY UST GOT EPLACED.
CHIEF JUDGE, WITH...WITH OUR CURRENT DEFENCE CAPABILITY...I MEAN, THERE'S NO WAY...
NO. WE CAN'T WIN THIS. BUT LET'S AT LEAST GO OUT WITH A ***STATEMENT.***
DO WE HAVE COMMS?
CONTROL IS IN ENEMY HANDS, CHIEF JUDGE, BUT I'VE GOT A LINK WITH OUR WEAPON PLATFORMS--
PUT ME THROUGH.
THIS IS THE CHIEF JUDGE.
IF IT ISN'T A NUKE, ***LAUNCH IT.***
"WILL THAT STOP THEM, MA'AM?"
NO.
AND I THINK THE TEN MINUTES BACHMANN GAVE ME ARE UP...

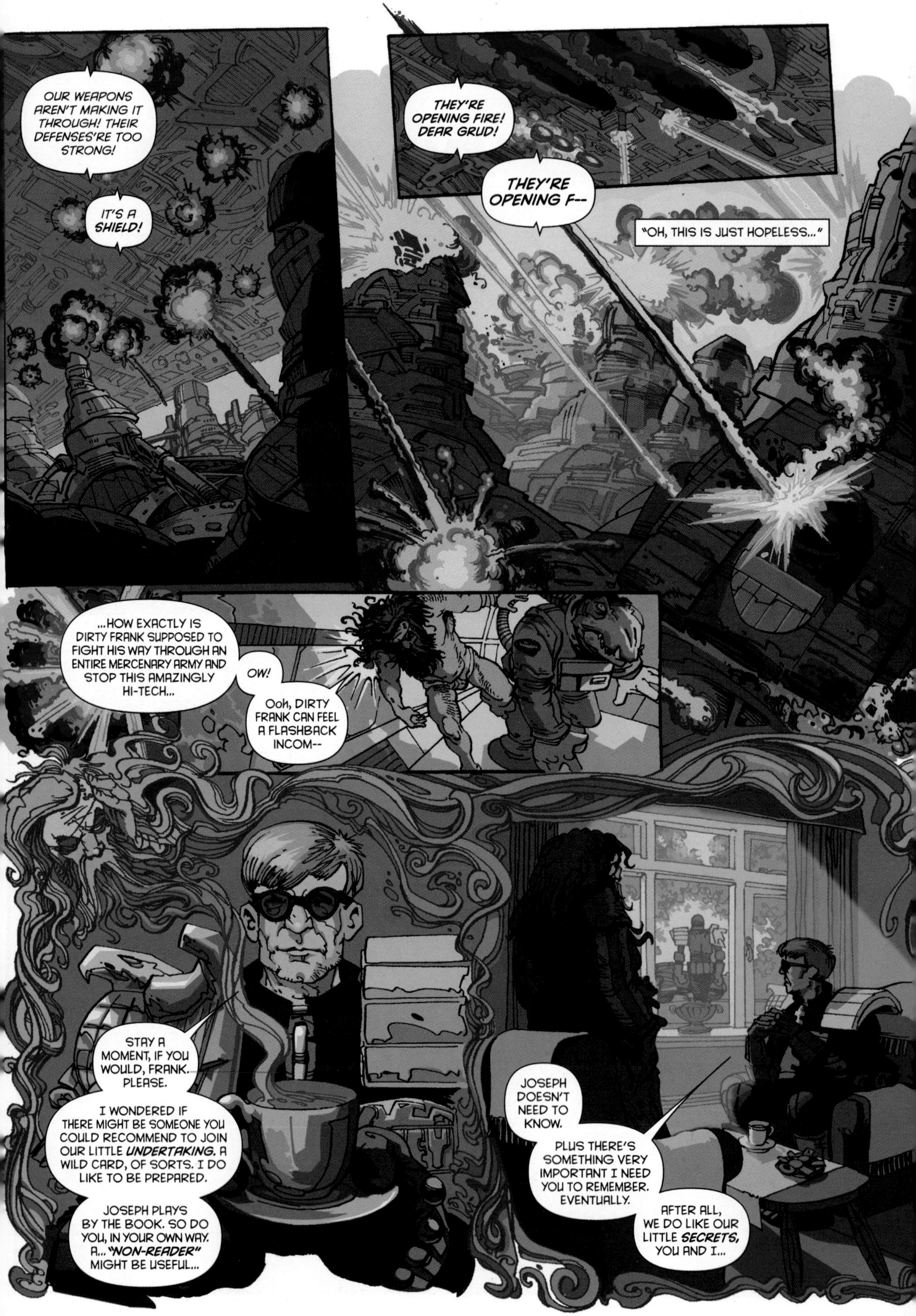

OUR WEAPONS AREN'T MAKING IT THROUGH! THEIR DEFENSES'RE TOO STRONG!
IT'S A SHIELD!
THEY'RE OPENING FIRE! DEAR GRUD!
THEY'RE OPENING F--
"OH, THIS IS JUST HOPELESS..."
...HOW EXACTLY IS DIRTY FRANK SUPPOSED TO FIGHT HIS WAY THROUGH AN ENTIRE MERCENARY ARMY AND STOP THIS AMAZINGLY HI-TECH...
OW!
Ooh, DIRTY FRANK CAN FEEL A FLASHBACK INCOM--
STAY A MOMENT, IF YOU WOULD, FRANK. PLEASE.
I WONDERED IF THERE MIGHT BE SOMEONE YOU COULD RECOMMEND TO JOIN OUR LITTLE UNDERTAKING. A WILD CARD, OF SORTS. I DO LIKE TO BE PREPARED.
JOSEPH PLAYS BY THE BOOK. SO DO YOU, IN YOUR OWN WAY. A... "NON-READER" MIGHT BE USEFUL...
JOSEPH DOESN'T NEED TO KNOW.
PLUS THERE'S SOMETHING VERY IMPORTANT I NEED YOU TO REMEMBER. EVENTUALLY.
AFTER ALL, WE DO LIKE OUR LITTLE SECRETS, YOU AND I...

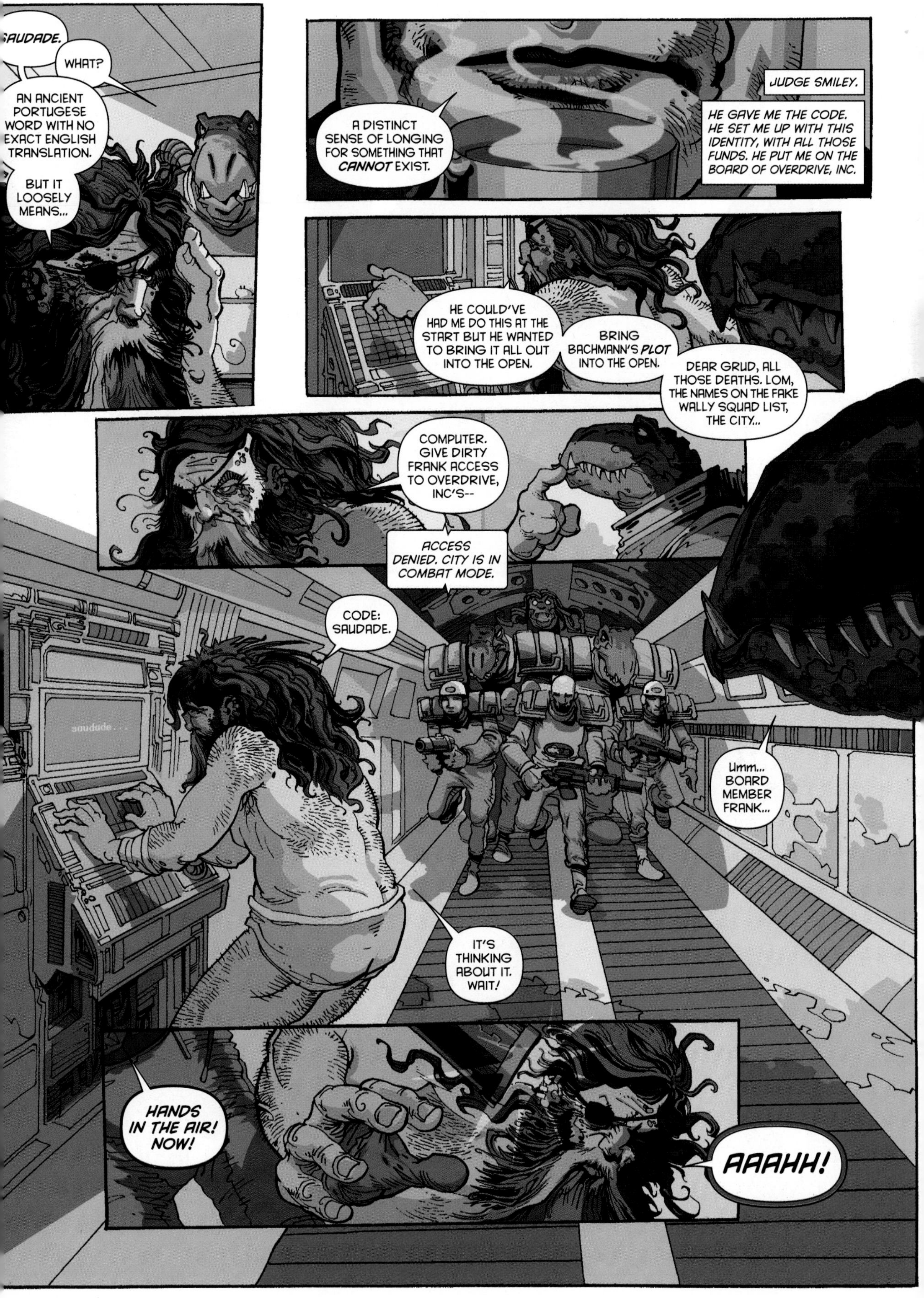
SAUDADE.
WHAT?
AN ANCIENT PORTUGESE WORD WITH NO EXACT ENGLISH TRANSLATION.
BUT IT LOOSELY MEANS...
A DISTINCT SENSE OF LONGING FOR SOMETHING THAT CANNOT EXIST.
JUDGE SMILEY.
HE GAVE ME THE CODE. HE SET ME UP WITH THIS IDENTITY, WITH ALL THOSE FUNDS. HE PUT ME ON THE BOARD OF OVERDRIVE, INC.
HE COULD'VE HAD ME DO THIS AT THE START BUT HE WANTED TO BRING IT ALL OUT INTO THE OPEN.
BRING BACHMANN'S PLOT INTO THE OPEN.
DEAR GRUD, ALL THOSE DEATHS. LOM, THE NAMES ON THE FAKE WALLY SQUAD LIST, THE CITY...
COMPUTER. GIVE DIRTY FRANK ACCESS TO OVERDRIVE, INC'S--
ACCESS DENIED. CITY IS IN COMBAT MODE.
CODE: SAUDADE.
saudade...
Umm... BOARD MEMBER FRANK...
IT'S THINKING ABOUT IT. WAIT!
HANDS IN THE AIR! NOW!
AAAHH!

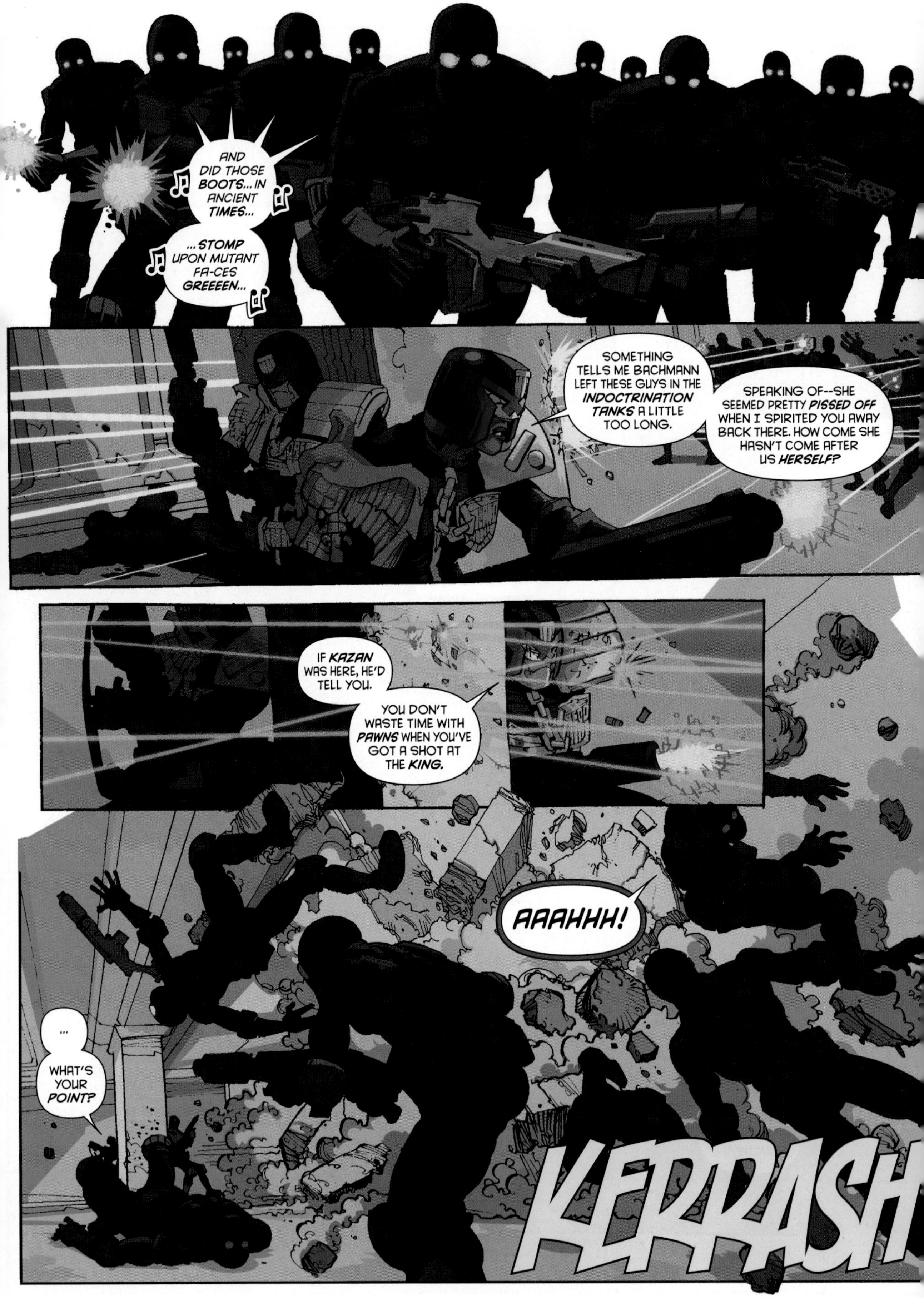
AND DID THOSE BOOTS... IN ANCIENT TIMES...
... STOMP UPON MUTANT FA-CES GREEEEN...
SOMETHING TELLS ME BACHMANN LEFT THESE GUYS IN THE INDOCTRINATION TANKS A LITTLE TOO LONG.
SPEAKING OF--SHE SEEMED PRETTY PISSED OFF WHEN I SPIRITED YOU AWAY BACK THERE. HOW COME SHE HASN'T COME AFTER US HERSELF?
IF KAZAN WAS HERE, HE'D TELL YOU.
YOU DON'T WASTE TIME WITH PAWNS WHEN YOU'VE GOT A SHOT AT THE KING.
AAAHHH!
...
WHAT'S YOUR POINT?
KERRASH

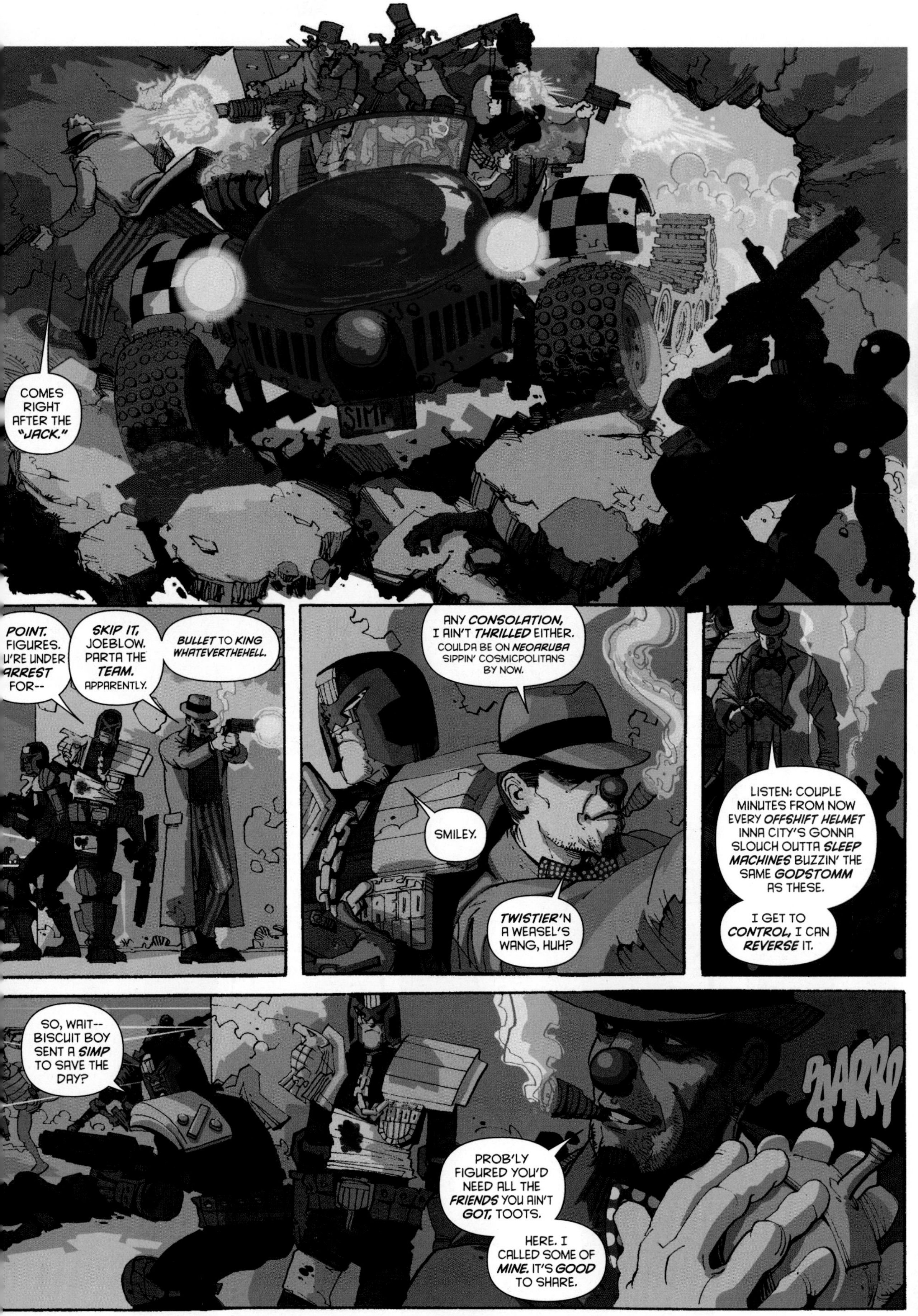
COMES RIGHT AFTER THE "JACK."
POINT. FIGURES. U'RE UNDER ARREST FOR--
SKIP IT, JOEBLOW. PARTA THE TEAM. APPARENTLY.
BULLET TO KING WHATEVERTHEHELL.
ANY CONSOLATION, I AIN'T THRILLED EITHER. COULDA BE ON NEOARUBA SIPPIN' COSMICPOLITANS BY NOW.
SMILEY.
TWISTIER'N A WEASEL'S WANG, HUH?
LISTEN: COUPLE MINUTES FROM NOW EVERY OFFSHIFT HELMET INNA CITY'S GONNA SLOUCH OUTTA SLEEP MACHINES BUZZIN' THE SAME GODSTOMM AS THESE.
I GET TO CONTROL, I CAN REVERSE IT.
SO, WAIT-- BISCUIT BOY SENT A SIMP TO SAVE THE DAY?
PROB'LY FIGURED YOU'D NEED ALL THE FRIENDS YOU AIN'T GOT, TOOTS.
HERE. I CALLED SOME OF MINE. IT'S GOOD TO SHARE.
PAARRP

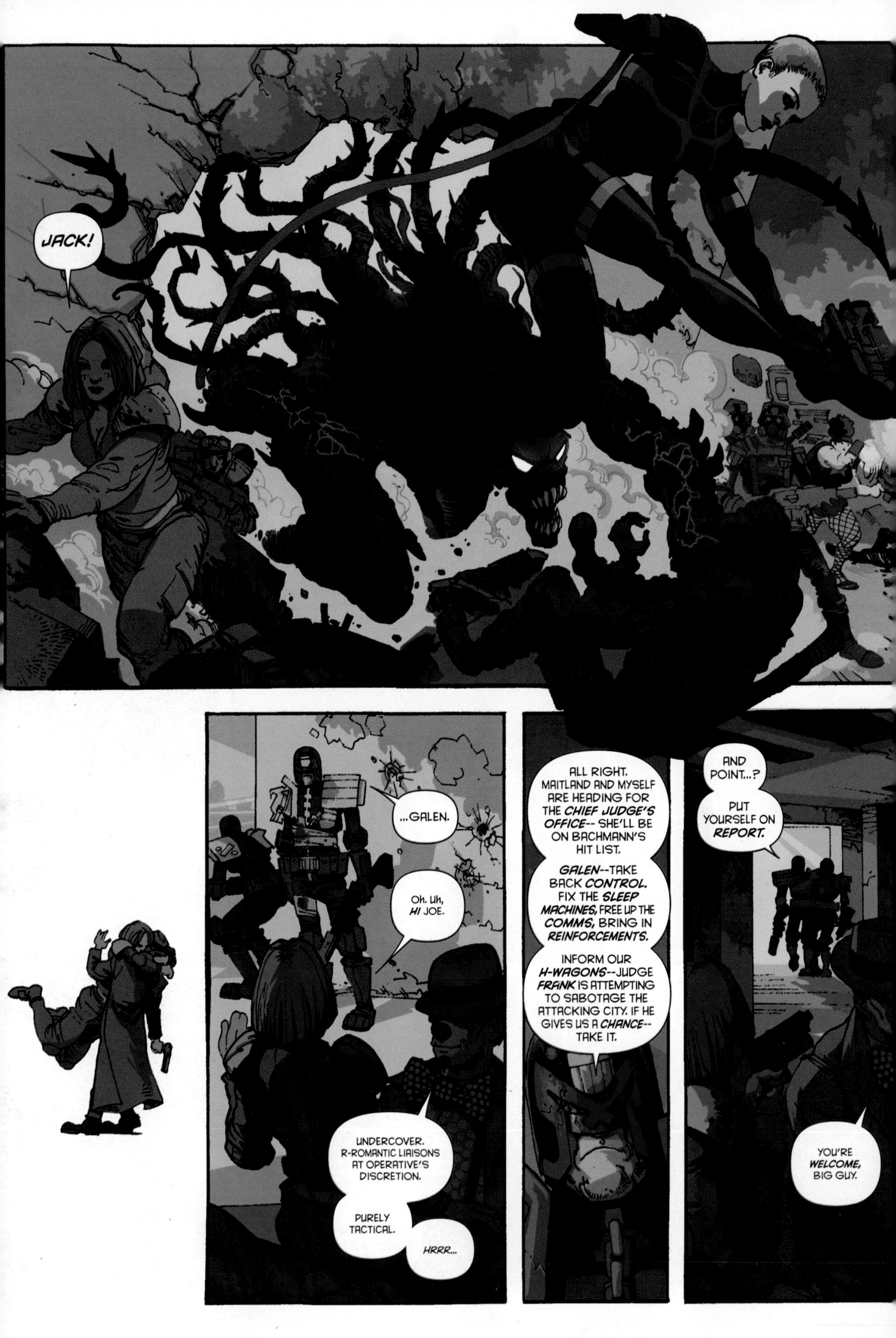
JACK!
...GALEN.
Oh. Uh, HI JOE.
UNDERCOVER. R-ROMANTIC LIAISONS AT OPERATIVE'S DISCRETION.
PURELY TACTICAL.
HRRR...
ALL RIGHT. MAITLAND AND MYSELF ARE HEADING FOR THE CHIEF JUDGE'S OFFICE-- SHE'LL BE ON BACHMANN'S HIT LIST.
GALEN--TAKE BACK CONTROL. FIX THE SLEEP MACHINES, FREE UP THE COMMS, BRING IN REINFORCEMENTS.
INFORM OUR H-WAGONS--JUDGE FRANK IS ATTEMPTING TO SABOTAGE THE ATTACKING CITY. IF HE GIVES US A CHANCE-- TAKE IT.
AND POINT...?
PUT YOURSELF ON REPORT.
YOU'RE WELCOME, BIG GUY.

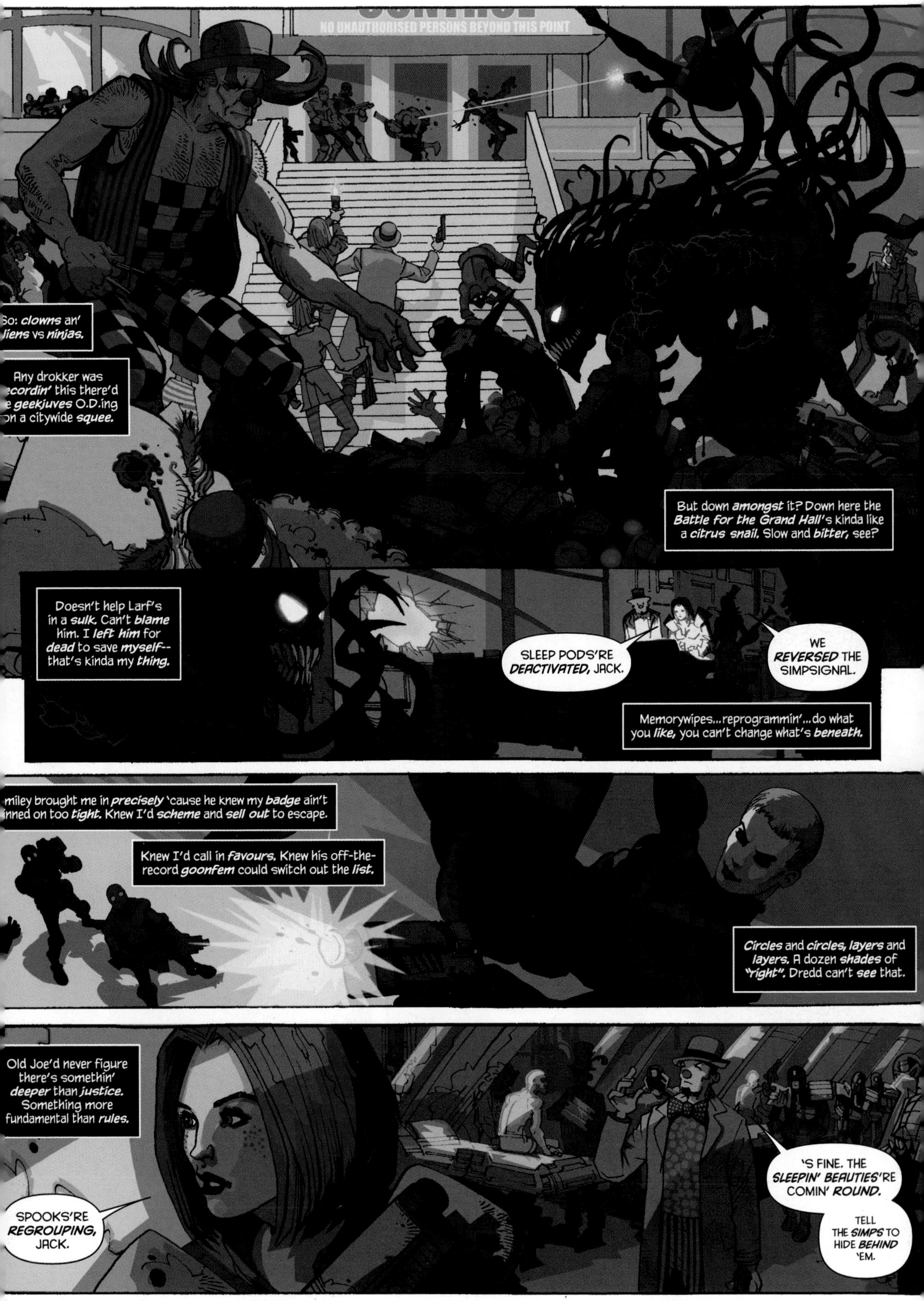

NO UNAUTHORISED PERSONS BEYOND THIS POINT
So: *clowns* an' liens vs *ninjas.*
Any drokker was ecordin' this there'd e *geekjuves* O.D.ing on a citywide *squee.*
But down *amongst* it? Down here the *Battle for the Grand Hall*'s kinda like a *citrus snail.* Slow and *bitter,* see?
Doesn't help Larf's in a *sulk.* Can't *blame* him. I *left him* for *dead* to save *myself*-- that's kinda my *thing.*
SLEEP PODS'RE *DEACTIVATED,* JACK.
WE *REVERSED* THE SIMPSIGNAL.
Memorywipes...reprogrammin'...do what you *like,* you can't change what's *beneath.*
miley brought me in *precisely* 'cause he knew my *badge* ain't inned on too *tight.* Knew I'd *scheme* and *sell out* to escape.
Knew I'd call in *favours.* Knew his off-the-record *goonfem* could switch out the *list.*
Circles and *circles, layers* and *layers.* A dozen *shades* of *"right".* Dredd can't *see* that.
Old Joe'd never figure there's somethin' *deeper* than *justice.* Something more fundamental than *rules.*
SPOOKS'RE *REGROUPING,* JACK.
'S FINE. THE *SLEEPIN' BEAUTIES*'RE COMIN' *ROUND.*
TELL THE *SIMPS* TO HIDE *BEHIND* 'EM.

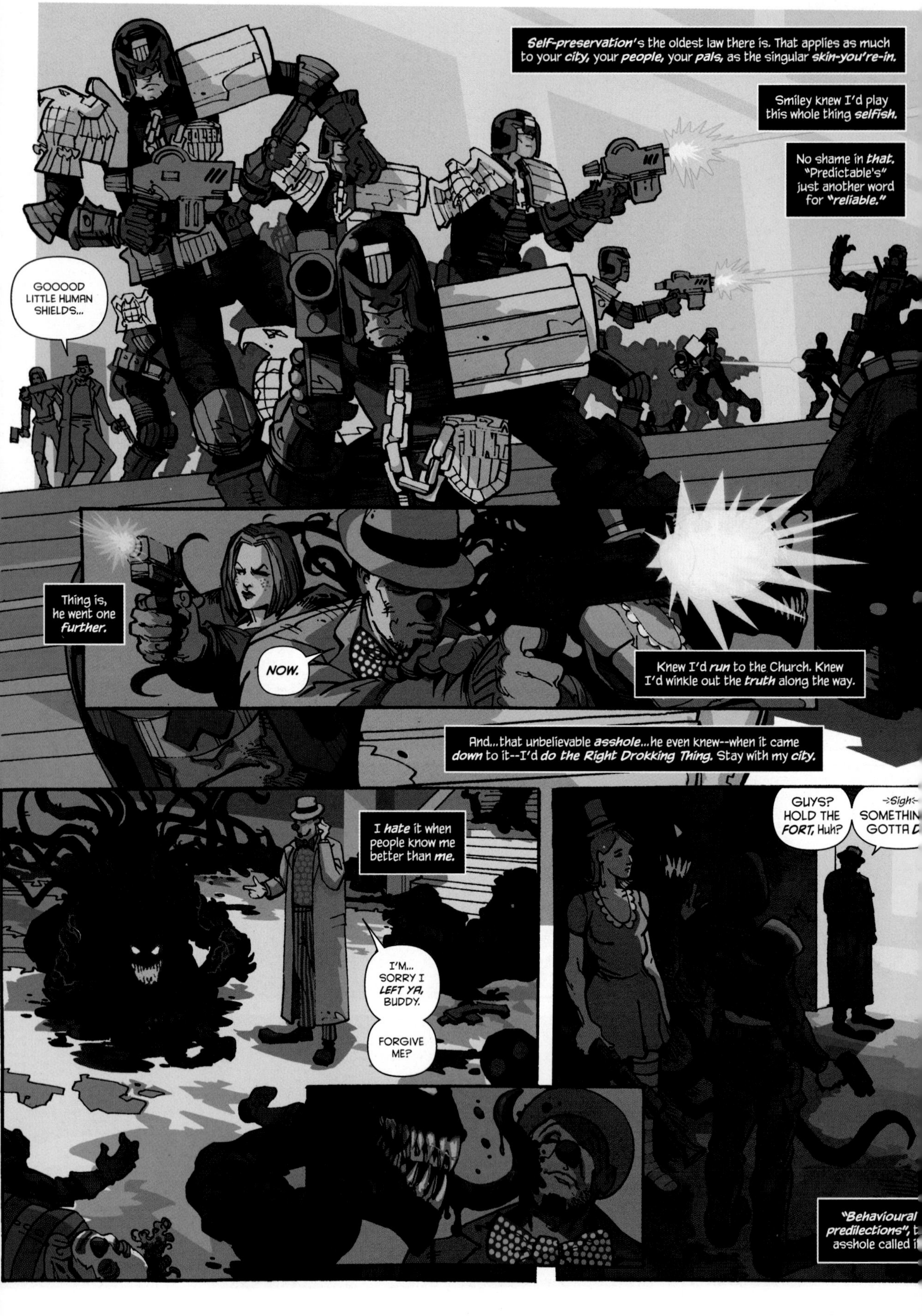
Self-preservation's the oldest law there is. That applies as much to your city, your people, your pals, as the singular skin-you're-in.
Smiley knew I'd play this whole thing selfish.
No shame in that. "Predictable's" just another word for "reliable."
GOOOOD LITTLE HUMAN SHIELDS...
Thing is, he went one further.
NOW.
Knew I'd run to the Church. Knew I'd winkle out the truth along the way.
And...that unbelievable asshole...he even knew--when it came down to it--I'd do the Right Drokking Thing. Stay with my city.
I hate it when people know me better than me.
I'M... SORRY I LEFT YA, BUDDY.
FORGIVE ME?
GUYS? HOLD THE FORT, Huh?
~Sigh~
"Behavioural predilections",
asshole called

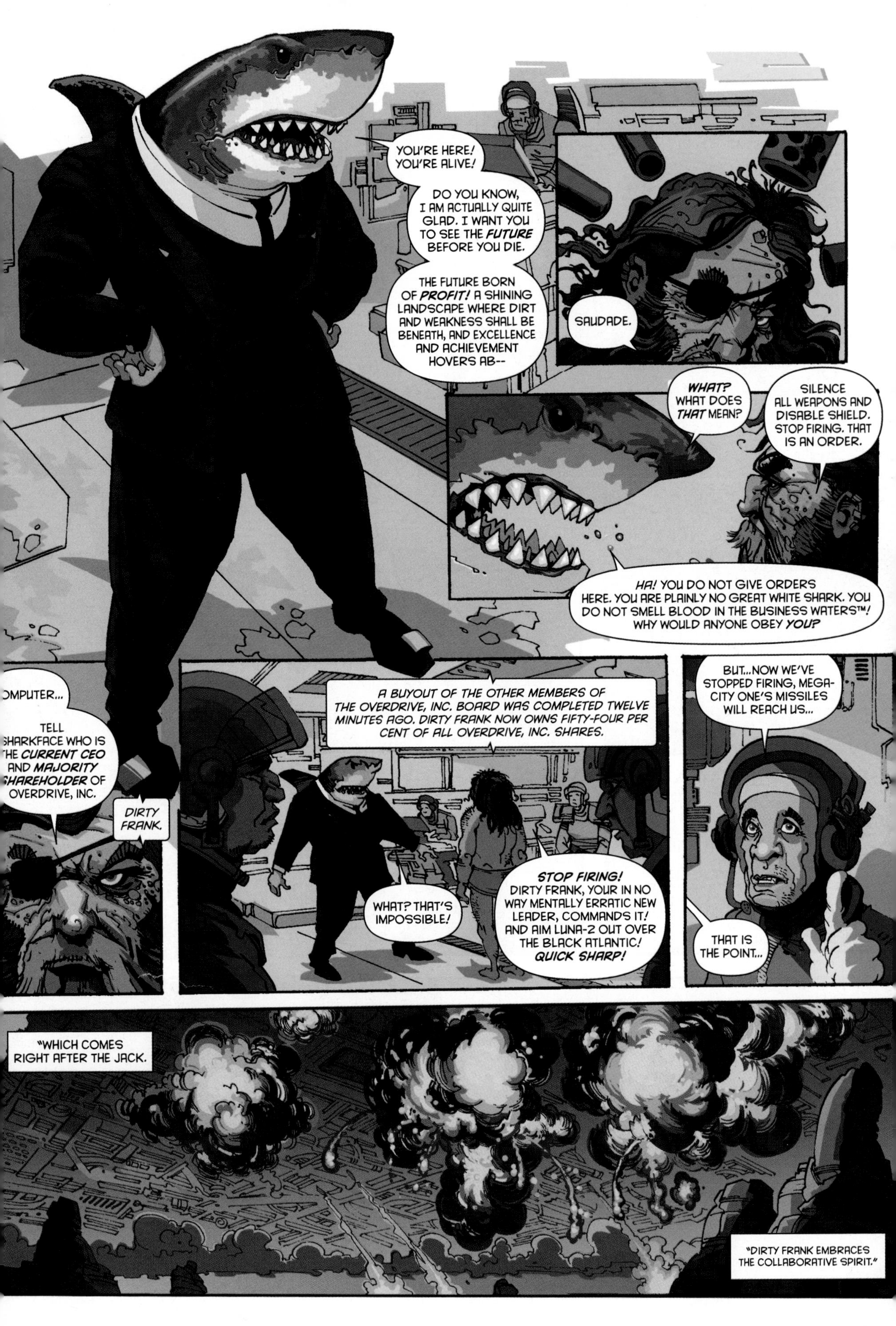
YOU'RE HERE! YOU'RE ALIVE!
DO YOU KNOW, I AM ACTUALLY QUITE GLAD. I WANT YOU TO SEE THE *FUTURE* BEFORE YOU DIE.
THE FUTURE BORN OF *PROFIT!* A SHINING LANDSCAPE WHERE DIRT AND WEAKNESS SHALL BE BENEATH, AND EXCELLENCE AND ACHIEVEMENT HOVERS AB--
SAUDADE.
WHAT? WHAT DOES *THAT* MEAN?
SILENCE ALL WEAPONS AND DISABLE SHIELD. STOP FIRING. THAT IS AN ORDER.
HA! YOU DO NOT GIVE ORDERS HERE. YOU ARE PLAINLY NO GREAT WHITE SHARK. YOU DO NOT SMELL BLOOD IN THE BUSINESS WATERS™! WHY WOULD ANYONE OBEY *YOU?*
OMPUTER...
TELL SHARKFACE WHO IS THE *CURRENT CEO* AND *MAJORITY SHAREHOLDER* OF OVERDRIVE, INC.
DIRTY FRANK.
A BUYOUT OF THE OTHER MEMBERS OF THE OVERDRIVE, INC. BOARD WAS COMPLETED TWELVE MINUTES AGO. DIRTY FRANK NOW OWNS FIFTY-FOUR PER CENT OF ALL OVERDRIVE, INC. SHARES.
WHAT? THAT'S IMPOSSIBLE!
STOP FIRING! DIRTY FRANK, YOUR IN NO WAY MENTALLY ERRATIC NEW LEADER, COMMANDS IT! AND AIM LUNA-2 OUT OVER THE BLACK ATLANTIC! *QUICK SHARP!*
BUT...NOW WE'VE STOPPED FIRING, MEGA-CITY ONE'S MISSILES WILL REACH US...
THAT IS THE POINT...
"WHICH COMES RIGHT AFTER THE JACK.
"DIRTY FRANK EMBRACES THE COLLABORATIVE SPIRIT."

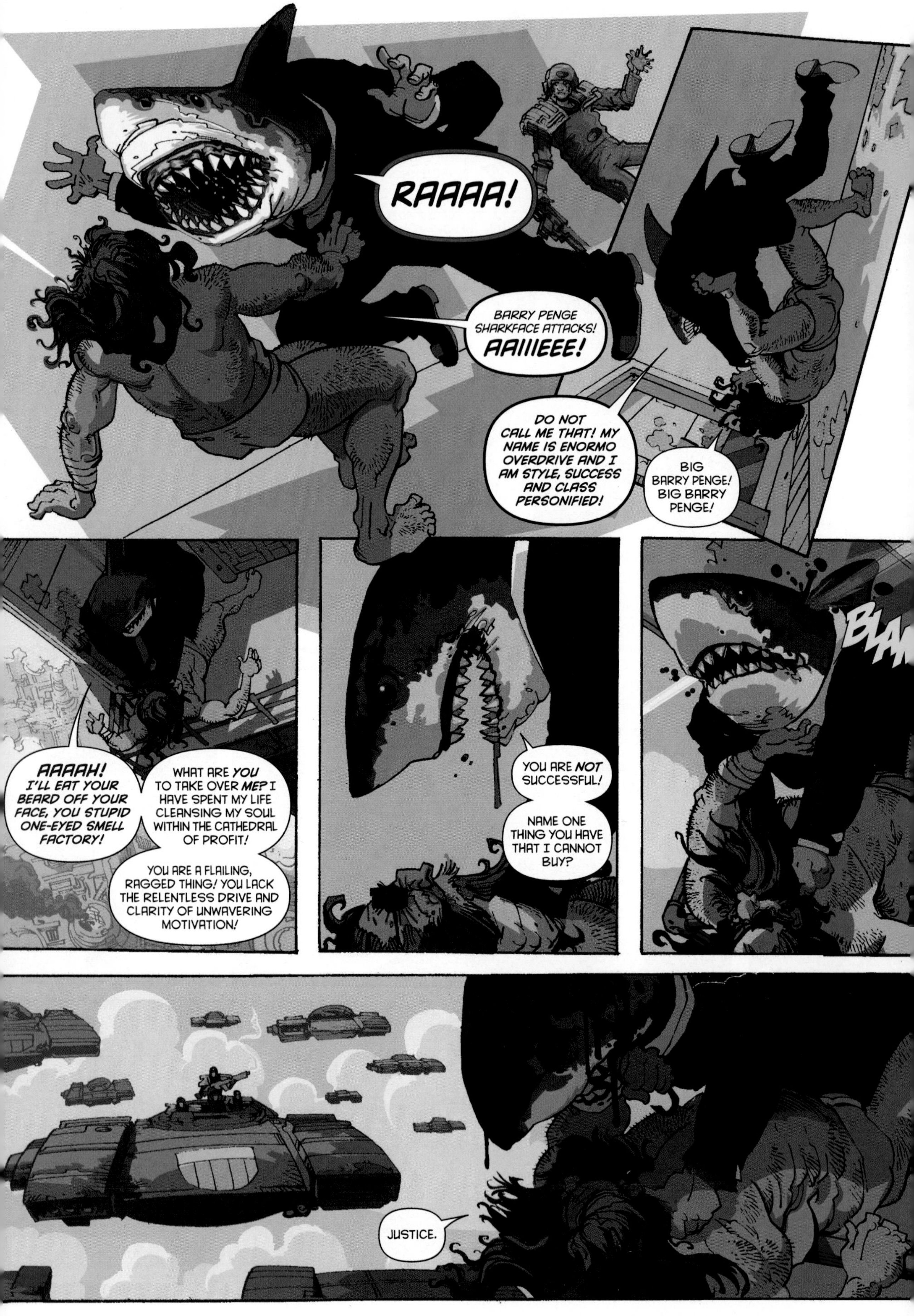
RAAAA!
BARRY PENGE SHARKFACE ATTACKS! AAIIIEEE!
DO NOT CALL ME THAT! MY NAME IS ENORMO OVERDRIVE AND I AM STYLE, SUCCESS AND CLASS PERSONIFIED!
BIG BARRY PENGE! BIG BARRY PENGE!
AAAAH! I'LL EAT YOUR BEARD OFF YOUR FACE, YOU STUPID ONE-EYED SMELL FACTORY!
WHAT ARE YOU TO TAKE OVER ME? I HAVE SPENT MY LIFE CLEANSING MY SOUL WITHIN THE CATHEDRAL OF PROFIT!
YOU ARE A FLAILING, RAGGED THING! YOU LACK THE RELENTLESS DRIVE AND CLARITY OF UNWAVERING MOTIVATION!
YOU ARE NOT SUCCESSFUL!
NAME ONE THING YOU HAVE THAT I CANNOT BUY?
JUSTICE.

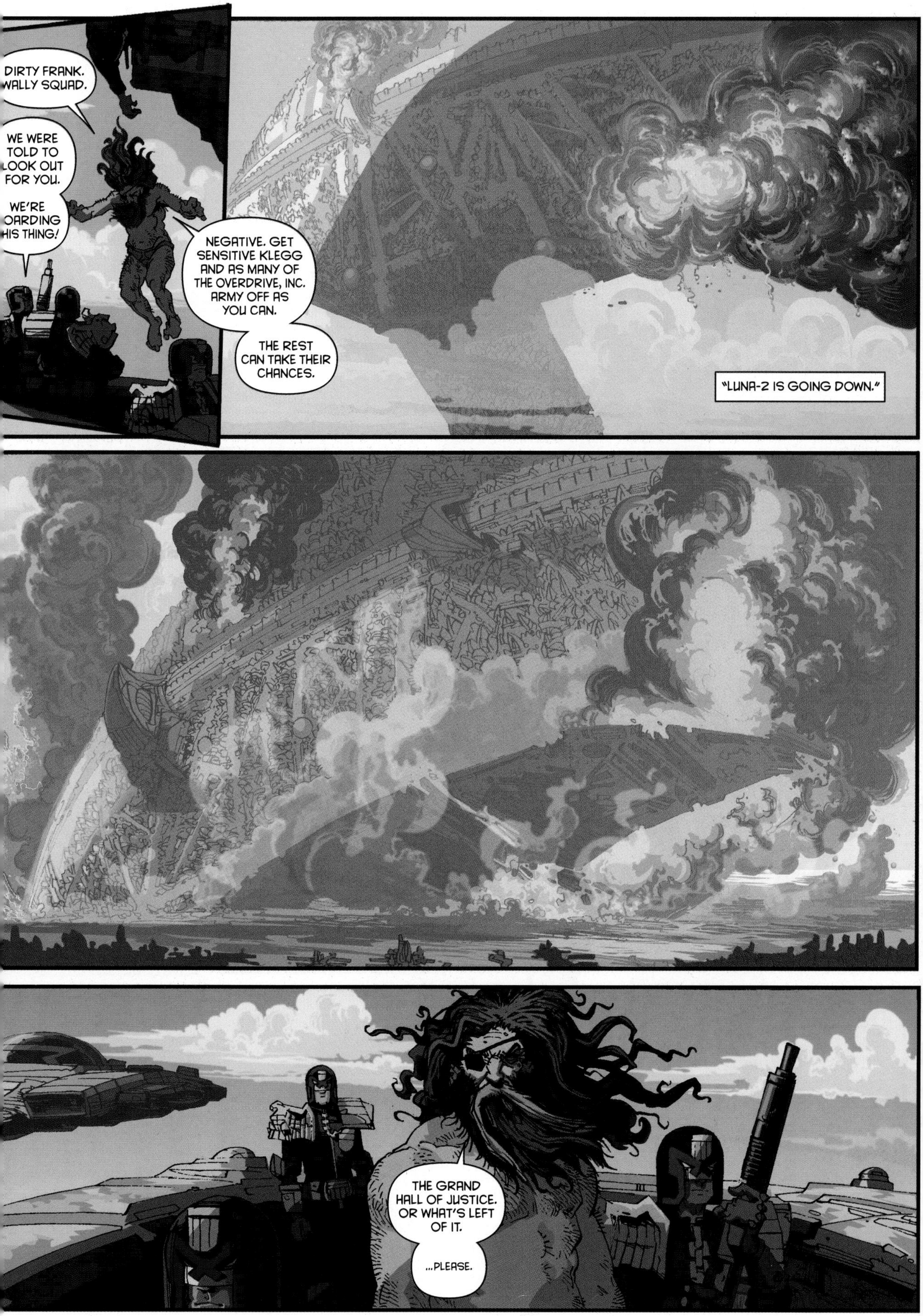
DIRTY FRANK. WALLY SQUAD.
WE WERE TOLD TO LOOK OUT FOR YOU.
WE'RE OARDING HIS THING!
NEGATIVE. GET SENSITIVE KLEGG AND AS MANY OF THE OVERDRIVE, INC. ARMY OFF AS YOU CAN.
THE REST CAN TAKE THEIR CHANCES.
"LUNA-2 IS GOING DOWN."
THE GRAND HALL OF JUSTICE. OR WHAT'S LEFT OF IT.
...PLEASE.

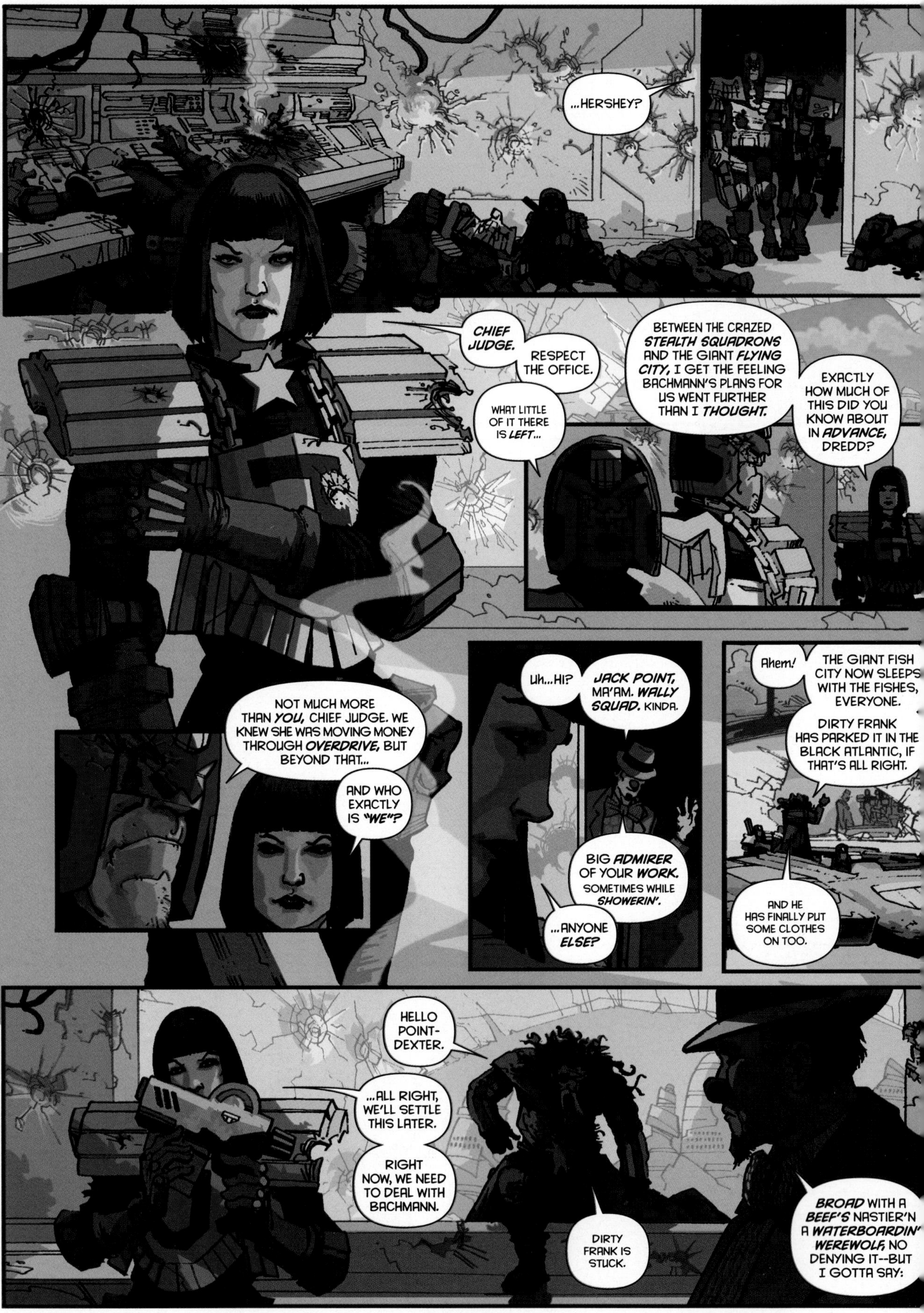
...HERSHEY?
CHIEF JUDGE.
RESPECT THE OFFICE.
WHAT LITTLE OF IT THERE IS LEFT...
BETWEEN THE CRAZED STEALTH SQUADRONS AND THE GIANT FLYING CITY, I GET THE FEELING BACHMANN'S PLANS FOR US WENT FURTHER THAN I THOUGHT.
EXACTLY HOW MUCH OF THIS DID YOU KNOW ABOUT IN ADVANCE, DREDD?
NOT MUCH MORE THAN YOU, CHIEF JUDGE. WE KNEW SHE WAS MOVING MONEY THROUGH OVERDRIVE, BUT BEYOND THAT...
AND WHO EXACTLY IS "WE"?
Uh...Hi?
JACK POINT, MA'AM. WALLY SQUAD. KINDA.
BIG ADMIRER OF YOUR WORK. SOMETIMES WHILE SHOWERIN'.
...ANYONE ELSE?
Ahem!
THE GIANT FISH CITY NOW SLEEPS WITH THE FISHES, EVERYONE.
DIRTY FRANK HAS PARKED IT IN THE BLACK ATLANTIC, IF THAT'S ALL RIGHT.
AND HE HAS FINALLY PUT SOME CLOTHES ON TOO.
HELLO POINT-DEXTER.
...ALL RIGHT, WE'LL SETTLE THIS LATER.
RIGHT NOW, WE NEED TO DEAL WITH BACHMANN.
DIRTY FRANK IS STUCK.
BROAD WITH A BEEF'S NASTIER'N A WATERBOARDIN' WEREWOLF, NO DENYING IT--BUT I GOTTA SAY:

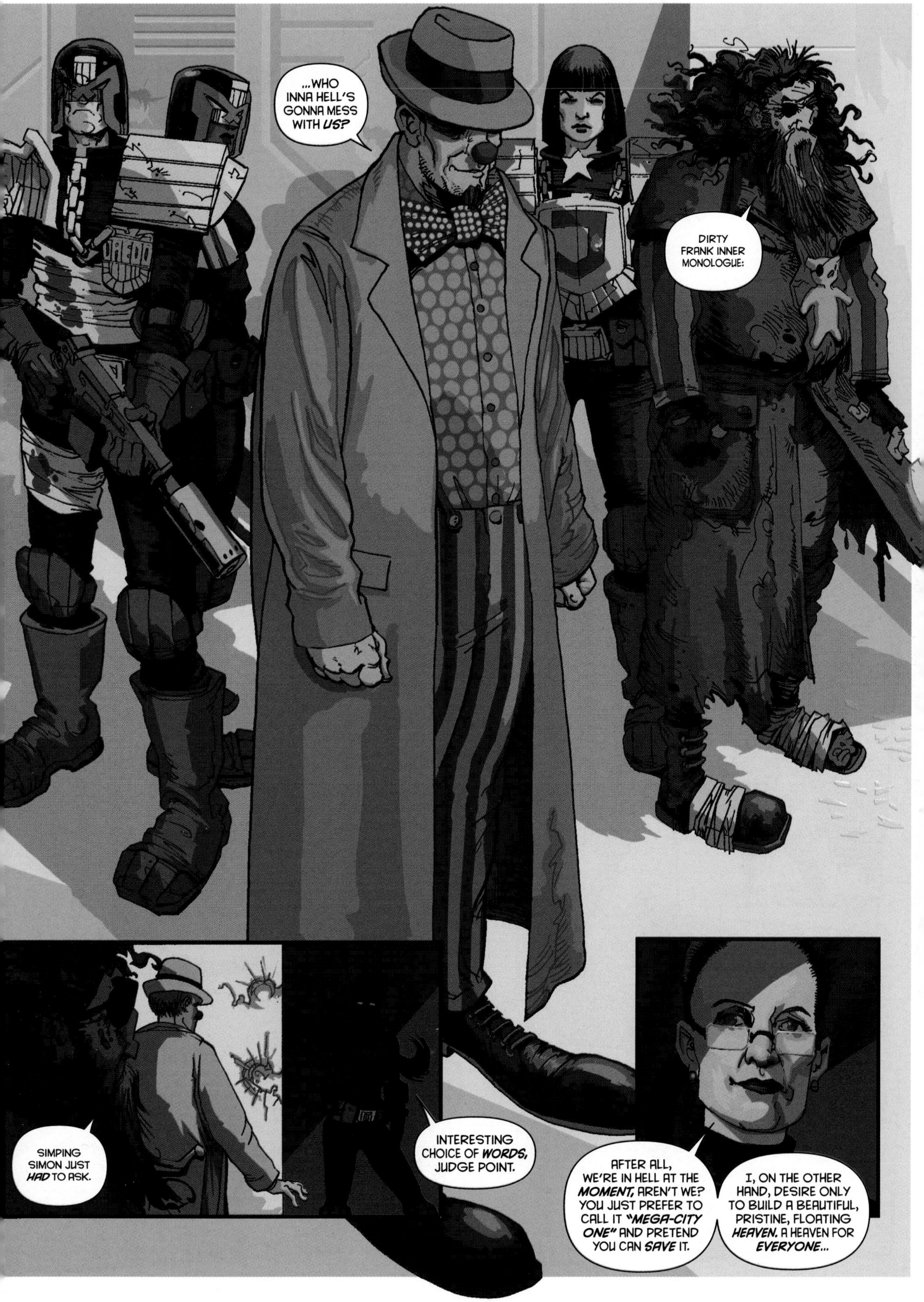
...WHO INNA HELL'S GONNA MESS WITH *US?*
DIRTY FRANK INNER MONOLOGUE:
SIMPING SIMON JUST *HAD* TO ASK.
INTERESTING CHOICE OF *WORDS,* JUDGE POINT.
AFTER ALL, WE'RE IN HELL AT THE *MOMENT,* AREN'T WE? YOU JUST PREFER TO CALL IT *"MEGA-CITY ONE"* AND PRETEND YOU CAN *SAVE* IT.
I, ON THE OTHER HAND, DESIRE ONLY TO BUILD A BEAUTIFUL, PRISTINE, FLOATING *HEAVEN.* A HEAVEN FOR *EVERYONE...*

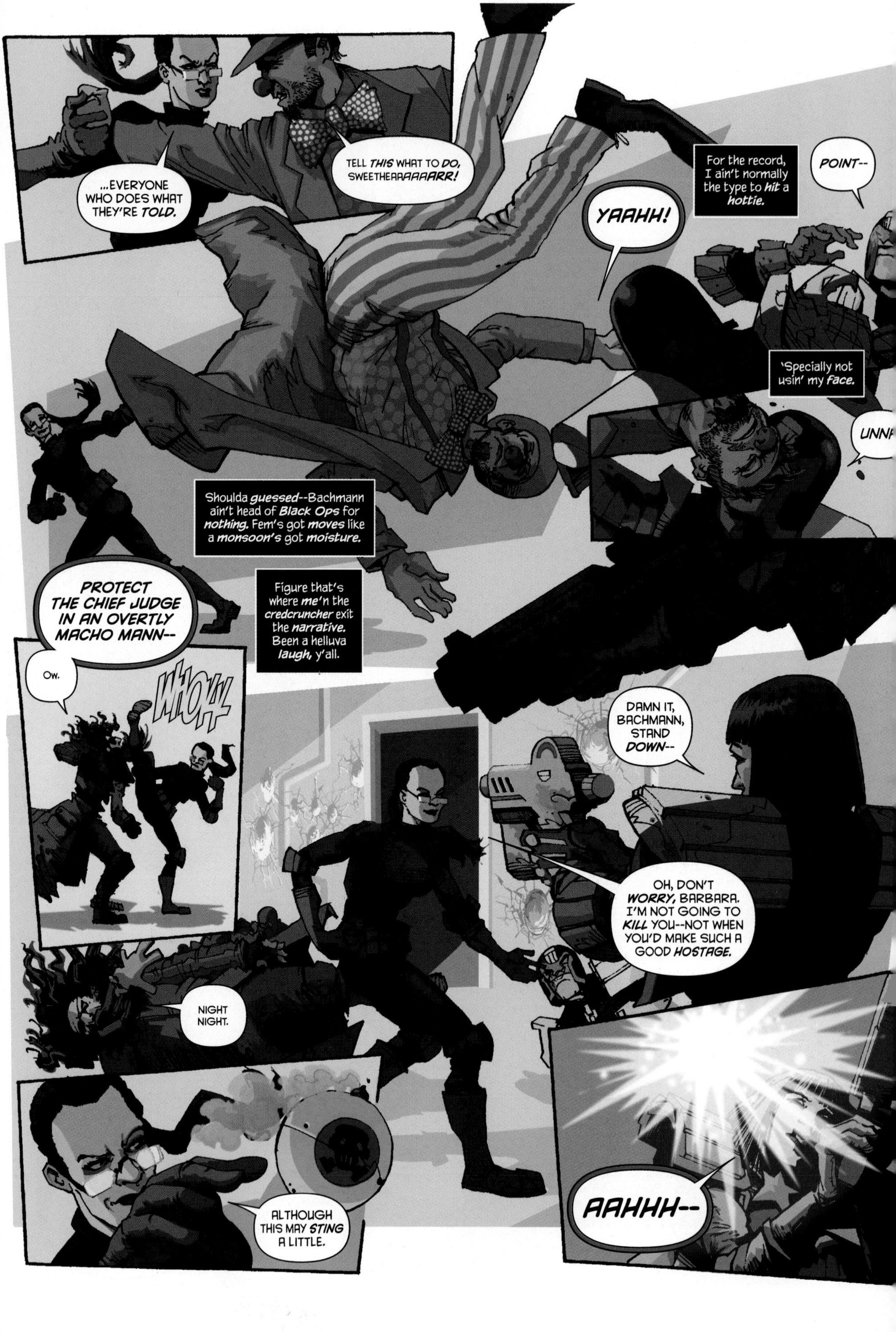
...EVERYONE WHO DOES WHAT THEY'RE TOLD.
TELL THIS WHAT TO DO, SWEETHEARRAAAARR!
YAAHH!
For the record, I ain't normally the type to hit a hottie.
POINT--
'Specially not usin' my face.
UNN
Shoulda guessed--Bachmann ain't head of Black Ops for nothing. Fem's got moves like a monsoon's got moisture.
PROTECT THE CHIEF JUDGE IN AN OVERTLY MACHO MANN--
Figure that's where me'n the credcruncher exit the narrative. Been a helluva laugh, y'all.
Ow.
WHOK!
DAMN IT, BACHMANN, STAND DOWN--
OH, DON'T WORRY, BARBARA. I'M NOT GOING TO KILL YOU--NOT WHEN YOU'D MAKE SUCH A GOOD HOSTAGE.
NIGHT NIGHT.
ALTHOUGH THIS MAY STING A LITTLE.
AAHHH--

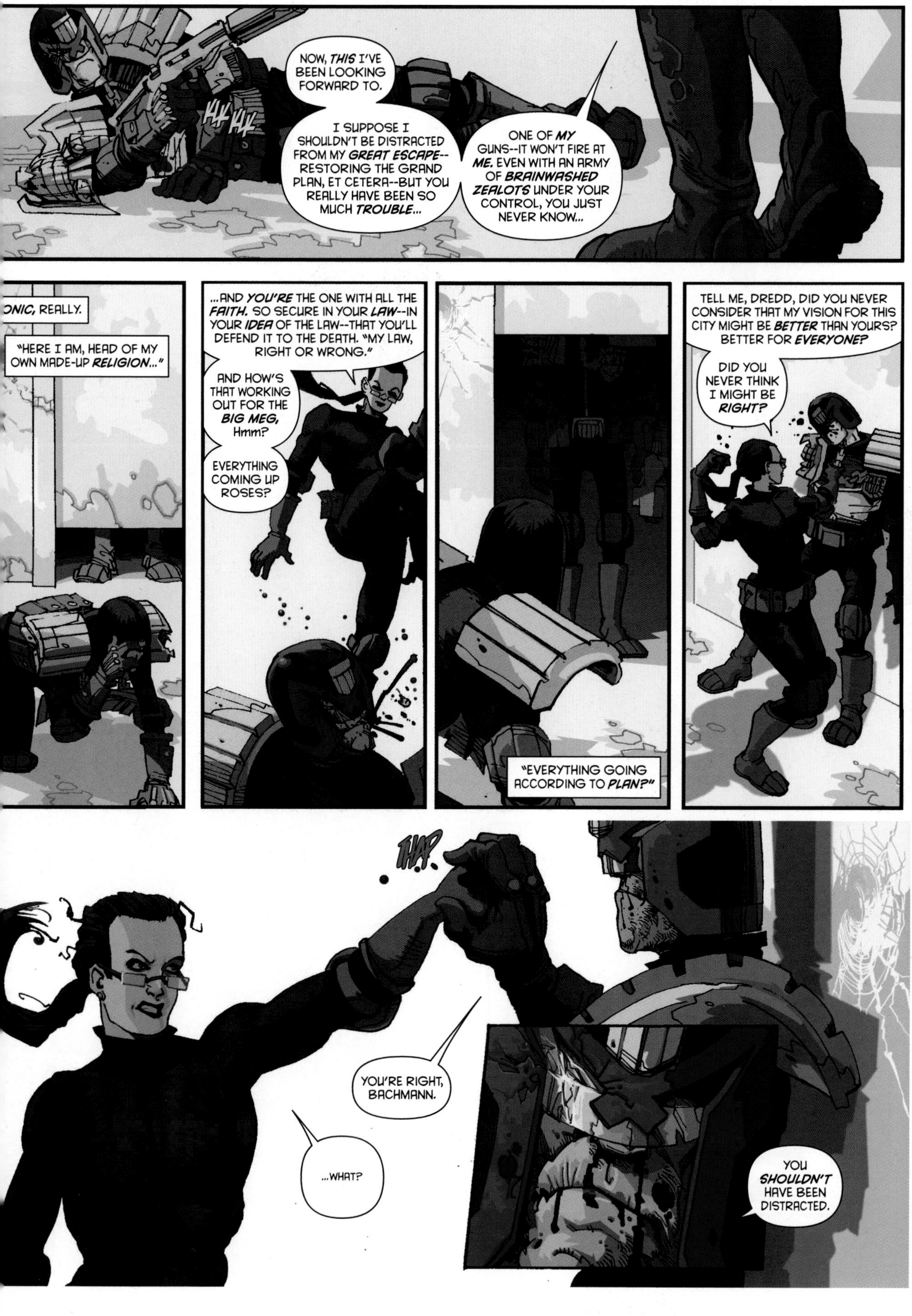

NOW, THIS I'VE BEEN LOOKING FORWARD TO.
I SUPPOSE I SHOULDN'T BE DISTRACTED FROM MY GREAT ESCAPE--RESTORING THE GRAND PLAN, ET CETERA--BUT YOU REALLY HAVE BEEN SO MUCH TROUBLE...
ONE OF MY GUNS--IT WON'T FIRE AT ME. EVEN WITH AN ARMY OF BRAINWASHED ZEALOTS UNDER YOUR CONTROL, YOU JUST NEVER KNOW...
ONIC, REALLY.
"HERE I AM, HEAD OF MY OWN MADE-UP RELIGION..."
...AND YOU'RE THE ONE WITH ALL THE FAITH. SO SECURE IN YOUR LAW--IN YOUR IDEA OF THE LAW--THAT YOU'LL DEFEND IT TO THE DEATH. "MY LAW, RIGHT OR WRONG."
AND HOW'S THAT WORKING OUT FOR THE BIG MEG, Hmm?
EVERYTHING COMING UP ROSES?
"EVERYTHING GOING ACCORDING TO PLAN?"
TELL ME, DREDD, DID YOU NEVER CONSIDER THAT MY VISION FOR THIS CITY MIGHT BE BETTER THAN YOURS? BETTER FOR EVERYONE?
DID YOU NEVER THINK I MIGHT BE RIGHT?
THAP
YOU'RE RIGHT, BACHMANN.
...WHAT?
YOU SHOULDN'T HAVE BEEN DISTRACTED.

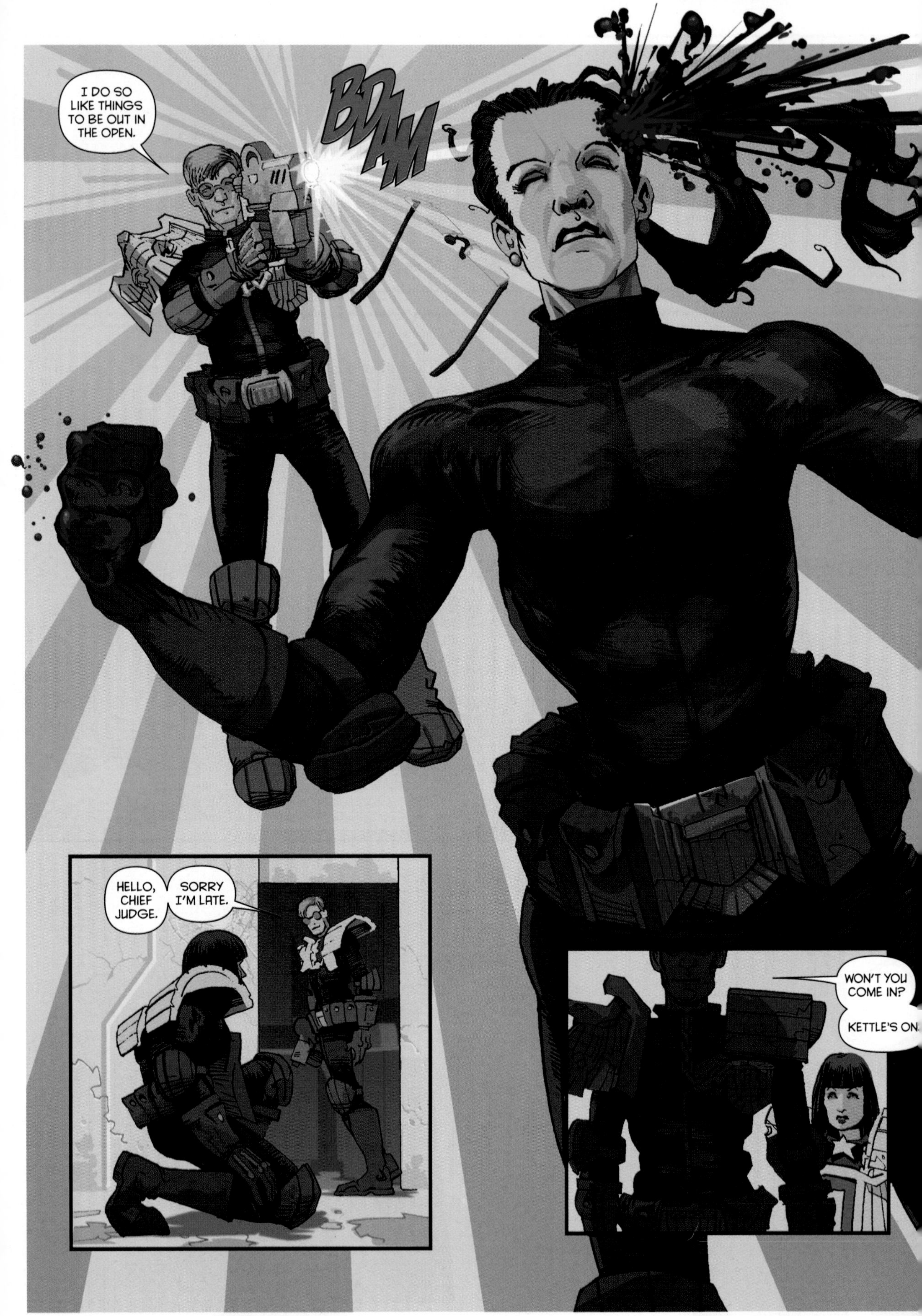
I DO SO LIKE THINGS TO BE OUT IN THE OPEN.
BDAM
HELLO, CHIEF JUDGE.
SORRY I'M LATE.
WON'T YOU COME IN?
KETTLE'S ON.

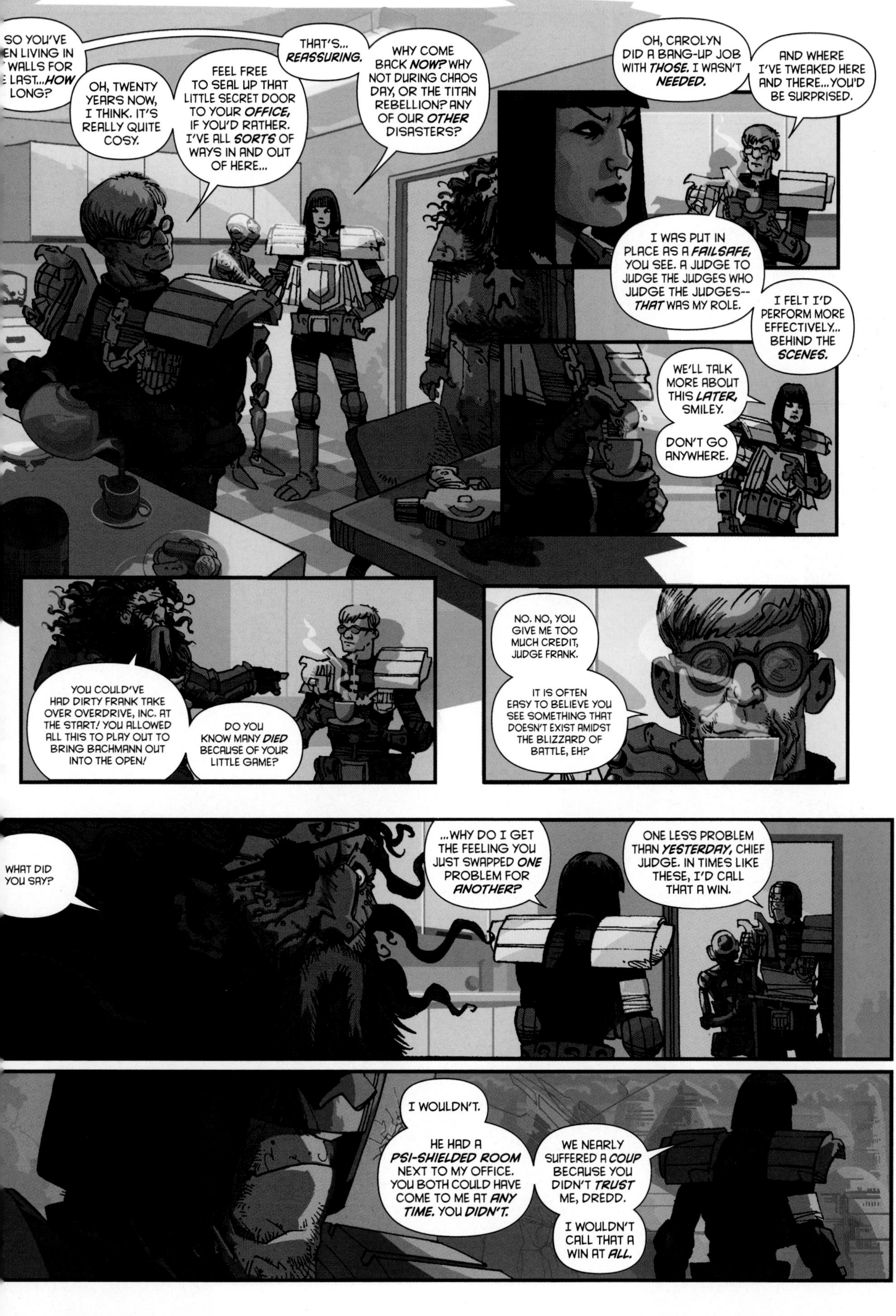
SO YOU'VE EN LIVING IN WALLS FOR E LAST...HOW LONG?
OH, TWENTY YEARS NOW, I THINK. IT'S REALLY QUITE COSY.
THAT'S... REASSURING.
FEEL FREE TO SEAL UP THAT LITTLE SECRET DOOR TO YOUR OFFICE, IF YOU'D RATHER. I'VE ALL SORTS OF WAYS IN AND OUT OF HERE...
WHY COME BACK NOW? WHY NOT DURING CHAOS DAY, OR THE TITAN REBELLION? ANY OF OUR OTHER DISASTERS?
OH, CAROLYN DID A BANG-UP JOB WITH THOSE. I WASN'T NEEDED.
AND WHERE I'VE TWEAKED HERE AND THERE... YOU'D BE SURPRISED.
I WAS PUT IN PLACE AS A FAILSAFE, YOU SEE. A JUDGE TO JUDGE THE JUDGES WHO JUDGE THE JUDGES-- THAT WAS MY ROLE.
I FELT I'D PERFORM MORE EFFECTIVELY... BEHIND THE SCENES.
WE'LL TALK MORE ABOUT THIS LATER, SMILEY.
DON'T GO ANYWHERE.
YOU COULD'VE HAD DIRTY FRANK TAKE OVER OVERDRIVE, INC. AT THE START! YOU ALLOWED ALL THIS TO PLAY OUT TO BRING BACHMANN OUT INTO THE OPEN!
DO YOU KNOW MANY DIED BECAUSE OF YOUR LITTLE GAME?
NO. NO, YOU GIVE ME TOO MUCH CREDIT, JUDGE FRANK.
IT IS OFTEN EASY TO BELIEVE YOU SEE SOMETHING THAT DOESN'T EXIST AMIDST THE BLIZZARD OF BATTLE, EH?
WHAT DID YOU SAY?
...WHY DO I GET THE FEELING YOU JUST SWAPPED ONE PROBLEM FOR ANOTHER?
ONE LESS PROBLEM THAN YESTERDAY, CHIEF JUDGE. IN TIMES LIKE THESE, I'D CALL THAT A WIN.
I WOULDN'T.
HE HAD A PSI-SHIELDED ROOM NEXT TO MY OFFICE. YOU BOTH COULD HAVE COME TO ME AT ANY TIME. YOU DIDN'T.
WE NEARLY SUFFERED A COUP BECAUSE YOU DIDN'T TRUST ME, DREDD.
I WOULDN'T CALL THAT A WIN AT ALL.

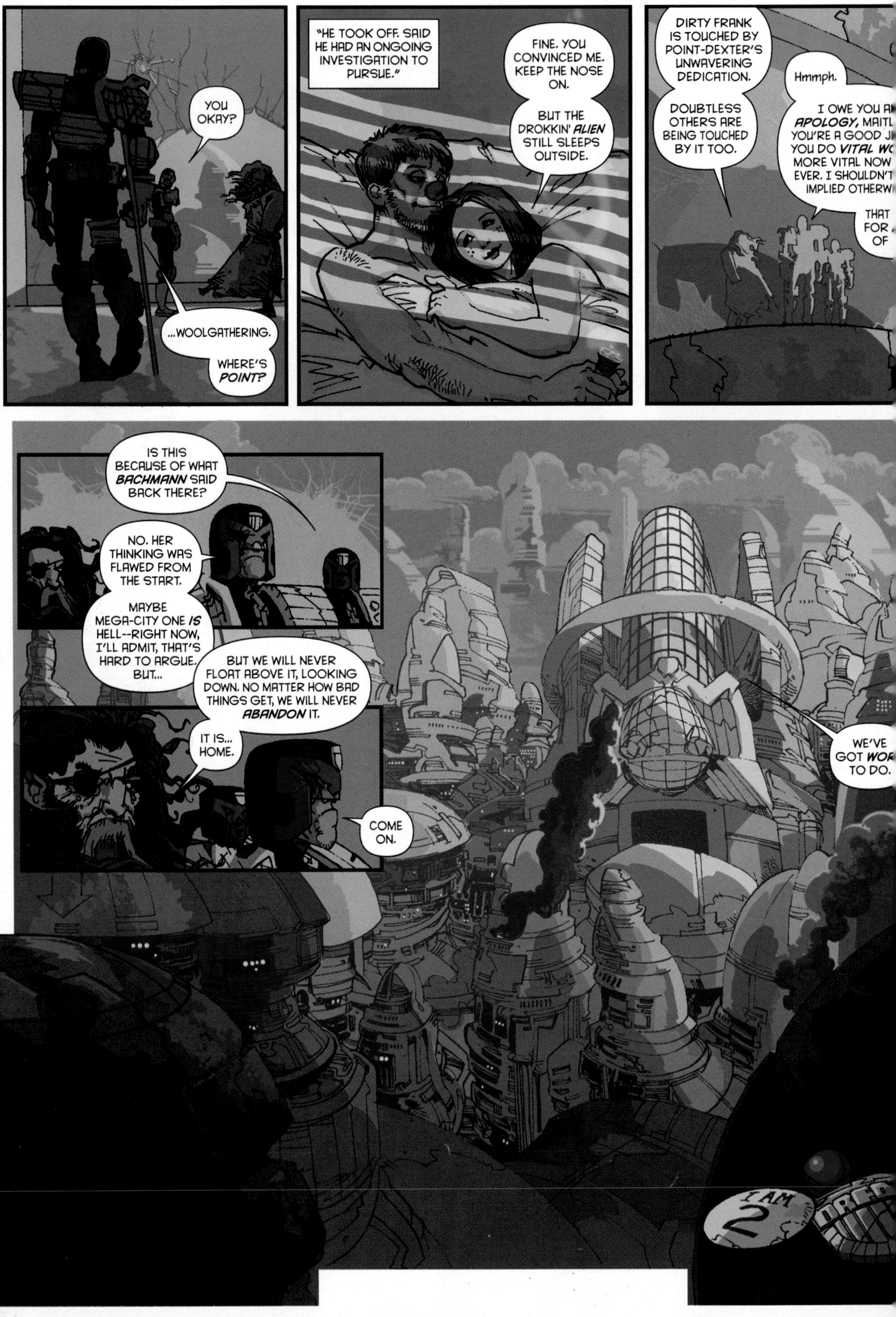

YOU OKAY?
...WOOLGATHERING.
WHERE'S *POINT?*
"HE TOOK OFF. SAID HE HAD AN ONGOING INVESTIGATION TO PURSUE."
FINE. YOU CONVINCED ME. KEEP THE NOSE ON.
BUT THE DROKKIN' *ALIEN* STILL SLEEPS OUTSIDE.
DIRTY FRANK IS TOUCHED BY POINT-DEXTER'S UNWAVERING DEDICATION.
DOUBTLESS OTHERS ARE BEING TOUCHED BY IT TOO.
Hmmph.
I OWE YOU A *APOLOGY,* MAITL YOU'RE A GOOD J YOU DO *VITAL W* MORE VITAL NOW EVER. I SHOULDN'T IMPLIED OTHERW
THAT FOR OF
IS THIS BECAUSE OF WHAT *BACHMANN* SAID BACK THERE?
NO. HER THINKING WAS FLAWED FROM THE START.
MAYBE MEGA-CITY ONE *IS* HELL--RIGHT NOW, I'LL ADMIT, THAT'S HARD TO ARGUE. BUT...
BUT WE WILL NEVER FLOAT ABOVE IT, LOOKING DOWN. NO MATTER HOW BAD THINGS GET, WE WILL NEVER *ABANDON* IT.
IT IS... HOME.
COME ON.
WE'VE GOT WOR TO DO.

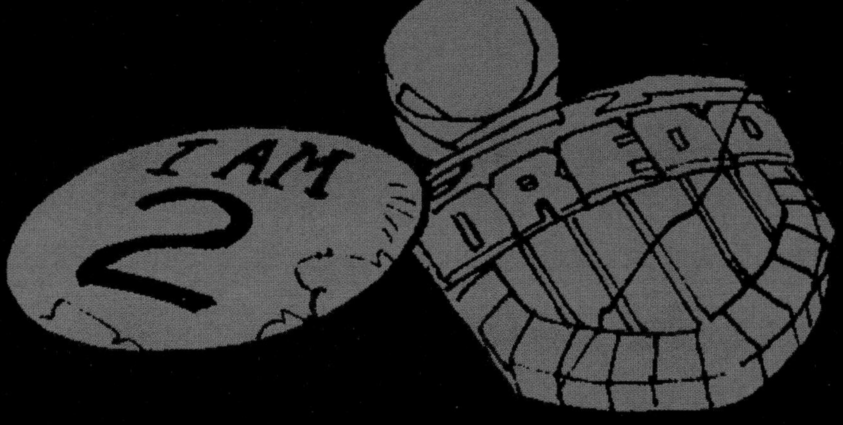
I AM
2
DREDD

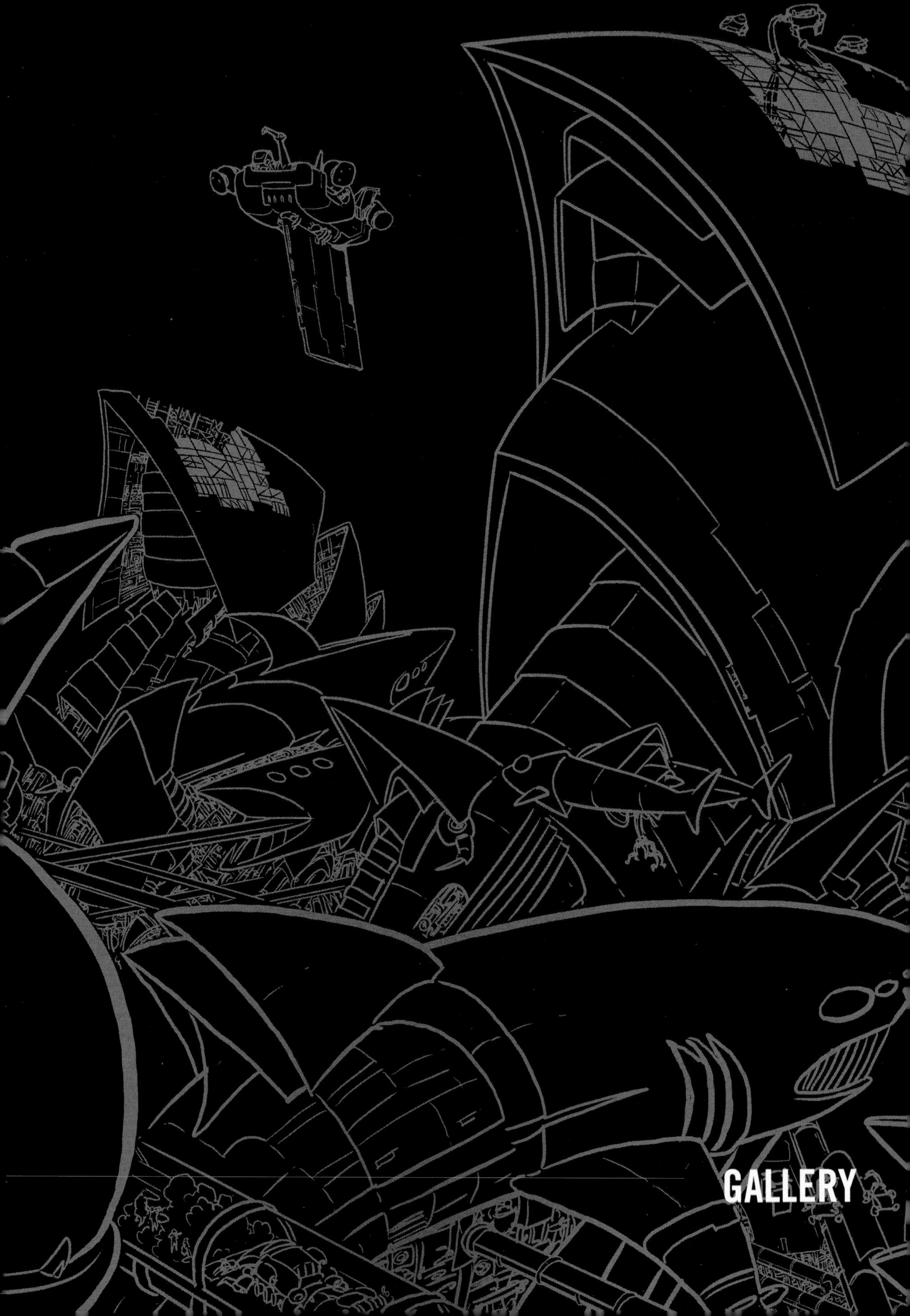

GALLERY

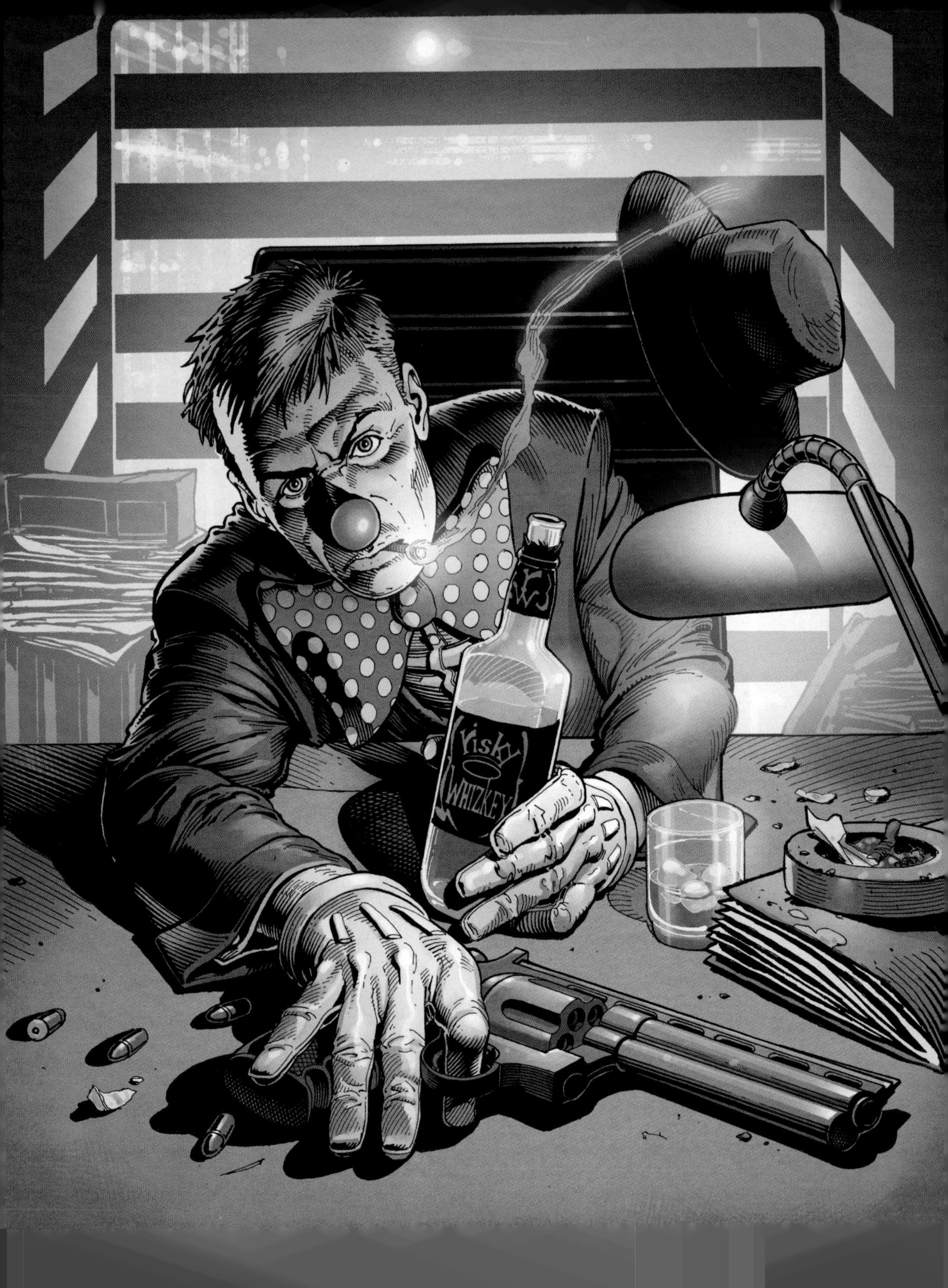
Risky
WHIZKEY

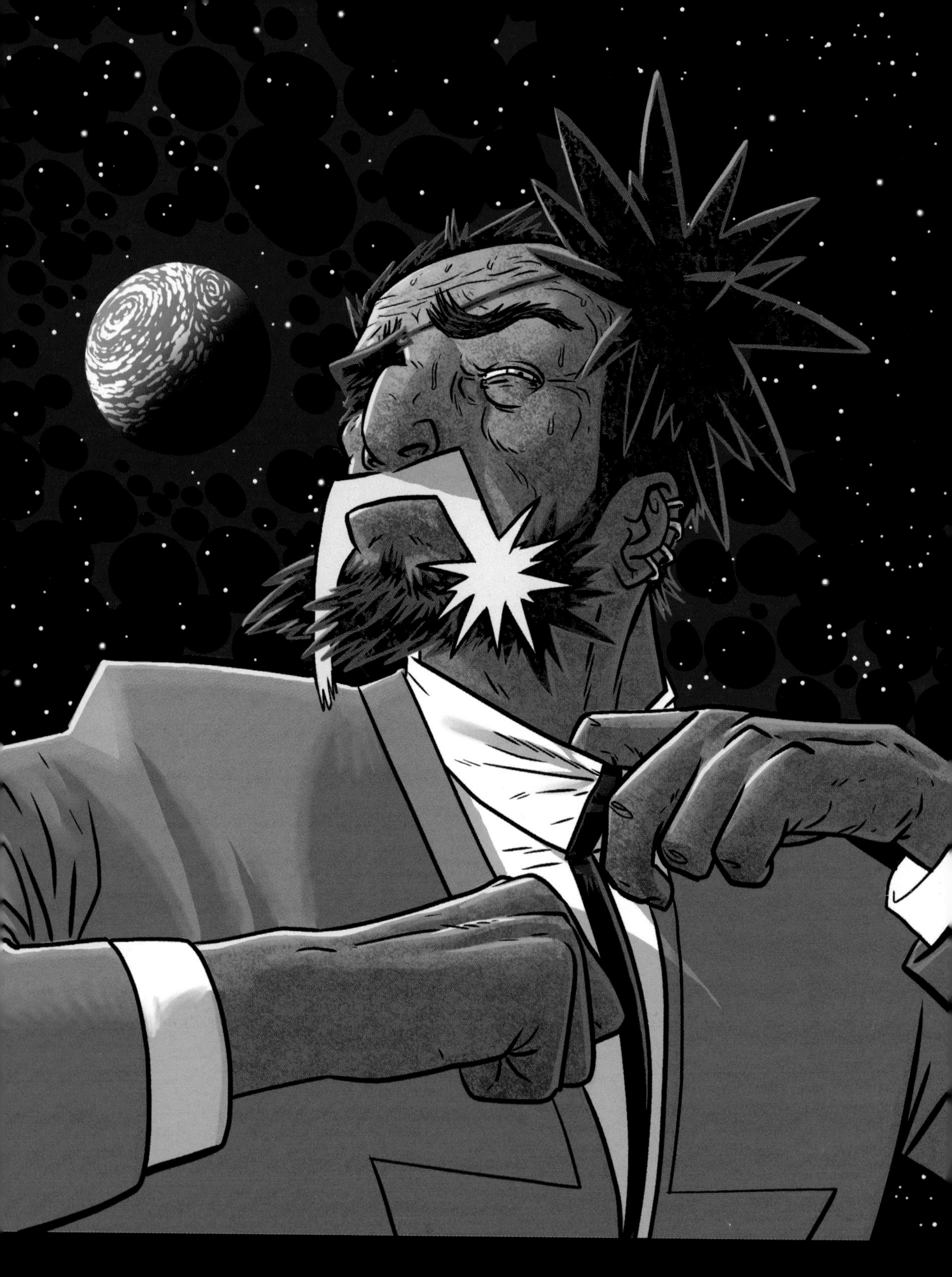

2000 AD Prog 1805. Cover by **D'Israeli**

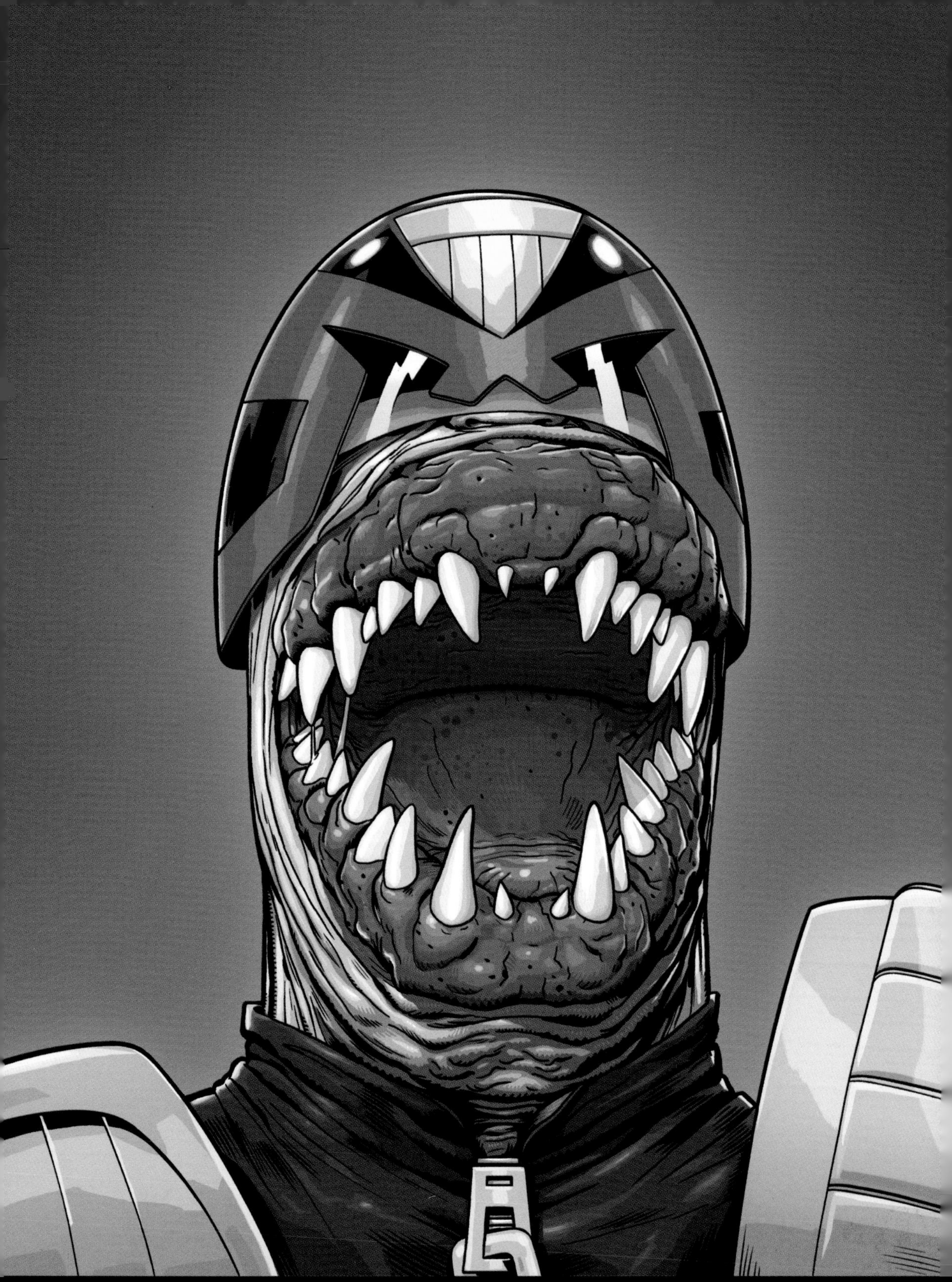

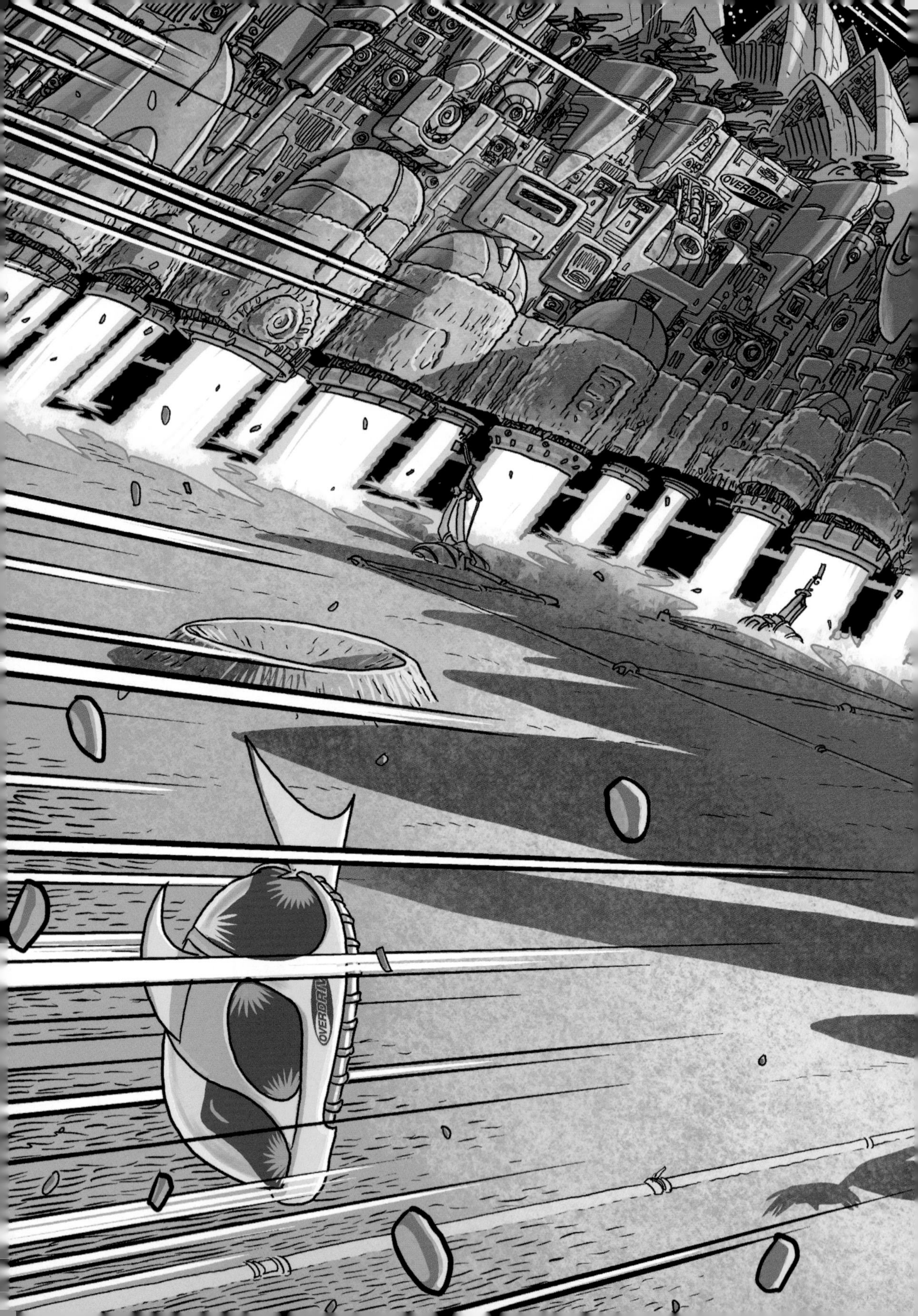
OVERDRIVE

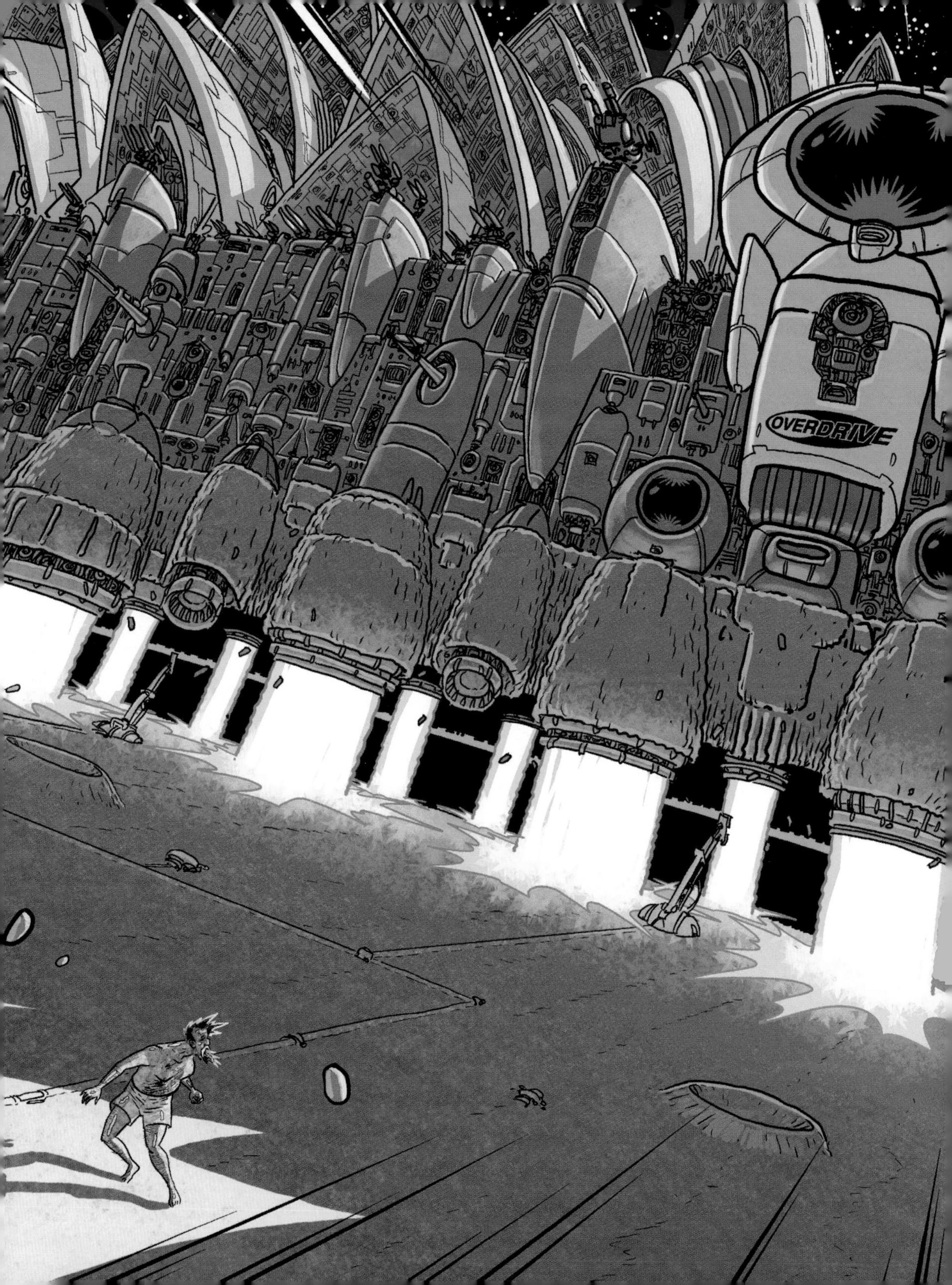
OVERDRIVE

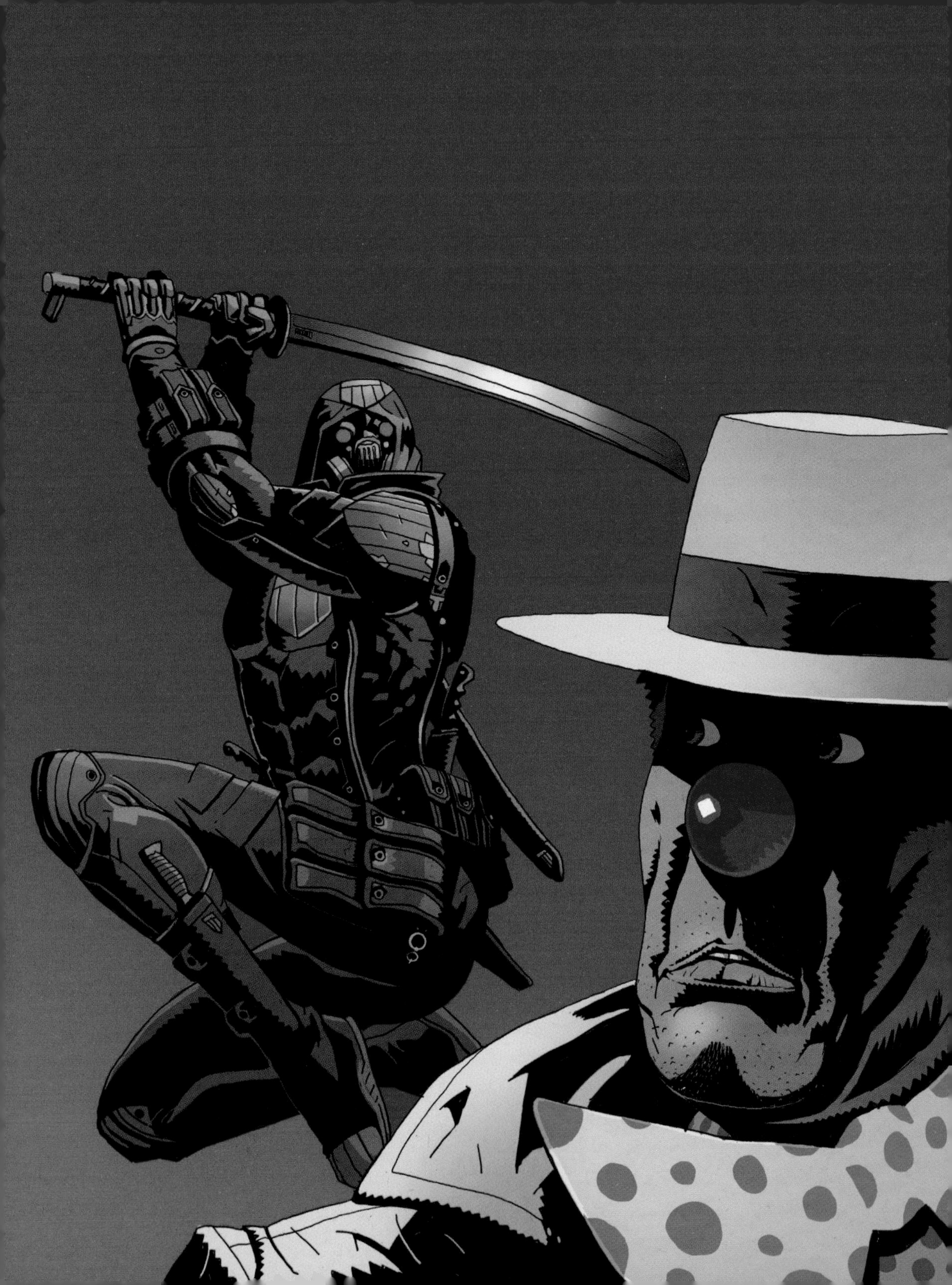

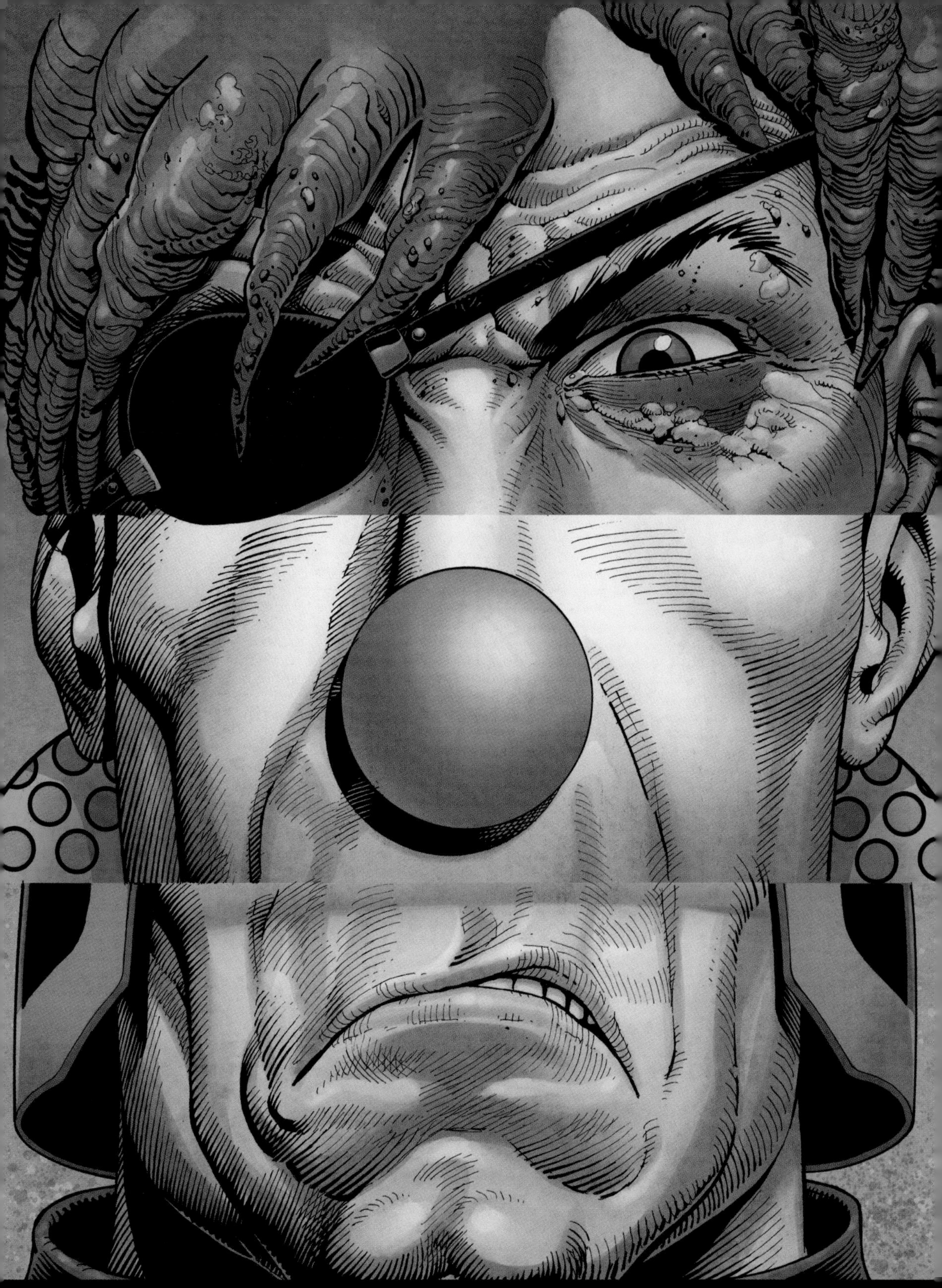

2000 AD Prog 1812: Cover by **Cliff Robinson & Dylan Teague**

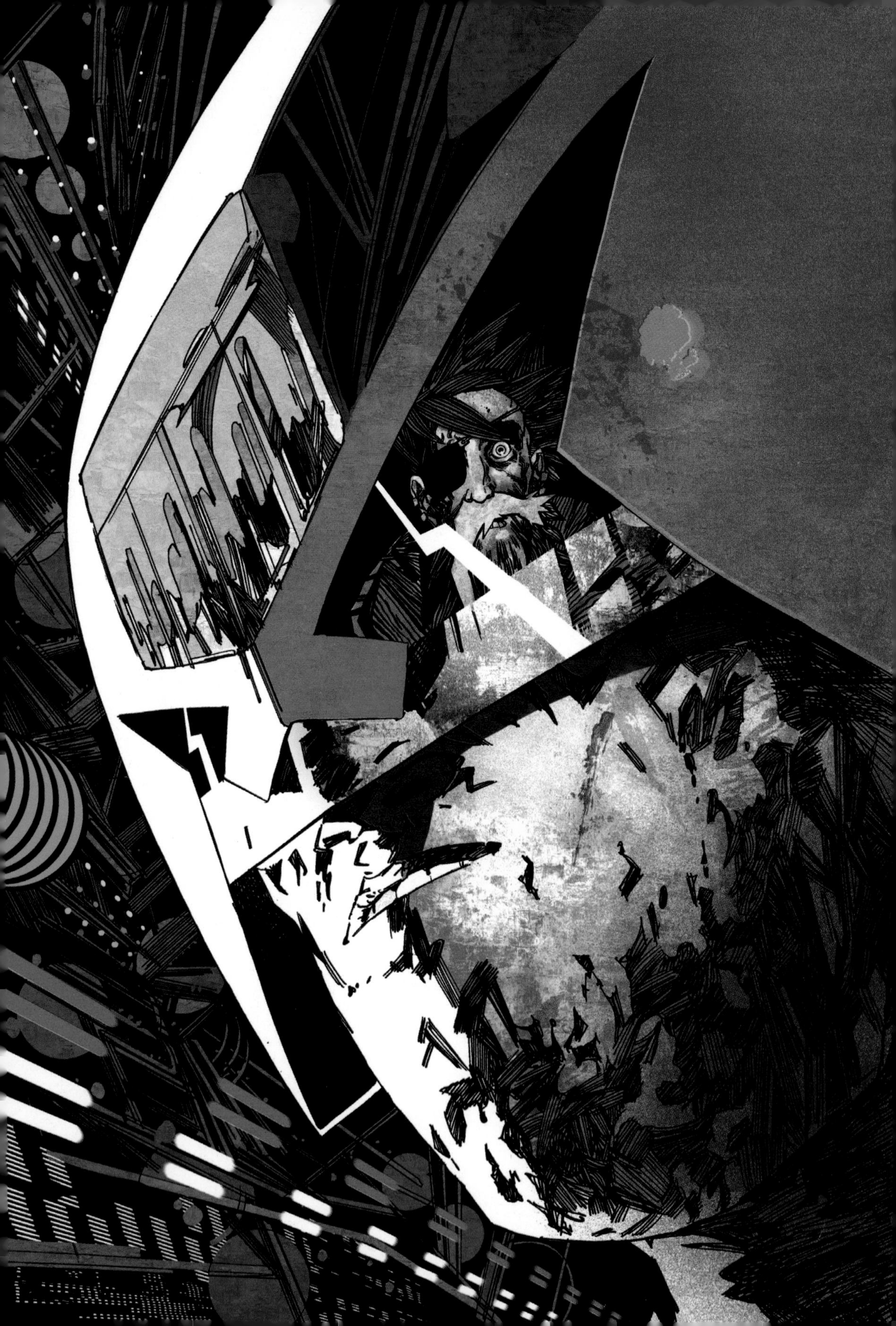

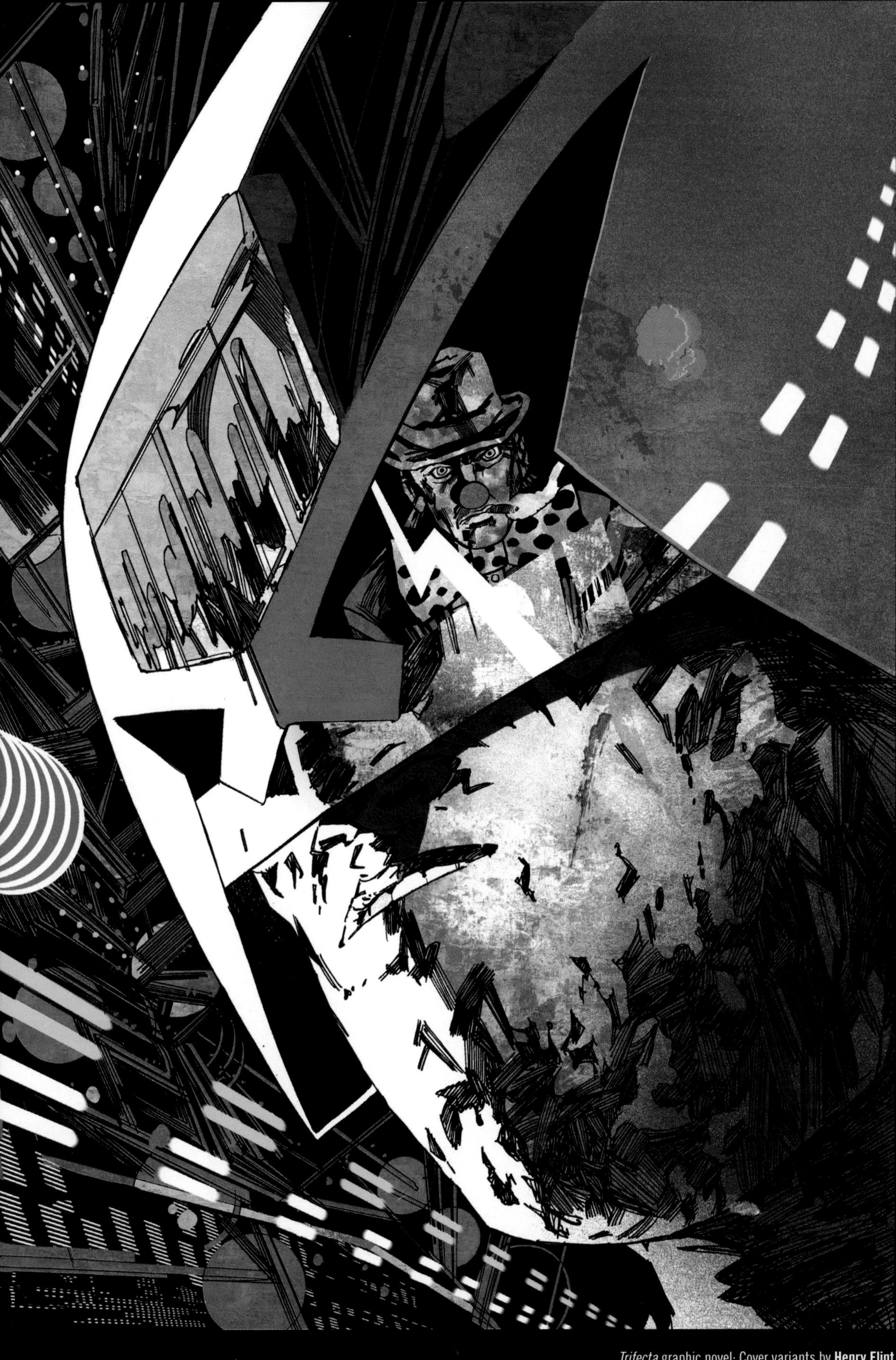

Trifecta graphic novel: Cover variants by **Henry Flint**

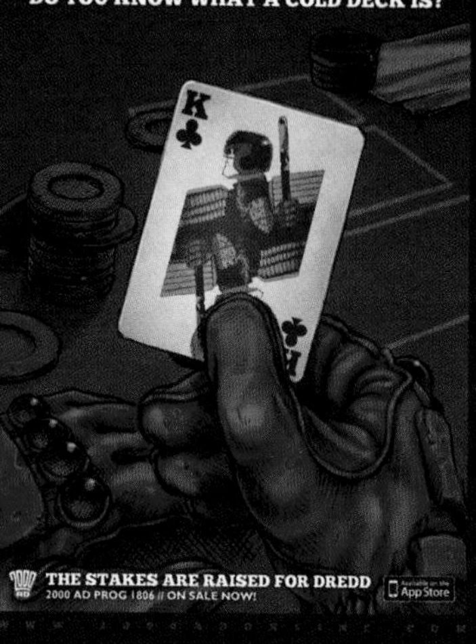
DO YOU KNOW WHAT A COLD DECK IS?
THE STAKES ARE RAISED FOR DREDD
2000 AD PROG 1806 // ON SALE NOW!
App Store

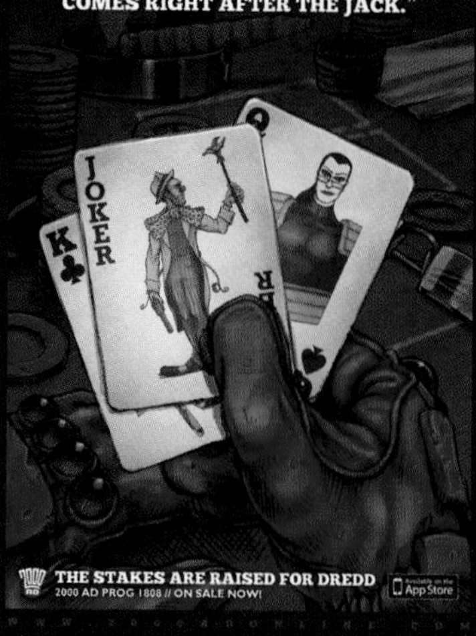
COMES RIGHT AFTER THE JACK."
JOKER
THE STAKES ARE RAISED FOR DREDD
2000 AD PROG 1808 // ON SALE NOW!
App Store

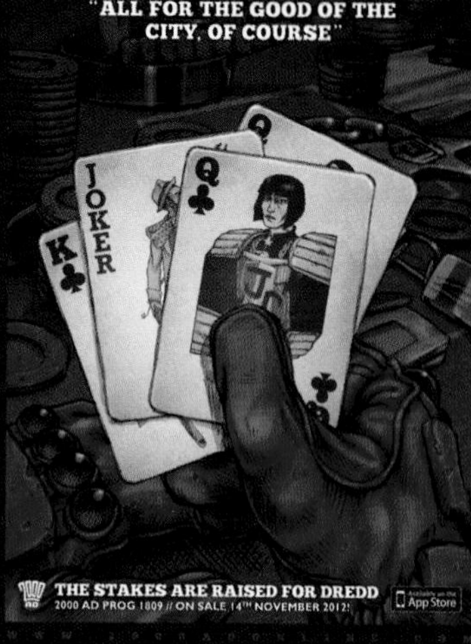
"ALL FOR THE GOOD OF THE CITY, OF COURSE"
JOKER
THE STAKES ARE RAISED FOR DREDD
2000 AD PROG 1809 // ON SALE 14TH NOVEMBER 2012!
App Store

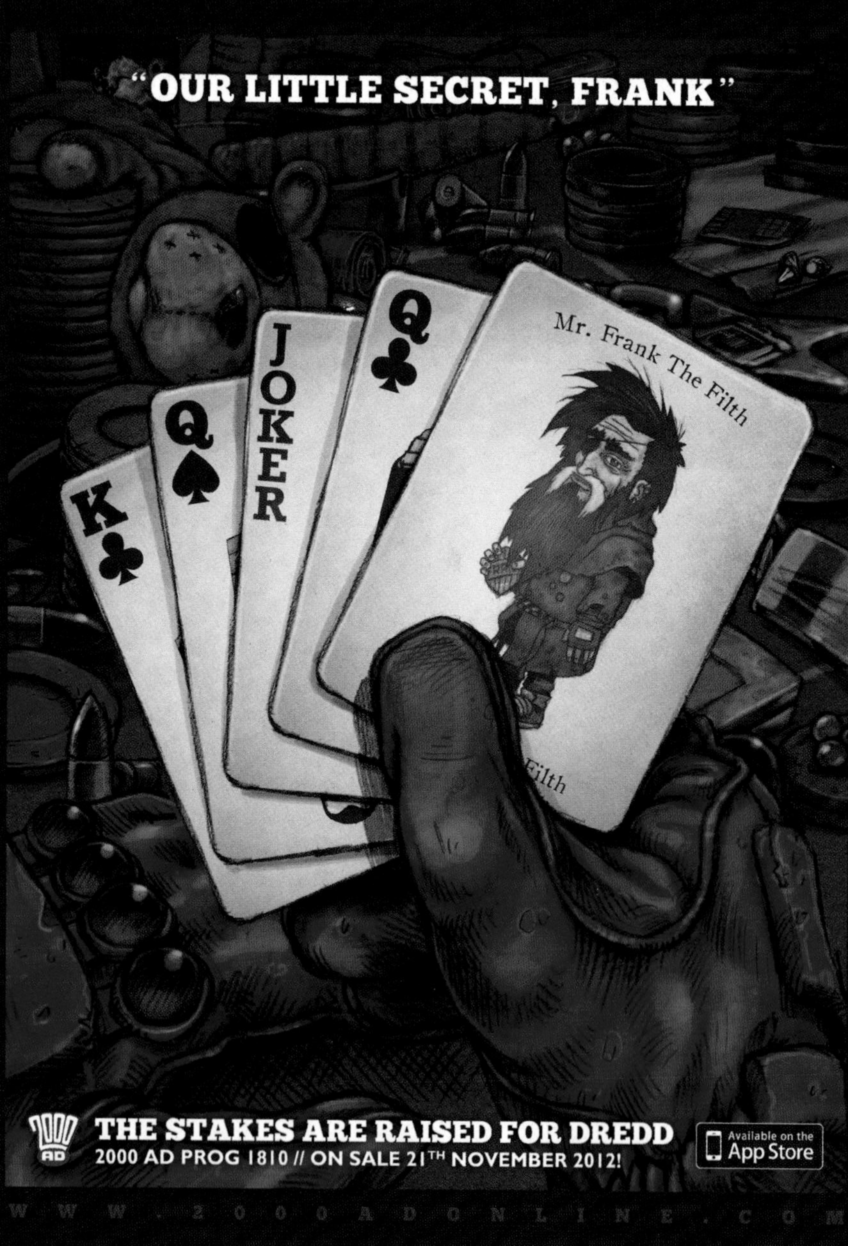
"OUR LITTLE SECRET, FRANK"
JOKER
Mr. Frank The Filth
THE STAKES ARE RAISED FOR DREDD
2000 AD PROG 1810 // ON SALE 21TH NOVEMBER 2012!
Available on the App Store
WWW.2000ADONLINE.COM

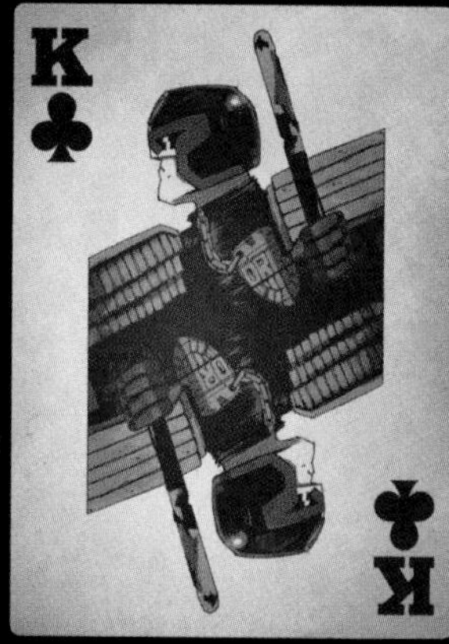

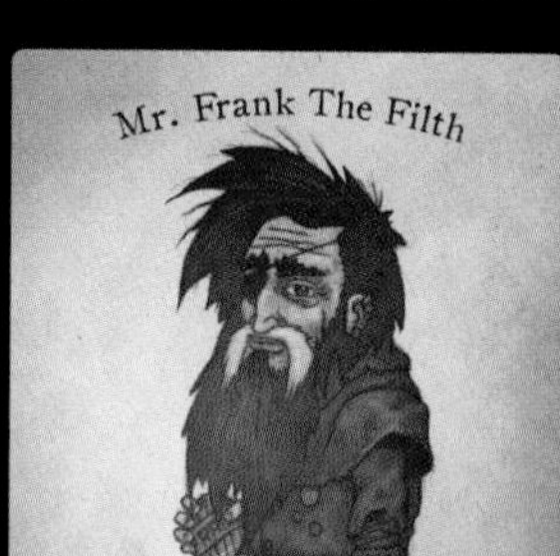
Mr. Frank The Filth
Mr. Frank The Filth

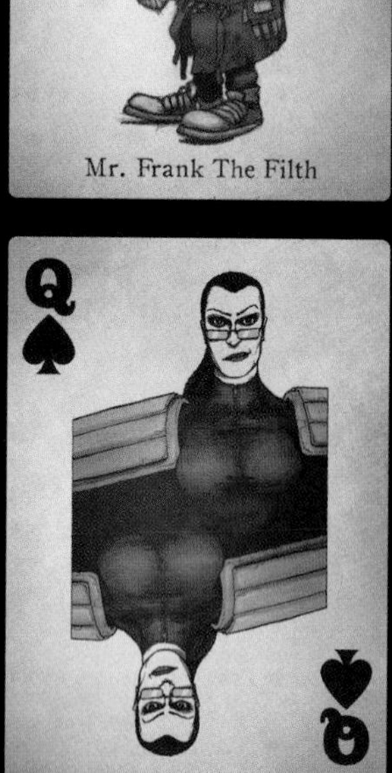

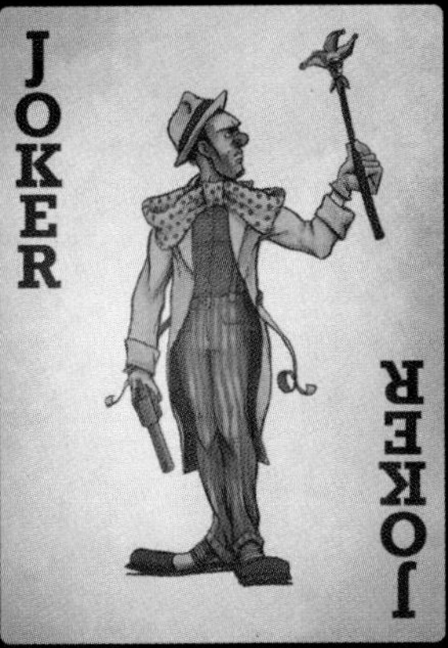
JOKER
JOKER

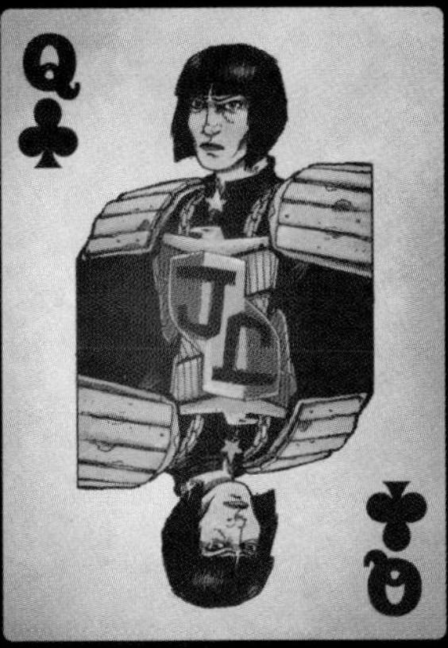
Q
Q

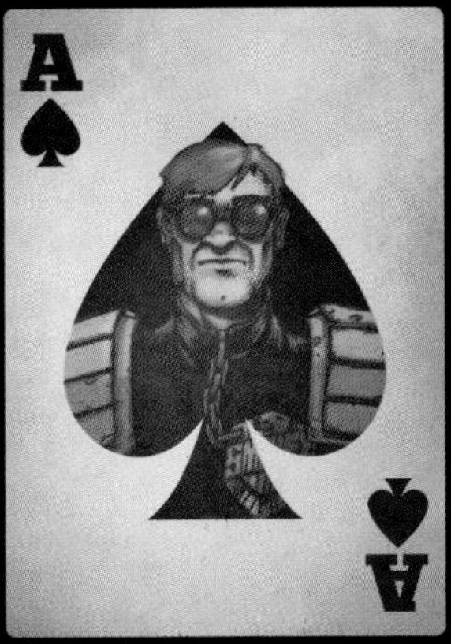
A
A

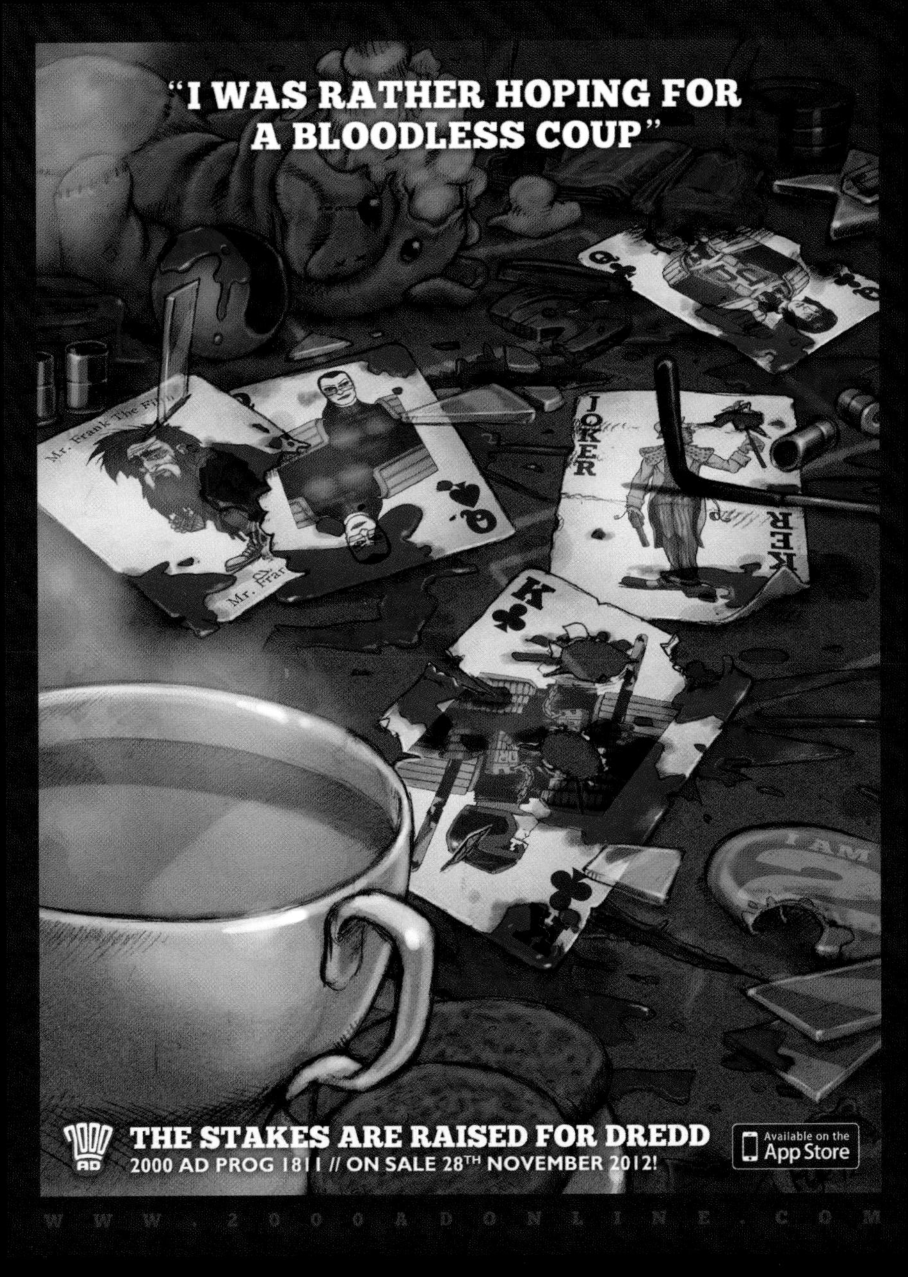
"I WAS RATHER HOPING FOR A BLOODLESS COUP"
Mr. Frank The Fifth
JOKER
K
I AM
2000 AD
THE STAKES ARE RAISED FOR DREDD
2000 AD PROG 1811 // ON SALE 28TH NOVEMBER 2012!
Available on the App Store
WWW.2000ADONLINE.COM

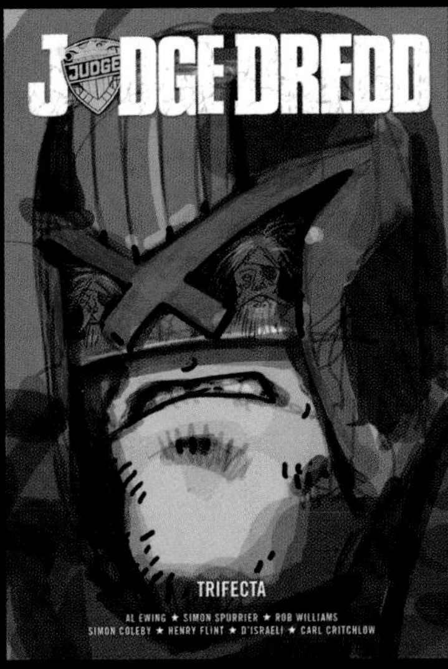
JUDGE DREDD
TRIFECTA
AL EWING ★ SIMON SPURRIER ★ ROB WILLIAMS
SIMON COLEBY ★ HENRY FLINT ★ D'ISRAELI ★ CARL CRITCHLOW

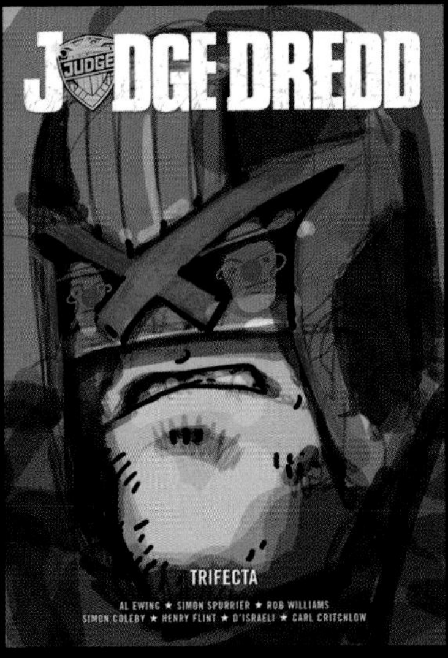
JUDGE DREDD
TRIFECTA
AL EWING ★ SIMON SPURRIER ★ ROB WILLIAMS
SIMON COLEBY ★ HENRY FLINT ★ D'ISRAELI ★ CARL CRITCHLOW

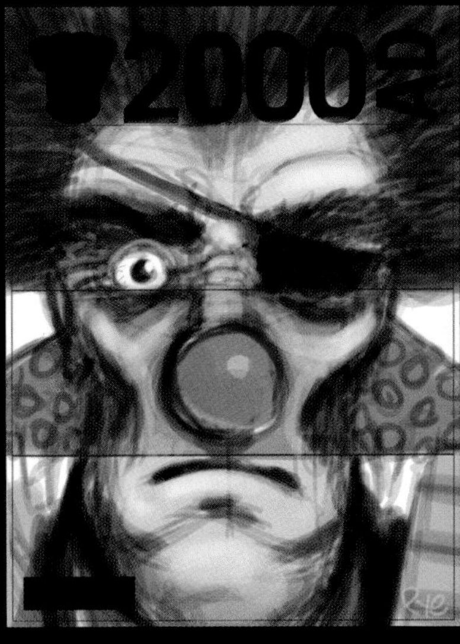
2000 AD

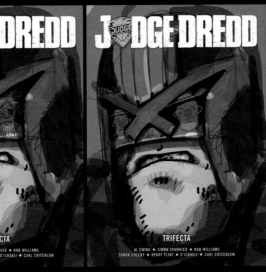

The Cold Deck/Trifecta: Advertising and cover concepts by **Pye**

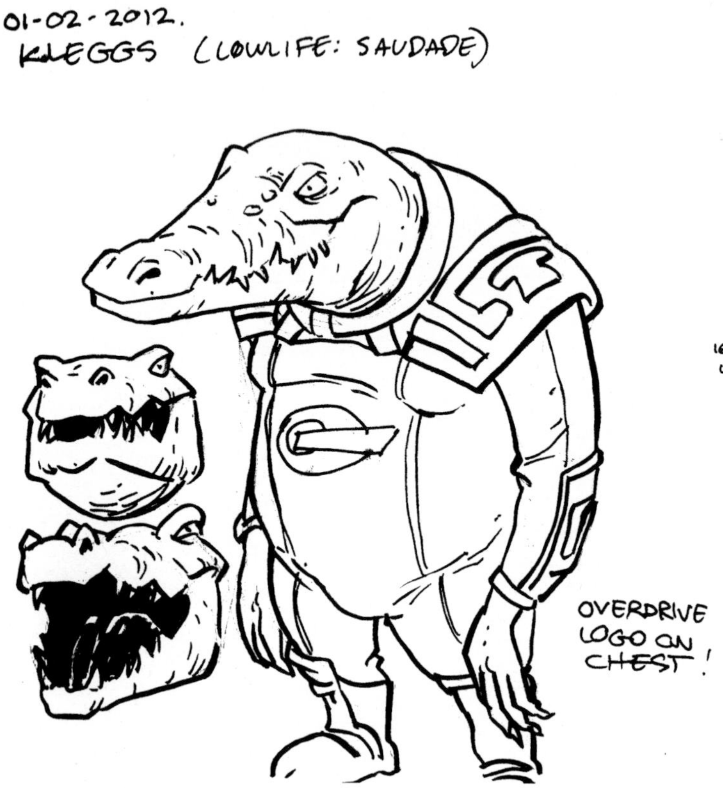
01-02-2012.
KLEGGS (LOWLIFE: SAUDADE)
OVERDRIVE LOGO ON CHEST!

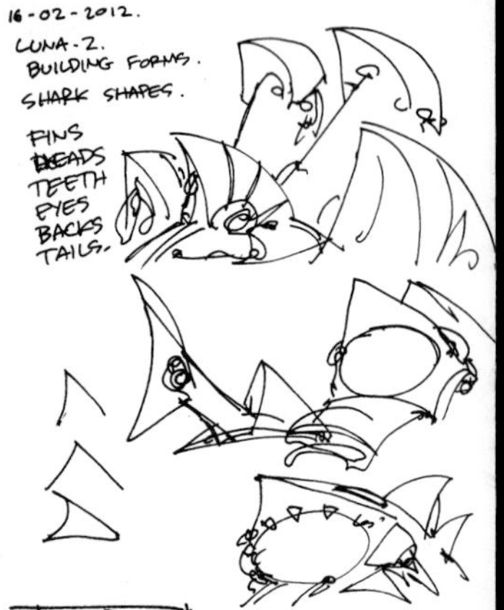
16-02-2012.
LUNA-2.
BUILDING FORMS.
SHARK SHAPES.
FINS
HEADS
TEETH
EYES
BACKS
TAILS.

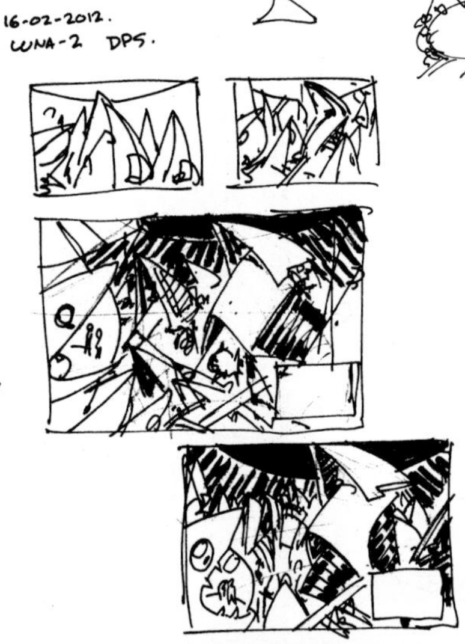
16-02-2012.
LUNA-2 DPS.

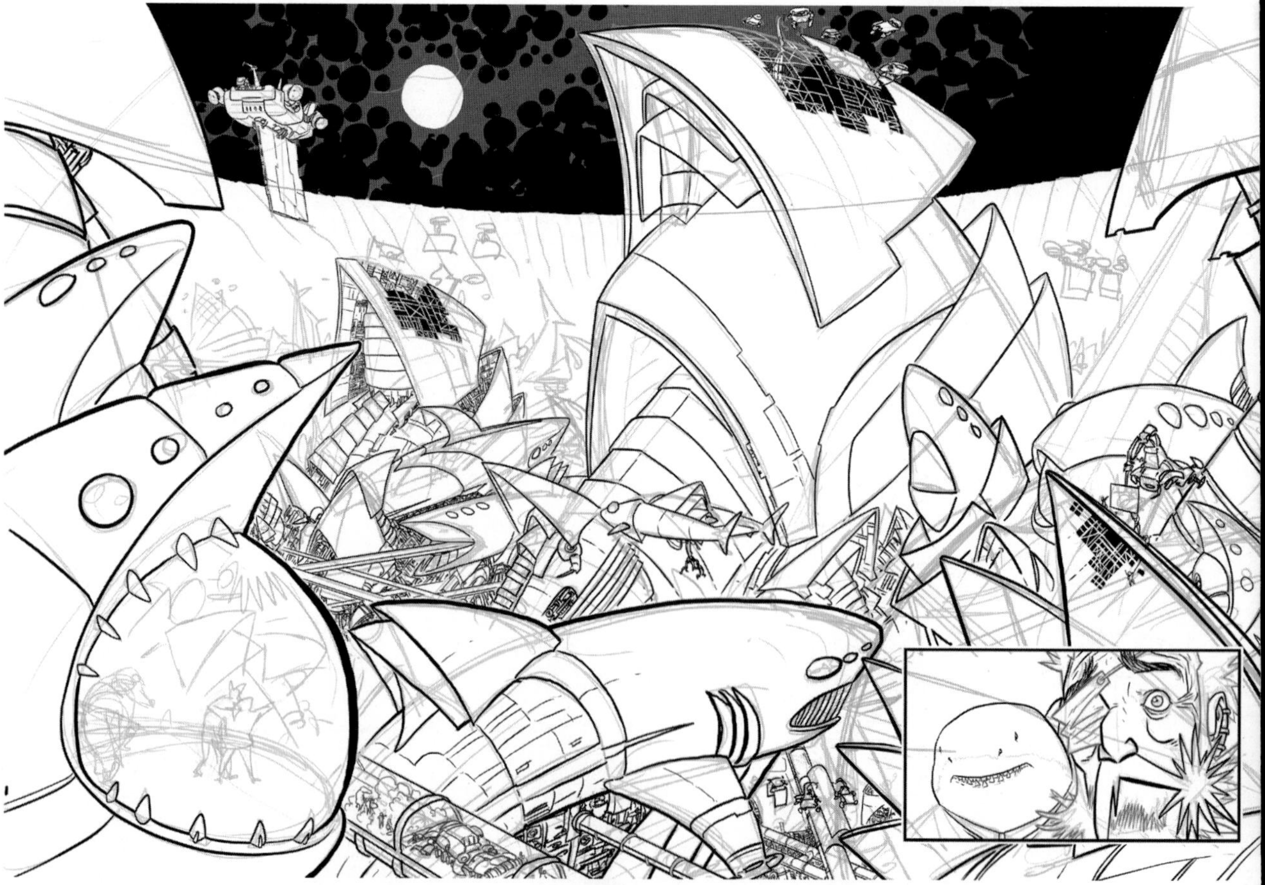

Saudade: Character sketches and an unused Luna-2 double page spread by **D'Israeli**

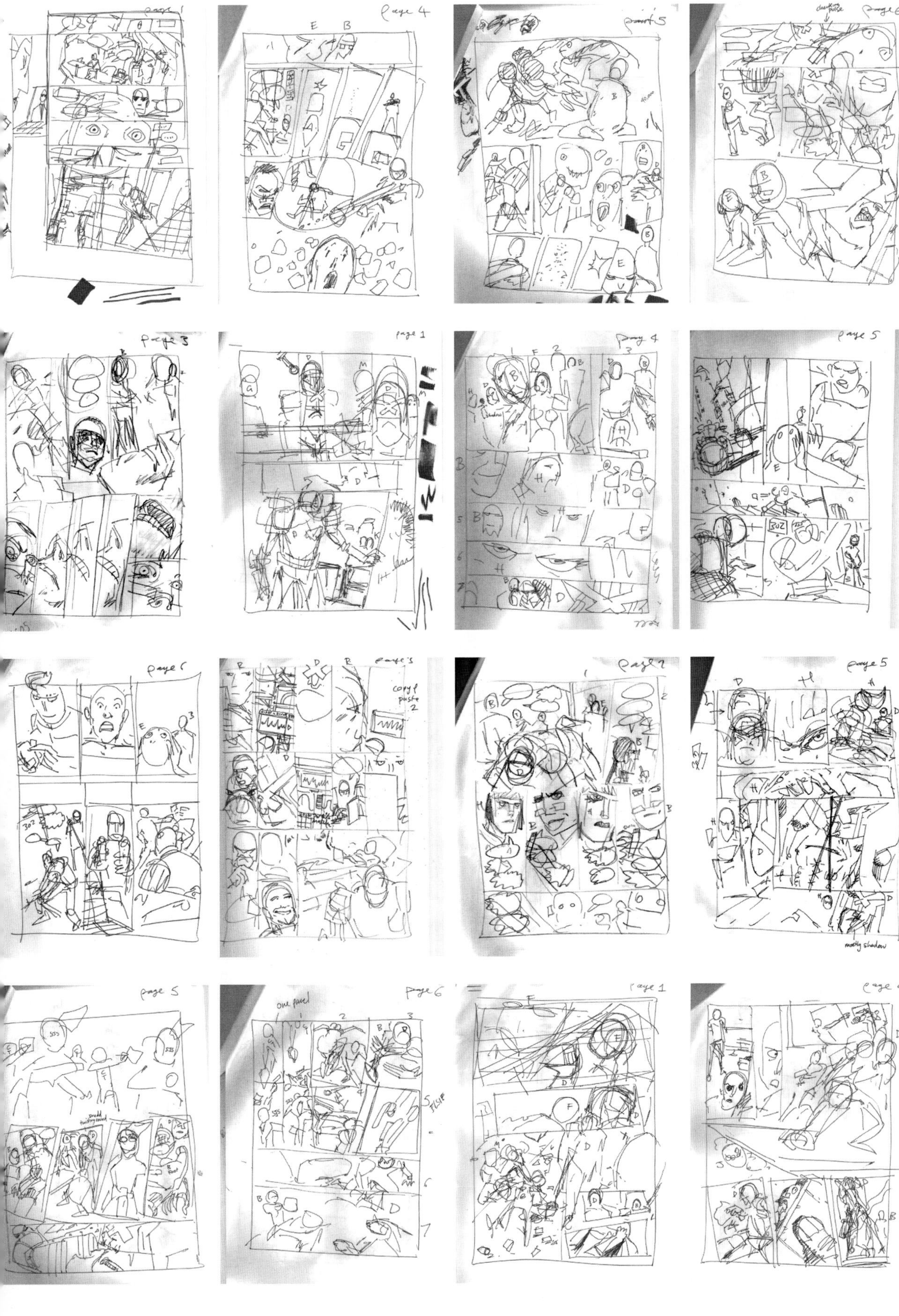

The Cold Deck: Page layouts by **Henry Flint**

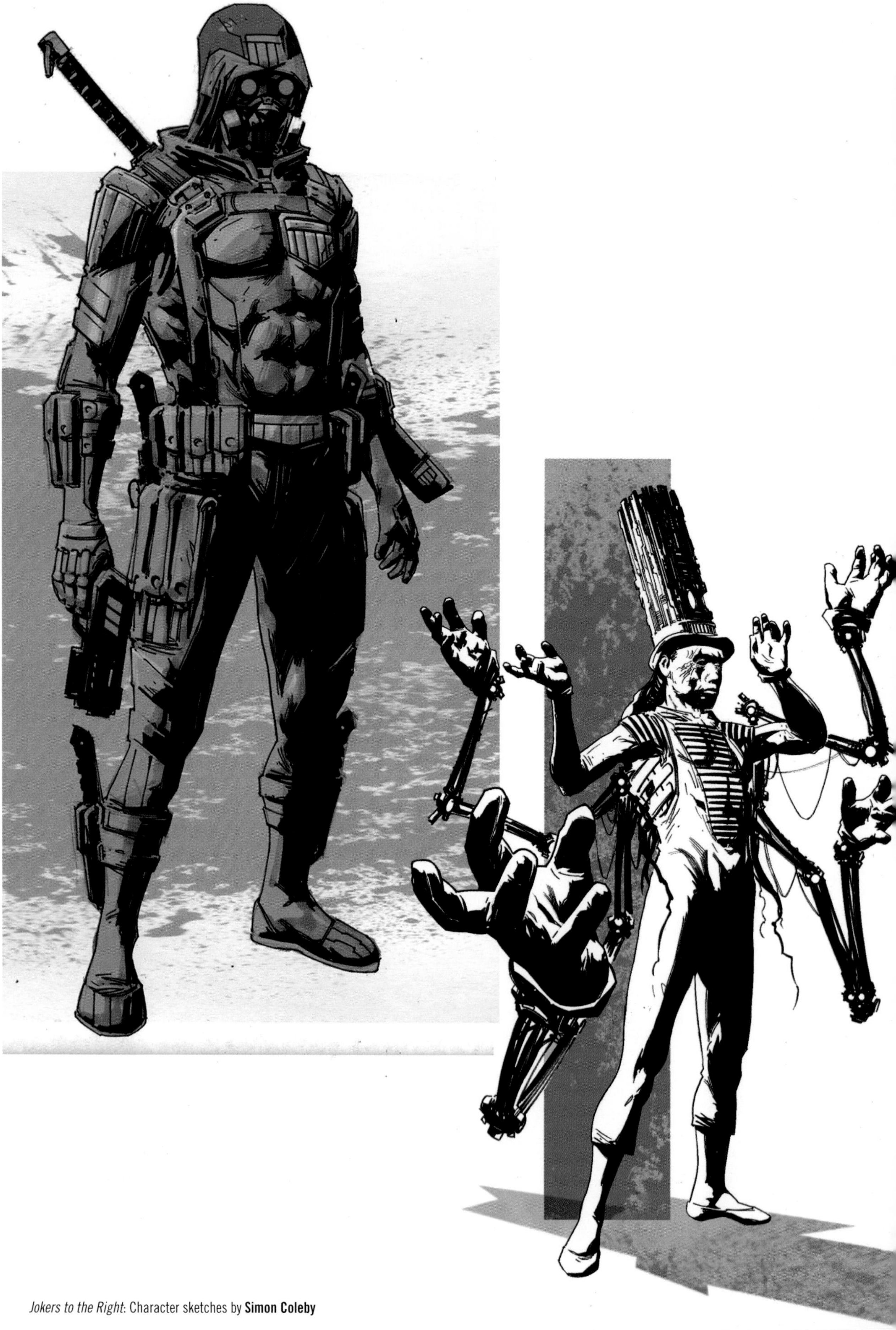

Jokers to the Right: Character sketches by **Simon Coleby**

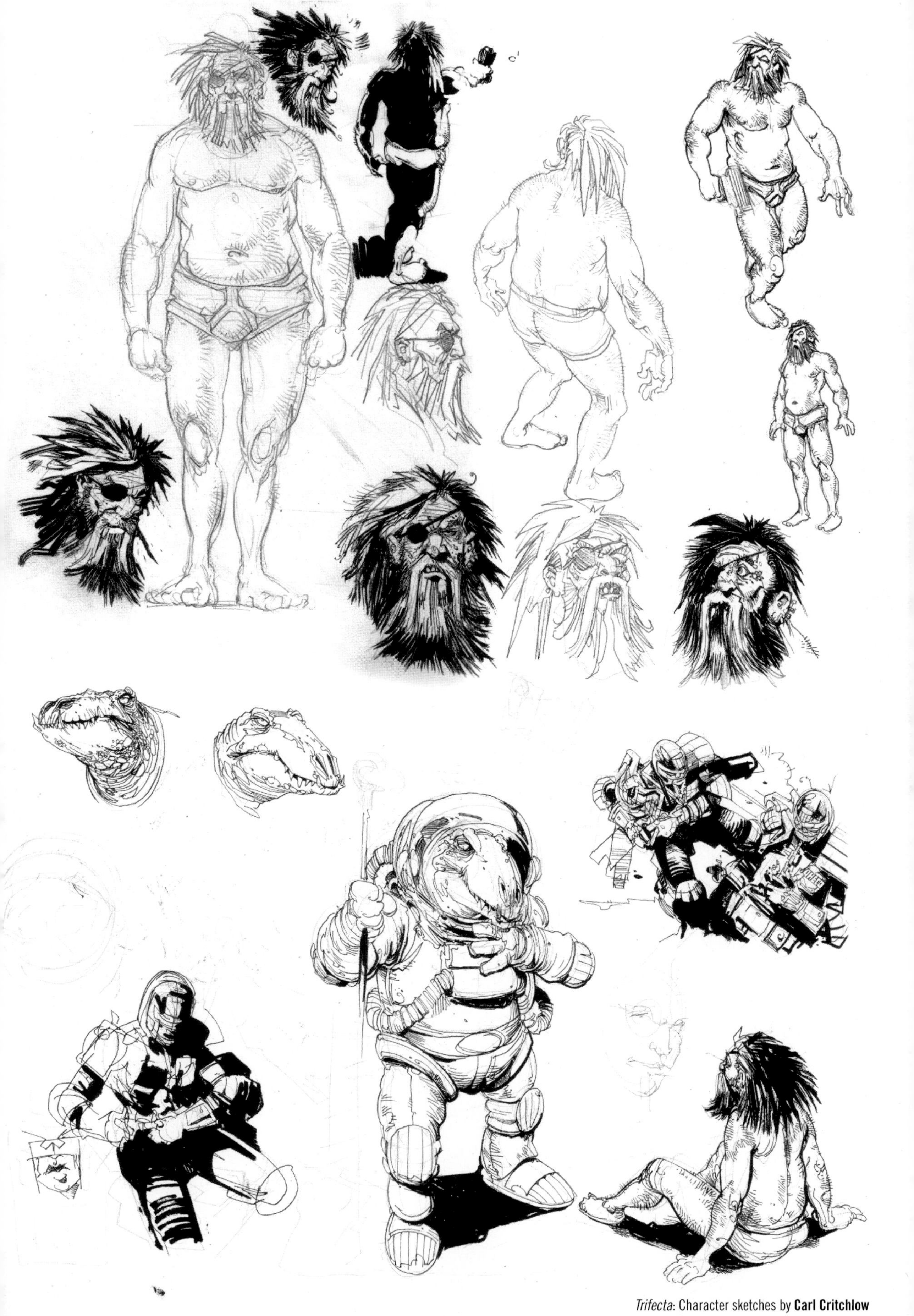

Trifecta: Character sketches by **Carl Critchlow**

AL EWING

Al Ewing's work for *2000 AD* has seen him hailed as a major voice in the field, bringing both fresh characters, a keen sense of comedy and a startling inventiveness to the UK comics scene. Now a seasoned *Judge Dredd* writer, Al's other work for the Galaxy's Greatest Comic includes various *Terror Tales* and *Future Shocks*, *Dead Signal*, *Damnation Station*, *The Zaucer of Zilk* and the hit series *Zombo*, while he has scripted several *Tales from the Black Museum* strips and *Tempest* for the *Judge Dredd Megazine*. He has also written five novels for Abaddon books, including *I, Zombie*, *El Sombra*, *Death Got No Mercy*, *Gods of Manhattan* and *Pax Omega*.

Comics veteran Garth Ennis picked Al Ewing to write a six-issue arc on *Jennifer Blood*, a comic published by Dynamite Entertainment. More recently Al has lent his writing talents to Marvel Comics.

SIMON SPURRIER

Simon Spurrier was physically born in the 80's but profiles an existential/curmudgeonly age of 103.

Working as an Art Director for the BBC in the armpit of the millennium, he took an unscripted tangent into the murky depths of Making Shit Up On Paper and has since become an award winning author and graphic novelist.

His latest crime novel, *A Serpent Uncoiled*, was released to great critical acclaim in 2011, while his comics works includes *Judge Dredd*, *Crossed*, *Gutsville*, *Six-Gun Gorilla* and the all-new, all-weird *X-Men Legacy* – part of the "Marvel Now" initiative.

He lives in a superpositional state of modern neurosis – both calm *and* biliously anxious up until one or the other is measured – and can be isolated on Twitter through @sispurrier

ROB WILLIAMS

Rob Williams is perhaps the baldest of Tharg The Mighty's script droids to appear over the last decade. He has written popular *2000 AD* series' including *Low Life*, *The Grievous Journey Of Ichabod Azreal (And The Dead Left In His Wake)* and *The Ten-Seconders*, amongst others. He has also written *Judge Dredd* and innumerable characters from other companies that you're possibly not interested in, because you read *2000 AD*. Things like *Spider-Man* and *Wolverine* and *Batman*. You know the sort. His really very good creator-owned series *Ordinary*, co-created with *Low Life's* D'israeli, is due in 2013. www.robwilliamscomics.co.uk

SIMON COLEBY

Simon Coleby's first work for *2000 AD* was a *Future Shock* – 'Rogan's Last Ride' – in 1987. Since then, Simon has illustrated *Judge Dredd*, *Rogue Trooper*, *Low Life*, *Universal Soldier* and *Venus Bluegenes*. He also co-created *Bato Loco*, with Gordon Rennie. Simon has also worked for Marvel Comics, collaborating with Pat Mills on the *Punisher 2099* series and *The Authority* for Wildstorm Comics. More recently he is enjoying critical success working on IDW's *Judge Dredd: Year One*.

CARL CRITCHLOW

Carl Critchlow made his debut in *2000 AD* working on *Nemesis and Deadlock*, then moving on to Batman/*Judge Dredd*, *Flesh*, *Future Shocks*, *Judge Dredd*, *Mean Machine*, *Lobster Random* and *Tales of Telguuth*. Outside of the Galaxy's Greatest Comic, he is the creator of the hugely popular *Thrud the Barbarian* - soon to be collected by Titan Books.

D'ISRAELI

Matt Booker, a.k.a. **D'Israeli**, is a current fan-favourite at *2000 AD*. His distinctive style has graced several strips in the Galaxy's Greatest Comic, including three *Tharg's Future Shocks* (which he also scripted), *The Vort*, *Stickleback*, *Low Life*, *Judge Dredd*, and *XTNCT* which he co-created with Paul Cornell for the *Judge Dredd Megazine*.

Beyond *2000 AD*, D'Israeli co-created *Lazarus Churchyard* with renowned comic writer Warren Ellis and the critically-acclaimed *Kingdom of the Wicked* and *Scarlet Traces* with his regular collaborator, Ian Edginton.

HENRY FLINT

Henry Flint, winner of the National Comics Awards for Best Comic Artist 2004, is one of the Galaxy's Greatest Comic's superstars. Co-creator of *Sancho Panzer*, *Shakara*, and the fan-favourite strip, *Zombo*, his incredibly versatile pencils have also graced *A.B.C. Warriors*, *Judge Dredd/Aliens*, *Deadlock*, *Judge Dredd*, *Rogue Trooper*, *Nemesis the Warlock*, *The V.C.'s* and *Venus Bluegenes*. He has even written a *Tharg's Alien Invasions* strip! He has also worked on several American comics including *Omega Men*, *Haunted Tank* and *Fear Itself: Fearsome Four*. Away from the comics industry, Henry produced art for the cover of D. Food's 2012 album, *The Search Engine*. His art book, *Broadcast: The TV Doodles of Henry Flint* is available from Markosia Press.

THE JUDGE DREDD COMPACT CLASSICS

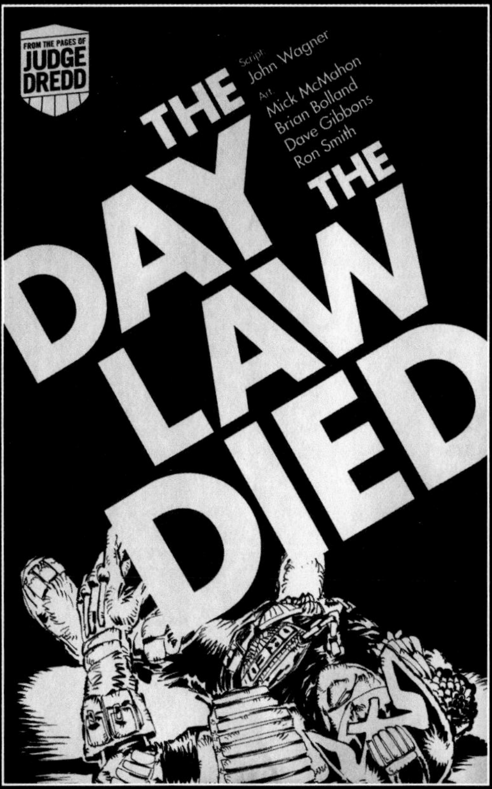
FROM THE PAGES OF JUDGE DREDD
THE DAY THE LAW DIED
Script John Wagner
Art Mick McMahon
Brian Bolland
Dave Gibbons
Ron Smith

£6.99 • SBN: 978-1-78108-009-2

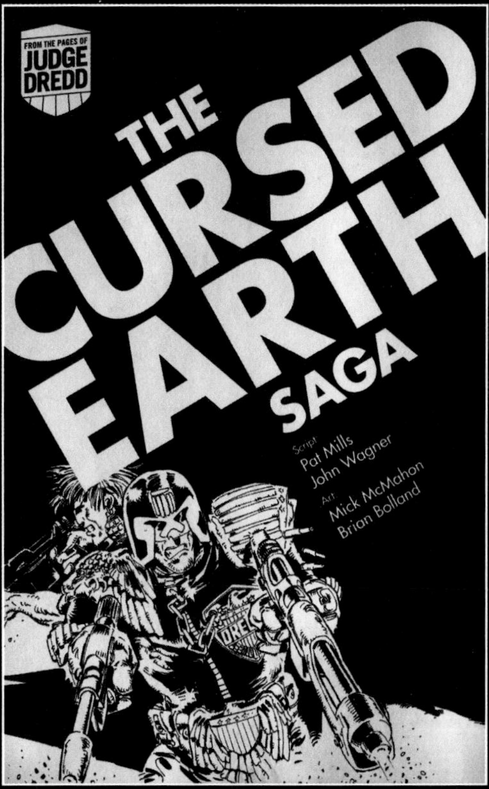
FROM THE PAGES OF JUDGE DREDD
THE CURSED EARTH SAGA
Script Pat Mills
John Wagner
Art Mick McMahon
Brian Bolland

£6.99 • SBN: 978-1-78108-008-5

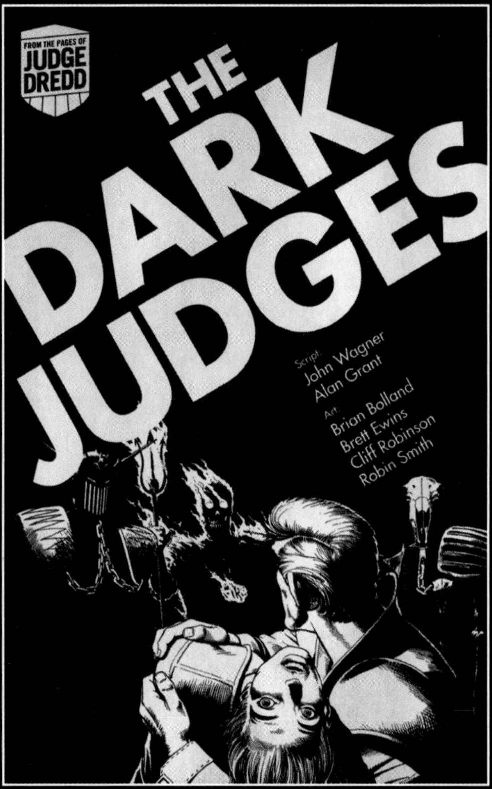
FROM THE PAGES OF JUDGE DREDD
THE DARK JUDGES
Script John Wagner
Alan Grant
Art Brian Bolland
Brett Ewins
Cliff Robinson
Robin Smith

£6.99 • SBN: 978-1-78108-045-0

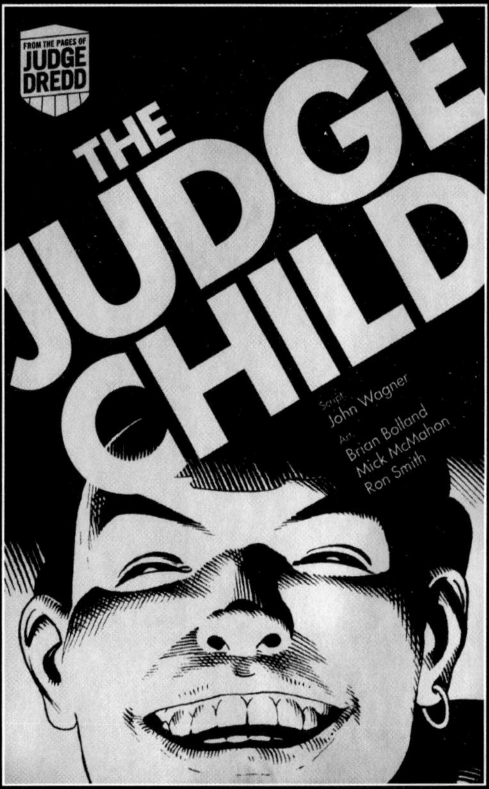
FROM THE PAGES OF JUDGE DREDD
THE JUDGE CHILD
Script John Wagner
Art Brian Bolland
Mick McMahon
Ron Smith

£6.99 • SBN: 978-1-78108-109-9

TO ORDER **2000 AD** GRAPHIC NOVELS, SUBSCRIPTIONS, BACK ISSUES AND MERCHANDISE

CALL **01621-877-250** OR VISIT **SHOP.2000ADONLINE.COM**